TALES OF GASLIGHT NEW YORK

COMPILED BY FRANK OPPEL

CASTLE

CONTENTS

1
The New York Cab Driver and his Cab

THE
OUTING
MAGAZINE

NOVEMBER, 1906

THE NEW YORK CAB DRIVER AND HIS CAB

BY VANCE THOMPSON

PHOTOGRAPHS BY ARTHUR HEWITT

THE cab is no integral part of New York life. Venice without the gondola were as unthinkable as a woman without hair. No little of London's compelling charm is in its swift-rolling hansoms. These things we know. But one can't think of New York in terms of cabs. Once upon a time I was an exile; only in memory did the great city rise before me; and what I saw was this: Huge cañons of stone and steel—filled with noise and darkness—through which great yellow worms crawled, one after the other, in mid-air. That is the picture of New York that haunts the exile, even as the outlawed Venetian is obsessed by slim, black gondolas cutting across lanes of moonlight. Your true New Yorker is a steam-projected, electrically-carted person; only in exceptional moments of gloom or gayety does he ride "in a carriage and pair." He is carriage-ridden to a funeral; he cabs it in winey moments, on dark errands, when the fear of God is not in him. The cab-instinct is but faintly developed in him. There are only two thousand licensed cabs and hacks on the island of Manhattan. Others there are, of course, plying piratically in the dark quarters; but even with these thrown in the reckoning is small. No, the New Yorker is not a cabby person.

And that is a pity.

Riding in cabs does much to soften the rudeness of the unintelligent man. It gives him a chance to commune with himself. Away from the swaying mob of an elevated train, away from the jostling democracy of the cable or trolley car, he has a chance to isolate his emotions and get acquainted with himself. The cabbies of New York are a small race, but when you come to know them you will discover that they are an efficient race, and efficient whether it be for business or pleasure. I have thought over this a great deal. In fact, the problem fascinates me. Why is it that the cabber—and by that I mean the man in whom the habit is strong—why, I say, is he usually a better man than his un-cabbing fellow? He may be no richer. He may have no more brains. Yet he is the man who accomplishes things. You will find that he is the kind of man who gets what he wants out of life. Faith, he whistles life to heel and makes it follow like a dog. I daresay the masterfulness was in him originally. The cab-habit has only brought it out more strongly. The cabber—the study of a few specimens will convince you —has a huge quantity of self-respect. He will not permit the body that incloses him to be elbow-rubbed and knee-kneaded in publicly promiscuous vehicles. And so he

It used to be part of a young gentleman's education to know how to dance well enough to win an heiress and shoot straight enough to keep her. It was a not unpleasant way of getting on in the world. Unfortunately it has gone out of vogue—like many another good old fashion. Much in the same way, it seems to me, the young gentlemen of to-day should be instructed in the art of using cabs. It may not lead to great fortune; it may not be the directest road

Police lines keep the cabby where he belongs.

cabs it. Fat with pride and self-respect, he is bowled along through what the old stage-directions used to call the populace; and we, trudging afoot or jolted along by electricity, give him the right of way. It is natural enough; intuitively we feel that the man who so evidently respects himself deserves a measure of respect from us. Thus he cabs himself into the good things of this earth.

to the Presidency; but it will inculcate self-respect and a certain fat way of taking one's ease in life, better than great fortunes (which are common and rather vulgar, anyway) or the Presidency. Like every other art, that of cabbing has its rules. In New York, I fancy, there are very few who are really adept in them. The youngest man-about-town knows, of course, the two elemental occasions for taking a cab—

when he wants to be alone, or when he wants to be alone with her. The other occasions shade off into subtleties. Taking a cab when no one sees you is as ridiculous as wearing an orchid in the buttonhole of your bath-gown. You ride in a cab in order to be seen riding in a cab. The only real satisfaction to be got out of being alone is to have other people stand, timid and afar, saying thoughtfully, "Ah, he is alone." I know a vehement and distin-

me as stylishly humorous. It is exotic, like the English rose and the French lily. It has not made itself at home yet. Indeed, the cab has not yet become an essential part of city life. It is casual. Nor is there any definite system, such as you find in older cities abroad. You see a wayfaring vehicle—it may be a public cab, duly licensed by the mayor's marshal, it may be a pirate, it may be a prowler from a livery-stable; there is no way of telling. Oh,

The cabby's "better half" takes breakfast.

guished novelist, who rides up and down Fifth Avenue for hours at a time, not only to think, but to let us see him think; he has mastered the art of cabbing as, in New York, it should be cabbed.

How little it takes to decorate life!

You may be trundled up and down Fifth Avenue for hours and the cost is only fifty cents for twenty blocks.

Upon the whole the New York cab strikes

there are laws and regulations enough! The city has ordained what fares shall be paid; it has enacted laws for the licensing of drivers and public vehicles; it has schemed out the prettiest plan in the world for regulating the cab service—only it has provided no method for enforcing its laws. It has designated certain public hack-stands. Having done so, it said that all was well; and rested. The cabs stood

Patrolling Fifth Avenue for victims.

where they pleased, or crawled unconcernedly in the avenues. One amiable pirate whom I know has taken out ten licenses; upon these ten licenses he sends out one hundred cabs to ply for hire. Let us descend to figures; he pays the city $2.50 a year; he should pay $25—and the difference seems wide enough to drive six grafts abreast.

In a word, the whole business here is loose and lawless. It is neither well-ordered nor well-kept. The private stables pay no heed to the legal rates. The hotel-cabs, upon the pretense that they are not "public hacks" within the meaning of the law, charge twice the legal fare. The pirates rob at will. And the public pays. It was brought out in court not long ago that during the first year of the existence of the Waldorf-Astoria hotel, the cabs—and only those standing on the Thirty-third Street side—paid $14,000 in commissions to the hotel. Now it is not easy to understand just why the public should be fined that amount for using public conveyances. The cab-privileges all around that gilded block will bring in a sum in thirty years or so sufficient to pay for the initial cost of the hotel. *Quid absurdum est*, as the children say. In every street the unlicensed cabs of the great stables go to and fro; their charges are exactly double that permitted by the law. Unless you have a fairly good cab education you will not often cab it at the legal rate of fifty cents a mile. And the fault lies not so much with the negligent public—not so much with the rapacious cabby—as it does with the city officials who are responsible for the slack enforcement of the law.

Personally, I am on the side of the cabmen. I know scores of them—Flynn and Gould and many another good man—and I think they act as fairly as they can under the bad existing circumstances. Probably the majority of them are as clean as that hound's tooth which has got itself into politics. Now and then you get into the hands of a wrong 'un——

It was only the other day——

I wonder whether the sun will ever shine so brightly, or so golden-brown a girl—for the hair and the eyes and the hat and the gown and the shoes and the gloves were golden-brown—express a wish to drink tea in the Casino of Central Park. Any-

way, that is where he drove us from lower Fifth Avenue, the cabby; he was wise and not unkind, for he drove slowly and found a circling way through the Park. Handing the golden-brown thing out, I asked: "How much?"

"Ten dollars," said the cabby.

"It was worth twenty," I said.

He went away like the young man in the parable; at night, I think, he wakes with a bitter and strong cry, cursing that time he dared not ask enough. I told this anecdote to Flynn over in First Avenue, there by Sixty-third Street, where the little Italiany children wallow in the gutters. I told it because we were talking cabs and also because I like to tell it as often as I can—a pleasant memory cannot be too often recalled.

"That was all your fault," said Mr. Flynn—he is gray-eyed and determined, and he said it as though he meant it—"all your fault. Why did you ask him what the fare was? You knew well enough. There should be a law passed making it an indictable offense for a man to ask what the fare is. It is putting temptation in the driver's way. Do you think you could resist that kind of thing yourself? You get into a licensed cab—the fares are posted up in front of you—and you get out and ask the driver, 'How much?' What do you expect the driver to say? Naturally he will look you over and decide that you are the kind of fool he can part from ten dollars of your fool money. Don't blame him. It is your fault. And you are simply educating him to be a robber."

Said Flynn—there was a pleasant evening light in First Avenue; 'tis a broad and spacious street, lined with smart little shops and homey tenements; then it was so blithe with Italiany children that one might well be content to settle down there and make friends; across the street from the doorway in which we stood was Flynn's stable, where a hairy old man, who would be the better for more teeth, was washing a hansom. Flynn, with an owner's eye, watched the operation.

"I have been twenty years at the craft," he said with a quiet sort of pride.

Do you remember the rat-catcher in "Lavengro," who maintained that his craft was immeasurably superior to any other? He had the right kind of pride.

The New York cabby is the most slovenly in the world.

driver has to have a license; that mysterious official, the mayor's marshal, grants one upon the pay-ment of twenty-five cents and two written testimonials of hon-esty. A man may come out of Sing Sing, whither he has been sent for highway robbery or stoning the minister's cat or any other crime; if he presents two greasy letters—one of any Jones and the other of any Smith—stating that he is an honest fel-low, he will get a license. No inquiry is made. His references are never looked up. Indeed, if you are a desperate criminal—guilty of mayhem or murder or failure to pay alimony—you can do no better than take out a license and hide on top of a cab. So, into the business drifts all sorts and conditions of rogues. Under the ægis of the law (the ægis being a twenty-five cent badge) they rob you, and me——

(The sun shone goldenly; and, eh, but she was a bonny lass, all golden-brown; she expressed

The man who doesn't think his business is the best in the world has no right to be in it—whether it be spilling the gaunt pot-hooks of literature on virginal white pa-per or blowing up *pommes de terre soufflées* through a straw. So, being proud of it, Flynn told me of the efforts he and a few others have been making to clean up the cab business. These men are they who own their cabs and horses. They have an association—that of The Public Hack and Cab Drivers. With great diligence they have been trying to get the city officials to enforce the laws—with no great success; on every cab-rank and hack-stand unlicensed vehicles jostle them. They have gone to the Board of Aldermen and asked for the enactment of sterner ordinances. They have urged the Merchants' Association to assist them in reforming the abuses of the business. And in one place as in another they have got about as much sympathy as re-formers usually get. They have been at the police and the aldermen and the mayor's marshal in an attempt to get the rogues innowed out of the fraternity of drivers; th what success you may imagine. A

But he keeps his top hat well brushed.

a wish to drink tea at the Casino—I beg your pardon; I forgot I had mentioned that already; it is a little like the head of King Charles, which insisted upon getting into Mr. Dick's narrative; but a prettier head, believe me.)

These things Mr. Flynn made clear to me as we stood in the doorway of the tenement in First Avenue, while succeeding waves of Italiany children broke and splashed at our feet. And I felt as he did; I thrilled with the same indignation; suppose you were one of the seven hundred good men and true, who own and drive their own cabs in this city of iron and of stone, would you not kindle against the knaves, big and little, who were dirtying your chosen trade? Here's more power to him; so far as I can I will help him out; never again will I ask how much; with an experienced cabber's wisdom I shall pay the fifty cents a mile, putting a quarter atop by way of tip.

There is lots of time for reading.

Off duty.

There are forty-five stables sending out cabs and victorias into the streets. In their employ are about one thousand four hundred drivers, who are members of the Coach and Cab Drivers' Protective Association, which is known in the trade as the "Liberty Dawn." They are part of the Team-Drivers' International Union, of the one hundred thousand drivers scattered from Maine to Hawaii. Edward Gould is chairman of "Local No. 607." He is a big, upstanding man with a good, wind-beaten face. In the bulk of him a fine sense of humor lurks.

"The object of our society," said he, "is to help out the landlords."

"That sounds good," said I; "go on."

"Well, it is this way," Gould explained; "before the association took hold the men were working twenty hours a day and sleeping in the stables. We brought the work down to fourteen hours a day and gave the men a chance to hire flats and cultivate domesticity."

There is a universal wage of $2 a day; and then there are the tips. Each member is taxed a monthly due of five cents;

The auto-cab is the hansom's chief rival.

"Doing" New York.

if he falls ill he receives $7 a week for two months; if he dies he is buried to the extent of $115. The "Liberty Dawn" is a notable institution. Its membership includes most of the drivers of the railway cabs. A man need not have gray in the hair—nor the shame of baldness on him—to remember the origin of this tolerable system of getting about. It dates back only a few years. The service is a good

the horses are good. No city can exhibit smarter public turn-outs. The best of it all is that these fast-faring, comfortable and cheap carriages are educating the public up to the proper use of the cab. Everything must have a beginning. Young Milo began by carrying a calf and in time walked lightly under the weight and bulk of a full-grown bull. The young man who begins timidly by cabbing it from the Grand Cen-

At the railway station 'tis: "Have a hansom—keb. keb, keb?"

one. You pay the fare to the agent of the railway cab service before you get in; it is as plain a business as buying a ticket to Canaan, Four-Corners, or any other metropolis; and you pay an exact legal fare.

If you do not tip the driver when you get out, you are a trifle the better and he, apparently, is not much the worse. Moreover, the vehicles are smart and new, and

tral Station—with trunk and bag atop—for seventy cents, will come, little by little, to displaying himself in the splendid isolation of a hansom in Fifth Avenue. A trifle later he will be 'phoning for a carriage from the jobber. In a few years he will not be content without a stable of his own

Frankly, a great deal of nonsense gets itself said and printed about the advantages of economy. The best equipment a young man can have, starting out in life, is a bundle of wants. He should want to smoke good cigars; want to get his clothes made by the best tailor; want to dine at the best tables; want to flirt with the prettiest women; want to belong to the best club; want to have his turn at Monte Carlo and spin his yacht in the Adriatic; want, in a word, the best and most of everything. Give a young man all the needs possible. Let him acquire the habit of living largely. That young man will be no idler. He will find the wherewithal to satisfy his needs. He will get together the kind of a fortune needed for his ample way of life. You say that he may fail to work out the equation? Then is he a yellow dog. By no chance could he have been any use to himself or society. He had best drop down and run in the common with the yellow-haired fellows of his breed.

Cabbing, I repeat, is for the young man the beginning of wisdom. Its study might profitably replace Greek in every college curriculum.

Some day the cab business of New York will shake itself down into an orderly trade; the various drivers' unions will be welded into one; the many owners' associations will combine; the idle aldermen will pass proper ordinances; the mysterious marshal of the mayor will see that only proper men are licensed; the police will exercise effective supervision; the public, enlightened, will not ask how much.

("How much?" I asked.

"Ten dollars," said he—she was an ardent and desirable girl, golden-brown from tip to toe, like a meadow-lark.

"It was worth twenty," said I.)

In the meantime, the poor, dislocated trade goes darkly through piracy and disfavor. He who comes oversea to us is beaten upon by the worst of it. You know the rusty hacks with the rusty horses and the rusty darkey that lie in wait at the docks. Even so, I have been informed by naturalists, the alligator *Mississippiensis*, more commonly called the *crocodilus Lucius*, lies basking on the muddy shore, waiting, too, for the unwary. If I were writing a five-act tragedy, "The Cab," I would put in just here very blood-curdling things. Many and many a young Englishman, rosy and fatted and innocent, has been seen

for the last time as a rusty darkey bundled him into a rusty cab at the dock. He never arrived at any destination. In faraway English homes they waited, heartsick and hope-sick, for news of him. No word ever came. He was never heard of, never seen. There was no trace—not so much as an *h* dropped from the hack-window as a signal of distress. He took a hack at the docks—and was not.

Only the native New Yorker (and preferably one with the stripes of the Bowery on him) should adventure his fortunes in one of the old arks that crawl about the docks or gather, when night is deep, in Chatham Square. If there be wicked old men in New York, they sit upon the boxes of these rumbling carriages. He is a strenuous criminal, too, who takes his seat by the driver as the hack starts off, toward what defiled paradise I know not. All will not be well with the countryman who sits, full of bucolic pride and wickedness, within; faster than he knows he is bearing down upon the zone of trouble. Some day they will drive away—rusty coachman and creaking hack—into half-forgotten local history. In the meantime they should be left to the kind of gentleman who sings by night and derives a subtle pleasure from riding with one leg through the window frame. It doesn't matter what happens to him anyway. But you and I, being self-respecting cabbers—proud of our clean bodies and our clean minds—will have none of this night-faring. Not even for the sake of acquiring "local color" will we go down into that nocturnal world where the night-hawk circles for his prey.

Arcadian airs are blowing in the Park; the sunlight falls prettily on pretty women and the lordly-shining coats of horses, bay and brown; let us go drink tea at the Casino —yonder at one of the white tables; and as twilight comes we shall go swaying home in a hansom down the gray reaches of the avenue, where only a few lights flicker here and there. (And if you are good— pray, when are you not good?—you may take the white beauty of your hand out of that brown glove and I will see that no harm comes to hand or glove. This is better; the rhythm of the flying cab; the gray beauty of the avenue we love—an ungloved hand.)

"It was worth twenty," said I.

2
Guarding the Gateway of New York

Guarding the Gateway of New York.

BY RUTHERFORD CORBIN.

WHAT MILITARY SCIENCE HAS DONE AND IS DOING TO MAKE THE AMERICAN METROPOLIS IMPREGNABLE AGAINST ATTACK— THE FORMIDABLE MODERN FORTS THAT WOULD CONFRONT A HOSTILE FLEET THREATENING THE CHIEF CITY AND PORT OF THE NEW WORLD.

QUIETLY but vigorously and thoroughly the army has gone about strengthening the defenses of New York harbor, along the lines of a systematic plan adopted many years ago. There is still much to be done, but as it stands the American metropolis may be pronounced absolutely impregnable against any force which any foreign power could send against it. When the scheme of defense is finished, it will be strong enough to defy the combined fleets of the world.

This has cost money, and will cost more, but the charge is not excessive when we regard it as an insurance upon the vast riches of New York. Harbor forts are like a " gun " in Arizona— when you need them, you " need them bad." The ugly bundles of mechanism which form the modern high-power disappearing gun, and the unlovely scars in the earth behind which it hides, do not make such ornamental pictures as the castellated defenses of olden times, but a day may come when they will be the most important things in the world to the community they protect.

WAR'S CHANGED ASPECT.

The pride and panoply of war has become a thing of the past. Fighting is a fierce, grim business now; and the only business in which advertisement has ceased to be a factor. Even the American army blue has gone. It made the men it clothed too distinct from the background of the green or brown or gray of the landscape. An army board spent several months testing every practicable color and every method of construction to find the uniform which presented the least possible contrast to its surroundings. The result was the selection of the olive drab in which Uncle Sam's soldiers are now clothed. At a thousand yards a column of men in blue shows distinctly to the naked eye. A similar body clad in olive drab is practically invisible at that distance without a powerful glass.

The incidents of the Spanish War are so well remembered that it is scarcely necessary to recall the contrast between the black powder of the old Springfield rifles used by our volunteers and the smokeless " Krags " of the regulars. The troops which formed the maneuvering corps at Manassas last summer were all armed with the improved rifle, which shoots only smokeless powder. The great guns in the forts around New York abandoned smoke powder six years ago.

THE DISAPPEARING GUN.

During the past decade, every government in the world has been experimenting with the disappearing carriage for the larger guns. The merits of the device are to a certain extent a matter of controversy, but it is safe to say that the United States has brought it to the highest degree of perfection attained anywhere. The carriage in use in our coast defenses is the product of the mechanical genius of two officers of our ordnance · department, Generals Buffington and Crozier. Its working is easily understood from the engraving on page 513. In its first position, the gun is swung low behind the rampart. It is loaded and sighted while in that position, being entirely invisible to the enemy, and protected from their fire. A mechanical device lifts the gun and throws its muzzle over the rampart for just the second necessary for its discharge, instantly bringing it back again to its former protected position.

Just as the "smoke of battle" and the "army blue" have become phrases of a glorious past, the picturesque ramparts marked with stone port-holes and black cannon muzzles are

THE OLD SOUTH BATTERY ON GOVERNOR'S ISLAND, NEW YORK HARBOR—THESE OBSOLETE MUZZLE-LOADING GUNS WOULD BE USELESS FOR DEFENSE AGAINST MODERN WAR-SHIPS. NEW YORK IS NOW GUARDED BY MORE POWERFUL BATTERIES AT A GREATER DISTANCE FROM THE CITY.

equally obsolete. The old south battery at Governor's Island, which in the war of 1812 covered the approach to Brooklyn and Manhattan Island, is being turned into a club for the soldiers and officers of the garrison. The old main redoubt at Fort Hamilton has become the post bakery, and children play about its stern portcullis.

The modern army's effort is to be as inconspicuous as possible. Soldiers clad in invisible uniforms fight with invisible cannon charged with invisible powder. Forts do not display their

ONE OF THE GREAT MODERN GUNS THAT GUARD NEW YORK—A TEN-INCH BREECH-LOADING RIFLE MOUNTED ON A DISAPPEARING CARRIAGE. THE ENGRAVING SHOWS THE GUN IN POSITION FOR LOADING; FOR FIRING, THE MECHANISM OF THE CARRIAGE LIFTS IT ABOVE THE PARAPET IN FRONT.

armament, but hide it. There is no prettier sight in the harbor of New York than the green ramparts of Fort Hamilton, at the Narrows. There is not a gun to be seen, and yet, crouching grim and silent behind the grass-grown embankments are the great rifles of the most powerful battery in the western hemisphere. A call of a bugle, a rush of men into the covered trench behind, a whir of electricity, and the scarp would bristle with the black muzzles, to fill the Lower Bay with a hail of shells, each capable of hitting a battle-ship at six miles or more.

INNER AND OUTER RINGS OF DEFENSE.

Both entrances to New York harbor are covered by two fire zones. On the north the city is still further protected by the fortifications which block the entrance from the Atlantic Ocean into Long Island Sound. A chain of seven forts stretches along the coast from Fort Rodman, near New Bedford, to Fort Trumbull, at New London; while Fort Wright and Fort Terry stand on the islands that divide the fairway of the Sound into comparatively narrow channels, easily commanded by the guns of the forts.

Should an enemy's fleet get into the Sound—a feat which, by the way, our North Atlantic Squadron was unable to do in the maneuvers of two years ago— it would still find its way to New York effectually barred. The northern approach to the metropolis is protected by heavy batteries at Forts Slocum, Schuyler, and Totten. Fort Slocum is located on David's Island, which lies in front of New Rochelle, and the guns of this, the prettiest of the harbor forts, sweep clear into the entrance of Long Island Sound. Five miles nearer the city, where the East River properly begins, are Schuyler and Totten, stern sentinels at New York's gateway. These stand on either side of the channel, Fort Schuyler a few miles from West Chester, and Fort Totten just below Whitestone, on Long Island.

At Fort Totten is located the United States Engineer School of Submarine Defense, and here, in time of war, would be the main torpedo field of the northern entrance. The range of the guns

from Schuyler and Totten reaches into the channel beyond Slocum, so that an attacking fleet, as it made its way along the deep-water channel, would be under fire for ten or twelve miles—an ordeal that no vessel could hope to survive.

NEW YORK'S MAIN GATEWAY.

This thorough protection of the northern approach—made doubly dangerous to an enemy by the difficulty of navigation—throws the chief burden of defensive preparation upon the southern fire zone, created by the guns at Forts Hamilton, Wadsworth, and Hancock. Cutting the clear channel into New York harbor from the Atlantic Ocean, there are only these three forts to put out of action, and the great city would lie at the mercy of a hostile fleet. But they are not ordinary forts. Every resource known to the science of war has been called into service to make them impregnable. A battle-ship fleet, entering ship by ship, in the long, thin line necessitated by the comparative narrowness of the channel, would for fifteen miles be exposed to the fire of twenty great guns. Moreover, it could not navigate the channel except on the supposition that the mines strung from the Romer Shoals to the Narrows failed to work. And the naval campaign about Port Arthur has shown how terribly destructive are these deadly implements of warfare.

Even without mines or forts, the winding course might well puzzle the pilots of an attacking fleet; for of course the buoys that now mark the fairway would be removed if hostile visitors were expected. With every precaution, an ocean liner sometimes runs aground on her way in or out of the harbor; and the fate of an enemy's warship that lay stranded and helpless in such a position can easily be imagined.

As the small map on page 516 shows, the channel runs close under the guns of Fort Hancock, and then, bending sharply northward, enters the narrow gateway between Forts Hamilton and Wadsworth. A new and more direct channel is now being dredged, which will pass Fort Hancock at a considerably greater distance. When this is opened, which will not be for several years, it is

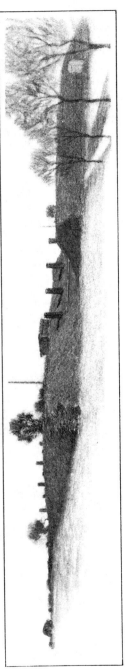

FORT HAMILTON, ON THE EASTERN (LONG ISLAND) SHORE OF THE SOUTHERN APPROACH TO NEW YORK HARBOR—WHEN THE PROPOSED WORKS AT THIS POINT ARE FINISHED, IT WILL BE THE STRONGEST FORTIFICATION ON THE COAST OF THE UNITED STATES. THE BUILDING ON THE LEFT OF THE UPPER ENGRAVING IS OLD FORT LAFAYETTE, USED AS A PRISON DURING THE CIVIL WAR, AND NOW OBSOLETE; ON THE RIGHT ARE THE EARTHWORKS OF THE MODERN FORT, OF WHICH THE LOWER ENGRAVING GIVES A NEARER VIEW.

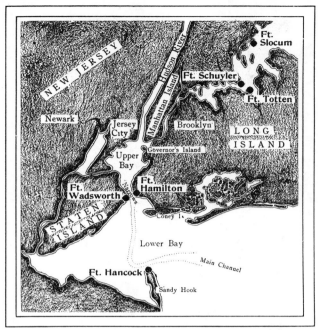

MAP OF NEW YORK HARBOR, SHOWING THE SIX GREAT FORTS THAT GUARD ITS NORTHERN AND SOUTHERN APPROACHES.

defense of New York. Here, under Colonel Greenough, a typical modern fighting man who does things out of his own brain and with his own hands, the artillery corps of the United States army is constructing its finest fort. It is a fine one already, but a scheme of improvement has been submitted to the War Department which will cost from two to three million dollars. This will include the building of a seaside park beside the fort, which in time of peace would be a public pleasure-ground of great value to the city and its people. Should war come, the park could be closed and used as a camp-ground for the five thousand men who would be needed to garrison the fort, and for whom there are now no available quarters.

The old forts in the inner harbor, which once formed the defenses of New York, are entirely obsolete. On Bedloe's Island a corporal's guard watches to see that the visitors to the Statue of Liberty do not break off pieces of the brazen goddess as souvenirs. Ellis Island is given over to the immigrant station. The Battery has reverted to the city; the old Castle Garden, originally called Fort Clinton, is now used as an aquarium. On Governor's Island old Fort Jay, built as a defense by the students of Columbia College a century ago, has succumbed to the law which scatters land defenses in proportion to the increased range of artillery. It is still the headquarters of the Atlantic Division, and with the new enlargement will form a magnificent base storehouse for munitions of war. The old house which was formerly the residence of the Dutch governors of New York still stands, and is now occupied by Brigadier-General Frederick Grant, in command of the Eastern Department. On its list of earlier tenants are the names

likely that the War Department will establish another battery on the Long Island coast, probably on Plum Island, which lies behind the eastern end of Coney Island.

Fort Hancock is on the long peninsula, or island, of Sandy Hook, which juts from the northeastern corner of New Jersey into the sea, separating the Lower Bay and the Shrewsbury River from the Atlantic Ocean. Besides the batteries of Hancock, the government owns a five-mile stretch of sandy waste which it uses as a proving-ground for the testing of guns of various kinds before their acceptance, and for experimenting with new models.

Fort Wadsworth is on the Staten Island side of the entrance to the Narrows, the inner gateway of New York harbor. Its guns control the horizon line from Fort Hamilton, on the Brooklyn side of the channel, to Sandy Hook, their muzzles sweeping over the white city of Coney Island.

AMERICA'S FINEST FORT.

Fort Hamilton is the central and most important point of the southern

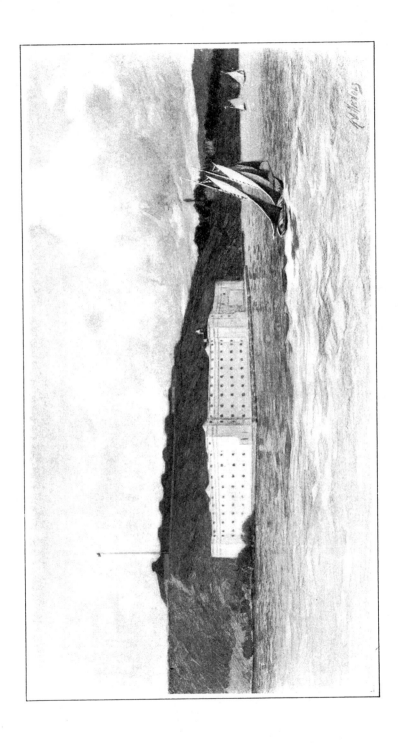

FORT WADSWORTH, ON THE WESTERN (STATEN ISLAND) SHORE OF THE SOUTHERN APPROACH TO NEW YORK HARBOR—THE MAIN SHIP CHANNEL, WHOSE ENTRANCE IS COMMANDED BY FORT HANCOCK, ON SANDY HOOK, PASSES CLOSE UNDER THE GUNS OF FORTS WADSWORTH AND HAMILTON, WHICH STAND ON EITHER SIDE OF THE NARROWS, LIKE SENTINELS GUARDING THE GREAT GATEWAY OF THE NEW WORLD.

THE COMMANDING GENERAL'S RESIDENCE ON GOVERNOR'S ISLAND—HERE, WHERE THE OLD DUTCH GOVERNORS OF NEW AMSTERDAM ONCE RESIDED, HAVE BEEN IN RECENT YEARS THE HEAD-QUARTERS OF LIEUTENANT-GENERALS SCHOFIELD AND MILES, AND MAJOR-GENERALS RUGER, MERRITT, SHAFTER, AND OTIS. IN THE ENGRAVING MAJOR-GENERAL CORBIN STANDS ON THE STEPS. THE PRESENT COMMANDER IS BRIGA-DIER-GENERAL FREDERICK D. GRANT.

of Schofield, Howard, Ruger, Merritt, Miles, Shafter, Otis, and Corbin, and it was in this house that Major-General Hancock resided while the Democratic candidate for the Presidency against Garfield in 1880.

Six thousand soldiers watch New York. Each day a thousand men mount guard in the fifteen forts that protect the great city and the waters around it.

Each day a hundred guns are cleansed and oiled and made ready for the time when the nation may need to call them into use.

As the sun sets in the west, the dull mounds of earth loom heavy in the twilight, monuments to the power of the Republic which goes its way, to guard its own borders and to assure peace in the western world.

3
The Renaissance of Coney

THE
OUTING
MAGAZINE

AUGUST, 1906

THE RENAISSANCE OF CONEY

BY CHARLES BELMONT DAVIS

ILLUSTRATED BY HY. S. WATSON

FAR down on the New York Bowery there exists to-day a highly colored poster of a young woman in an abbreviated skirt, a décolleté waist and a plumed picture-hat. The poster is pasted on a billboard and the board leans against the front of a dance hall. In the mornings the place is quite deserted, but during the late afternoon hours and again at night the little tin tables which are scattered about the room are fairly well occupied; there is a rush of waiters in soiled coats between the bar in front and the groups about the tables, and a young woman sings ballads and comic songs from a little stage in the rear of the hall. This young woman has a hard, rasping voice, but sufficient in volume, however, to reach the passers-by on the street. Like the lady on the picture outside, she has a short skirt, but there the resemblance ends, for the poster outside is usually of some well-known celebrity such as Lillian Russell or a divinity of the French music halls. There is no intention on the part of the proprietor to deceive, for his class of patrons probably have never heard of Miss Russell or the divinities of the French music halls; the poster is simply the emblem, and the east-side tough and the sailor ashore for a spree know it and know that within they can find wine, women and song, and all of the three in their most degraded forms. The day has not long passed when the Bowery was fairly rich in such resorts, but now they are gone, and so far as I know all that is left is the dive of which I have spoken and which still hangs out its brazen banner on the sidewalk.

When the traffic deserted its old haunts the managers of the dance halls gathered up their paraphernalia and the greasy-coated waiters and started a new Bowery far from the old stand—a land unknown to the reformer and where law and justice cut but a sorry figure. This chosen spot was called Coney Island, and they christened that part of it which they chose to degrade the Bowery—probably in grateful memory of the palmy days when they were allowed to ply their trade much nearer to City Hall, even in the shadow of the Tombs. They opened the doors of the dance halls, and either side of the single street which constituted the town were lined with the three-sheet posters of the gaily bedecked artists who were supposed to perform within. In addition to the dance halls there were a few "shows" to which an admission was charged, but the shows were "fakes" of the most pronounced kind and their managers pretended them to be little else. Two classes of people supported these shows and dance halls —innocent souls from the country who believed that they were seeing city life in its most devilish form, and thoroughly knowing men and girls from the city who knew just how soiled "Coney" was and liked it for that very reason. It became the meeting place of the city's petty thieves, the touts from the neighboring race tracks and the lowest social strata of the Metropolis. Sometimes little parties of sightseers of a better class dined at Brighton Beach and drove over afterwards for a look at "The Bowery." They went there prepared to buy gold bricks, and they were not disappointed. Coney Island in those days was synonymous for everything that was corrupt and lawless—and then there came the reformation, for the change seemed to have happened over night. From a social sore Coney Island was

м·Ј·W
One of Coney's "children."

turned into the most extensive and best show place in the world. I have no interest, I regret to say, in any of the numerous enterprises which constitute this amusement village, nor any particular desire to advertise any of its attractions, but it is a pleasure to speak truly about a place which can give so much happiness to children of mature years. There is a theory that crime must be conceived in darkness, and it is an old practice of the authorities to clean up a vicious neighborhood by hanging

up a particularly bright electric light in its midst. It is highly improbable that the men who reformed Coney Island had this idea in view when they threw their network of millions of electric globes across this end of the Island, but the result was the same. Any one who can rob or even practice the mildest deception under the present white light of publicity is deserving of the swag.

There are several ways to reach Coney Island, at least New Yorkers will tell you there are, but the average New Yorker is for some reason wholly ignorant of the geography which immediately surrounds him. In a general way he knows that there is a North and an East River and a Bay and a Sound, but their exact location is usually rather hazy to his mind, and he differentiates them solely by the friends he happens to know who own summer homes on their various banks. When I first sought information as to the best mode of reaching Coney Island I am sure twenty different routes were presented, and each was guaranteed to be the safest and best. They included trips by excursion boats, ferry-boats railroad trains, trolleys, elevated trains, hacks, automobiles and combinations of a part or all of these. I believe I tried every one of them, and eventually found that the only logical route is to take an elevated train at the Brooklyn Bridge; ask every guard's, policeman's and official's advice in sight, and then by taking the trains you are told not to take you will eventually arrive at Coney Island. This route costs but a dime, and includes a trip across the bridge and a wonderful view of the chimneys and second-story bedrooms of all Brooklyn. The chimneys are distinctive in the fact that each one is decorated by a billboard painted to represent a huge human molar, and in the center of each is the picture of the painless dentist himself with a large black moustache. The Brooklyn second-story bedrooms assert their similarity to each other in that whatever the hour the chambermaid seems to have always neglected to make up the bed since the previous night, and each room contains one occupant—a man sitting in his shirt-sleeves, always collarless, and reading an evening paper. The chimneys and bed-rooms extend for many miles, but at last we get into the open and a land of semi-de-tached villas and arid acres, identified solely by large signs whereon real estate agents tell us that on these very acres great cities will soon arise. And then at last across the meadows we see the towers and the bizarre-shaped walls of the play-houses of the city of pleasure.

We enter Coney Island by the stage door as it were, and as the train slows down we find ourselves surrounded by the unpainted backs and wooden frame-work of the can-vas walls of tinsel villages. The first thing that impresses us about this pleasure ground is that it is un-like the other "Midways" and "Pikes" and county fairs we have seen, in that it is a city and not the temporary show-place of the fakirs. The one street of which the town practically consists is paved, and there are ca-ble cars and electric-light poles and policemen and all the other signs of the organized common-wealth. It is only in the architecture and the uses of the buildings that line the little street wherein we see the difference. Every house seems to be either a restaurant or a so-called amusement-palace. Here and there we find a modest little haberdasher or a trim-ming-store tucked away between the gaudy en-trance to a scenic-railway or a "Johnstown Flood," but these little shops ap-pear very insignificant and seem really sadly out of place. Even the res-

taurants afford some kind of entertainment —if it is only a gentleman who bangs out "rag-time" on a bad piano. Some of them rise to the dignity of the employment of so-called Hungarian bands, but these are all wide open on the street, and all are free and most of them are decorated with signs which announce that "basket-parties are wel-come." Some day there will be a good res-taurant at Coney Island, but that day is not yet. Several of those now existent have red lamp shades and one has beardless waiters, but the old régime had a keen disregard for fresh tablecloths, and its feelings are still respected. The same old régime also left a few of its members, who have tried to give the old tone to the new town. This rem-nant of the past has built its home on a little street just back of the main thorough-fare and directly on the sea, and here one finds a very mild and wholly uninteresting view of what was once typical of Coney Isl-and. There are open dance halls and open

The main street in the "City of Fun."

Anything for a "sensation."

variety performances, where a lot of woodeny chorus girls and very dull comedians attempt to lure the passer-by in for a glass of beer. But the white light of the new town shines fiercely down upon them and upon their poor entertainment, and must eventually drive them as it did the other cheap and bad shows to another hunting ground.

It would be as difficult, in a short article, to describe, even enumerate, all the shows which line the main thoroughfares as it would be to see the sights of a world's fair in twenty-four hours. The best one can do is to wander along until he or she finds an electric sign which promises something to their taste. Should the visitor have a delight for horrors there is a rare choice of historical mishaps such as the Johnstown or Galveston floods, the Mount Pelee Eruption, The Fall of Pompeii, or several realistic exhibitions of whole blocks of burning build-

ings. The year of 1904 will be memorable, if for nothing else than those two terrible disasters, the burning of the Iroquois Theater and the excursion boat *General Slocum*. So great was the supposed revulsion of feeling on the part of the public after the first of these disasters that theatrical managers found it necessary to cut out any use of flames in a stage performance, and in several instances when a "fire-scene" was necessary to a production the whole play was abandoned. And yet, perhaps, the two most successful shows at Coney Island last summer were the exhibitions, really terrible in their realism, of burning buildings, which seems to show that the morbid love of the public for devastating flames is just as great as it ever was, only the public must be guaranteed absolute personal safety.

In addition to these grewsome exhibitions of disasters there are many other independent shows of a lighter nature such as trips through imitation coal mines and canals and even the sewers of the great cities. But the foundation of Coney Island's success is not so much in these independent shows as in the three great so-called "Parks" which form the nucleus of the pleasure village. Each of the three is a Midway in itself, and the only difference between them is the very natural advantages which the last two have gleaned from the successes and failures of their predecessors. The same crowd visits all the three, and each has its own particular attractions and faithful admirers. On a fine day or still better on a fine night these parks, which are incidentally built with solid floor foundations, and each covering as much space as a "Midway" or "Pike," are crowded with a great surging mass of men, women and children, and all with but one purpose—amusement.

That is where the showman of Coney Island has the advantage of the city theatrical manager. When a man or more especially a woman pays two dollars for an orchestra seat he or she becomes the critic and mentally demands the full worth of the money expended. The same public goes to Coney Island, spends many times the money it would at the theater, smiles continually and tries to see the best there is in everything. Coney Island is regarded as a lark, and it is treated with the same joyous regard as is the annual visit to the circus.

Old men and old women come with their children and grandchildren, and according to their worldly goods dine at a restaurant or bring their suppers in a basket and afterwards go to one show or fifty as the case may be, but they always go with the spirit of the holiday upon them, and it is this great mixed mass of humanity and the good-will that pervades it that more than all else make Coney Island what it is to-day. Just as the best scenery yet devised was arranged by the Creator of this world, so its best shows are those wherein the people are the leading actors. It is not the long-tailed thoroughbreds with their midget jockeys that make a Derby or a Grand Prix or a Suburban, but it is rather the waves of human beings frenzied with the love of gambling; it is not the broad roadways nor the overhanging trees of the Bois that make the show, but the women in the carriages and the clothes the women wear; the best part of a prize fight is not the sight of two human brutes pounding each other into insensibility on a resined floor, but rather the yelling, crazy mob with its innate love of carnage that the two brutes have turned into the principal actors. It is the same at a stock exchange or at Monte Carlo or a court ball—the people make the show. All it requires is a little stage-management, and this the promoters of pleasure at Coney Island well understand.

A clever person once devised a fire-escape for use in schools, which consisted of a huge metal tube containing a smooth spiral slide. It was only necessary to put a child at the top of the spiral slide, and it would eventually come out at an open doorway at the bottom. From this has been evolved one of the delights of Coney Island. In place of the metal tube there is but a low wall to keep the people from shooting out into space as they slide down the spiral chute. There is even a later development of the same idea at Dreamland. Instead of the spiral chute there is a broad slide glass-like in its smoothness, with raised obstacles placed at intervals. The slidee starts at the top and endeavors to avoid the obstacles. As this is quite impossible, the said slidee, after being turned around three or four times, usually reaches the bottom of the slide head-first. At first glance this would seem to be an unnecessary mishap, and yet hundreds of men and women slide down all day and night, to the delight of the gaping thousands. It is surely a strange pastime for the sane, but the spirit of joy is abroad and the sight of a serene-looking and elderly fat lady bumping her way down this wooden hillside and ending with a couple of somersaults to finish off with seems but a proper and legitimate pastime after one has grown accustomed to the true spirit of the place. And yet these elderly Jacks and Jills pay for the pleasure of the bumps, while the crowd below watches the fun with shouts of glee and pays nothing. The fat lady would probably excuse herself by telling you that she was enjoying a new sensation, and in this perhaps is to be found not only truth but the great secret which underlies the success of Coney Island's pastimes. There may be cynically inclined worldlings who contend that it is not possible to obtain a real sensation for a dime. If such there be I am sure that one properly conducted visit to Coney Island will cure them of this idea. For many years our simple tastes were content with the merry-go-rounds still sacred to county fairs and cheap watering resorts. The

It takes a clever man to be a fool.

sensation was distinctly mild even in the case of children, and grown-ups were usually attacked with *mal-de-mer*. To offset this mildness the showman eventually built his merry-go-round with horses which plunged about independent of the general rotary movement of the whole concern. It is true that a child was sometimes thrown, but it was that little element of danger that made the game worth while. The same mental reasoning is what makes automobile-racing and tiger-hunting amusing.

But we eventually outgrew merry-go-rounds—children tired of them and old people could ride them without being ill—and so the scenic-railway was introduced. Statistics would probably show that accidents are about as rare on scenic-railroads as they are on hearses, but the effect, exhilarating to most people, is quite equal to that of going in an automobile at the rate of fifty miles an hour. It has one infinite advantage over the automobile, for by going down a grade it can drop you into apparently limitless space. The same effect could probably be obtained by an automobile being driven over the Palisades and dropping into the middle of the Hudson River. And yet it is this sensation of immediate disaster caused by scenic-railways, chute-the-chutes, loop-the-loops, all variations of the one idea, which takes most of the people to Coney Island. After some experience I am personally convinced that one can get a sensation for a dime.

A friend who had recently "done" Coney Island said to me one day: "Easily the best sensation at the Island is the scenic-railway with the wooden beam that looks as if it were going to hit you on the head. It's great." My friend was a somewhat soured person and satiated with the world's

sensations, and for several days I searched for the scenic-railway with the beam that looked as if it were going to hit me on the head. At last I found it at an independent enterprise a short distance from Dreamland. It was called a musical railway for some reason I could not understand unless the music was out being tuned. The name, however, may be just a whim of the manager, who I know has a real sense of humor for at the entrance of the first tunnel to his infernal railway there is a sign. The inscription is simple—"No Kissing Allowed in this Tunnel." The tunnel is built on the general plan of an artesian well and about as dark, and it seemed to me that the car dropped down the grade at the rate of several hundred feet a second. If an elevator containing a man and woman, complete strangers, were allowed to fall from the top floor of the Flatiron Building to the cellar it would be just as reasonable to accuse them of kissing during the fall as it would be to post such a notice in front of that tunnel on the Musical Railway. The real sensation of the beam, however, comes much later in the trip. It is at the end of a dark tunnel, and one sees it just after rounding a particularly dangerous curve. There it is, barely discernible through the darkened space—a great rough beam, built right across the tunnel and just low enough to knock our heads clear off our bodies. Of course we dodge instinctively and the beam passes over us many inches, perhaps feet away, for all I know. But the effect in the darkness and at the rate at which the car is rushing is most deceptive. Many people speculate at one time or another just what they would do if face to face with certain death. There is no longer any reason why they should have any doubt on the subject—the sensation can be obtained

HY S WATSON

Listening to the Barker's story.

at my musical railway, and for the small sum of ten cents. But I think the thing that annoyed me most about that beam was the nonchalant manner with which the gentleman who drove the car approached it. He not only refused to dodge, but not for a moment did he cease chatting with the beautiful lady on the seat back of him, and who I suppose must have been a friend of his as she seemed to be on the free list. There is an authentic case of an English officer who, having very narrowly escaped death on several occasions from flying shrapnell feared that he was losing his nerve. To definitely ascertain the truth in the matter he went up in a balloon and then descended to earth by means of a parachute. Then he was satisfied that he was all right. On somewhat the same principle I took five successive trips over that musical railway and four times I dodged the beam, but the fifth time I found my nerve and sailed under it with head erect. Another five rounds and I believe I could have bandied a few words with the charming lady who rode free. This statement is intended for those who visit Coney Island and tempt each sensation but once. If tickets are bought for a sensation by the strip I honestly believe any one can become callous to any shock.

There are, of course, a great many ways to spend one's time at Coney Island, quite free from shocks. For instance there is the gigantic Ferris wheel, ponderous in its movement and most admirably suited for those sentimentally inclined, especially as the guards always seem to arrange that each car shall hold but two passengers although they are really built for twenty. This, incidentally, has nothing whatever to do with that other most excellent revolving machine, "the Barrel of Love." The barker here will tell you that "the ladies like this show the best of all." Here is the reason for this statement given by the student of nature who wrote the official guide: "The young men (and every man is young when there is a woman in the

Everywhere there are children.

case) like it, because it gives them a chance to hug the girls; the girls (and every woman is a girl when there is a man in the case) like it, because it gives them a chance to get hugged."

The same author a little further along in the guide drops his psychological studies and does a little descriptive work in regard to the Mirrored Ball-Room:

"An enchanting evening sight is the numerous handsomely gowned ladies accompanied by gentlemen in full dress. With an attendance of nearly two million during the season of 1900, the services of a police officer were not at any time required.

"There are four bands of music; but the music created by our patrons themselves, by their spontaneous laughter, their sounds of merriment and harmony of action displayed, excel by far in volume and tone the creation of any band."

Here is one more morsel touching on the engine-room of the same park:

"The engines and dynamos are enameled in white with gold mountings. A Vernis-Martin curio table holds the tools, and a beautiful mosaic table, the oil cups. The white-gloved engineer, uniformed in white duck with brass buttons, has a Vienna desk for his special use. He is a college graduate, qualified to lecture upon his plant as well as to operate it."

Surely there is no "shock" or sensation here for the visitor so long as he does not touch the dynamos and contents himself listening to the lectures of the "white-gloved engineer." Indeed, for the young fiancée who demands no greater shock than a gentle pressure of her lover's hand much has been done at Coney Island. The sewers with their dark tunnels and stealthily moving, self-propelling skiffs may be highly recommended. Also a trip over the glistening Alps or through the canals of dank Venice surely breathes sentiment to those whose nostrils are constantly inflated for that modest passion. And again, for those averse to the strenuous life of the "shocks" and "thrills" there may be found in the various parks hanging Japanese tea-gardens, where elderly Geisha girls abound; a modest representation of the last Durbar; an array of infant incubators, and a fish-pond. For those not satiated with a knowledge of science and literature there is a good sample of a flying-machine, a papier-maché try at the infernal regions with a running lecture on the life and deeds of Dante, who we are told (the gentleman first having collected our dimes) was "a born poet who once lived in sunny Italy."

The one entertainment, whose title perhaps appeals to those whose tastes lead them to witness the *danse du ventre*, as given on the Chicago Midway, is "The Temptation of St. Anthony." But as a matter of fact it is not at all like the Midway shows, nor in fact are any of Coney's entertainments at present in the slightest need of Women's Leagues or Mothers' Clubs. In the present instance when the snickering audience has been relieved of its dimes and gathered in a small room, a curtain is withdrawn and a large oil painting disclosed. On the right we note the good saint praying hard, and standing back of him and quite beyond his vision is a lady draped in a garment modest only in its limitations. The gentleman who has sold us our admission tickets and who later pulled back the curtain, then disappears behind the oil painting, and continues to growl out a life and history of the times of St. Anthony. At such intervals as the audience seems to become a trifle peevish, the panel on which the siren is depicted is removed and another one inserted. If the first lady was a blonde the painted lady of the second panel is sure to be a brunette, and equally ill-clad even for a Jersey summer resort, but it makes no difference to St. Anthony at all for he is painted to look the other way, and the merest layman who has paid his dime is really in more temptation than the good Saint. Even the darkened room and the rumblings of the gentleman back of the picture fail to create much illusion, as the ladies were not painted by even a Bougereau, and in the flesh would have considerable difficulty in securing places as show-girls in a musical comedy.

I must confess to a great admiration and a feeling of personal esteem for a successful barker—the gentleman who by his antics and nimble wit tries to allure the passer-by into the particulars how he happens to represent. The barkers at Coney Island are of many kinds and have been gathered from very divergent callings. For instance, one gentleman in front of an alleged humorous show did nothing but laugh. He happened to be a bad actor from a bad variety show, but his laugh was loud and infectious, and as he stood on the plaza laughing violently at the mere thought of the entertainment within, he was really not without his usefulness. There was also an animal actor who posed in front of a menagerie and called the attention of the public to his show by emitting very good imitations of the low growl of the King of the Forest, as well as the fiendish screech of the hyena, but the barker I liked much the best was one I first discovered in front of "The Fall of Pompeii." He was a smooth-faced, sad, cadaverous-looking young man who seemed to regard the calling of which he was so excellent an example as a terrible bore. It seemed to make but little difference what show he happened to represent, and I doubt if he had ever seen any of them. His methods varied greatly, but most of his effects were produced with a huge paper megaphone and a pointer such as are used in school-rooms. He would wait until a party had passed him, and would then bring his pointer down with a resounding whack on the megaphone, and cry aloud, "look, look." The noise sounded exactly like a rifle-shot and the passing party would invariably start to run and eventually turn to find the sad-faced young man pointing at the entrance to his show. Sometimes he would run behind people and bark like a dog or growl like a carnivorous animal, but having once thoroughly frightened his prey he always returned to complete silence and the same interested pose. The second time I went to Coney Island I found that he had left "The Fall of Pompeii" and was selling tickets from a high stand in front of "The Canals of Venice." He had, however, not completely lost the love of his old calling, and during an occasional lull in business would once more attract attention to himself and the show by his unique methods. When I inquired why he had left "Pompeii," the erstwhile barker leaned over his stand and sighed deeply.

"There's nothin' doin' over there, and I tried so hard to get 'em in I lost my voice. I 'talked' fifteen hours a day in front of that show and still they wouldn't come. So they gave me a chance over here sellin' hard tickets, but the boss won't let me work any short change games, and all the graft I get is the change the men leave when they're in a hurry."

"How about the change the women leave?" I inquired.

The barker grew reflective and gazed for long across the park. "I can't remember a case now of a woman ever leavin' change."

"And you have been in the business a long time?"

"Twenty years," he sighed. "The men left four-thirty today, but that isn't cigar money to me. Why, I had the ticket privilege every other day with a circus last summer. The ticket-wagon was supposed to open every night at seven, but I kept it closed 'til about seven-twenty. By that time there was a howlin' crush outside, and as soon as a rube came along with a girl and would hand me a big bill just to show off I would give him short change. You see the crowd back of him would push him on, and he generally didn't set up his holler till he was about twenty feet away. Then he would run for a cop that was standin' just opposite my window and want to have me arrested. But the cop he was a partner of mine, just dressed up like, and we divided the graft. Sometimes the partner would only tell the rube to shut up, and sometimes he would beat him insensible just as occasion required." The barker gazed upward at the white lights that blazed down upon him and his open stand and the little bunch of tickets he held in his hand.

"It's a little too respectable for me down here, I guess," he sighed. "Four-thirty a day ain't enough for a good grafter—next summer it's me for the white tents and the red wagon; and where you can change the money under an old kerosene lamp."

As I said before, there are a great many ways to see the Coney Island of to-day, but after many visits I have concluded that

Where dignity can be ignored.

HT·S WATSON

there are two vantage points better than all the rest, and neither requires an outlay of very much energy or expense. One is from a seat on a bench facing the vaudeville stage in the center of the great plaza at Dreamland. In front of you there are hundreds of people sitting at little round tables watching the performance. From one end you can hear the laughter of the brave people who are sliding down over the bumps and the thousands who are watching them, and from the other end come the shrieks of the merrymakers in the boats racing down the water chutes. And all about you there is a great surging mass of men and women and little children. And all of them are laughing and talking to their neighbor and guying each other, and all of them are equal. The millionaire with his wife and children has run down on his private car, and the clerk from the city who has come in a crowded steam boat with his best girl and the stout party he hopes to have for a mother-in-law, and there are many young men who wander in little groups and are rich enough to go from show to show, and there are crowds of girls from the city stores happy enough to get away for a breath of fresh air and arm-in-arm to march up and down the broad walks of this white city of pleasure. And above it all there rise the shouts of the barkers and the confused music of many bands of all nations mingled with the growls of strange animals from the me-

nageries and the babel of loud voices of a great army of merrymakers.

The other point of vantage is from a seat on the back porch of a bathing pavilion at the very end of the village. It is a very dark, deserted little place at night, and in all respects most suited for a clueless murder. On either side it is flanked by tenantless bath houses, and in front long, crescent-shaped tiny breakers creep up the sand to one's very feet. On a clear night one can look out on the swift moving yachts with their rows of electric lights, and the heavy sailing boats with their green and red signals, plowing their way to harbor. If you look to the right there is nothing but a deserted beach and endless black water and a darkened sky; but to the left one sees blazoned against the blue sky a beautiful white city with high walls and towers and great wheels revolving in the air and balls of scarlet flame and minarets of many colors, and all glistening in the rays of a fierce light whiter and clearer than the sun of noonday ever knew. This age of electricity and science has certainly done much to overthrow the superstitions of our youth, but to the sailorman at sea or to any one who sits on my little bath house porch at night it would seem that this same age which has destroyed our illusions has created in its place something which is as near Fairyland as we ever dreamed of in our days of tops and pinafores.

4
The Story of the Slocum Disaster

MUNSEY'S MAGAZINE.

DECEMBER, 1904.

The Story of the Slocum Disaster.

BY HERBERT N. CASSON.

THE EXACT FACTS OF THE MOST SHOCKING AND PITIFUL
TRAGEDY IN THE ANNALS OF THE SEA, WITH THE DAMNING
EVIDENCE OF CRIMINAL INDIFFERENCE AND DESPICABLE DIS-
HONESTY ON THE PART OF DIRECTORS AND INSPECTORS.

THE article that follows is published to make people think, and to point out
with awful emphasis the criminal indifference on the part of directors, managers, and inspectors whose duty it is to safeguard the American public.

Every day some fresh disaster is recorded. We read of almost ten thousand
people killed on the railways within a year; of a thousand passengers drowned on
a New York excursion steamer; of nearly seven hundred pleasure-seekers burned
and crushed to death in a Chicago theater; of workmen caught in falling buildings or suffocated in mines; of men killed by explosions resulting from sheer

THE BURNING OF THE GENERAL SLOCUM, IN WHICH ONE THOUSAND AND TWENTY PERSONS, MOSTLY
WOMEN AND CHILDREN, WERE KILLED ON JUNE 15 LAST—THIS ENGRAVING SHOWS THE
WRECK OF THE SHIP AFTER SHE WAS BEACHED AT NORTH BROTHER ISLAND.

carelessness in handling dynamite or dangerous chemicals; of tenants roasted to death in fire-trap tenements; of people poisoned by adulterated food, liquors, and drugs. Many of these disasters are so directly due to disregard of the ordinary dictates of prudence, and even to breaches of the written law, that they are not accidents, but crimes. It is the purpose of this article to bring at least one such crime home to the criminals, and to awaken the public conscience.

In 1902—the latest year for which figures are available—fires in the United States caused the loss of $154,600,000 of property. It is estimated that considerably more than a hundred thousand operatives are killed or injured annually in our factories. In the ten years ending with 1903, seventy-eight thousand people lost their lives on the American railroads. The actuary of a leading life insurance company states that eight per cent of the deaths reported to his company in 1909 were due to accidents. It is a fair inference that of every dozen adult persons now living in the United States, one will die a death that might and should be prevented.

Not only is this vast destruction of life and property appalling in itself, but its secondary results are still more far-reaching. They form a grievous tax upon the whole community. We all pay more for rent, more for insurance, more for taxes, more for every railway or steamship ticket, because of the costly accidents which proper precautions would not permit to happen.

It is a fact that few passengers traveling in Pullman cars lose their lives in accidents. These cars are strongly built, and do not break up like dry-goods boxes in a collision. The Pullman passenger, because of the extra price he pays, is entitled to finer chairs, better upholstery, a more handsomely finished car, and porter service. But is he entitled to greater safety? No, emphatically no. The life of the poorest passenger traveling in the plainest car should be as safe as that of the rich man in the Pullman. This can be brought about, and should be.

The awful story of the GENERAL SLOCUM DISASTER which follows this introduction shows the wretched indifference and dishonesty of our inspector guardians. But the responsibility for the slaughter of these one thousand and twenty people does not rest alone on the inspectors. The fullest measure of blame is theirs. If they had done their work faithfully, there would have been no drowning and burning of a thousand women and children in New York harbor on the 15th of last June.

Primarily, however, and to a far greater extent, the responsibility rests upon the directors and managers of the Knickerbocker Steamship Company. It is on their hands, rather than on those of the inspectors, that the deeper and more damning bloodstains are found.

And yet these men are doubtless good neighbors, good friends, good fathers and husbands, and, in other respects, good citizens. THEY ARE MARKED EXAMPLES OF THE CRIMINAL INDIFFERENCE OF THE TIMES TO RESPONSIBILITY. Here we have the key-note of the whole question. This is the day of the director, and the director habit and the director curse are upon us. Men by the thousand become directors in corporations who never give a thought to their responsibility to the public or to their employees. They think only of directors' fees, of fat dividends, and of a successful handling of their property. They take the chances that accidents will fall to some other management than their own, and go on recklessly skimping and saving and deceiving. The greed for dividends has them body and soul, and they become desperate, daring gamblers with human lives, forgetting their individual responsibility.

The corporation is an inanimate thing. What if it does cause a dozen lives, or a thousand, to be blotted out? It is a dumb, stupid, stolid, indifferent creature,

THE STORY OF THE SLOCUM DISASTER.

on which responsibility rests lightly. And even if the responsibility does reach back in some slight degree to the directors and management, why, they are not, as they see themselves, individually to blame—only collectively. The real blame is on the corporation—not on them.

Isn't it time for an awakening on the part of directors to a full sense of their individual responsibility when they accept positions that involve dealing with human lives? And isn't it time for the public to awaken and demand that corporations be in the hands of men of conscience and keen sense of their responsibility to the people? And isn't it time we should insist that our inspectors be honest, faithful men instead of time-serving hypocrites?

When men can become so base, so depraved, as to load life-preservers with iron instead of filling them with the proper amount of cork; when they adulterate our foods and our drugs; when they haul us in cars that break like kindling-wood; when they lodge us in deadly fire-traps and invite us on board of tinder-box excursion boats—when this condition is as rampant as it is to-day, isn't it time for the pulpit and the press all over the land to stir the public conscience?

ONE THOUSAND AND TWENTY human lives destroyed by greed and criminal negligence, and yet no one has been made to suffer, no one will be made to suffer, the penalty for this unspeakable crime!

The story of the General Slocum disaster is one which cannot be written without emotion, which can scarcely be read without tears. A packed ship-load of happy, unsuspecting women and little children trapped without a moment's warning in a blazing furnace, without help, without hope, without the possi-

GATHERING THE SLOCUM'S DEAD—ONE MORE BABY WASHED ASHORE, BROUGHT TO THE SURFACE BY THE FIRING OF CANNON NEAR THE WRECK.

ONE OF THE PADDLE-BOXES OF THE WRECKED EXCURSION BOAT, WHICH, WHEN CUT OPEN, WAS FOUND
TO BE CLOGGED WITH THE BODIES OF WOMEN AND CHILDREN.

bility of escape! Children perished before the eyes of parents. Husbands witnessed the sudden destruction of their wives and families. Mothers, with babes at their breasts, were swept by the flames into the sea.

All this, and more; yet the men who are responsible are still unpunished. Half a year has passed, but the guilty directors, steamship officials, and inspectors are unharmed and free—as free as though there had been no drowning and burning of innocent and helpless people, sacrificed to fill the treasury of a heartless and brutal corporation.

For thirteen years the General Slocum has been one of the largest excursion steamers of New York harbor. She was licensed to carry twenty-five hundred passengers. Between nine and ten o'clock on the morning of June 15 she took thirteen hundred and fifty-eight people aboard at the East River pier at the foot of Third Street. They were members of a Lutheran church —St. Mark's, on Sixth Street—and their friends, bound down Long Island Sound on their annual outing. There were comparatively few men in the

party. It was a boat-load of women and little children—a defenseless gathering that was absolutely dependent upon the protection afforded by the vessel.

As the boat steamed up the East River, between the tall buildings of Greater New York, the band played Luther's majestic hymn, " Ein Feste Burg ist Unser Gott "—" Our God is a Mighty Fortress." The four hundred children romped on the decks. It was ideal weather for such an excursion. The sky was unclouded, the flags fluttered their stripes and stars in the summer breeze; and with land close on either side, the fear of death or danger occurred to no one.

THE FIRST ALARM OF FIRE.

Ten minutes after leaving the dock, fire broke out in a storeroom near the bow. A fourteen-year-old boy, named Frank Perditski, saw the smoke and ran breathless to the pilot-house with the news.

" Shut up and mind your own business! " snapped the captain.

This first alarm was given when the boat was opposite Eighty-Third Street, nearly three miles from the island where the boat was finally beached. A quarter of a mile farther on, William Alloway, a dredge captain, saw a puff of smoke break from the lower deck. He blew four quick blasts of his whistle. The warning was echoed from other boats; but all alike were unheeded. The Slocum steamed straight on, away from the Astoria shore, straight on as if she had no captain, no rudder, no crew.

Another boy rushed to a deckhand, who was drinking in the barroom, and pointed to the fire. The muddled laborer ran into the storeroom, picked up a bag of *charcoal*, and threw it on the fire.

"That did no good," he admitted at the inquest; "so I ran out and notified the mate."

Mate Flannagan, totally ignorant of fire-drill methods, wasted several invaluable moments by hurrying to the burning storeroom. He gazed at the blaze in open-mouthed consternation, and then shouted the news up the captain's tube.

As if fire were a sluggish enemy, Captain Van Schaick delayed a little longer in a trip of investigation. By this time the boat had reached One Hundred and Tenth Street. The yellow flames were leaping upward and aft, toward the unsuspecting passengers. Not until then was the fire-alarm

SEEKING FOR THE VICTIMS OF THE SLOCUM DISASTER—THE FLEET OF VOLUNTEER SEARCHERS, WHO GATHERED IN THE HARVEST OF DEATH AROUND THE SUNKEN VESSEL.

rung by the captain, who appears to have been as dazed as any green member of his crew. "Go slow! Full speed! Stop! Go ahead!" he signaled frantically to the engineer; and the doomed vessel zigzagged on and on for another fatal mile.

A CRAVEN AND COWARDLY CREW.

Meanwhile the mate and a half a dozen clumsy, undrilled deckhands were

were shot into the water like a cartload of refuse. Then a sudden burst of flame tumbled all three decks into a pit of fire. Twenty or thirty feet above the smoke-stack rose the flames, yet on and on, in the face of the wind, went the death-ship.

"My children! Save my children!" was the cry which tore the hearts of half a thousand mothers. It is not true that these women were afraid. Women

THE GENERAL SLOCUM ON THE BEACH AT NORTH BROTHER ISLAND, AS SHE APPEARED ON THE MORNING AFTER THE DISASTER.

fumbling with the hose. At last a line was fastened to the standpipe and the water turned on. The flimsy hose promptly burst in three places, and tore itself loose from the standpipe. There were other coils of hose and other standpipes, but none were used by the panic-stricken crew. Absolutely nothing was done to check the fire until the fireboat hose at North Brother Island threw water upon the ruined hulk.

The panic of the crew at once became contagious. Several women and children on the lower deck were caught by the fire, and their screams terrified the others. A fear-crazed deckhand sprang overboard, and many rushed to follow him. Three little girls, their clothes flaming, jumped over the rail and floated past, one with a red wound on her forehead.

"*Frieda! Meine Frieda!*" screamed a mother, leaping into the water.

From this moment horror was piled upon horror. The port rail of the after deck gave way, and a hundred people

who are afraid do not rush with passionate eagerness into a red cavern of fire because they see a boy's cap or the flutter of a yellow curl. The young mother who sprang from the high upper deck straight into the dark, swirling water because it had revealed for a moment the white face of a little girl, was not afraid. Such is not fear; it is love. And there is no pain in the world like the agony of the love that is losing its dear ones.

"Just as the upper deck was falling, I saw my two sisters upon it, kneeling in prayer," says George Heinz. "I leaped to save them, but in a moment was swept into the river. My sisters and my mother perished in the fire."

Children whom the flames had caught on the forward decks rushed, blazing like torches, to their mothers. Many women, maddened by the desperate choice between the fire and the deep water, flung their children overboard and leaped after them. There was no help. There was no hope. They were in

WHEN THE WATERS GAVE UP THEIR DEAD—THE CORPSE-STREWN BEACH OF THE EAST RIVER, WHERE THE VICTIMS WERE WASHED ASHORE WITH THE BROKEN FRAGMENTS OF ROTTEN LIFE-PRESERVERS.

a circle of death that closed upon them with each agonizing moment.

THE FATAL FOLLY OF THE CAPTAIN.

Was the captain mad? Why did he steer on and on, in the middle of the river, when the shores were so near? Women threw themselves on their knees in front of the pilot-house, and begged him to turn the vessel toward

crowned the tragic scene on the Slocum with a halo of heroism that should ever be remembered.

High above the clamor of the whistles rose the shrill screams of the dying. There are no letters in any language to spell such sounds. Once heard, they are seared upon the memory as with white-hot iron. They moved every heart—every heart except the captain's. Noth-

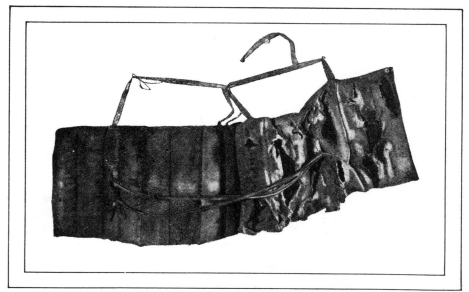

ONE OF THE ROTTEN LIFE PRESERVERS DECLARED TO BE SAFE BY INSPECTOR LUNDBERG, THOUGH THEY WERE THIRTEEN YEARS OLD, AND FILLED WITH CORK-DUST.

the land. Men, struggling to save their families, cursed him. One, crazed by the death of his child, drew a revolver and fired twice at the captain's head. Yet on went this floating inferno, away from the fleet of sloops and tugs that whistled messages of help—away from the piers where men stood ready and willing to give assistance.

Pastor Haas stepped from the side of his wife and daughter for a moment and tried to calm his people. When he turned, his wife and daughter had disappeared. Next day he found them with a thousand other lifeless ones. The battle for life became fiercer, as the oil-fed flames approached. But it was not a death-grapple for personal safety. It was a struggle of husbands to save wives, of mothers to save children, of children to save parents. This family devotion

ing on earth, apparently, could convince him of the fatal folly of his course.

And in the midst of this carnival of death—how shall I tell the story of such a motherhood?—a new life came into this merciless world for a few moments. A few tiny breaths of hot and smoky air, and then it was asleep in its young mother's arms on the cold, black bed of the deep river! Surely, surely, we have reason to be kind to one another in a world of such mysterious and unbearable sorrows.

When the Slocum was beached at North Brother Island she was a roaring furnace, with hundreds of frantic women and children clinging, like swarming bees, to every uncharred refuge. No prearranged scheme for wholesale slaughter could have been more deadly than the two-mile run of

IN THE GHASTLY ACRE OF THE DEAD—THE TERRIBLE SCENE ON NORTH BROTHER ISLAND AS THE BODIES FROM THE SLOCUM WRECK WERE BROUGHT ASHORE AND LAID IN ROWS ON THE GRASS—THE ENGRAVING SHOWS LESS THAN ONE-TENTH OF THE TOTAL NUMBER OF VICTIMS.

THE COFFIN-SHIP AFLOAT AGAIN—THE HULL OF THE GENERAL SLOCUM ON ITS WAY TO A SHIP-YARD
FOR REPAIRS, AFTER BEING RAISED AT THE PUBLIC EXPENSE.

the blazing vessel. As long as our race exists, it will be remembered as the most terrible and the most needless of recorded disasters.

To those who ask: " Why did the captain run a burning vessel two miles up a narrow channel instead of beaching her at once?" there is no satisfactory answer. It was one of many criminal and inexplicable mistakes.

AN HOUR WHEN HEROES WERE MADE.

Nothing was done as it should have been done, in this tragedy of blunders. The vessel was run straight upon the shore, leaving the fire in front of its surviving passengers, and deep water on both sides of the stern, to which they were hanging in despair. Had it not been for the arrival of the fleet of tugs, which had been almost bursting their boilers in the race to reach the runaway steamer, it is not likely that more than a few dozen would have been brought to land.

Here, for the first time, came help to the few who were not forever beyond it. Jim Wade, owner and captain of a tug, ran his grimy little boat straight against the burning steamer. His tug represented the savings of ten years of hard work, but Jim Wade was a man, not a corporation.

" Let her burn," said he. " What's a tugboat to human life?" And a hundred people or more were helped across this tug-bridge to a place of safety.

Then came nurses from the near-by hospital, fishermen, policemen, wharfrats—to bring to shore the dead and the living. Mary McCann, a young Irish patient, forgot her illness and rushed into the water again and again to rescue babies and children. The captain and the two pilots jumped from the upper deck and were pulled to land with slight injuries. The head wind, which had swept the fire back upon the decks crowded with women and children, had made the pilot-house the safest refuge on the boat.

When it was thought that only the dead remained upon the burning wreck, there was a sudden shout of surprise and agony from those on shore. A little boy was seen to be climbing the flagstaff to escape from the furnace below. Sharp spears of flame were thrust at

THE PIER AT EAST TWENTY-FOURTH STREET, TRANSFORMED INTO A VAST DEATH-CHAMBER—FROM ALL PARTS OF THE LONG PIER CAME CRIES OF ANGUISH, AS RELATIVES IDENTIFIED THE WHITE-ROBED VICTIMS.

him as he shook his yellow curls and worked his way a few feet higher. It was a brave fight. For a dozen seconds his little body was outlined against the lurid glare, and then the flagstaff toppled slowly and fell into the crack-

charred bodies were laid out in long rows on the grass. More and more were found. This was not murder, it was massacre. By midnight six hundred and eleven lay on the lawn and four hundred more were still in the river.

THE LONG PROCESSION OF HEARSES BEARING THE DEAD OF THE SLOCUM FROM THE MORGUE TO THE LUTHERAN CEMETERY—EVERY HEARSE IN NEW YORK CITY WAS IN LINE.

ling pit. He was the last of four hundred child-martyrs, sacrificed to swell the dividends of a callous corporation.

THE AWFUL HARVEST OF DEATH.

Then came the most ghastly horror of all, the gathering and labeling of the dead. North Brother Island is used as a place for the city's sick, but it now became a place for the dead. The limp,

The dead lay in family groups in this island morgue. There were four of the Strickroth family, five of the Dieckhoff family, six of the Gress family, ten of the Weis family, eleven of the Rheinfrank family, and so on. Many entire families were destroyed, and remained until late next day unidentified. Practically the whole church kindergarten was wiped out; out of fifty-one little

THE DOOR OF THE NEW YORK MORGUE, ON THE MORNING AFTER THE SLOCUM DISASTER—THOUSANDS OF FRIENDS AND RELATIVES, TOO CRAZED WITH GRIEF TO STAND IN LINE, FILED IN AND OUT THE HALL OF THE DEAD.

ones only a dozen remain. The doomed ship had scattered its living freight over two miles of the river's length, and for days the bodies were picked up and brought to the island of sorrow.

After the heart-breaking work of identification had ended, there remained many whose names could not be learned. These were buried by the city in a wide, deep trench—the Great Grave, as the survivors call it. The others were taken, in a seemingly endless procession, to the Lutheran garden of sleep, on Long Island, and laid there together, a town of the dead, on the sunny southern slope.

Human sympathy, " swelling like the Solway tide," poured in its messages from all parts of the globe. "Accept my profound sympathy for yourself, church, and congregation," telegraphed President Roosevelt to Pastor Haas. "I send to the families of the victims the expression of my sorrowful sympathy," said President Loubet, of France. "Heartfelt prayers that the Father may vouchsafe comfort and sustaining grace," cabled the British Sunday School Union, then in session in London. Truly, New York's grief was a sob " heard round the world."

THE SOCIETY OF THE STRICKEN.

Welded together by their common sorrow, those who escaped death on the Slocum have organized an association under the name of " The General Slocum Survivors." It is the most unique and somber of all representative bodies. It represents a thousand and twenty dead. More than seven hundred relatives are mourned by its three hundred members.

" I lost my wife and daughter." said its president, Mr. Charles Dersch. " Our secretary lost his wife and two children, our treasurer his wife and four children. We are three homeless men, but we have suffered no more than many others."

To describe the bi-weekly meetings of this singular association would require the pen of a Dante and the brush of a Doré. All the members are clad in black. The walls of their hall are shrouded in mourning, and the strained, intense silence conveys the appalling impression that a thousand

A FEW OF THE THOUSAND COFFINS IN WHICH THE PASSENGERS OF THE GENERAL SLOCUM
RETURNED TO THEIR HOMES.

THE "GREAT GRAVE" IN THE LUTHERAN CEMETERY, IN WHICH WERE BURIED THE UNIDENTIFIED VICTIMS—ONE HUNDRED AND SIXTY GRAVE-DIGGERS WERE NEEDED TO MAKE GRAVES FOR THE SLOCUM DEAD.

wronged spirits are in some way a part of the assemblage.

Letters are read from German societies, from survivors of the Iroquois disaster, and from eminent men in public office. Short speeches are made—short because many of the speakers suddenly lose control of their voices and sit down.

"I saw my four children pushed overboard, and I could not help them," says

a woman whose eyes are cavernous with weeping.

"This morning, in the hospital, my wife died of a broken heart," says a white-haired man.

A HOUSE OF MOURNING—NINE EXCURSIONISTS WENT UPON THE SLOCUM FROM THIS HOUSE, NO. 104 FIRST AVENUE, NEW YORK; NONE CAME BACK ALIVE.

"They call us good-natured Germans," asserts President Dersch; "but we have determined that our dead shall be avenged, and that other homes shall not be destroyed as ours have been."

All are on the verge of tears. Even

the hard-eyed reporters are affected by the atmosphere of sorrow. A little boy is called to the platform. He is the last to come from the hospital. The whole side of his head is one livid, glistening scar; and grief blends with joy in his mother's eyes as she leads him back to his seat. A woman brings a poem to the president.

" This poem is about our dead. Shall I read it ? " he asks.

" No, no; don't read it," cry a dozen voices.

" Let us adjourn," suggests the secretary, " for we cannot endure this! " And the silent, tearful Germans file out into the crowded street, back to their stricken homes.

THE RESPONSIBILITY FOR THE SLAUGHTER.

To-day the passion of indiscriminate blame has passed. Two responsible bodies, the coroner's jury and the Federal commission appointed by President Roosevelt, have investigated the disaster and made known their reports. It is now clearly seen that this slaughter of the innocents was the natural and inevitable product of criminal negligence on the part of the Knickerbocker Steamship Company and the United States steamship inspection service. It was the reckless, irresponsible director, who takes the rewards of his office without performing its duties, and the slipshod, negligent public official, whose aim in life is to get the highest possible salary for the least possible exertion, who are equally guilty of destroying the happiness of a thousand homes.

The Knickerbocker Steamship Company, which built and operated the Slocum, is capitalized for two hundred and fifty thousand dollars. Its officials are as follows:

President, Frank A. Barnaby.

Secretary, James K. Atkinson.

Directors—Frank A. Barnaby, James K. Atkinson, Charles E. Hill, C. De Lacy Evans, Robert K. Story, Floyd S. Corbin, and Frank G. Dexter.

These men are, first and foremost, the men who are responsible for the Slocum disaster. The members of a steamship company cannot shield themselves behind a corporation charter, nor behind a careless inspector's certificate.

The United States Supreme Court holds that where the owner of a vessel is a corporation, the president and directors are not merely the agents of that corporation, but the corporation itself. *A corporation may be fined, imprisoned, or executed, according to the crime of which it is found guilty.* The State law of New York is equally definite in holding the individual members of a corporation responsible for all corporate acts.

GAMBLERS IN HUMAN LIVES.

In the thousand pages of evidence taken at the coroner's inquest, it did not appear that the above seven owners of the Slocum had any intimate knowledge whatever of the condition of the vessel. President Barnaby, who draws a salary of six thousand dollars a year for his services, testified that he had not been aboard the boat this year. The equipment of the two vessels in their fleet was left entirely in the hands of two aged captains, John A. Pease and W. H. Van Schaick.

The system of evading responsibility went from top to bottom. The directors appointed the president, paid him twenty dollars a day, and told him to do as he pleased. The president appointed the captains, and told them to do as they pleased. The captains appointed the mates, and told them to hire the cheapest deckhands in the labor market.

The mate of the Slocum was found to be an unlicensed iron-worker, inefficient and cowardly. The crew he engaged consisted of a medley of truckdrivers, laborers, and dockmen. This picked-up gang of landsmen, hired for twenty-five dollars a month apiece and their keep, were absolutely unskilled in the task of protecting the boat and its passengers from fire or from any of the dangers to which such vessels are inevitably exposed.

OPEN CONTEMPT FOR THE LAW.

Although the law requires a fire-drill at least once a week, with a test of the hose and life-boats on every occasion, the Slocum had been sailing since the season began without putting water through her hose, without lowering a life-boat, and without having a fire-drill of any kind. Captain Van Schaick weakly protested that three fire-drills had been held.

" I can't go into details; I'm getting tired and restless," he said when he was asked to give the dates and particulars of these drills.

In direct contradiction of his evidence, every member of the crew who was put on the witness-stand swore that no drill had been held. While captains of ocean liners consider it necessary to have emergency drills during each voyage, and in some cases every day, even with a crew of professional sailors, Captain Van Schaick permitted his score of laborers to remain in ignorance of all emergency measures.

Instead of springing to appointed stations, this crew jumped overboard when the fire-alarm was rung. Two stand-pipes were lifted from the wreck by divers, and both had *closed valves*, proving that no hose had been attached. The hose that was rescued by the divers was burned black on the edges only, showing that it had never been uncoiled. This circumstantial evidence, by mute witnesses that cannot be impeached, demonstrates that no effort was made to fight the flames. With such a crew, a vessel made of steel and asbestos would be in danger; much more a newly painted, wooden tinder-box like the Slocum.

The law declares that no hay shall be carried on an excursion steamer, yet there were seven barrels in the Slocum's store-room, all of which contained more or less hay, used as a packing for glassware. Side by side with these stood three barrels of oil, and scattered about the floor were paint-pots, scraps of canvas, and other bonfire materials. The door of the room was never locked. The deckhands hung their wet clothes in it, because " it was the warmest place on the boat." The law requires that in every compartment in a steamer's hold there shall be a steam-valve, so that it can be flooded with steam in case of fire; but there was no steam valve in this dangerous store-room.

Under such conditions, a fire must have occurred sooner or later. Gather together hay and oil and paint and matches and cigarettes and reckless deckhands in a twelve-by-twelve room, and the result can be easily foreseen.

THE SLOCUM'S WORTHLESS HOSE.

If the Slocum had possessed every known life-saving device, if her hose and her life-preservers had been first-class, if her crew had been well drilled and courageous, she would still have been a dangerous boat with more than a thousand women and children aboard. But a bill obtained by the coroner from the New York Belting and Packing Company showed that the " new hose," of which the steamship company had boasted, had been bought for *sixteen cents a foot*. The cheapest garden hose costs more. For the hose now in use by the New York Fire Department a dollar and ten cents a foot is paid.

A half-burned yard of this worthless stuff, brought up from the wreck by a diver, proved it to be two-thread linen hose, without any rubber lining. Such " hose " was hose in name only. It was bought to deceive passengers into a sense of security, and with the knowledge that the inspectors would pass anything. It was never tested until the fatal morning in June, when it burst into rags before the water could reach from the standpipe to the nozzle.

The only excuse offered by the company for this fraud was the suggestion by one of its lawyers that sixteen cents a foot was five cents more than the price paid for hose by several other steamship companies of New York. Though this may well be, it cannot excuse the slaughter of a ship-load of women and children.

USELESS LIFE-BOATS AND RAFTS.

The ten life-boats and rafts on the Slocum were as useless as uninflated balloons. Neither crew nor passengers knew how to launch them. Several passengers almost succeeded in getting one life-boat to the water, but a frenzied deckhand sprang into it and capsized it. The rafts were fastened to the deck with wire at which the passengers tugged and tore in vain. Like the hose, they were for purposes of exhibition only; when the time for service came, they were worthless mockeries.

A life-ring, which should have been sufficiently buoyant to sustain a dozen people, was found by a diver at the bottom of the river. It was still grasped by four women, who had entrusted their lives to this treacherous sham and gone down with it as it sank.

"That life-ring was the finest anchor I ever saw," exclaimed the indignant coroner.

ROTTEN, DUST-FILLED LIFE-PRESERVERS.

As for the life-preservers, they, too, were false as Dead Sea apples. The coroner placed one in a tub of water and it sank like a stone before the eyes of the jury. The life of an ordinary life-preserver is from seven to eight years, but nine-tenths of those on the Slocum were *thirteen years old*. "Some life-preservers will get mildewed in a single season," testified an experienced sea-captain.

The Knickerbocker Steamship Company offered several invoices to prove that new life-preservers had been purchased for the Slocum; but the invoices were found to have been *altered by the use of acid*. The name of the Grand Republic, another vessel belonging to the company, had been erased and that of the Slocum written in its place. This clumsy deception was easily exposed by several detectives sent from the District Attorney's office, who found that all the new life-preservers were on board the Grand Republic. Barnaby, the president of the corporation, was pilloried by the coroner for trying to shield himself behind this shameless fraud.

There was abundant evidence to prove that the Slocum's life-preservers were thoroughly worthless and rotten— "life-destroyers," as one survivor bitterly phrased it. They, too, were fastened to the ship with wire. A deckhand testified that "a considerable pull" was necessary to loosen them.

"We couldn't budge the wire," said a survivor who was compelled to jump overboard without a life-preserver.

"I tried to pull down three," said another, "but they all split and let the cork fall on my face."

In all the preservers the cork was of the cheapest granulated kind.

"I thought it was sawdust," said a witness.

"When the vessel was beached there was floating cork an inch deep on the water," remarked Coroner O'Gorman.

This powdered cork was scattered upon the decks; it was thick in the hair of every victim who was brought to shore. Of course, life-preservers filled with it were useless, and even worse than useless.

"I saw women and children wearing life-preservers sink the moment they struck the water," asserted R. A. Tudor, the captain of a sloop.

Steward Graham, the only member of the crew who failed to escape, fastened a life-preserver about his waist, jumped overboard, and, in the words of the mate, "went to the bottom like a stone." The other members of the crew knew better than to hamper themselves with these death-belts. Only two men, both good swimmers, dared to put them on. The captain wore no life-preserver. The pilots wore no life-preservers. The rotten bags of glue and cork-dust were for the passengers only.

Such was the "life-saving" equipment of the General Slocum. Linen hose, wired rafts, unlaunched life-boats, rotten life-preservers, unopened stand-pipes, contraband hay, and an undrilled crew of landsmen! All this with thirteen hundred people aboard, including more than a thousand women and children. And all this made possible by a lawless greed that places little value upon human life when a fatter dividend can be gained by reckless and fraudulent parsimony—made possible by directors who have been allowed to think that the profits are for them and the responsibility for their subordinates!

"PERMITS" TO TAKE HUMAN LIFE.

The law in this case is adequate and unmistakable. No new law is needed. More than a hundred pages of law relating to steamship inspection and life-saving apparatus have been enacted since 1852. Apparently every danger has been foreseen. Every steamship must have "good and suitable hose," and "good life-preservers of suitable material." Not even a friction match can be carried; and criminal negligence is defined as manslaughter, whenever loss of life is its result.

But up to the present time this last statute has been as harmless as the leather cannons of Tibet. It was enacted thirty-four years ago, yet not one owner, not one captain, not one inspector, has been convicted under its provisions. Both the steamship companies and the inspectors regard this law as practically non-existent.

Twenty-five years ago the Seawanhaka was burned, with sixty-two lives lost, in the same East River. Those responsible for the disaster escaped punishment. A few years before, the boiler of the ferryboat Westfield exploded, and eighty-five lives were taken. There was the usual public clamor in both cases, and the usual public forgetfulness. No one was fined, imprisoned, or discharged.

In 1901, when the Northfield, a Staten Island ferryboat, sank like a seive— fortunately, near her dock—thirty-three of the New York ferryboats were found to be more than thirty years old. Yet no action of any consequence was taken at the time, and none has been taken since. Year after year these dangerous hulks have their certificates renewed, and the peril is never abated. Practically, they have permits to run until wrecked.

THE DISGRACE OF THE INSPECTION BUREAU.

In fact, the Slocum disaster has revealed the United States inspection service to be a helpless and perfunctory bureau, shackled by red tape and serving mainly as a refuge for aged officeholders. " General " Dumont, the septuagenarian who was in charge of the New York district, held office continuously for twenty-seven years. He was in office when the Seawanhaka proved to be a coffin-ship for sixty-two of its passengers. No accidents, whatever their number or their nature, have ever produced any apparent effect upon this inspection department, which costs the taxpayers three hundred and sixty-nine thousand dollars annually.

In the past twenty years, thirty-six hundred lives have been lost and more than sixty-five million dollars' worth of

shipping and cargoes destroyed, all within the jurisdiction of the bureau. In New York harbor alone, one hundred and seventy-three accidents were reported in 1903, yet *not one license was revoked.* In a few cases the negligent captains and engineers were suspended, but every one was allowed to retain his license, no matter what loss of life had resulted from his carelessness. *Only three licenses have been revoked in three years, in spite of the occurrence of more than five hundred accidents.*

Once an inspector, always an inspector, appears to be the rule. The yearly reports of the bureau expose the fact that only nine inspectors have been " removed " during the last three years. The word " removed," as used in the reports, is ambiguous. It may mean discharged, or it may mean promoted. As to the imprisonment of criminally negligent inspectors, such a danger is no more feared in the department than the possibility of a collision with the planet Mars.

It is difficult to write with calmness of this cold-blooded officialism, this automatic and shameless inefficiency. Some possible excuse might be found for it, if it were not so vociferous in making excuses for itself. Temporary lapses from vigilance might be forgiven, but what shall be said of officials who protest that their slothful blundering is the faithful performance of duty?

The self-justifying report given out by the New York board of inspectors asserts that "the life-saving apparatus of the General Slocum was *entirely adequate.* Before the coroner, " General " Dumont had not been so positive, refusing to answer when he was asked if he believed the vessel to have been honestly inspected. " No dead bodies were found with life-preservers on," says this extraordinary document; therefore " not a single life was lost by reason of the inefficiency of the life-preservers." Marvelous logic, indeed!

INSPECTORS WHO DID NOT INSPECT.

According to their own reports, the inspectors of the New York district are most industrious. They inspect forty-seven steamships a week; but, if we may judge from the inspection of the Slocum by Inspector Lundberg, the work could be done quite as satisfactorily by telescope from the roof of a Broadway skyscraper.

"I *looked* at the hose," said Lundberg, when at bay before the coroner's jury. Although the law requires that all hose shall be tested, he wrote "hose in good order," without making any test whatever. "I never seen anybody test the hose since I've been around New York harbor," said he. "Provided that the steam pump would work, it would work all right," was his remarkable answer when asked how he had tested the pumping apparatus. His "test" of the life-preservers was merely to poke a few of them with a stick. In less than six hours he had completed his inspection of this two-hundred-and-fifty-foot vessel, with its twenty-five hundred life-preservers; and left it in the condition which, forty days later, caused the disaster.

Inspectors Dumont and Barrett accepted Lundberg's report without question, although he was but a probationer of four months' standing. Eighteen days afterwards they received a warning from Mr. Cortelyou, head of the Commerce and Labor Department, suggesting that special steps should be taken to protect the passengers on excursion steamships during the overcrowded summer season. This warning was disregarded. There was no further examination of the Slocum. Inspectors Lundberg and Fleming, who pretended to have inspected the vessel; Dumont and Barrett, who were in authority over them; Rodie, who was in authority over Dumont and Barrett; Frank A. Barnaby and his six fellow-directors of the company owning the boat, who were the first violators of the law; are all partners in the terrible responsibility of having caused a thousand deaths.

THE MEANEST FRAUD OF ALL.

Emboldened by the feebleness of the inspection service, all manner of deceptions are practised by steamship corporations and those who furnish their supplies. Life-rafts are found to have wooden pegs made in such a way as to imitate iron rivets. Absolutely worthless fire-hose is exhibited on the decks of many steamers, as there is no fear that the lazy officials will test it.

As this article is being written, the officers of the Nonpareil Cork Works, Camden, New Jersey, are being arraigned for *inserting bars of iron in the life-preservers* which they manufacture. More than two hundred and fifty cork blocks have been seized, every one of which contained a seven-inch bar of cast iron. Iron is cheaper per pound than cork, and as the law requires that every life-preserver shall weigh six pounds, a few cents of blood-money can be gained by making up the weight with bars of iron.

Instead of supporting a dead weight of twenty-four pounds, as the law demands, a test shows that one of these iron life-preservers will sustain no more than sixteen pounds. Any full-grown person who trusted to one of these death-decoys would sink under the waves like a stone. Yet this ghastly fraud was discovered, not by a steamship inspector, but by an outside governmental department.

THE ACTION OF PRESIDENT ROOSEVELT.

The Federal commission appointed by President Roosevelt submitted its report to him on October 17, and he at once issued an order to remove from office the negligent inspectors. The report would fill forty pages of MUNSEY'S MAGAZINE. In every point it corroborates the verdict of the coroner's jury, in placing the blame directly upon the owners, officers, and crew of the Slocum, and upon the New York board of inspectors.

Agents of the commission made the first thorough inspection that has ever been made of two hundred and sixty-eight vessels in New York harbor. More than one-third were found with defective life-preservers. One quarter had defective hose, and less than half of the vessels had as many feet of hose as the law requires. Yet every one of these dangerous boats showed certificates of inspection signed by the New York officials.

But why continue to pile fact upon fact? The first supreme fact is that a thousand women and children were slaughtered. No legal sophistries can give back the breath to their moldered bodies. And the second fact, shameful and incredible, is that the men who were proved guilty six months ago are still, as this is written, untouched by any agency of justice.

"THE PUBLIC BE DAMNED!"

This nation remembered the Maine. It was willing, even enthusiastic, to shoulder the ponderous burden of war because of the destruction of a battleship and two hundred and sixty men. But what about the Slocum? What about this loss of life that is almost four-fold greater and incomparably less excusable? How shall this mystery be explained—that we rush to battle to avenge the death of two hundred and sixty young men, who had knowingly enlisted in a perilous calling, and then sit as helpless as a colony of rabbits when a treacherous and law-breaking corporation burns and drowns a thousand of our women and children?

These seven directors of the Knickerbocker Steamship Company have no excuses which they dare to offer to the public. They know that for the sake of three hundred and fifty dollars they sent a ship-load of human beings into the jaws of death. They know that none of their wives or daughters were on the Slocum. Once only did this corporation venture to open its mouth, to have its deceptive testimony and its fraudulent invoices flung in its face by an indignant coroner's jury.

They cower behind their bodyguard of legal janizaries, these blood-guilty directors. They have no answer to make when six hundred husbands cry, "Give us back our wives and our children!" They scheme for delay. They manufacture protests, quibbles, technicalities. If half of the money now being spent to defeat justice had been spent for life-preservers that would float and hose

that would carry water, there would not be so many blighted homes to-day on the East Side of New York.

This Slocum disaster was the most terrible of all the world's tragedies of the sea. Never before were the victims so helpless or the harvest of death so great. If such a catastrophe will not move the slow machinery of the law, what will? Must other thousands be slaughtered before one of these reckless corporations can be checked in its murderous career?

Now that the hull of the Slocum has been raised—at public expense—shall we expect to see it next summer rebuilt, repainted, and refitted with rotten hose and dust-filled life-preservers, with another thousand woman and children on its flimsy, inflammable decks, and with Captain Van Schaick, the Charon of the East River, at the helm?

PUNISH THE GUILTY MEN!

Such corporations care nothing for words. Denunciations are no more serious to them than a volley of goose-feathers to a battle-ship. Fines are easily paid and charged to legal expenses. The only way to take the sneer from a guilty director's lips, to give him a very little of the suffering that he has caused to others, is to show him an open prison door. Accident will follow accident until the irresponsible directors are taken from their corporation pedestals and treated like ordinary breakers of the law. In short, this aristocracy of crime must be destroyed.

Both the safety of our people and the integrity of our institutions demand that no man shall be below the law and that no corporation shall be above it. They demand the arrest, prosecution, and imprisonment of all whose greed and criminal recklessness caused the burning of the General Slocum and the loss of a thousand lives.

5
A Unique
New York Club

A UNIQUE NEW YORK CLUB.

BY CLAY MEREDITH GREENE.

THE LAMBS—THE RECORD AND THE PURPOSES OF THE CLUB, ITS
MEMBERSHIP, ITS GAMBOLS, AND ITS SUMPTUOUS NEW FOLD,
DESCRIBED BY THE WELL-KNOWN PLAYWRIGHT WHO IS NOW
SERVING HIS TENTH TERM AS ITS SHEPHERD.

DURING the Christmas week of 1874 a little coterie of souls congenial and temperaments analogous foregathered at the Delmonico's of the time, to despatch a midnight repast at the bidding of George H. McLean. Long after the streets had grown silent under the mantle of an incipient dawn, the feasters tarried, and thought not of sleep.

There is an indefinable something, almost akin to magic, which breeds rebellion against the edicts of the hours in such a gathering. The host eloquently voiced a deep regret that the night and its entertainment must have their ending; that such a company, where actor and author, manager and banker, painter and poet, could sit in complete social harmony, must soon tread its several pathways in directions that had no common trend, to vanish among the shadows of the unknown future.

But before he had finished, fruitful suggestion deferred the dissolution of the gathering. It was pointed out that future regrets of the same nature might be permanently avoided by organization. This was at once effected, and Henry J. Montague—at that time leading man of

THE FIRST QUARTERS OF THE LAMBS AT 848
BROADWAY, IN A TINY BUILDING NEXT
DOOR TO THE OLD WALLACK'S
THEATER.

Wallack's Theater—was chosen as presiding officer. Being asked to name the new organization, Mr. Montague called it "The Lambs" after a dining-club in London of which he was a member; and it was decided that the bantling should preserve the same customs and purposes as its parent.

At a subsequent meeting, held early in the January of 1875, the following officers were elected: Shepherd, Henry J. Montague; Boy, Harry Beckett; Corresponding Secretary, George H. McLean; Treasurer, John E. I. Granger; Recording Secretary, Arthur Wallack.

For some time the Lambs met only at monthly dinners in the various hostelries surrounding Union Square, but these gatherings soon became so popular, and the roster of membership so large, that in 1877 the society became a corporation under the laws of the State, and began to record its achievements on the pages of metropolitan club history.

On this page there is a picture of the club quarters of 1876, at 848 Broadway, over a saloon next door to Wallack's Theater—the old Wallack's at Thirteenth Street and Broadway. The accommoda-

61

tions of this place, however, proved so inadequate, as indeed did every attempt at the one-room club idea, that annually the Lambs folded their tents and stole away to some other convenient spot, equally confined, until 1880, when they rented the entire house at 34 West Twenty-Sixth Street. Here began what must be called the true history of The Lambs as a club proper, with all of the accommodations furnished, in greater or less degree, by other clubs.

Here, too, began what must remain in the memories of those who fought it as the most heroic battle against adversity that it or any similar organization has ever known. The club succeeded, and yet it failed; it prospered, and yet it languished; its dinners became the definitive unit of functions of that nature, as did its ledgers the glaring proofs of a too prodigal liberality.

SOME FAMOUS MEMBERS OF THE CLUB.

The best-known actors, littérateurs, *bon vivants*, wits, and orators of their time were either its members or its guests. Among them may be mentioned Edwin Booth, John McCullough, Mark Twain, Lester Wallack, Daniel Dougherty, Steele Mackaye, Charles A. Dana, Charles R. Thorne, Robert Ingersoll, William J. Florence, John R. Brady, John R. Fellowes, Tom Ochiltree, and Dion Boucicault. All who came beneath its roof were safe from notoriety or public criticism. The Lambs have never admitted a journalist to their gatherings, except under the distinct agreement not to mention any of their doings in the public prints.

On one occasion Charles A. Dana, John R. Fellowes, and John A. Cockerill —all dead now—sat together at a dinner given to Henry Irving. From these redoubtable antagonists a fine display of mutual vituperation was expected, and the expectation was not disappointed. Colonel Fellowes was called upon first, and began:

"Shepherd Wallack, guest of the evening Irving, and gentlemen—I thank God that for the first time in my life I am in a gathering where whatever may be in my mind to express will not be garbled, distorted, and destroyed in the newspapers. Mr. Cockerill and Mr. Dana are both publishers, but as gentlemen

THE GRILL-ROOM IN THE LAMBS' NEW FOLD, ONE OF THE PRINCIPAL ROOMS ON THE GROUND FLOOR OF THE BUILDING.

they cannot, they dare not, violate the sanctity of the rule that guarantees to all speakers within these walls immunity from public comment."

What followed may well be imagined. Fellowes flayed Cockerill with his wonderful powers of invective; Cockerill showered on Fellowes stinging blows of eloquent sarcasm, and then turned his stream of venom upon Dana. The veteran of the *Sun* retorted in kind, amid wild cheers and applause, until the allotted time had expired, when the Shepherd declared the contest a draw.

But these functions were expensive, and even through the administrations of such capable Shepherds as Harry Beckett, Lester Wallack, William J. Florence, John R. Brady, and E. M. Holland, the club's debts steadily accumulated. As bankruptcy became more and more certain, the personal liability of responsible members was avoided by numerous resignations. By 1891 it had become impossible to secure a meeting of the council for the purpose of nominating officers, and an obscure member of the club, Paul Arthur by name, himself placed a ticket on the bulletin-board, nominating the writer as Shepherd; Augustus Thomas, Boy; Thomas B. Clarke, Corresponding Secretary; John A. Stow, Treasurer; Fritz Williams, Recording Secretary; and a council consisting of Clarence L. Collins, Samuel Bancroft, Jr., Thomas Manning, Norman F. Cross, Charles W. Thomas, Charles Frohman, and himself.

FROM POVERTY TO PROSPERITY.

To these men, share and share alike, must be given the credit for the work that lifted the society from bankruptcy to affluence, from a position of social decadence to one that ranks it high among the unique and unconventional clubs of the world.

One of their number drew the check that prevented service of a sheriff's writ.

THE NEW FOLD OF THE LAMBS, A SUMPTUOUS CLUB-HOUSE AT 130 WEST FORTY-FOURTH STREET, WHICH IS TO BE OPENED EARLY IN JULY.

A meeting was called, and subscriptions obtained for the purpose of paying the most pressing debts. A public entertainment was given, and with the proceeds settlement was made with the creditors on the basis of thirty-three and one-third per cent. Then, with three hundred dollars in its treasury, the club moved to more economical quarters on West Twenty-Ninth Street.

Then came the wave of prosperity which from that moment has not for one day receded, save to return freighted with greater promise. Within a year a larger house became necessary, and this was secured at 26 West Thirty-First Street; the old debts, though legally released, were paid off in full; and the Lambs' Gambols, at which original plays written and acted by members were produced, became town and country talk. The legal limit of membership being nearly reached, in 1897 property was purchased at 70 West Thirty-Sixth Street, and a club-house of the society's own was erected.

In the next year the mortgage of thirty-six thousand dollars was cleared by what became known as "the Lambs' Star Gambol," an entertainment in which all the prominent dramatic and operatic stars of the club participated, and which, in eight cities of the country, played in a single week to the enormous sum of sixty-seven thousand dollars.

A SUMPTUOUS NEW FOLD.

During the administrations of Thomas B. Clarke and De Wolf Hopper the membership continued to increase. The limit was raised by one hundred and fifty, but still there was a long waiting-list of applicants for admission who could not be accommodated. Under these conditions, Shepherd Hopper called a general meeting for the purpose of securing an appropriation to erect a permanent home that would meet all the requirements, both material and artistic, of an organization that had rapidly and completely outgrown its surroundings. The proposal met with unanimous indorsement, and when Mr. Hopper surrendered his crook to the present incumbent he clothed him and his council with the authority to spend three hundred thousand dollars for a permanent fold.

This is now nearing completion at 130 West Forty-Fourth Street. The architects, McKim, Mead & White, say that of thirty-three club-houses they have created, that of the Lambs will be the most novel, artistic, and complete. The building, with its façade of brick, terra-cotta, and marble, is an imposing combination of the Colonial and Renaissance schools. It occupies two city lots, and is six stories high, with basement, cellar, and sub-cellar. Passing through the marbled vestibule into a capacious corridor, containing offices, guest-chamber, letter-boxes, and telephone booths, one is immediately struck with the prevailing air of space, convenience, and comfort. Beyond is the grill-room, a hall thirty-four feet square, in dark woods, with red tiled floor, and an enormous fireplace, and a carved stone mantelpiece from a medieval Italian palace. Behind this are the billiard-room and bar, which are

similar in general appearance and decoration to the grill-room. The second floor is devoted to the dining-rooms and lounging rooms, richly decorated in white, red, and gold, with furniture of mahogany, and capable of expansion, by the removal of partitions, into one great banquet hall twenty-five by ninety feet in size.

On the third floor, in front, is the library, with shelves, paneling, and rafters of dark oak, relieved by colorings of green in carpets and drapery. Behind this is the theater, the main feature of the club, where the gambols, which have been so potent an agent in securing its success, may be produced with as much perfection of detail as can be secured in any public playhouse. As an example of the enthusiasm of the membership, it is worth recording that this room has been completed in all of its features—scenery, draperies, seats, and decoration, besides a grand piano and a large pipe organ—by a special voluntary subscription, and that the subscribers insisted that no reasonable expense should be spared.

Below the gallery, the room is paneled in dark oak, and gallery front and proscenium are of the same material with appropriate carvings, and lightly lined with gold. Above the gallery the walls are to be decorated with mural paintings by a committee of which Robert Reid is chairman, and the ceiling work will be designed and executed by James F. Finn. Draperies and carpets are of a green shade in harmony with the woodwork, and at the back of the room is placed the organ, which is operated by motors hidden in the sub-cellar.

The remaining floors of the club-house are devoted to living-rooms, sumptuously furnished, and supplied with every convenience known to the builder's art.

THE SPIRIT OF THE CLUB.

Early in July the informal opening will take place. On that occasion no one who is not a member may be informed as to the ceremonies that take place. More than ever before will the Lambs be jealous of what they say to one another, because they believe that sentiment is not for ears to friendship unattuned. But in the early fall the first gambol and banquet will be given, where he who is friend to the Lamb may feast with him, laugh with him, and pledge with him success to the continuance of that spirit of social democracy which has been his shibboleth through all his struggles.

THE MAIN FEATURE OF THE LAMBS' NEW FOLD—THE COMPLETE AND HANDSOMELY DECORATED THEATER IN WHICH THE CLUB GAMBOLS ARE TO BE GIVEN.

This spirit was most aptly expressed by one of the characters in a play at a recent gambol.

"A democracy that knows no distinction between star and support, banker and book-keeper, the captain of a man-of-war and the youngster from the steerage. Friendship is friendship whether it be clothed in broadcloth or flannel; Bohemia is Bohemia alike on floors of deal or of marble; and the good Lamb is a Lamb be he in rented lodging-house or in palace all his own."

These, in short, are the principles on which the foundation-stone of this merry convocation of convivial spirits was laid, and it has grown, course by course of friendship's solid masonry, without cliques or politics, until it now stands an enduring monument to the sentiments that inspired the little coterie down in Fourteenth Street thirty years ago.

6
American Cities in Pencil — New York

Everybody's Magazine

MAY, 1904.

American Cities in Pencil

Drawings by Vernon Howe Bailey

III. New York

GRANT'S TOMB.

Grant's Tomb, on Riverside Drive at 123rd Street, occupies a commanding site overlooking the Hudson. The corner-stone of the Tomb was laid by President Harrison in 1892, and in April, 1897, the monument was dedicated with imposing cere-monies. The view looking up the river from Claremont, the old family mansion standing north of the Tomb, now "Claremont Inn," is justly famous. A steel viaduct one-third of a mile in length, spanning Manhattan Valley, provides for a northern exten-sion of the Drive to connect with the Harlem Speedway.

ST. PAUL'S CHAPEL AND PARK ROW SKY-SCRAPERS.

St. Paul's Chapel on Broadway, between Vesey and Fulton Streets, is a cherished relic of Colonial days. Built in 1766 as the chapel of Trinity Parish, it is the only church edifice in New York which has been preserved from the pre-Revolutionary period. Towering behind the church are seen the Park Row and St. Paul Buildings, the former being the tallest building in the world. To the left is the Astor House, for fifty years Manhattan's most famous hotel. The front of St. Paul's faces towards the river, and in the old days the lawn sloped down to the water's edge, then on the line of Greenwich Street.

FIFTH AVENUE, BROADWAY AND TWENTY-THIRD STREET.

The intersection of Broadway, Fifth Avenue and Twenty-third Street, popularly called "The Flatiron Corner," is the best known corner in New York City. It is near the shopping district, and is singularly animated at all hours, particularly during the afternoon. On certain days it is discreetly avoided by those who object to the pranks of sudden gusts of wind. The accompanying view was made from the balcony of the Fifth Avenue Hotel, looking south on Fifth Avenue, Broadway being on the left, and Twenty-third Street crossing the foreground.

71

THE PLAZA.

At Fifth Avenue and Fifty-eighth and Fifty-ninth Streets is "The Plaza," an open square remarkable for its architectural and social surroundings. On the east are the great hotels, the Netherland and the Savoy. On the south is Cornelius Vanderbilt's house. On the west is the Plaza Hotel, and to the north lies Central Park. The principal entrance to Central Park is here; and the Metropolitan Club overlooks the square.

LOWER MANHATTAN FROM
BROOKLYN BRIDGE.

The accompanying drawing includes the territory between Brooklyn Bridge and the extreme end of Manhattan Island at the Battery.
The outlook is south over the Upper Bay; to
the left is the Statue of Liberty, and South
Street, noted for its wharves and shipping
lines, is below the observer in the foreground.

"OLD FIRST CHURCH."

Foreign critics who are in the habit of saying that New York possesses few architectual features of merit, invariably make an exception of The First Presbyterian Church, widely known as "Old First." Founded in 1716, it stood originally in Wall Street, near Broadway, but now occupies the block on Fifth Avenue, between Eleventh and Twelfth streets. It is beyond doubt one of the most distinguished and distinctive edifices of its class in the country. Nine pastors have succeeded one another there, the present incumbent being Howard Duffield, D.D.

BROAD STREET AND THE STOCK EXCHANGE.

This view shows Broad Street looking north towards Wall Street, which is the financial centre of the country. An imposing succession of bank and office buildings are massed in this neighborhood. The sidewalks and street are crowded with alert, jostling throngs of bankers, brokers, lawyers, clerks, and messenger boys. On the left is the new building of the New York Stock Exchange. Across from the Stock Exchange, on the corner of Nassau Street, is the sixteen-story Gillender Building, and opposite is the United States Sub-Treasury, with its Doric portico, overlooking Wall Street.

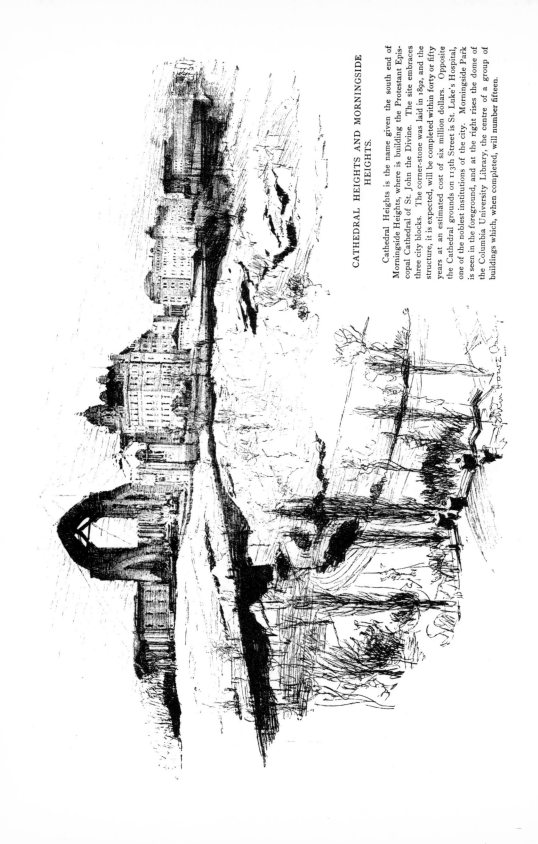

CATHEDRAL HEIGHTS AND MORNINGSIDE HEIGHTS.

Cathedral Heights is the name given the south end of Morningside Heights, where is building the Protestant Episcopal Cathedral of St. John the Divine. The site embraces three city blocks. The corner-stone was laid in 1892, and the structure, it is expected, will be completed within forty or fifty years at an estimated cost of six million dollars. Opposite the Cathedral grounds on 113th Street is St. Luke's Hospital, one of the noblest institutions of the city. Morningside Park is seen in the foreground, and at the right rises the dome of the Columbia University Library, the centre of a group of buildings which, when completed, will number fifteen.

7
The Black Hand

EVERYBODY'S MAGAZINE

SEPTEMBER, 1908

THE BLACK HAND

By LINDSAY DENISON

EDITOR'S NOTE.—The Skull and Cross-bones flag of piracy is gone from the seas. But in our cities flourishes the Black Hand, a symbol every bit as significant of greed and cruelty—even more an emblem of cowardice and treachery. The scoundrels who lurk behind the terror of the Black Hand wax fat and daily grow more arrogant in their contempt for American law and order. Their wicked prestige has been fostered by the hysteria of the newspapers and the self-sufficiency and ignorance of the police, until security of property and safety of living are disappearing from the tenement and small-shop districts of our cities. The well-to-do will not long be immune. Here it is told how these graduates of Italy's penitentiaries escape to this country; what evil they have done; and how the Black Hand may be suppressed by sending its devotees back to the Italian government, which yearns for them.

A LETTER shoved through the crack under a door or dropped in a tenement letter-box, bearing the dread symbol of the Black Hand and the signature *La Mano Nera,* and containing a demand for money under threat of death or disaster. A few weeks later, if the demand in the letter is ignored, a knife-thrust in the dark, or, more commonly, the explosion of a crude bomb, which wrecks the first-floor front of the house.

That is the Black Hand: the extortion of money by the certainty that a refusal of blackmail will be followed by bodily violence and disaster—a certainty kept terribly alive by a daily succession of assaults, murders, and explosions under the very noses of the police. It is evidence that our immigration laws are not stringent enough to keep out of this country the very worst of the bad

79

ITALIANS ON TRIAL FOR SENDING BLACK HAND LETTERS.

people which those laws were made to exclude. It represents the transferring to this country of the most lawless men and methods of the Camorra of Naples and the Mafia of Sicily.

The existence and growth of the Black Hand is not only a demoralizing disgrace to our system for maintaining public order. It is an affront to the hundreds of thousands of useful, honest, happy-tempered Italians who have come to this country to take up the work from which the prospering Irish immigrant turned a generation ago. It is a deterrent to their progress; the price of prosperity as a merchant or as a barber or in any decent business is a blackmailing demand from the Black Hand.

How rich is the field in which the Black Hand garners its harvest is indicated by the fact that the bank deposits of Italians in the United States in the past five years have amounted to three hundred millions of dollars—one hundred millions of dollars in New York state. And there is hardly a dollar of all that honestly earned total that is not

ONE OF THE FIRST BLACK HAND MEN ARRESTED.

at the mercy of this system of blackmail.

The terror of the Black Hand now is tremendously increased by its mystery. The mystery will never be revealed, because there is nothing tangible to reveal. If you, the reader, were an Italian who had accumulated some money, and I, the writer, were an Italian criminal, associating with other criminals, and wanted your money—I should write you a Black Hand letter. It would mean to you (being an Italian) that all the stealthy ruthlessness and cruelty and devilish persistence of an Italian criminal, or a band of Italian criminals, were to be turned loose on you if you did not submit to blackmail.

And if you were unusually brave and took the threats to the police, you would know that testimony given against me in court would mean that my family and my criminal friends would follow you and yours with the *vendetta*. In fact, even though Italian detectives had surrounded you and had persuaded you that this wasn't Italy, and that the bearing of evidence in court was not an act of shameless and reprehensible indecency, one or more of my friends would certainly be in court to remind you of another opinion. The form of the reminder would probably be the drawing of the fore-finger across the throat. And it would come over you that for your own immediate per-sonal prospects this *was* Italy—and you would refuse to testify, and I would go free. Where-upon the newspapers would boil over with indignation against "the wonderful criminal intricacy of the Black Hand organization." Which would be nonsense. For the force that really operated would have been the Italian, and especially the south Italian, tem-perament. The law and the police have not been battling with a great, complicated, and secretly united murdering graft-machine, but with individual products of the opportunities for criminal education afforded by southern Italy for hundreds of years.

It is all very true, as well as very amusing, that this murderous sys-tem was presented with its name by a reporter of a New York newspaper.

There was a histori-cal foundation for the name. Back in Inquisi-tion days in Spain there was *La Mano Nera*, a secret society which fought the government and the church. It passed, and the secret societies of southern Italy were its heirs. Twenty years or more ago a false report was raised in Spain that *La Mano Nera* had been revived. The story lin-gered in the brain of a *Herald* reporter, and one fine day he at-tempted to rejuvenate waning interest in a puzzling Italian murder case by speculating as to the coming to life of the Black Hand among Latin immigrants in America. The other newspapers seized on the idea eagerly, and kept it going.

Nor did the police withhold their good offices in aiding the sin-ister exploitation of the name. The policemen who have been entrusted with the regulation of Black Hand crime are mostly of north Italian parentage. They do not understand the south

ELIZABETH STREET, NEW YORK, WHICH IS THE HEART OF THE ITALIAN DISTRICT.

DEPOSITORS SURROUNDING THE PATI BANK—SCENE OF A BLACK HAND BATTLE.

Italian criminal, but they fear him. And they were only too willing to foster the invention of a Black Hand of marvelously intricate and compact organization; no reporter has ever suggested any detail too mysterious for instant police verification.

Now, your transplanted Italian is no more a born fool than your transplanted Irishman. The free advertising which the non-existent Black Hand was receiving was almost too good to be true. If you happen to be a breakfast-food manufacturer, just sit down and figure out in cold cash what you would have been willing to pay for that exploitation which the name Black Hand got for something less than nothing.

THIS YOUNG MAN IS SERVING A 15-YEAR SENTENCE.

There were in New York then, and had been for many years, a great many Italian criminals — not two per cent. of our Italian population did they form, perhaps, but nevertheless there were more of them than would be allowed at large in Italy. There were blackmailers, swindlers, counterfeiters, kidnappers, robbers, and murderers among them. Coming from the same ports in southern Italy, most of them, they had a general intercommunication, the same lounging places. Why should it not be so, when they spoke the same dialects and had the same neighborhood gossip from home to talk about — and lived by the same crimes? As at home, there were chiefs among

82

them—men known for desperation, cruelty, and records of murder. But they had no fixed hours of meeting; and no lodge rooms. They had no gang names; they had even no prestige as a body.

And along came the benevolent and intelligent New York newspapers and gave them a name and then exploited it. And did the inchoate Italian criminal gangs grab the chance and keep it going? For an answer glance over the head-lines of any New York newspaper any day.

It must be remembered that such crimes as are there chronicled are but the exponents of a hundred or a thousand efforts at blackmail. Refusals of the demands are few and scattering. Therefore it is impossible to compute the extent of Black Hand crime —except that there is hardly an Italian, from contractor to fruit-stand keeper, who has not been coerced into paying blackmail.

There are already indications that the loot hunger of the Black Hander will make him

AN ITALIAN LABORER CONVICTED AS
A BLACK HAND CRIMINAL.

bold enough to look for victims outside of the Italian-born population. In the first stages of his hunting, his victims have always been those who have learned to fear him and his vengeance in Italy. But as the number of his unpunished outrages increases, the terror of his pirate name is becoming potent to frighten any timid American reader of the newspapers. Sooner or later, if the Black Hand is not checked, it will be a menace not only to Italian-born Americans, but to all of us; it is bound to grow with what it feeds on. Within the past few weeks an alleged Black Hand assault was perpetrated among the summer dwellers in the Berkshires, in Massachusetts. A large plot is reported as in operation against a number of wealthy families in Mexico. Time and patient investigation will determine whether these are machinations of Black Hand gangs or the schemes of other desperadoes who have adopted the Black Hand symbol.

THE RUINS OF A FRUIT STORE DESTROYED BY BLACK HAND DYNAMITERS.

TWO ITALIANS ACCUSED OF SENDING BLACK HAND LETTERS, AND THEIR INTERPRETER
(THE MAN IN CENTER).

For of course not all of the crimes bearing this emblem have anything to do with the real Black Hand gangs. A jealous girl may use the symbol to frighten her lover. It is but a few weeks since two Russian Jews in New York used it to scare money out of a real-estate dealer of their own race, and since then two Greeks were caught trying to blackmail another Greek with a letter signed Μαυρὰ Χείρ. But the more the symbol is used by outsiders, the greater its value to the Italian Black Hand. This is the one secret society on earth—if one may call it a society—which can afford to encourage the pretensions of spurious members.

It is very hard indeed for the native-born American to puzzle out the psychology of the great body of respectable, law-abiding, hard-working, thriving Italians

AN ITALIAN BARBER NOW A BLACK HAND RESIDENT OF SING SING.

who submit as tamely as they do to the Black Hand imposition. One must go to Italy for the explanation.

The secret society of Sicily, for instance, is the Mafia. Take the word of an Americanized Sicilian for it, and it is just about as much of a dyed-in-the-wool criminal machine as is our own dear old Tammany Hall—no more and no less. The nobility belong to it, and men of high standing throughout the community —just as the William C. Whitneys and Bourke Cockrans and Francis Burton Harrisons and James W. Gerards and Robert B. Roosevelts belong to Tammany Hall; likewise there are in the Mafia persons like Yakie-Yake Brady and Paul Kelly and Monk Eastman—leaders of gangs of bad men who call them chief. But it is by the acts of the gang leaders that the

Mafia is known on this side of the ocean. The gentle and nobly born members of the Mafia, according to this version of the tradition, endeavor to restrain their bad brethren—and have so far succeeded that the worst and wickedest of the "Low Mafia" are now in and about New York and Chicago, St. Louis and Denver.

The Camorra of Naples is very much the same sort of an organization. The native spirit of intrigue of the man of south Italy works out in pretty much the same way, whatever the town. The Mafia man will tell you that there is a difference between the Mafia and the Camorra; that it is the tradition of the Mafia that a man shall meet his enemy and fight him in the open, face to face, after a warning; whereas the Camorra countenances sneakings-up in the dark, and stabbings in the back, and the poisoned cup proffered in ostensible friendship. But the Camorra man will bite the back of his fingers when this is repeated to him, and say that the Mafia man is many kinds of a liar.

However that may be, hereafter in this article the names Mafia and Camorra will be used as though they referred only to the criminals of those organizations.

The recruits of the societies are men who have committed small crimes of violence and dishonesty. They sell their souls to the chiefs of the bands for protection from the police. If in spite of this aid the criminal is arrested and brought to trial, the Mafia supplies a crowd of willing perjurers to support his innocence; the state's witnesses are scared nearly out of their senses by threats, which will be only too grimly fulfilled if the accused is convicted; and five times out of six he goes free.

It is but justice to the Italian government to acknowledge here, parenthetically, that in the past ten years it has been getting the better of the societies; the proportion of those who are saved from the penalties of their crimes is waning—and, of course, the power of the gang chiefs is waning, too. For this very reason, as will be shown later, the menace to America has increased.

But to return to the criminal recruit: after pledging himself to the chief, he is a bad Mafia or Camorra man. He must take orders from the chief. He is tested lightly at first—he is merely sent as a witness to a forthcoming affray, or into court as a perjurer. Later he is commanded to join with a crew who are to beat up a man

who has disobeyed the chief's orders. Moreover, if he has occasion to commit small crimes on his own hook from time to time, he has that semi-immunity which Mafia brings. He proves himself deft, trustworthy, desperate. Murders are entrusted to him. If he commits enough of them, if the whole community begins to fear him, if the time comes when peaceable citizens regard his slightest intimations as orders to be obeyed implicitly—he is himself a gang chief, than whom there is no more reckless, ruthless, arrogant scoundrel in the world.

It is men trained in such societies who are terrorizing the Italian settlements in America by the use of the Black Hand. It is the long habit of submission to such tyranny which makes Italians here submissive to this similar, though comparatively unorganized, system of blackmail. Now it is time to look into the reasons why these bloodthirsty Italian scoundrels come here, and into the means of their coming, despite the laws of both Italy and the United States.

Let us suppose that at some time in his bloody career the Black Hand assassin is caught or convicted. There is no death penalty for murder in Italy. And even if his society has not been able to save him, it has almost certainly been able to effect a modification of the degree of his conviction so that the murderer has to serve but from two to ten years. Until he gets out again, the society forgets him. There are practically never any escapes from the Italian prison to which Mafia and Camorra convicts go. A rocky island, well out in the sunny bay of Naples, surrounded day and night by an armed patrol, with searchlights playing out over the water and a torpedo-boat lurking in the shadows—no, the secret organizations do not try to rescue their brethren who fall by the wayside.

And even after the sentence is complete, the societies can be of comfort to the convict in only one way. They can help him get out of Italy. This becomes his one desire, for no desperado ex-convict can be even bearably near comfort in Italy. Here are some of the restrictions laid upon him when he is discharged from his prison sentence, under *sorveglianza speciale* (special surveillance):

He must tell the police where he is going to live. He must not venture out of his dwelling-place between eight at night and eight in the morning—for if he is caught out during the prohibited hours he is sent back to prison. He cannot obtain employment without the permission and approval of the chief of police—and even then the employer must give a bond that the ex-convict will abide strictly by the police restrictions. He cannot change employers except under the same conditions. He must report at police headquarters at frequent stated intervals, and there have his call recorded and the record countersigned in a book which he must have always on his person, subject to the inspection of any policeman who may demand a look at it. He must not carry any deadly weapon; the discovery of even a pen-knife in his pockets (and he is always subject to search) renders him liable to an especially long term in prison. He must not frequent drinking-places; the first sign that he is intoxicated is as bad as the possession of a weapon. If he is involved in a street broil the law assumes that he is the aggressor and that he is in the wrong, no matter how innocent he may actually be.

It is enough to drive a criminal of any spirit quite mad. He must get out of Italy. But the law says he may not leave Italy. He may not pass the frontier nor take passage on a foreign-bound ship without a passport. The Italian government is more enlightened than the governments of our own states and municipalities, whose ideal method of dealing with undesirable citizens is that of Mr. Dogberry:

"The most peaceable way for you, if you do take a thief, is to let him show himself what he is and steal out of your company"

Though it is not a penal offense for the ex-convict to attempt to leave Italy, it is a misdemeanor, punishable with sufficient severity to make him beware of being caught at it.

Accordingly, on every vessel sailing from Palermo or Naples are a dozen or more members of the Camorra or the Mafia, employed as sailors, coal-heavers, and stewards. It is their fraternal duty to aid their brethren to evade the passport law. If there are six or more members of a ship's company earnestly desirous of concealing a stowaway, the thing can always be done. There are recorded instances where a stowaway has been hunted for three hours by twenty men, after all the officers and crew have been sent ashore, and has remained undiscovered—because he was sewed up in a mattress in a bunk. When the steamship has tied up at her berth in an American port, the fugitive puts on the uniform or overalls of one of his confederates and easily makes his way off the pier. And thus, a seasoned and hardened criminal, his blood-stained hands against all the world as the world's hands are against him, he is turned loose in the land of the free and the home of the brave. Every steamship man concerned in the Mediterranean trade knows something of the system; one of them has admitted these facts. It is the theory of the professional policeman of America that the Italian criminal comes to us through France and Canada. That is nonsense; he has neither the intelligence nor the means.

The ex-convict has the New York address of one or more former members of his society in Italy. He makes his way to this address as quickly as he may. He is without work and in a strange country. It may be that happy chance will find honest work for him at once. But usually it is not so. He becomes, more likely, a willing and useful tool of the Black Hand, a dependent on the generosity of more thoroughly acclimated criminals. The stealthy delivery of blackmailing letters, the stabbings, the bomb plantings, and even the murders of the Black Hand type are done by men who are so ignorant and so helpless that they face starvation if they do not carry out the orders of the Black Hand thugs who house and feed them after their surreptitious entry into the United States.

Ordinary police methods are of no avail in tracing such a criminal. The very men whose tool he has been and whose behest he has obeyed probably do not know his name—with the exception of the gang leader who has given the order. The honest and peaceable Italians, even if they dared reveal him, do not know his face nor his habits nor even of his arrival in this country. The very law here is a protection to him. In Italy the giving of a false name to a policeman is a crime. The burden of proof of identity is on the suspect; if he cannot prove his right to his name, he goes to jail. In America he may change his name every day, without penalty or even the necessity of an explanation.

Not always is the Black Hand recruit an ex-convict. As the pressure of the Italian police has borne down more and more heavily on he Mafia and the Camorra, unconvicted criminals have been fleeing before the wrath to come and making their way to the United States in the full comforts of the steerage while there is yet time. But the

FACSIMILE OF A TYPICAL BLACK HAND LETTER, WHICH, TRANS-
LATED, READS:

This is the second time that I have warned you. Sunday at ten o'clock in the morning, at the corner of Second Street and Third Avenue, bring three hundred dollars without fail. Otherwise we will set fire to you and blow you up with a bomb. Consider this matter well, for this is the last warning I will give you.
I sign the Black Hand.

proportion of these is small as compared to the number of stowaways who slip down the gang-planks of every Mediterranean steamer.

And so it is that the Italian criminal does get out of Italy and into the United States despite both governments. And in the fulness of time it has come to pass that there are more Italian ex-convicts at large in the United States than there are in Italy—that all the daring, reckless, unreformable desperadoes of Italy are in this country, taking not only the purses but the good names of their former compatriots by means of the Black Hand.

It is not possible to speak certainly of the way in which the spoils of their plots are divided. It seems most likely that the "divvy"

is governed by the generosity of the head "bad man" and the risks taken by the members of the gang in accumulating the loot—and as well by the prevailing prosperity or poverty of the gang as a whole. The worst and greediest scoundrel in the plot takes all he dares. Most of the rest goes to the men who have made the threats. Half of what the chief takes goes "higher up." There are at least two or three old graduates of south Italian crime who never sully their hands with the commission of actual crimes nor trouble their brains to plan them, though occasionally the big chief or one of his nearest lieutenants may drop in on an Italian banker and ask for a thousand dollars or so. He gets it, quick. He doesn't have to make any threats; the mere appearance of his face in the place is a threat. There is no talk of notes or security. The transaction is almost as simple as when one of the Bosses of High Finance drops in on a bank outside the New York clearing-house and asks for a few extraordinary favors. The very names of the Black Hand's big chiefs are names of terror. They know the little chiefs. They know the gossip in Italian blackmailing circles. And the little chiefs give up a moiety to them meekly and with dispatch.

So loosely formed are the component parts of the Black Hand that sometimes they work at cross purposes. Not very long ago in New York one Pati, who had a little Italian bank, was singled out as a victim by a Black Hand crew for the most part made up of former Mafia men. He had associations which made him feel that he ought to be immune from Black Hand interference. Some of his own friends shared his indignation. Representations were made to the Mafia band that, really, old Italian enmities ought to be forgotten in this country. There was a plenty of Italian bankers to be preyed upon who were not dearly beloved brethren of the Camorra. But the Mafia crew was hungry. Pati was rich; Pati had been warned to give up; discipline must be upheld, let the bombs fall where they might. All right, said Pati's Camorra friends, go ahead! The Mafia sent their collector around to the Pati bank. He had hardly entered the door when he was shot dead in a fusillade of bullets which were fired not only by Pati and his son, but by half a dozen friends of Mr. Pati, who significantly happened to be present and armed.

The admirable character of the banker is perhaps best shown by the fact that after being patted on the back by the police of New York as a brave man and the first of his race to face the Black Hand issue squarely, he went away secretly, and at this writing some scores of depositors mournfully regard the closed doors of his bank and wag their heads in sour satisfaction as they contemplate the certainty that the Mafia will find him somewhere some day, and exact its grimly sentimental dividend from his person in full.

This falling out on lines of cleavage drawn by the old Italian society bonds is most unusual. For the most part, traditional transatlantic enmities are forgotten and reappear only when word comes from over sea that the Mafia or the Camorra has decreed the death here of one who has fled from Italy to escape feud vengeance. The closest students of Italian crime believe that the famous "barrel murder" was the outcome of a Sicilian love affair. The old Jew peddler whose body was packed in a trunk and humorously set out under the windows of a New York police station, not many years ago, paid the price of unfair dealing, either by himself or by a relative, in conducting fence negotiations with a robber in Italy.

Such crimes, however repugnant and sensational they may be, are of small importance when one contemplates the growing power of the great blackmailing mill which adopted the American suggestion of naming itself the Black Hand.

As I have set down before, there are no fixed meeting-places, no oath-bound pacts, no elected or appointed officers. What need? A Black Hand "bad man" walks into an Italian saloon; he may greet the bartender; he may ignore him. But a sign is given; it may be the scratching of an ear; it may be the rearrangement of a necktie; it may be the picking of a thread out of a sleeve. It is enough. Notice has been given that certain persons are to meet the chief to-night at a certain place. Perhaps it is to be in that same saloon, perhaps in another saloon miles away. That doesn't matter. At the rendezvous at the appointed hour the summoned men are present. Some one proposes a game of *zecchinetta*, which is not unlike the American game of faro. Inasmuch as the police of America have prejudices against gambling, will the proprietor kindly furnish a private room with a secure inside lock? He does. The plot is outlined, the assignments are made, the dole from the last effort at blackmail is distributed or the bomb is produced which is to punish its failure.

The *zecchinetta* game thus having been properly concluded, the members of the gang separate—perhaps without knowing one another's names. And the next night the same chief may call a similar conclave made up of altogether different men, or in part of the same men, and line out another crime. There is little fear of treachery in the heart of a man whose minions know that he has a score of others just as ready to revenge treachery at his bidding as are they themselves.

It is little wonder that the American police have not been able to make much headway against so indefinite an organization. But it is the disgrace of our police authorities that, except by Commissioner Bingham of New York (who has been disgracefully hampered by a trivial and stupid board of aldermen), no intelligent warfare has been made on Black Hand crime. If the thing is to be done, it must be done by the same methods which the Italian government has found effective against the same sort of people at home. First of all, there must be developed a uniformed corps of police, made up of men —south Italians—as brave and as reckless and as honest as were Wild Bill Hickok and Seth Bullock and Colonel Sanders and Bat Masterson and the others who terrorized the road-agents and the cattle-thieves of our own wild West forty years ago. There are plenty of such men in Italy and here.

But, in addition, they must know the secret language of the Italian secret societies—the most complicated thieves' jargon in the world. The mongrel dialects of the Mediterranean ports are puzzling enough, anyway, made up as they are of bits of all the Latin languages, Greek, Arabic, and their variations. But the banded plunderers of the Camorra and the Mafia superimpose on this tangle a code of their own which can be learned by only the most patient, intelligent, and daring detective study.

The members of this police corps must be no respecters of tradition or of persons in authority. In the great Camorra trial which seemed to be the end of the Camorra in Naples, the thieves and thugs of the society were found to use priests and the nobility as cogs in their mill; and even now the value of the whole proceeding is shaded by the suspicion that the Camorra was represented in the prosecution, and had shielded some of those on whom the greatest real guilt rested.

There must be also an Italian detective bureau, working in secret concert with the uniformed Italian police; its members, too, must needs be south Italians, who have the instincts inherited from generations of the darkest intriguers of Europe. For instance, if a well-trained Mafia or Camorra member be on his way to Elizabeth Street, in New York, from his home in Harlem, to buy his week's groceries, he would as soon cut off his right hand as go direct to his destination. He rides about on different lines of surface cars, transferring with economical carefulness, until he gets into the dry-goods district. He passes through one or more department stores, using the elevators freely. He takes to the elevated railroad or the subway. He doubles back on his tracks as often as he may without paying an extra fare. He mixes with the seething crowd at the Brooklyn Bridge entrance. He loiters on the upper floor of an office building, and walks down twenty weary flights of stairs, and emerges from an entrance on another street than that from which he entered. When he has reached Elizabeth Street and his favorite grocery-store, he has spent four hours on a journey which he might have accomplished in half an hour. He is always in practice. No national board of strategy was ever so ingenious in the devising of war games. Such a man cannot be kept in sight by the keenest American shadower alive, nor even by a north Italian. But a south Italian detective, whose mind works just as does that of the prey he is pursuing, has a chance.

Cooperation between this government and the government of Italy has done some good and will do more. Italy is very willing to take back to her own tender mercies the ex-convicts who have come to America. It is the official Italian theory that crime will be discouraged in Italy once it is understood that even America is not a safe refuge. Italy has complete records and descriptions of all her missing convicts. A wise appropriation of money on this side of the water for the hunting out of Italy's missing criminals would clear our Italian settlements of a shameful scandal and terror.

The Black Hand must go. The use of the symbol must become a guarantee of imprisonment or deportation as certain as is now its promise of plunder and bloodshed. The development of the Black Hand system of contempt for law is demoralizing to all the better ideals of our foreign born population. Soon it will be, if not suppressed, a menace to the native born as well. Moreover, the elimination of the Black Hand we owe to Italy nearly as much as to ourselves. It will be an inestimable favor to a nation to which we are indebted for the uplifting of our ideals of art, for the labor which has helped develop our national resources, and for the infusion into our blood of the sturdy, thrifty strain which becomes strikingly apparent as soon as the normal, industrious, simple-souled Italian immigrant begins to make himself at home.

8
East Side Considerations

EAST SIDE CONSIDERATIONS.

BY E. S. MARTIN.

THE BOY WHO KNEW WHERE THERE WAS A TREE.

AN enlightened official of New York said, the other day, "The happiest people in town live on the East Side." He did not speak officially, and not without knowledge that a great many very wretched people also live there, but very likely what he said was the truth, though not, of course, the whole truth. The ordinary impression of people who don't live on the East Side and who don't go there is that it is a painful quarter of the city, where all the people are poor, and live huddled up together, and nearly die every summer, and have a pretty bad time all the year round. The East Side is associated with misery; is looked upon as a consequence of the imperfect apparatus now in use for distributing money. To sink layer by layer down the strata of society and finally to bring up in an East Side tenement is the conventional, well-to-do New-Yorker's conception of an awful fate. Persons who might live in a good part of town, and who, from pious motives or because they are tired of conventional society and manners, go over and take up with the East Side, and live in tenements there, are looked upon as people who have made an enormous sacrifice. No doubt it is true that the majority of East-Siders don't live on the East Side absolutely from choice, but because life there best suits their incomes and occupations. Most of the people who live east of Broadway and south of Houston Street are poor, and live where they do not so much from any special prejudice against the Fifth Avenue side of Central Park as to be near their work, or because in the tenement-house streets they get more for their money. They are not all poor, by any means. Some East-Siders stick to the East Side because they are used to it and belong to it—yes, and because a good deal of it belongs to them, as is the case of that East Side woman whom report which seems veracious credits with owning (last year) no less than sixty-four double tenement-houses, the rents of which are said to run up to sixty thousand dollars a year. Their owner manages her own property, collects her rents, bosses her tenants, and personally postpones repairs on her property; and it suits her convenience

THE BEGINNING OF A MERCANTILE CAREER.

as well as her taste to be a resident landlady, and to live where she has her own under her eye, and can better appreciate the blessings of means.

There is misery on the East Side, of course, because there are a great many more people there than should be, and because there are sickness and extreme poverty there, as well as evil passions and sin, and all the painful things one finds wherever human beings are gathered in considerable groups. But there is unquestionably unhappiness also on Fifth Avenue. Among all the wretched people in New York it would be hard to match the apparent wretchedness of some persons whom one sees driving in closed carriages in Central Park in winter. They look as if they never had had any fun, or known any emotion of real happiness. They look stunted and comatose. No doubt many of them are sick people; but many of them, too, are overfed and overcoddled citizens who have missed the joy of living from too great solicitude to retain the comforts of life.

Whatever pangs a thorough knowledge of the East Side may involve, the superficial observer does not find it sad to look upon. It happened once in April to a visitor to New York to have to make a call at the University Settlement in Delancey Street. He started early in the evening from one of the respectable residence streets on Murray Hill, and being about to penetrate he knew not how desperate and lawless a quarter, he took along a stout stick as a means of self-protection against marauders. When he got there he found a quarter where clean streets paved with asphalt were brilliantly lighted and swarmed with people. It was one of the first mild evenings of spring, and a large part of Delancey Street was sitting out-of-doors. Mothers were sitting on door-steps gossiping with one another and watching children who ought doubtless to have been abed. There were life, action, and social activity everywhere. Saloons and billiard-rooms seemed crowded—indeed everything seemed crowded—and to all appearances an immense amount of entertainment was in process of distribution among a great number of people. When the visitor got back to his respectable Murray Hill street it was uncommonly like returning from the land of the living to the abode of the departed. Murray Hill was ditch-water after Delancey Street. Nobody in the side streets; nothing going on. Not so much light; not so good a pavement; nowhere near so much fun in sight.

He smiled when he put his heavy cane in the corner, and then he sighed at the realization that there are losses for all our gains, as well as gains for all our losses, and that people who have their choice, and families who have whole houses to themselves, and live in-doors even on pleasant evenings, do not enjoy all those advantages without paying for them to some extent in the loss of easy fellowship, and also of many pleasant social opportunities.

Mankind is not only the noblest study of man, but the most entertaining. People are more interesting than things or books, or even newspapers. The East Side is especially convenient for the observation of people because there are such shoals of them always in sight, and because their habits of life and manners are frank, and favorable to a certain degree of intimacy at sight. Where each family has a whole house to itself and lives inside of it, and the members never sally out except in full street dress—hats, gloves, and manners—it is hopeless to become intimately acquainted with them as you pass on the sidewalk. You may

AN ORIENTAL TYPE.

walk up and down Fifth Avenue for ten years and never see a Fifth Avenue mother nursing her latest born on the doorstep, but in Mott or Mulberry or Cherry Street that is a common sight, and always interesting to the respectful observer. When the little Fifth Avenue children are let out, if they don't drive off in a carriage, at least they go with a nurse, and are clothed like field daisies, and under such restraint as good clothes and even the kindest of nurses involve. But the East Side children tumble about on the sidewalk and pavement hour after hour, under slight restraint and without any severe amount of oversight, hatless usually, barehanded and barefooted when the weather suffers it. It is the children that constitute the East Side's greatest charm, and no doubt it is especially due to them that a veracious man who often walks northward or eastward from Mulberry Bend late in the afternoon is able

A LITTLE FATHER.

to testify that he invariably reaches Bleecker Street with modified and softened sentiments toward his fellows, and increased tolerance for creation and its perplexing incidents. It cannot be said that the East Side children are clean. Some of them are clean sometimes. It is stamped upon an observer's memory that on a Saturday early in April he passed a little girl in Hester Street who had one of the cleanest heads of sunshiny hair he ever saw. Some East Side children are cleaner than others, but as a rule they are pretty dirty. The streets are clean for streets, and the children are clean for children who play in the streets.

To be very clean indeed is a luxury of high price. People are apt to look upon it as a mere virtue, but that is a modern notion born of hot and cold running water and a bath-room on every floor. Saints in old times usually went very dirty from religious conviction. East-Siders don't do that, but they put up with a moderate amount of dirt because it is one of the unavoidable conditions of their existence. Their children are usually dirty, but only

moderately dirty, as any normal child will be after playing in the street or anywhere out-of-doors. Dirt or no dirt, in good weather the children of the East Side are very interesting to watch. Some of them look sick, and a sick child is a pathetic sight wherever seen, but except in midsummer the great majority of them seem to be in good health and well nourished and lively. They play together very much as children do everywhere, and if they are more amusing than a lot of Fifth Avenue children, it is doubtless because they are under less supervision and are more natural. The most natural behavior we are used to see obtains in a cage of monkeys. The East Side children are nearly as untrammelled as the monkeys, but they are a great deal kinder to one another. Little girls tending babies and carrying them from door-step to door-step are a common sight. The little mothers are famous, but it seems to be in the nature of little girls to love babies and be good to them. What is more remarkable, and yet not uncommon on the East Side, is kind and responsible little boys who look after still smaller children, and drag them around in ramshackle carts or amuse them and keep them out of harm's way. Of course one sees something of the other side of human nature too. There are crying children, and mothers whose patience is worn out, and bullying older boys, but the East Side would not soften the heart of the sympathetic passer-by, and make him happier for passing through it, if the evidences of human kindness were not more plenty than the signs of the other side of human nature. It is what you see in people's faces that affects your spirits, not what they wear on their backs, or even on their heads. Fine birds in fine feathers are a gladdening sight. Really fine people with proper souls, whose faces show really superior qualities, and whose clothes and cleanliness and gentility are becoming to them, adorn creation in their way, and are folks that observers looking on at life are thankful for. You do not see people of that sort on the East Side;

but, on the other hand, you are not shocked there by the contrast between the individual and his circumstances. There are no "chappies" there; there is nothing to be seen there quite so astonishing and amusing and queer and pathetic as such chappies as one may sometimes see sipping green mint and smoking cigarettes in the purlieus of the Waldorf Hotel. The East Side is thoroughly disciplined. Faces there show rarely dejection, except what comes from illness, but endurance, patience, the practical education that comes of daily labor. In front of an uptown club is a cab loaded with travelling-bags. Inside are two young fellows just starting for some railroad station. A servant stands bareheaded at the cab door. One of the young men inside is dissatisfied with something. His arrogant face, as he makes complaint, is the face of a youth who has never earned his salt; who has been overfed, overstimulated, overamused; who has always had all material luxuries within his reach, has accepted all as his due, is grateful for nothing, is appreciative of nothing, and whose conception of his obligations in life is pretty well fulfilled if he does what he considers his part in keeping club servants thoroughly well up to his notion of their duties. Faces of the type of his face are not prevalent on the East Side. Persons whose business in life is to be carried, and to kick at their carriers when they stumble, do not abound down there. There are coarse people there, but they wear cheap clothes and work hard. There is no such disconcerting contrast between their outside and what one reads in their faces as afflicts the observer in more opulent parts of the town. If their looks are often enough commonplace and sometimes disagreeable, their environment and their clothes modify instead of aggravating them. Beggars may be pic-

turesque, but beggars on horseback are grotesque.

It may be true that fleas have still smaller fleas to bite 'em, and even on the East Side there may be a tyranny of things and a constant effort to maintain a scale of living that is uncomfortably high. But certainly it is not noticeable. The scale of living on Mulberry and Mott and the other tenement-house streets seems simple and easy. One is not perplexed and oppressed as he walks through that quarter of the city with constant recurrence of the query, where do the people who live in all these houses get the money to maintain them? The imagination which is stumped by the problem of the maintenance of miles of dwellings at from ten to fifty thousand dollars a year apiece, easily copes with the problems of paying rent for a tenement-house apartment and buying bread and simple food

FEATHER-BED DAY.

for a working-man's family. It is easy to see how East-Siders manage. The eternal servant problem never troubles them. Their social duties seem not to be exacting. Lo! on the fire-escapes and balconies, on Mondays or any of the various wash-days that race or creed or custom prescribes, their garments flap in the wind, and, on some streets, lend human interest to continuous frontages as far as the eye reaches. Food is convenient at every turn. Mott Street market-men sell Chinese roast pig already roasted, and Heaven knows what curious Oriental dainties that look as though they had crossed the sea. Mulberry Street abounds in sidewalk venders of bread which seems to have no remarkable quality (except, maybe, its cheapness), and strange white Italian cheeses, made evidently in America for the Italian market, encased in skins and shaped like tenpins. The great Jewish quarter has its butcher shops with Hebrew signs, and, in the spring, its provision of unleavened bread for the Passover. Hebrew housekeeping has other peculiarities. The street-cleaning men will tell you that after Easter it rains straw from mattresses in that part of the town, and that beds by the thousand change their stuffing.

A remarkable neighborhood is that Jewish quarter lying south of Houston Street and between the elevated railroads and the East River. On week-days parts of it swarm with push-carts. On Saturdays there are none to be seen, but thousands of orderly people in their Sabbath-day clothes meet in the streets and in the synagogues. There are synagogues of all grades and sizes, from the little room over a shop to the erstwhile church which has lost its Christian congregation and been sold to new worshippers, who have adorned it with just enough Hebrew architecture to make its change of owners and uses apparent. Religion receives profound attention in the Jewish quarter, and its interests and consolations seem to be thoroughly appreciated. One sees remarkable faces in the synagogues—rabbis with robes and stove-pipe hats manipulating ancient scrolls, and rows of men with hats on finding apparent satisfaction in ceremonies that seem curiously antiquated and perfunctory. The Jews of that quarter are usually not of the hook-nosed type familiar and accepted, but the marks of their race appear rather in the formation of the jaw and mouth and in the general facial aspect. No doubt they are largely recruited from Russia and southeastern Europe. Occasionally one sees the old familiar type—venerable, most respectable in dress and aspect,

clean, neat, bearded, and curved as to the nose. This seems like an old friend or a character out of a story-book.

And then there are the Jewish women, with lines of profound patience in their faces, and invariably false fronts of brown hair smoothed above their foreheads. They go to the synagogues too, but sit by themselves, screened off out of sight from their husbands and masters. The brown wigs abound everywhere, and are doubtless a religious requirement which the air of America has not yet availed to modify.

Life on the lower East Side is even more transitory than most life in New York. Most of the population there is of comparatively recent acquisition. Habits of life are more often brought there than formed there. It is not like the East End of London, where the people who live there now were born and have always lived. Signs abound of customs born elsewhere. The May-day parties of the East Side children are reminiscent of village life. If you see a troop of children in May, far downtown, following some leader and marching off with a definite purpose, the chances are it is a May party. A lover of the East Side, who had followed one of the parties a block or two, audaciously accosted the leader, a bright-eyed Jewish youngster, who evidently knew perfectly what he was about.

"Where are you bound for, Johnny? You can't get up to Central Park, can you?"

"Park! No; but I guess I know where there's a tree."

He did. He led his young troop through street after street, and by devious turns and twists, to the tree, a poor stunted wreck of a tree, slanting out of the sidewalk with that list away from the house fronts which city trees are wont to have. It was not much of a tree, but it answered the purposes of a May party, and what it lacked was made up by childish imaginations.

There are evidences all through the East Side of thought taken and money spent for the welfare of the dwellers there. No part of the town needs clean streets and smooth pavements so much, and no part of the town shares more fully in those blessings. Wagon traffic does not abound excessively in the streets

THE SABBATH—A SYNAGOGUE THAT WAS ONCE A CHURCH.

where the population is most dense. Most of these streets have been asphalted; all of them will be in time; and children play over their whole width. When a horse passes through, the driver picks er, big enough to hold 2500 visitors—a ministration to need by authority which it does the heart good to witness.

There are conscientious democrats who find comfort in maintaining, in the face

THE SACRED SCROLL IN THE SYNAGOGUE.

his way. The two new parks at Mulberry Bend and Corlears Hook are admirable breathing-places. In both of them the walks are lined with seats from end to end, so as to afford resting-places for the greatest possible number. Corlears Hook Park, at the bend in the East River and opposite the Brooklyn Navy-Yard, has a most interesting water-front and view. All the water traffic between the Bay and the Sound passes there. The Grand Street Ferry is close by, and all day long the river provides its entertainment for the park population. Newer still and near by is the Dock Commissioners' Recreation Pier at the foot of Third Street, with its great upper story, covered play-ground, reaching far out into the riv-

of indications to the contrary, that there are no classes in this country. The contention is praiseworthy, and persistence in it is praiseworthy too, for it helps, like Jefferson's declaration of the equality of men, to keep alive an idea that needs to be sustained. But even if there are not classes in the republic, disparity of estate and training have begotten varieties, and the tendency of each variety to herd with its own sort is always in sight. It is a tendency that is based on convenience; but it has its drawbacks. It narrows our experience and impoverishes our view of life. People who live and work in big cities fall into the way of following a little daily round, which takes men down town at a certain hour and by a certain route, and back at another hour, and which confines most women to rounds of the shopping and residence streets, where they see the same sights and the same sort of people every day, month after month and year after year. It is so much easier to follow a rut than to make a track for one's self that of course most people follow ruts. But for those who appreciate the wholesomeness of variety and the value of new sensations and suggestions, the East Side is an amazingly rich field. Not only is the contemplation of the poor a relief after the contemplation of the rich, but to get our minds off

world we live in. It is only a matter of three miles or so from Madison Square to Hester Street, but who would dream, who had not seen it, that the same town held within so short a distance scenes and people so contrasted as the shops and shoppers of Twenty-third Street and the hucksters of Hester and Ludlow? Not to have seen those hucksters, and their carts, and their merchandise, and their extraordinary zest for bargaining, is to have missed a sight that once seen declines to be forgotten. If there is the like of it anywhere in Europe, there is a better chance that the uptown New-Yorkers will see it

THE ENVIRONMENT OF SCHOLARSHIP.

ourselves and our ways, and those of our immediate neighbors, gives us a wholesome jolt, and helps to adjust them to a realization of the characteristics of the

there than in their own town. The locksmiths and jobbing tinkers and plumbers, with their keys and their tools strung on a wire hoop that rests on one shoulder;

the itinerant skirt-peddlers, with their stock in trade strung along on a pole, parading along the street and searching the faces of women for the signs that bespeak the possibility of a sale—how queer they are, and how inspiring to the observer who sees them for the first time!

son can see them often enough to keep them in mind without taking thought about the social and municipal problems that they suggest. What needs to be done for the East Side? What can be done? What is being done? The observer ponders all these questions, and if

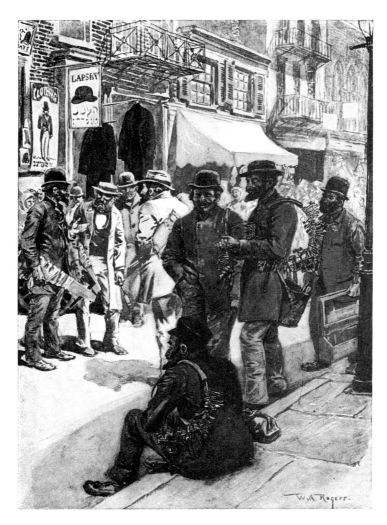

A TINKERS' EXCHANGE, HESTER STREET.

There is much more than mere entertainment to be got out of sights like these. Familiarity with them breeds neither contempt nor indifference, but rather increased interest. No thoughtful person

he goes far enough into them they lead him into acquaintance with a net-work of enterprises in which public officers and private charity work together. Everywhere he goes the signs of this co-operation appear. The public schools, big, substantial, and often handsome, still insufficient but all the time increasing; the churches, parish-houses, libraries, kindergartens, vacation schools, dispensaries, college settlements, hospitals, fresh-air funds, and scores of other enterprises and establishments attest the persistence of the East Side in the public memory. Thousands of well-to-do New-Yorkers rarely give it a thought; but there are hundreds, not themselves members of its family, who brood over it and plan and act in its behalf. Not that it cannot help itself. The East Side, stretching from Franklin Square to the Harlem River, harbors the greater part of the manual workers of New York, and the bulk of its great population is thrifty, industrious, self-respectful, and self-sustaining. But because Manhattan Island is narrow it is crowded, and because Europe is constantly pouring needy emigrants into it who cannot speak our language, and are used to a very low scale of living, it needs an exceptional amount of help from outside. There are great areas of it, indeed, which are more justly to be

A SKIRT-VENDER.

regarded as training-schools for American citizens than as mere residence quarters for working-people. It is the crop that the East Side raises that makes it important—the great crop of American voters, from the reaping of which there is no evasion or escape.

9
Park Driving

OUTING

JUNE, 1905

PARK DRIVING

By JAMES H. TUCKERMAN

PHOTOGRAPHS BY ARTHUR HEWITT

DURING the two brief months of spring and the three longer ones of autumn, when Central Park, from a social world's point-of-view, is formally "at home," the average attendance of horses within its gates is roughly estimated at from eight to ten thousand a day.

In some respects the exhibition in New York is as remarkable as any to be seen in the world. It could not be American and be otherwise. It is remarkable for its amazing incongruities. In few civilized lands can there be found examples of a more ignorant or a more vicious disregard, not only of the ethics, but of the common civilities of the road; in few places can there be seen traps with pretentions to smartness turned out with such ingenious ideas of smartness. One might travel far before discovering a poorer quality of horsemanship.

And in no place, moreover, where horses play a part can there be found a more thorough understanding, a more punctilious observance of those laws and courtesies which gentlemen have framed for the use of those who go in for this sort of diversion. Neither in the Row nor on the Bois nor in the König-Strasses of Continental cities can there be found a park coach, a gig, a victoria, or a brougham turned out with such nicety in detail or with a keener knowledge of form. As for horsemanship,

even a bred-in-the-bone Englishman will acknowledge quite freely that more really first-rate whips come from New York than from any other city, barring London.

To the mind of the casual stranger the equine exhibition in the Park, no doubt, is confined to that impressive pageant which is put on each afternoon between the hours of four and seven, and which is fondly and frequently referred to by the newspapers as "the fashionable Park parade." To one, however, more familiar with the Park routine and with the intricacies of its drives and bridle-paths the exhibition may be divided, not only into three separate and distinct performances, but into an old-fashioned one-ring circus as well.

Obviously the parade as a spectacular affair is the most popular of the three. All that is loveliest in womankind, all that men envy most in their fellowman, all that is best in horseflesh, is represented. Measured by length and breadth, there are seven continuous miles of it. It is not, however, until the big city is retreating Harlemward, and the elms have stretched their quiet shadows across the meadow, that the parade gathers in its glory.

As England dictates the fashion in equine affairs, some comparison between the driving in the Park and the driving in the Row seems inevitable. That the London function should be endowed with a solemnity

The tandem lends its bit of smartness to the show.

and pomp which is, in a measure, lacking here, is to be expected. For an American to take his pleasure in tranquil and un-hurried mood is a task still beyond his strength. So far as the actual science of driving is concerned, honors between the two cities may be said to rest easy. To be sure, the skill of the English servants, taken as a whole, is superior to those of New York, but that superiority, like the quality of some of their thoroughbreds, may be attributed to the fact that as a people we have not gone in much for the breeding of servants, and importation of good ones is of very recent habit. Even now the ma-jority of grooms and coachmen in private stables are little better than the riffraff from London.

If a test were to be made of the compara-tive numerical strength of the London horsewoman and the horsewoman of New York, the latter would lose almost by de-fault. Of the hundreds of women who take their lives and their reins in one hand —preferably the wrong one—and with or without servants work their horses through the dangerous afternoon traffic in the Park, it is probably safe to assume that not more than ten per cent. are equipped with any-thing more useful than a gee and haw know-ledge of driving. That so many continue to drive and to add their fresh loveliness to the beauty of the Park must be due in part to providence and in part to the police. When a New York woman, however, recog-nizes that driving one, two, or four horses is quite as much a science as a diversion it is a difficult task to find her superior. And the same thing may be said with equal truth of her brother. As a matter of fact, the most finished horsemen as well as the green-est are to be found in Central Park. The former may still be deficient in quantity but in quality it is distinctly at the head of its class. At present there are a score or more of American men and women who have made driving in some form or other the reason for a prolonged stay in England, and are admitted to be capable whips either in town or road work. It is in nicety of detail and in the correctness of his appoint-ments that the New Yorker excels. So scrupulously does he observe the laws of equine fashion that when his trap is turned out, only the most experienced servant can be of service to him. For this increasing

The banker seeks recreation in his spider phaeton.

tendency towards good form, the National Horse Show Association, in taking into consideration the appointments as well as the quality of an exhibit, is deserving of much credit. Since Park driving became a recognized factor in the day's fashionable routine, there have always been plenty of good horses. It is only comparatively recently, however, that owners have come to properly classify different types and to appreciate the fact that putting a coarse-necked, awkward-moving horse to a gig does not necessarily make of him a gig horse, nor that a brilliantly acting, beautifully modeled little cob is not a brougham horse merely because he is drawing one. So well understood has this fact now become that even the runabout horse—that quaint blending of the dilettante and the utilitarian—has a place all to himself. He should show more breeding, the experts say, than he does at present. He should be a little heavier and he should possess plenty of speed with not too much action.

Each year the cast in the Central Park parade is becoming more cosmopolitan in character. It was not more than twenty-five or thirty years ago that the long-tailed,

long-barreled and long-pedigreed horse, put to a mail phaëton, was the only animal that aristocracy would recognize, a dock-tailed horse was looked upon with abhorrence, an actor with pitying mirth. Nowadays the drives contain a heterogeneous collection that would be hard to duplicate, and the present market value of a horse is strikingly illustrated in at least two examples of different types which are to be seen in the drives almost daily. One is an eleven-hand Welsh pony which cost $2,500, the other is a sixteen-three Russian coach horse which weighs 1,350 pounds and cost $2,000.

Save when a horse is ailing and is out for a whiff from the dew-wet meadows, a majority of the performers are novices—unsophisticated young country fellows getting their first glimpse of town life and its strenuous way. Many of them, even those that are ordained for harness careers, are taken out under saddle. The majority of them are still tired and fretful from long unaccustomed journeys. Fresh from quiet country towns, the tumult of the city has got onto their nerves and they are ready for anything—to sulk, to strike, to turn rogue altogether. And it is this critical

The showiest feature of park driving.

"The flower of the New York police."

period which calls for all that a horseman has of delicacy and diplomacy. To return a frightened, peevish pupil to his stable after an hour's work, his mind quieted, his temper and his appetite restored, and his heart partially reconciled to the new order of things, seems to many to be the refinement of the art of horse handling.

It is well worth braving a 5 A.M. call to witness such a demonstration. One morning I shared a bench with two men, one an Easterner and dyspeptic, the other a Westerner and profane. Apparently the two men were strangers. Presently a big-boned, straight-backed bay gelding, carry-

face, whose hands were on a level with the horse's withers, gave him his head, and for a moment both remained quite motionless.

Suddenly the gelding, obviously having made up his mind that he would take no chances with such monstrosities, whirled and bolted, apparently with no nearer destination in view than the Battery. The young man took him in hand leisurely, stopped him in his flight in the course of a hundred yards and brought him back to the jumping-off place. Neither in the tone of his voice, the attitude of his body nor in the use of his hands did he betray the slightest evidence that he was conscious of

Where two's a "crowd" in a runabout.

ing a lean-faced, stooped-backed young man, came swinging around a curve in the bridle path a hundred yards or more below the bench. The horse's ears were darting forward and back with the precision and swiftness of steel-shuttles; his eyes were dilated and in them were fear, distrust and deviltry. The moment he espied the figures ahead of him, weirdly outlined in the morning mist, he stopped abruptly, his eyes became focused on the bench and he gave utterance to a loud snort, which translated into English might have stood for a brief but pertinently profane interrogation. Instantly the young man with the lean

his mount's state of mind. In a second or two the horse repeated his first remark, less emphatically, however, and started to whirl again. The young man caught him this time and in the next line up he had gained half a dozen yards toward the bench. This performance was repeated until finally the horse was juggled to a point in the path almost opposite the men. It had taken the young man some thirty minutes or more to accomplish this trip, but his lean face remained wholly impassive, quite as though he had just been trundled through the Park in an electric hansom. Nor did his tranquillity desert him when the horse suddenly took to the lawn and, placing his steel trade-mark indiscriminately over yards of new spring turf, darted for the reservoir.

The Eastern man was the first to comment upon the exhibition. "A wonderfully pretty bit of horsemanship," he remarked to his neighbor, and a great deal of the native austerity in his voice, the third man noted, had melted into something like actual fervor. "As clever a piece of jollying as a man would care to see," he added. The Westerner gazed at him earnestly and long in the hesitating perplexity of one trying to determine whether he had a hopeless

The color had slowly mounted to the Easterner's face, and when he made answer his sentences were punctuated with icebergs. "It is one of the curious anomalies of nature, I suppose, that a grand, broad country should produce small, narrow men. Take your own case. You seem quite incapable of differentiating between a stone mason and a diamond cutter. To be explicit, your 'puncher' is the stone mason; that 'baked-faced-monkey' is the diamond cutter. What would your puncher have done with that sensitive high-bred horse? He would have jammed a six-inch rowel into his ribs, cut him open with his quirt

A "pocket edition" turn-out.

fool or a droll jester to contend with. He evidently decided upon dealing with the first proposition. "Horsemanship!" he echoed. "Pretty bit of horsemanship! Why, do you know what we'd do out in my country with a foolheaded hoss like that? We'd just turn him loose on the prairie with a puncher on him, empty a couple of guns so he could hear 'em distinct and when that hoss got back from the horizon he'd know what business and manners was or he wouldn't know nothin.' Good horsemanship! Why, I wouldn't let that baked-faced monkey ride a Newfoundland dog o' mine."

and brought him back in an hour and announced with a complacent grin that he was broke, and the statement would have been quite correct. If you could have found an eighty-dollar buyer for him you would have considered him well sold. When that 'baked-faced monkey' is done with his pupil one thousand dollars should not be an exorbitant figure."

The Westerner turned an aggressive front toward the slight-framed man beside him, but the other went bravely on. "You chaps boast of your horsemanship," he exclaimed, "and when it comes to brilliant dare-devilishness I grant you are justified;

but what do you know of horsemanship viewed as a science or an art? You can stay with a bucking, pitching bronco, but that is merely a trick—an act which any longshoreman with courage could acquire in a month. Of what avail would your busters and their stock saddles be with a clean-bred hunter that had become sour and sulky with bad handling or over-work? How would they go about to make a woman's saddle horse from the raw material? I promise you they would be as helpless as children. It is here in New

Between the first and the second enter-tainment, ample time may be had for break-fast. It is not until after ten o'clock, in fact, that the drives are again filled with performers. This show is distinctly vau-deville in character. On its program are juvenile artists, green women on melan-choly mounts, and the horses that are working for that post-graduate degree, the initial letters of which stand for Fearless of All City Sights. An amateur rode out one day behind a pair of these pupils and in the course of their instruction he obtained

The Victoria—Fifth Avenue's chariot.

York—in the heart of the effete East that you sneer at—that the best horsemanship on this continent is to be found."

"We ain't got time enough to fool away on any one hoss," said the man from the West. "We'll sell a bunch of them while you're getting rid of one."

"A statement," interrupted the other, "which altogether substantiates my views. You go in for quantity, we for quality. You are the miners, we are the artisans."

"I'll bet you any part of a thousand," shouted the Westerner, as his critic dis-appeared round the bend in the path, "that we've got a hoss with the C.R.X. outfit that can gallop rings around anything you dudes can lead out."

from their tutor a few elementary points in horse-schooling that may not be value-less to others. He learned, for instance, that the old theory of accustoming a horse to an object he is inclined to be afraid of by forcing him up to it and compelling him to give it a minute inspection is a wholly ex-ploded one. The proper method is to ig-nore the fact that the pupil is frightened at all or that he has anything to be frightened at. Let him shy and lunge, but under no circumstances take him back to the object that has caused it. To do so merely gives him reason to suppose that the thing is something he has a right to be afraid of. By taking the objects as they come without first warning the pupil by a firmer hold on

New fads cannot crowd out old fashions of "buggy-riding."

his mouth that here is something to be wary of, the theory is that he will soon realize himself the folly of going into hysterics over it. Another point which the amateur learned was the dexterous twist of the wrist by which a horse was foiled in his attempt to shy over an embankment or into another vehicle. Instead of pulling a horse's head toward the object he was preparing to shy from, according to the orthodox method, the handler, just at the psychological moment, jerked the animal's head away from the object and in the direction he was intending to jump. This sudden and wholly unexpected concession so diverted the pupil's mind that he forgot all about shying in any direction. If this trick is performed at precisely the right second it will work nine times in ten.

It is during these later hours of the morning that the mounted squad—"the flower of the New York police"—is most frequently in action. In his long, grotesque coat, his ordinary street trousers, with the official stripe down the leg, the lack of straps and boots or anything pertaining to the trooper, the mounted policeman presents a picture that belies his character as effectively as a Prince Albert coat and a white cravat disguises the confidence-man. In repose he is not an object to thrill the spectator with martial pride; in action he

is worthy to ride with Charles O'Malley's Irish dragoons. There are just twenty-seven of him on duty in the Park and in the course of a year he has on an average two runaways a day to stop. When he fails it is pretty safe to assume that death has cut him out of the running. When one is seated safely on some driveway bench, not even a fire down in the city affords a spectacle more potent to stir sluggish blood than a runaway chase in the Park. The instant an animal breaks away from its driver, the nearest mounted man slaps heels into his horse's ribs, sounds a shrill note from his whistle and with all his Irish sporting blood up enters the race. In a moment his alarm has been answered and the whole Park is ringing with whistles. It is like a covey of quail on an immense scale calling to one another after the guns have scattered them. Sometimes the chase continues the length of the Park, more often it is stopped before it has really gained headway.

There have been cases where two policemen, each clinging to opposite sides of a runaway's bridle, have been dismounted and dragged a quarter of a mile under the horse's flying feet, the thought to let go never entering their heads. One forgets the grotesque coats and the ludicrous riding breeches then.

10
Campers
by the Sea

CAMPERS BY THE SEA

By J. W. MULLER

PHOTOGRAPHS BY ARTHUR HEWITT

ALONG the south shore of Long Island, from within the very limits of the City of New York to where old Montauk thrusts his brave sand cape into a most lonely ocean, there stretches a sleepy world enchanted by the sea, of which men have still to learn the use.

Defended from the outer deep by an almost unbroken ribbon of sand nearly a hundred miles long and in places scarcely as many feet wide, lie immense lagoon-like bays holding an archipelago of islands and bars that offer camping ground for many thousands without crowding. There may be had in full measure the twin qualities that make a camp—adventure and loneliness. There may be had a life as free from civilization as in the Adirondacks, the North Woods or the Canadian Provinces. In the sea-camp a man may dwell as if he were a lonely sailor on a ship.

For these campers there is no waiting for seasons, no long voyaging by rail or ship. Whenever they tire of the town, be it summer or winter, they can shut down their desks and in an hour be pushing out over broad waters to where the shanty camp stands lonely, rising out of a shining plain of sea.

From some of these camps one may see glimpses of the city. At night its throbbing lights flame on the sky. But though the town may be in sight, it is in sight only to enhance the delight of loneliness, as rain falling on the roof serves but to make more evident the cosiness of shelter.

So great is this expanse of inland seas, that all the sportsmen of New York might build themselves camps there and yet hardly affect the condition of individual solitude. Even Jamaica Bay, lying partly within the municipal boundaries of New York and, therefore, a popular resort for as many as five thousand fishermen and yachtsmen every day in the summer, offers miles of lonely water where a man may loaf all day, and even in holidays, hardly see another human being.

The true sea-camp must not be confounded with the many settlements of anglers and small-boat sailors that are grouped on the mainland all along this stretch of bays. These are not true campers, although they enjoy many of the pleasures of the life. They are amiable souls but gregarious, too much in love with the social life to care to intrude on the solitude of the true camper. Not for them is the content of sitting alone in a box of a hut, ringed around by a black midnight sea, with the cry of the wind and the beating waves outside for sole company. Rather, they aim to build their shanties and clubhouses close together, so that, as one beholds them clinging to each other where they stand on their long-legged spiles, the observer is reminded of roysterers who sally out fearfully into dark lanes at night, after the feast of ghost stories in the tavern.

Every year these waterside communities grow. They form real villages within and near New York in such places as Canarsie, Old Mill, Ramblersville and Rockaway Beach. But they hold fast to the solid and respectable mainland.

It is a fine world, really very well adjusted. If everybody loved loneliness, there would be no loneliness left. As it is, most men love the close neighborhood of their kind too much to push out into the water and live the life of the prehistoric lake dwellers. So islands and bars away from the shore still lie virgin. Here and there stands a rough shanty, cocked jauntily on spiles, or a stranded canal boat supports a hut that looks over the bay like a primitive Martello tower; and these are inhabited by baymen or by campers and sportsmen whom the chance visitor cannot distinguish from the baymen, because they live and dress just like them. Some of them have even achieved the language and dialect of the bays.

There a man may "drowse the long tides idle," gazing through long sea-noons over the endless sweep of undulating, ever-fresh grass—the strange, dear sea meadows that twice a day sink beneath the sea and twice a day emerge in new beauty. There a man may lie for days with no sound to touch his ear except the cry of gull or quawk; no sight to remind him of men, except the sight of calm sails passing far beyond the reach of a hail; no sign to mark the lazy passage of time except the subtle changes of the mighty, unhaltered tide. Every day as the tides change, his world changes with them. When the flood comes sweeping in from the dancing inlet, green and fresh with the ocean wind behind it, imperceptibly the lands that dot the bays lessen and lessen, till, lo! at once there are no lands and all the world is one great, glassy sea.

With the brimming flood the big game of the sea comes ploughing in—dripping black backs of porpoises bob up and sink again as swiftly as they rise; wagging triangular fins show where sharks are swimming, lumbering and clumsy until some sudden need sends them darting as swiftly as a torpedo boat and as surely, with all its wicked power of destruction. Or a great width of channel suddenly turns oily and yellow, where a school of mossbunkers, with heads and fins just showing above the water, work slowly in on the young tide; and wherever they swim, their curious fluttering motion keeps the sea in a steady ripple. Suddenly, the school cascades on the surface in flashing masses; shining, lean things leap among it, spring out of their element, hurtle over and over in the air and fall back with a smash that sets the sea a-frothing. They are bluefish, hunting savagely as wolves, swimming swiftly as light, destroying with bloody jaws and blind wrath. Now the silver-banded spearing stream into coves and creeks in unnumbered shoals. Minnows, orange and bottle-green and striped, crowd in. Crabs and eels, shrimp and crustaceans, flock to shelter, for the big hunters have arrived. They sweep to and fro in the deep water with beats of tireless fins and winnowing of mighty tails—the weakfish, striped bass and sea bass, fresh from the open sea and keen for the chase.

So it streams by for six hours of tide—a mighty half-seen life. Then, for a time, when the tide is full, the bay lies scarcely breathing, with not a ripple to break a single inverted image of buoy or hut or vessel on the great mirroring surface. Again, slowly, wondrously, the waters stir; the

grasses bend again; the buoys, that stood straight out of the water, careen once more. Solemnly, immense, the flood turns and moves toward the sea.

Not only in summer is the sea-camp beautiful. When the first hint of spring comes into the town, while the streets are full of slush and blackened snow, the channels beckon. Still rimmed with ice, they flow black and mysterious and luring; the breeze still blows cold and boisterous; across the outer bar the coasting vessels labor hard in the winds of March. But the summer gulls have begun to flock in, and the shoals are white with their dainty persons. Drawing black lines across the clear sky, the wild fowl scurry, flying north. In the holes along the channels the flatfish, fat and lusty after their winter sleep in the rich mud, are biting fast and furious. One may sit on the leeward side of the shanty and smoke a pipe while the sun burns into the winter-dried bones and skin and sinews till they stretch in the generous heat.

And in the autumn when the nights begin to close in early, of a sudden comes the thought of the cozy shanty, standing alone in the dark and windy night; the miles of brown sedges stretching far; the birds flying; the fire of drift-wood, burning green and blue and red, while the North wind shouts outside and hurries the fowl southward—where are there camps in mountains or in forest that offer more?

Even the might of winter need not deprive the sea-camper of his solace. It is delight to face the wicked sea, shaking a few square feet of hammering sail into the white face of the storm, driving through the rollers with dripping decks and, at last, to tumble home in camp with shining oilskins, and to lie at ease before a rousing fire while Winter beats outside in vain. There are days then when the sportsman sees great birds drop heavily into the open water, and he works his way through ice and half-frozen marsh until he gets a shot at a wild goose or a swan. Sometimes he can win across broad channels, whose covering ice sways and rocks beneath him as he speeds; or he can half run and half flounder, holding fast to his flat-bottomed skiff, as he alternately drags it over the ice that breaks as he jumps, or poles and paddles it through open waters covered with floes, as if he were in Baffin Bay.

An Old South Bayman and his pets.

A "shanty" which rises to the dignity of a cottage.

To own such a camp demands no heavy purse. The house itself may be of the most simple construction, strength being the one needful quality, and the acquisition of the land is within the reach of almost any person.

The land under water in the bays on the South Shore, with a few exceptions where ancient grants and privileges still hold good, is under the jurisdiction variously of the Land Office of the State of New York,

Cabin of a camper who doesn't care for style.

the Shellfish Commission of the Forest, Fish and Game Commission, or the township and County authorities of the territory bordering on the water. A great part of this is at least possible ground for oyster or clam culture and, therefore, under the Shellfish Commission.

These lands may be leased for the cultivation of shellfish to persons who have lived in the State for one year or more. Before the lease can be granted, a notice of it must be posted for at least three weeks in

of acres find no bidders, since oyster and shellfish culture are the only purpose for which the baymen desire land under water. The leases may be made for a term up to fifteen years. In some localities the leases may be made as long as fifty years, but fifteen years is the maximum term almost everywhere. As soon as the lease has been granted the lessee must begin to mark the extent and boundaries of his grounds with stakes and buoys which must be maintained in good condition. Grants of land under

Out for bait.

the office of the town clerk and in the post-office nearest to the lands for which application has been made. The letting is then done at public auction and the lands go to the highest bidder. The minimum rental is twenty-five cents an acre annually. Of course, desirable oyster bottoms bring much greater rentals than that, running as high as five and eight dollars an acre for choice ground. But much of the land is worthless or nearly so, owing to unfavorable currents or to poor bottoms, and thousands

water not available for oyster culture are made both by the Land Office and the local authorities. The applicant must file an affidavit with the Land Office stating the purposes for which they are desired. The application must be accompanied by accurate maps showing the lands and by a full description. The minimum sum that can be charged by the State is fifty dollars in addition to a patent fee of five dollars for each parcel. The applicant must advertise his notice of application and attend to

Perched on a narrow sand-bar in the full sweep of the winds.

Sampling their jugs of "bait" between bites.

a number of other formalities stipulated by law, and in his application he must state the sum that he is willing to pay for the land.

If the ground is leased from the Shellfish Commission, the lessee must work it regularly, that being the requirement of the lease. As this involves a great deal of detail, and as the camper really needs only enough land to build his camp, the best and most satisfactory way is to rent a site from a bayman who already has oyster ground under lease. Many of the oyster planters who have hundreds of acres under cultivation are always ready to rent a part of the marshes bordering on their beds, and some of them will go farther and rent their shanties for a term of years. If they get a satisfactory offer they will build a new shanty for themselves somewhere else, and for a trivial consideration they will also act as caretakers and wardens of the camp.

One simple and highly satisfactory way that was adopted by some sportsmen a few years ago was to pay the annual rental of a small oyster ground for a bayman who had a particularly good house on a fine fishing channel. This made the sportsmen tenants of the house. Then they agreed with the bayman to let him occupy it also, in return for taking care of their boats and gear and rendering other services, such as going ashore to meet them when they alighted from the train. This proved to be an ideal arrangement, as the man was a splendid type of his class, and before long his personality had given added charm to the camp.

A system of signals was arranged. A flag hoisted over a house on the mainland in the daytime, or two red lanterns hoisted on the staff at night, informed him that the members of the party were waiting for a boat. No condition of weather ever kept him from answering the summons, and many were the wild trips that were made in his stout little sloop over the four miles of water that lay between the shore and the little marsh where the camp stood.

He was a cook of parts. His eel stews and clam fritters, his baked bluefish and roasted oysters were dishes that it would be selfish to describe unless one were ready to appease the appetites that the description would surely arouse. He spared no time or efforts to provide everything besides food to please his friends, and would get up in the middle of the night and work in mud and water up to his waist in the dark to assure the camp of an abundant supply of choice bait for the early morning fishing.

The baymen as a whole are thoroughly honest and sturdy men—the kind you can live with for weeks at a time without growing weary—and it is not difficult to find just the right person who has the very sort of a shanty fitted for such a camp.

If one wishes to build his own camp, the most important matter is the selection of the site. In the bays along the south shore there are comparatively few sandy islands that are not completely submerged at high tide, and most of them are practically submerged even at mean low water. The best locations, therefore, for bay camps are the marsh islands, scores of which are so high that their summits at least remain above water at all stages of the tide.

To select a site demands an intimate knowledge of the conditions of these big inland seas. He who knows them only as they sleep, peaceful and placid in long summer calms, has no conception of the power that lies concealed beneath the pond-like surfaces. When the tempests of autumn and winter drive them, they roll with seas that make well-found schooners labor and thresh. When the ice goes out, its broken yellow floes come a-roaring and a-thundering with the ebb, like the wreckage of bursted dams, and go tearing along on the loosed waters, shearing off points of land and cribbage work as a tinner snips a piece of tin.

When the spring tides rise, they swell to amazing volume and cover places that lie high above the lip of the highest flood during the rest of the year. Therefore, the aid of a good bayman is almost indispensable in selecting a good site for the camp.

A location to be avoided by the camper is a marsh or bar that has enough shoals around it to make it hard to approach at low water. Study of the government coast charts, one series of which gives the soundings for bays on the south shore, will give valuable help in this. Almost equally undesirable is an island that has only a narrow or tortuous channel leading to it. To find that channel, or having found it, to follow it in a sea fog or a dark and stormy night, is a task so difficult that even experienced baymen fail now and then, and it has often happened that a bayman owning such a shanty has had to spend the night afloat in a fog because he missed the channel.

If the boat happens to lose the channel when the tide is ebbing, the chances are that it will be impossible to get back to it, because the falling tide will hold her on the shoals, and then there is nothing to do except to sit and wait until the flood comes in and floats her off. Therefore, the proper location is a high marsh with the channel flowing close at its edge, or with a cove or deep creek making toward it from the channel. This creek should have at least two feet of water in it at dead low tide, which not only makes the camp approachable at any stage of water, but also offers shelter for boats—a consideration that is not appreciated fully until a man has been routed out of warm blankets a few times in the middle of a tempestuous night to save the boats from knocking to pieces in a roaring gale of wind and rain. That kind of thing remains a romantic experience to think of afterwards, but it is not so charming at the time, when one is laboring in a rolling small boat, smothered by combers, trying to herd a lot of craft that drag like mules in a dozen directions at once.

"Happy days."

A creek also offers a natural home for bait fish. A net can be stretched across its mouth at high tide and without labor further than to raise it at low tide, an abundance of the best kind of live bait, from killies to shrimp and shedder crabs, can be obtained over night.

So great are the uses of a little creek that it pays to cut one if a natural one does not exist. By planning so that it will lie in a general direction parallel, or partly so, with the course of the tides, the current will do a great part of the work of cutting it, and year after year it will grow larger and better. Often a few hours of intelligent ditching at low water will make an opening into which the sea will pour with a rush when the tide changes, and the man who has not had experience will be astonished to see how much work can be done by a few tides.

Spiling is the most expensive part of building the camp proper. The cutting and undermining of bank and shore is a process that goes on ceaselessly, steadily, minute after minute, year after year, for the sea is never still, and there is no part of the bays where tide or wave do not bite and grind at the land. So the banks must be well protected by logs and timbers, driven deeply into the mud or sand. Behind the spiles there should be deposited as many tons of oyster shells as can be packed in.

This makes a foundation for the house that is not only solid and well drained, but it also aids in solidifying the marshy ground.

There are men in every fishing village who make it a business to build these island shanties, and their charges are extremely reasonable. A very good shanty can be erected for $300, which contains from two to four rooms, though the ordinary one rarely has more than two. A small shanty may be erected for as low a sum as seventy-five dollars.

A shed to store driftwood should be

built alongside of it, that an abundant supply of dry fuel may be assured. Farther away, at a distance great enough to prevent danger from possible fire, a small structure should be built to hold the kerosene oil, of which a good supply is always needed for lanterns and for cooking when the firewood is damp.

The construction of everything may be rude, but it must be solid. The island camp has to be able to withstand storms strong enough to blow a flimsy structure down and carry it piecemeal off to sea. The entrance must face south, if possible, and the outer door should open at right angles to an inner door, so that it will be possible to enter or leave the house without exposing the rooms to the force of the wind. This also makes a little vestibule that is protected from the heat of the stove, thus furnishing a good, cold storage house for fish, meat and liquids.

The roof must be a sloping one, and so built that all the rain will run off at one corner. Under this corner a great cask is placed, for there is no way to get fresh water on the marshes except by gathering the rain. The water cask should be well charred and the bottom kept sprinkled with clean charcoal so the contents will be pure and sweet.

In such a camp the writer spent many happy seasons. Storm bound through three weeks of equinoctial gale, he lived like a shipwrecked mariner without seeing a single human being in all that time. He lay before the fire in his blankets through roaring winter nights. He drifted from the little pier through mysterious nights of summer, far out to sea and into the mysterious dawn. Through glorious days of August he rolled in the open sea off the shoals with the baymen, and built rafts of driftwood, with wild gymnastics in the tidestreak.

That tide-streak set in from Sandy Hook and swept for miles beyond the reach of eye, along the beaches. It lay on the ocean a wide, lazily moving, yellow band, with its ends lost in horizons. In it one was sure to find, sooner or later, everything that was lost in all the world. Once we picked up a home-made cradle there, that had been rudely carved from Norwegian pine; whether it had been dropped from some immigrant ship or by what other sea-chance it had floated in, the ocean only knows, as it knows so many things and will not tell. Sometimes we found tropical fruits; once or twice we discovered tropical birds and fishes.

All the ships steering in from the seven seas contributed something toward our trove of tide-streak. Our most important find was a noble mast from some great clipper, that drifted into our ken by who may tell what strange adventuring. It stands in front of the shanty now, and the flag breaks from its halyards as the dawn opens the black sea-gate of the wet east; and all around the bay other flags rise to answer it —the morning talk of the lonely men of the marshes

11
Games
of the
City Street

Marbles—And He Takes the Alley.

GAMES OF THE CITY STREET

By ROBERT DUNN

The wind blows East,
The wind blows West,
The wind blows over the Cuckoo's Nest;
　Shall he go East?
　Shall he go West?
Shall he go under the Cuckoo's Nest?
　Hon-pon-kuck-a-da-hook!
　Hon-pon-kuck-a-da-hook!!

AS long as spring in New York is still the old spring of warm days and many long twilights, you cannot pass such a place as Tompkins Square, at Avenue A and Tenth Street, without hear-

ing that song and that refrain some afternoon when school's just out. Or, skip over a great distance and many nations and pass Hudson Park, the queer polygon where Eighth Avenue begins, or Bayard Park on the lower East Side, or any of the green oases, uptown and downtown, in the tenements deserts of the city.

In hon-pon, two boys are "it": master and cuckoo. The cuckoo is picked by a round of "Eeny Meeny," or of fist-knocking for the pebble; and he, in turn,

Cold Enough for a Fire.

chooses his master, who stands erect against a park fence or house wall. The cuckoo, facing him, bends forward at right angles, and rests his head against the master's stomach. He is blindfold, and the master lays his fists on the cuckoo's back. And now the littlest boys, a-tiptoe, shrill and lithe, and the big boys, long-trousered and loungy, scheming how to "put up a game" on some mamma's pet—the thin, freckled, spectacled lad who lives in awe of a window opening down the block and a shriek coming from home—all are shouting "*Hon-pon-kuck-a-da-hook! Hon-pon-kuck-a-da-hook!*" with mixed vigor and falsettos.

The master, choosing a certain boy in the crowd, patent to all but the cuckoo, repeats the rhyme

> Shall he go East?
> Shall he go West? etc.

and pauses for the cuckoo to name the direction. Then the master leans over and whispers to the boy chosen to run to some point east or west within the bounds of three or four blocks agreed on for the game, and wait; around the corner, or in a far tenement hall or a doorway. If the cuckoo's order is to go under the nest, the master has nothing to say, and the boy must double himself up and crawl beneath the cuckoo. It's best to be sent there, as will be seen, and wonderful how many small bodies can squeeze under him.

So all the boys are disposed of one by one, jointly by master and cuckoo, neither (save in going under the nest) fixing by himself any boy's fate. The rhyme is repeated to each by the master, the refrain by the crowd; and by this time every boy is supposed to have one good hard knot in his handkerchief, or a rag of some sort; but double knots, or knots with stones in them or knotted straps and ropes, are not allowed.

When all are out, the master cries, "All out"; the cuckoo stands erect, tears off his bandage, and the real play begins. The master shouts, "*Hon-pon-kuck-a-da-hook!*

Hon-pon-kuck-a-da-hook!! Hon-pon-kuck-a-da-hook!!!" The third repetition is a signal for every one in hiding to foot it, fast as legs can carry him, back to master and cuckoo at goal. Fun and confusion begin. The last man back is the proper mark for a good beating with every knotted handkerchief; but as every man is the last man in, until the one next him in hiding distance from goal shows up, every player as he arrives gets a good beating. The first get fewer knots on their polls, and the later ones more and more; for, as soon as one boy has run the gauntlet, he turns in to chastise his successors. The actual last man gets a long basting from the whole gang; but as for the men under the nest, they come in for no trouncing at all, and have nothing to do but to wield their knots, while the actual last fellow is rewarded by being made the next cuckoo, with choice of a master.

No test of strength or skill enters a game like this, and that is why it is typical of city boys. Look close, and you will see that hon-pon offers countless chances, as the boys say, "for a whole lot of skin." Chums and enemies, personal likes and dislikes, divide every street gang. So the city boy uses his games to rub in or to avenge prejudice and preference; and for the humor therein—now, don't call it bullying. In hon-pon, for instance, the master will send a boy he has a grudge against, or the sweet child for whose benefit the game may have been proposed —who'd have been called cry-baby if he'd refused to play—to the most faraway corner in bounds to make sure he'll be the last victim of the knotted handkerchief. And the blindfold cuckoo, after a friendly whisper, gets a nudge on his knee from a chum to signal *he* must be sent under the nest.

Games like this are more popular in the heart of the city than the local variations to be mentioned on prisoner's base, hi-spy, and cops and robbers (these the most eclectic terms, I hope). For this, city conditions are responsible; not so much

An Exciting Moment in the Game.

that narrow and crowded streets, cranky old men who live alone and rush out at you, fuming in spectacles and carpet slippers, at the least noise on their door-steps, or the mountainous hydra-clubbed blue-coats, ponderous of motion and with no sense of humor — with whom every gang has its vendetta — are dampers on manlier games. The rings and

Top-spinning in the Park.

horses and horizontal bars that ornament the sward of Mr. Riis's parks and school yards are field enough for competition in muscle building. But they are no outlet for the big per cent. of devil in every boy. Horseshoe-the-mare gratifies the deuce in a boy even better than hon-pon; and grown-ups, not too grown, who know the carpet-slippered old fossils of a neighbor-hood, have been known to laugh as they passed and saw the prank in swing. And unless it were for teachers' favorites, boys weak-eyed from overstudy and too much home supervision, horseshoe-the-mare would be impossible. It is played thus:

The gang is in a restless mood. "Let's go get Georgie," says one of the crowd; "he's never been shoed." George is the teacher's favorite, the inoffensive innocent. He is waylaid on the way home from school and coaxed to come play. It is proved to him the crowd can't possibly live unless he's with them, and maybe flattery like that isn't irresistible, coming from boys George has always feared and looked up to, imagining they have despised and

One Pair of Roller Skates can be Made to do for Four.

looked down on him. So Georgie agrees to play. Some one suggests horseshoe-the-mare as a good game, and after one or two boys have pooh-poohed it—for a blind—it's agreed to be all right for a dull afternoon. Instantly a clamor rises; every boy wants to be the mare, until a big one in the gang, with the big boy's lazy halo of authority grounded in rumors that once in a while he smokes a cigarette, settles the matter by patronizing George, saying it's only polite and nice to let little Georgie be the mare.

"You be gentleman"—"I'm blacksmith," a couple shout, and gentleman and blacksmith scuttle off to return with a long piece of some mother's clothesline. The gentleman harnesses Georgie, knotting the rope so hard about his chest that he never can undo it alone; and while he puts his mare through her paces, making her stand, rear, trot, and gallop up and down the block, the blacksmith is off for his shop. Now the game must be played in a dwelling-house district; for, of course, the blacksmith's shop is the front stoop of the carpet-slippered fossil.

The gentleman reins in his prancing mare before the blacksmith in his shop, and shouts that her off hind foot needs a new iron. He shouts loud in case Mr. Carpet-slipper is asleep. "Who-a! who-a!" he calls, backing the mare into the bottom step, *backing her*, remember, "who-a! who-a!" as the blacksmith rubs the mare's mane and fetlocks cautiously, lifts up a foot and hammers away at the boot-sole with a chunk of coal. Whereupon the gentleman sneaks up the steps and ties the reins to the fossil's door-knob.

"It's a fine mare you have," says the blacksmith behind her back as the gentleman descends.

"Sure, that it is," replies the gentleman, "and how much do I owe you?" he asks.

"Oh, five dollars I guess," says the blacksmith, and a beer-keg stamp is handed over.

"Get-arp, get-arp!" both shout, hitting the mare over his shins, and little Georgie makes a plunge forward—stumbles—yanks the bell knob. . . .

The old duffer from behind the bell is doing for Georgie, invoking God, the police, parents, the devil, and untying the harness knot all at once. Wild cries of "Horseshoe-the-mare! Horseshoe-the-mare!" make hideous every corner.

Franker games, many like those we've all played, have been grouped into three classes, and the names simple variations of each will pass under in separate sections of the greater cities is curious.

The hi-spy class includes, among many others, ringalevio (Brooklyn name), kick-the-wicket, sixty-o, throw (or fling) the stick, I-spy-the-wolf (East Side), Yankee-dar-oo, (or nar-oo) (Harlem and Bronx) and Yoller. The rules of each merge and conflict with the rules of all. No one differs very much from plain hide-and-seek, but hide-and-seek is a girl's game, where you have to "lie low" until you're found, I believe.

The "it," for instance, in ringalevio stands up against the goal or base, blind-fold or "not peeking," and counts while the crowd hides. (If he counts sixty, the game may be sixty-o.) When he starts to hunt, he shouts "ringalevio" for warning. Generally the common rules of hi-spy are followed, except in yankee-dar-oo, which is in some ways more like hare and hounds. The hiders in yankee-dar-oo are given two blocks' start, and whenever one turns a corner he must shout "yankee-dar-oo" to give the "it" or "hound" the scent; and each one caught has to be tagged three times, not simply seen, and the goal raced for. In throw-the-stick, the boy who touches base before the "it," grabs a stick there, and hurls it as far as he can, freeing those already caught, and giving each time to hide again while the "it" is "shacking" it back to base. In yankee-dar-oo, as the hiders, or hares, are caught they have to pitch in and help the hounds; and yoller is a version of yankee-dar-oo for after-dark use, in which the hound need only see the hare to have caught him.

In some cities, prisoner's base is despised as a girl's game, but though New York boys feel they do not compromise themselves by playing it, its versions, under names like ring-rover or come-over, grand-daddy, corey, and pump-pump-pull-away, are more popular. Two opposing goal lines, often street curbs chalked off for ten yards or so, with a danger area between in which the "it" tries to catch the players as they run from goal to goal, is the principle under

An Alert Type of Street Urchin.

all. In ring-rover, whenever the "it" yells,

"Ring-rover, ring-rover,
Come over, come over,"

every player must make a dash for the other side, past the "it," who tries to catch and tag him three times. In versions that allow you to cross at your own sweet will, the "it" only has to tag to catch; and in nearly all versions the boys caught stay between the goal to help him. Other rules vary minutely according to the name and locality of the game, though nearly everywhere the custom is for the first man caught

An East Side Newsboy.

to be "it" the next round, and for the catchers to rush in and grab whom they can when all the players are on one side; this provided, he shouts the title of the game, "Pump-pump-pull-away!" or "Corey!"

Hop-a-da-goose (Brooklyn version) is more distinctive and has a lyric as well.

A rectangle, about six by ten feet, is marked on the sidewalk with chalk, or coal, or arc carbon. This is the den in which the "it" can walk on both feet, but may leave only by taking a hop-skip-and-jump. If he wants to go farther than that he must hop on one leg.

The players to be caught crowd around him, shouting,

> Hop-a-da-goose, hop-a-da-goose,
>   Come out of your den,
> Whoever you catch
>   Is one of your men.

"It" doesn't take his hop-skip until the players, getting braver and braver, crowd closer and closer upon the den. Then he makes a dive for them with the hop-skip, chasing beyond by hopping on one leg within bounds. But if he lets the other foot touch ground, he can catch no one until he has run back to his den, before which every player may pile in and beat him with a knotted handkerchief. As he catches each man he must shout

> Hop-a-da-goose, hop-a-da-goose,
>   I'm out of my den,
> For I have just caught
>   One of your men.

Versions of hare and hounds, like cops and robbers, and chalk-corners, in which the scent is given by arrows marked on walls or pavements, need no description. Where rocks are scarce, duck-on-the-rock has become a game played with a baseball —roly-boly. The crowd's hats are lined up on one curb, and a boy with the baseball from the other tries to toss it into some one's hat. Whoever gets it so, runs to get the ball while the crowd scoots the other way. As he picks it up, he shouts, "Stand!" at which all must stop in their tracks, while the ball is hurled to "sting" any one in sight; and the boy hit "rolls" for the next round. A baseball is used, too, in "over," which is played only on the city's skirts, where you live in low frame houses, gabled and with yards. The gang divides into two sides, the one given the ball throwing it over the house-top to the crowd on the other side. If the ball isn't caught the first time, it is thrown back; if not the second time, it passes to the other side. When it is caught, the crowd having it stampedes around the house, and whoever is caught and tagged by the boy holding the ball under his coat —the point is, the other side never knows who holds it—goes over to the invading party. The game is won by the side which takes all the players.

But as Fourth-o'-July is peer of all holidays, so the doings of Launchin' Day excel games of any sort whatsoever.

Launchin' Day (in pronouncing *don't* Boston the "au") is the greatest East Side field day, Durbar, Derby Day—what you will—and it comes on August first; why, no one knows, except it has to come in summer.

The grounds are all East River docks, haunted by longshoremen and by dock rats, who will tumble overboard, all dressed, for anything from a peanut to a penny; especially the bulkheads around Fulton Market and the Dover Street dock, just up from the Brooklyn Bridge, which the crazy bridge jumpers intend—before-hand—to strike for. On August first, the longshoremen are out bright and early to egg on the carnival. The first victims are the very poor urchins sent out at dawn to spear drift-wood in the river by bending a horseshoe nail and fixing it to the end of a broomstick.

"Better get yer clodes off," advises a slouchy truck-handler, to the poor child tying up his bundle of rocket sticks drifted in from Coney on the early tide. But before the boy can cry out or run or peel off, the dock rats are on him with a whoop.

"Over wid ye," they shout, and "Over wid ye," echo the 'shoremen. The kid whimpers he can't swim. "Can't help," says a big rat; "dis is Launchin' Day."

The rats watch him shriek and splutter in the wash among the piles, until the psychological moment of the third sinking, when all hands dive over with another whoop, and make the gallantest, splashiest sort of rescue. "D——n, why don't youse learn to swim?" is the leader's sympathy to the sobby, shivery kid on the pierhead, as he avenges himself with all his father's oaths, and as his head is full of proper resolutions about learning to swim. And ten to one, by next Launchin' Day he's a rat himself.

And by noon every boy who has poked his nose out of doors within three blocks of the river has had his ducking and made his resolutions to be a swimmer. The rats are bored, fearfully bored, and no reform school holds anything more vicious than a dock gang bored on Launchin' Day. In the afternoon you will notice rats snooping around lumber piles and hiding in saloon doorways across the street on the lookout for something. And generally it is found. Past will walk a kid rather better dressed than any rat, maybe with a dash of Grand Street ribbon in his sailor hat, or a little velvety Fauntleroy effect to his trousers. But the rats know he can't swim. He is seized, and over he goes, ribbons and all. The rescue follows at the psychological moment. Then, dripping and weeping on the bulkhead, he gets no advice about learning to swim. He is left alone, and maybe he isn't lonely.

In a while a crowd of strange faces, pitying and sympathetic, gathers about him. They ask where he lives, and if he wants to go home. Boo hoo! Indeed he does. They lead him, with cusses for the rats and "de cruelties of Launchin' Day," to his mother's door. The bell is rung. Then,

"See here, Willie," they say, "we've a-rescued youse from drownin', ain't we? An' youse stick to telling your mother dat, and not peach on us. We've a-rescued you, see, and we'll kill youse if you tell her we ain't."

Mother appears at the door and grasps her lost child.

"Missus, your kid was shootin' craps on de Dover Street pier dis afternoon,"

says the leader, "an' he tumbles overboard, an' Mike an' us jumps in, an' saves his life. We don't know what he's worth to youse, an' mebbe his clothes is all spoiled, but our gettin' wet is worth about two dollars' doctor bills to our healt'."

Very often the gang—for of course it's a relay of the same crowd that chucked Willie over—gets the two dollars. But there are some wise mothers, even mothers of Fauntleroys—particularly if they have had other children treated so. One thing is certain, by next August Willie can swim, even if he has had to tease his mother to take him to Brighton Beach to learn.

So the day ends, as the rats locate the cop's favorite saloon and strip for a last swim, doing the "front air" and the "back air" (back and front double somersaults). Some one says, while all are playing porpoise, "Let's chaw 'em," and half the gang scrambles ashore and knots up all the clothes of the other half, and shouts, "Cheese it—the cop," to put him on that swimming without tights is going on; and the cop chases off all to hiding.

" Heads or Tails ? "

12
Building New York's Subway

Difficult Engineering in the Subway

BUILDING NEW YORK'S SUBWAY.

BY ARTHUR RUHL.

WITH PICTURES BY FERNAND LUNGREN AND C. A. VANDERHOOF.

AYLIGHT was half a mile or more behind. In front a narrow arched passage, so low that the jagged roof just grazed one's head, followed a thin vista of hazy electric lamps farther into the solid rock. The heavy air was chilled with the breath of the under earth, and every now and then from under the tramway ties, or out of the indefinite darkness, came the *drip-drip-drip* and gurgle of water.

A thudding murmur in the distance suddenly grew more insistent and distinct. The shapes of men, of a swinging crane, of a tram-car mule, appeared under the flare of torches. The reverberations, locked between the narrow walls of rock, swelled into the deafening pounding of a steam-drill. Then a glimmer of daylight revealed the mouth of the shaft, and a moment later, clambering up into the open, I found myself in the lazy warmth of a summer afternoon and blinking at the velvet verdure of Central Park.

Now, the designers of that great underground railroad which is to bring Harlem within fourteen minutes of the City Hall and to extend for more than twenty-one miles just beneath the upper cuticle of New York city proper and the borough of the Bronx— not to speak of the extensions which are yet to be built to Brooklyn—would very earnestly explain at this point that tunneling, in the strict interpretation of the word, forms so small a part in the construction of the road that one may rightly speak of it only as a covered way. The motive for this distinction of terms is that those who know all about the new subway do not want those who know nothing about it to get creepy notions of dampness and "cellar air" and such lugubrious things, when some of the most characteristic features of New York's underground road, as compared, for example, with London's "Tuppenny Tube," are its nearness to the surface, its dryness, its airiness, and its light.

I have chosen to begin a visit to the subway in the branch that leads away from One Hundred and Fourth street and the Boulevard, and actually does tunnel under Central Park, to point out a bit more easily than could be done in some other places the contrast between the upper and the under cuticle of Manhattan, and the ignorance which the average uninquiring citizen of this town is likely to be in of all the hidden toil and turmoil that is constantly going on to provide for his comfort.

He is accustomed to take most things for granted and to neglect to accord wonder to the material achievements of his town, except to enlighten the mind of an occasional country relative. This is an attitude which he would find more difficult to maintain if he understood the personal, almost human, quality which these big things possess for many of those who know them only as among the facial characteristics of the great city they have never seen, or if he felt the personal quality which they equally possess for many of those who live beside them. In the imagination of the average untraveled son of the prairies who has never seen the skyline of Manhattan, it is much to be doubted if the Brooklyn Bridge or the elevated railroad is not quite as vital and human as, let us say, the Few Hundred or the Hon. Richard Croker. Many a prose vignette of Manhattan would have done just as well for Boston or Philadelphia had it not been for the presence of the "L" trains and their squealing brakes, while one's fancy can scarcely conjure up a printed picture of wintry New York which did not have its trail of steam from an L locomotive swirling about the heads of Christmas shoppers. And here is this great new hole-in-the-ground, stuffed with one knows not how many potential reactions on the life and the look of the town, and yet every day we ride over miles and miles of it with scarcely more than a languid musing as to the likelihood of dynamite explosions, or a peevish interest in magic devices by which contractors manage safely to support the pavement over which we ride, the L structure, or whole sheaves of underground pipes.

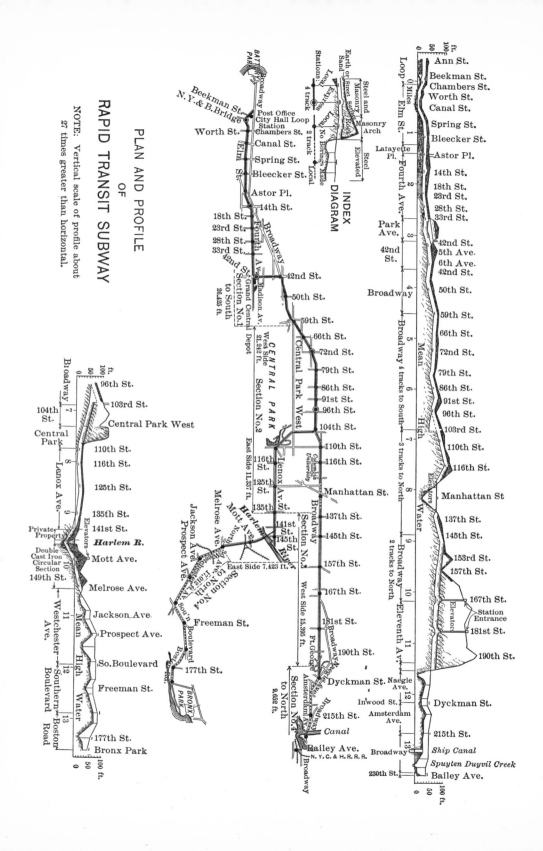

This Rapid Transit Subway, to give it its official name, is an underground railway running along the backbone of the narrow island of Manhattan, and, as now being built, extending on into the borough of the Bronx. From its southern terminus to the branch at One Hundred and Fourth street it will consist of four tracks, the outer two of which will be used for local trains, the inner two for expresses. From One Hundred and Fourth street, which is seven miles from the southern terminus, the main line with three tracks, of which the middle one will be used for express-trains, continues northward seven miles more to Kingsbridge, while a branch line of two tracks will swing off to the right, pass under the Harlem River at Bronx Avenue and One Hundred and Forty-fifth street, and thence on to Bronx Park and the Zoo, also a distance of seven miles. The local trains will be run at an average speed of fourteen miles an hour, stopping at stations one quarter of a mile apart, just about as the present elevated trains are operated; while the express-trains will have stations only about every mile and a half and be capable of attaining a speed of at least thirty miles an hour.

It is now fourteen years since the first bill providing for this underground railroad was sent to the New York legislature. In this time, so amazingly have the needs of the Greater City expanded that even with the Brooklyn extension, which was added to the original plan, the new subway, far from solving the problem, is only the first of many other similar systems which must be built in order even tolerably to dispose of the abnormal passenger traffic which at certain hours and at certain points on the narrow island reaches an excess of congestion to be met with in no other city in the world.

The great subway begins down by the City Hall, and it was into the plaza in front of that beautiful old building that the Hon. Robert A. Van Wyck, mayor of the city, inserted the official pickax in March, 1900, and thereby began the work of excavation. The bronze tablet which was immediately placed over the spot used to be surrounded morning and night by patriotic citizens who gazed down at it as though they were looking at Niagara, until it was presently removed to a contractor's shed, where it spent last summer waiting for the City Hall station to be done. The plaza itself has endured equal vicissitudes, now looking like a mining-camp, now roofed smoothly over, as when Prince Henry came and the escorting cavalry clattered gaily over the planking.

Although the City Hall station is intended to be rather the show station of the line, with its symphonic curves of roof and platforms and track, — "not a straight line in it," as one admirer has observed, — the main terminus and down-town station is a stone's throw away, over by the old Hall of

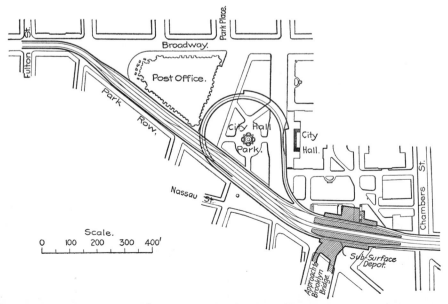

PLAN OF LOOP AT CITY HALL PARK. (ADAPTED FROM A DRAWING PUBLISHED BY THE "ENGINEERING NEWS.")

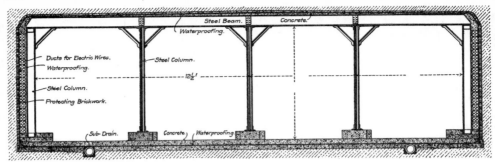

TYPICAL STEEL STRUCTURE.

Records and in front of the entrance to the Brooklyn Bridge. Both local and express trains will run to and from this station, and down its stairways late in the afternoon and early in the evening will pour part of the thousands who block the Third and Sixth Avenue L trains and the surface lines on their way up-town and to Harlem and the Bronx. Eventually the four-track route will extend straight on down to South Ferry and the end of the island, and thence by tunnel to Brooklyn, but at present the southern terminus is the City Hall. Curving out to the right from the four-track line, under the mayor's office in the City Hall, under the Post Office and some of the buildings of Newspaper Row, and thence back to the up-town track, is a single-track loop which is one of the most interesting engineering devices of the subway. This loop is designed to receive the down-town trains as fast as they come in from the north, and to bring them around to the up-town tracks without the delay of switching. When the line is completed through to South Ferry, a train may be run off the main track and around the loop, or it may be continued straight on, and as the loop is made to pass beneath the down-town track as it curves around, a grade-crossing is avoided and one of the more important tasks of constructive engineering which the subway presented is solved.

Morning and night the hordes of clerks and stenographers and business men who fill the offices of down-town New York have poured across Newspaper Row and City Hall Park with scarcely a glance at the labor progressing underfoot that is going to bring them so many minutes nearer their work in the morning, and at night so many minutes nearer their play. I recall one day, however, when several hundred of them, with equal enthusiasm, gave up almost all of the precious noon hour to tell the subway men just what to do and how. A team of white horses had

been drawing a load of green bananas across the chute which had hemmed in the car-tracks along Park Row. A wheel slued, the fence gave way, and a second or two later one of the big white horses was lying on his side across a gas-pipe over the subway ditch, like a sack of oats flung over a rail fence. With rare equanimity of temper and only an occasional kick the animal allowed his legs to be tied together and the canvas

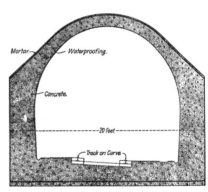

CROSS-SECTION THROUGH THE LOOP.

sling to be put about his belly, and presently, after three or four men had worked for an hour, and some hundreds had shrieked advice, a derrick which happened to be near was brought into requisition, and, with everybody cheering, the animal was hoisted up bodily and set on his feet on the pavement. Horses have fallen clear to the bottom of the subway ditch and have been hoisted out unhurt; others have not been so lucky. People have fallen in many times, and burglars have jumped in and escaped their pursuers. A rather suggestive comment on the liveliness of existence in New York's streets during the building of the subway was the remark of one of the workmen who officiated at this episode that in every section-shed such a sling or else one of the mats used to hold down flying rock in blasting was kept in readiness for just such emergencies.

From the City Hall up to Thirty-fourth street, where real tunneling began, the excavation has all been done from the surface, and any citizen who took the trouble during the last summer to step from his car and peer over the subway fence along this part of the route could grasp the salient features of the subway construction.

On account of the abnormal pressure of traffic at certain places in certain hours, a maximum of speed and a maximum of facility in operation were the first essentials. For this reason anything like London's Tuppenny Tube, with its slow-moving elevators carrying passengers far below the street-level, was out of the question. The road was therefore planned to run just beneath the surface of the streets, and as the stations are now built, it is decidedly nearer from the sidewalk to the subway platforms than to the platforms of the elevated road. If the disturbance of street traffic and pipe-lines which this scheme involved meant a maximum of inconvenience in construction, it also meant a maximum of convenience and cheapness in operation when the work was completed.

Another marked characteristic of the Rapid Transit Subway, as distinguished from most other underground railroads, is that the principles of the modern sky-scraper are applied in its construction, the roof and sides being supported by steel frames composed of transverse steel beams and light steel columns. With a cement floor and the sides and roof made waterproof and even damp-proof, and then lined with cement, the interior of the tube when completed will, as a matter of fact, look like solid whitewashed stone, but, as in the case of the sheathing of the sky-scraper, this will be only a shell. The elimination of grade-crossings and the insertion of "islands" between the tracks at the various express stations, so that by the means of raised passages passengers may transfer from local to express trains, and vice versa, at will, are other noticeable features of the design. It is by such a scheme that the engineers hope to attain a maximum of speed and carrying capacity. Neither the plan nor the carrying of it out in steel and blasted rock could be spectacular. It is rather a task requiring vast patience and the ability to simplify a mass of intricate details.

The work of steam-drills and traveling dumping-cars and the methods of supporting myriads of undermined pipes, all of which has been visible for a couple of years to every one who rode up-town from the Brooklyn Bridge in a Fourth Avenue car, have been about what most people have noticed in the construction of these lower and more prosaic parts of the subway. Few know that in order to cross Canal street, which at the subway grade is below the tide-level, a sewer which drained a greater part of the lower East Side into the North River had to be carried clear across the island in the opposite direction and into the East River. Quite as few ever heard of Aaron Burr's water-pipes, which were unearthed as the excavations proceeded up Elm street near Reade. These pipes, which were laid in 1799, to supply "the city of New York with pure and wholesome water," were merely logs with a longitudinal hole bored through the center of each and hollowed at one end and sharpened at the other, so that they could be fitted one into the other, just as glass tumblers may be piled. The story goes that the wily Burr inserted a "joker" in the act providing for his water company, by which he was able to break the monopoly then held by the Bank of New York and the New York branch of the United States Bank, and found a bank for himself and his friends. The bank thus organized is one of the well-known city banks to-day, and Burr's water-pipes, as dry as bones these many years, were tight and seemingly as good as new when they were uncovered. The unearthing of "Cat Alley" recalled, to those who remembered, the time when the sidewalk rendezvous of actors, called "the Rialto," was along Houston street, a day no less interesting than Aaron Burr's, if less classic.

Though solid rock is found at Union Square, where it is worked from the surface, real tunneling, through darkness and solid rock, begins farther up-town, at Thirty-fourth street. The short section of eight blocks from Thirty-fourth street under Park Avenue to the Grand Central Station has not shared that happiness which comes to tunnels as well as nations that have no history. It will remain long in the minds of the generation who saw it built as the "hoodoo" part of the tunnel. So persistently did a perverse fate follow the footsteps of the contractor who had this section in charge, even to his death from a fall of stone, that the happenings in these short blocks passed from tragedy almost to the point of burlesque, and I recall a paragraph printed in one of the papers in which a woman who happened to be present during a trolley-car smash-up in the depths of Harlem, one evening, was made to say, as she

DRAWN BY FERNAND LUNGREN.   HALF-TONE PLATE ENGRAVED BY F. H. WELLINGTON.

AT THE FOOT OF THE SHAFT, ONE HUNDRED AND FOURTH STREET.

pulled the conductor by the arm: "I am a stranger in this dreadful city. Tell me, Mr. Conductor—oh, *do* tell me—are we now on Park Avenue?"

Of the explosion of blasting-powder at Forty-first street by which eight were killed

which, were it not for one's sympathy for the ill-starred contractor, might well conduce to the gaiety of nations. The tunnel here burrows under the existing subway used by the Fourth Avenue surface-cars, and its floor is about sixty feet below the sur-

DRAWN BY FERNAND LUNGREN.   HALF-TONE PLATE ENGRAVED BY GEORGE M. LEWIS.

HOW THE WATER-PIPES ARE SUSPENDED.

The water-pipes in service under heavy pressure are temporarily suspended from beams at the street-level. After the subway is completed, masonry piers will be built on its roof to support them.

and hundreds endangered, about the only thing that can be said is that it might easily have been vastly more horrible. The carrying away of the subway roof, however, and the consequent fall of the fronts of several of the brownstone houses on the avenue just above Thirty-seventh street, was an episode

face. It had been carried about half-way between Thirty-seventh and Thirty-eighth streets, at what was thought to be a safe distance from the stoop-line of the row of houses above. But the rock, apparently as solid as Gibraltar, lay in slanting strata, and one day, almost without warning, a huge section of one of these slanting strata simply slid diagonally from the easterly roof as a card slips out of a loosely shuffled pack. Every workman on the section was rushed to the spot in the hope that the damage could be repaired before it became apparent on the surface; but before the break could be properly shored, the areaways and front steps of the houses came tumbling down into the chasm. Parts of the front walls soon followed, and the crowd of idlers and nurse-maids and delivery-boys who gathered a few minutes after the first cave-in enjoyed the delectable experience of gazing into the very heart of each house, just as you look at an interior on the stage.

One gentleman was in his bath-tub at the time. His valet burst into the room. "Quick! quick! You must get out of here, sir!" cried that worthy. "There's been an earthquake, sir, and the house is falling in!" "Indeed!" observed the gentleman with interest, and he finished his bath. He dressed himself, and loading his film camera and lighting a brier-wood pipe, he sallied forth, and when his wife's mother arrived on the scene from a distant part of town, whence she had driven at breakneck speed to save her child, she found her son-in-law standing on the brink of the chasm in front of his door-step, pointing down into it a film camera, the shutter of which he was working with the liveliest enthusiasm and delight. This teaches us that a bucolic equanimity may be preserved even on a metropolitan street beneath which a tunnel is building, and that nerves may be suppressed even in New York and in a somewhat neurotic age.

When the walls ceased to crumble away and the people had moved out of that block, —some of them, it was said at the time,

DRAWN BY FERNAND LUNGREN.   HALF-TONE PLATE ENGRAVED BY WILLIAM MILLER.

NIGHT-WORK IN FORTY-SECOND STREET NEAR FIFTH AVENUE.

This view shows the narrow trench under the sidewalk excavated through twenty feet of earth to rock and lined with heavy timber; steam-drilling and blasting of the rock bottom, and tunneling laterally under the surface tracks.   The materials are handled by cableway over the open trench.

demurely demanding both that the contractor buy their houses outright and that he pay their rent in new ones,—pipes were sunk from the surface, and watery cement was pumped down them to harden until the fallen rock was virtually restored. But fire and falling ruins were yet to descend on that unhappy section, and so timid was its contractor forced to become that when you visited it during the last summer, and saw the workmen pegging away under the acetylene lamps in the "waist" of the tunnel heading, you

and solved along almost every yard of this part of the underground road. The first of the subway stations to be finished was that under the Circle, at the southwest corner of Central Park. At the time these lines were written it was the only one completed, and from it visitors to the subway gathered their impressions of that lightness and general cheerfulness which it was one of the main

DRAWN BY C. A. VANDERHOOF.

STATION AT COLUMBUS CIRCLE, IN COURSE OF CONSTRUCTION.

The steel work is here shown in place, and the concrete roof, floor, and walls are finished.
The walls are not yet faced with glazed tiles, and the station-work is unfinished.

were likely to be reminded not so much of the strenuosities of engineering as of an operation in dental surgery.

From the Grand Central Station, where, of course, one of the main subway stations will be built, the road proceeds again by surface excavation west on Forty-second street to Broadway, and thence northward to One Hundred and Fourth street, where comes the parting of the ways. No one who has seen the subway pass beneath Forty-second street, the monument at the Circle, the elevated structure at Sixty-sixth street, and the surface car-tracks to the northward toward the Boulevard, needs to be told of the complex difficulties which have been met

desires of the engineers to provide in planning the work. Not only light, but sunlight, pours into the place from the ground-glass sidewalk overhead, and with its walls lined in enameled brick and tiles, and the white cement tube of its subway stretching north and south ablaze with electric lights, this station illustrates how successfully this desire has been achieved. As it is not an express station, there are only the two long and spacious platforms next to the outside, or local, tracks, and the express-trains will whisk by on the two inner tracks without a stop. When I visited the station they were experimenting with enameled bricks and tiles of various colors to see which were most likely to arouse enthusiasm in the esthetic sense of the traveling public.

"It reminds me," observed a foreman of that section, "of a cheap-lunch restaurant." The imagination staggers at the thought of higher praise than this. To those who

In the Circle, just below this station, rises the tall column on the top of which stands the statue of Cristoforo Colombo, given to New York by its residents of Italian birth. The subway passes directly under this column, and the difficulties and delicacies of

DRAWN BY FERNAND LUNGREN.   HALF-TONE PLATE ENGRAVED BY J. TINKEY.

DESCENDING THE SHAFT TO THE TUNNEL-LEVEL.

Showing the platform of the steam-elevator used to raise excavated rock,
and miners waiting in the tunnel to ascend for dinner.

are not familiar with the "unsurpassed coffee" refectories of the metropolis, it may be as well to explain that in these resorts survives for a modern age an oppressive cleanliness and a riot of onyx, glittering tiles, and enameled brick, which one is wont to associate with the baths of Pompeii and ancient Rome.

the task of shoring up this monument while the excavation was going on were not lightened by the fact that the foundation of the column rested partly on rock and partly on sand. "His head is just one hundred feet above yours," said the foreman, as we stood on the tunnel floor.

The embarrassments which such landmarks as these have suffered in preserving their dignity during the exigencies of subway construction were plain to any one who saw the statue of Samuel S. Cox, "the letter-carriers' friend," in Astor Place, or who crossed Union Square, where the Father of

to dip beneath Central Park, emerge at One Hundred and Tenth street and Lenox Avenue, and proceed thence to the Bronx. The problem that met the contractors in this part of the work was to pass under Central Park without disturbing a tree or a blade

DRAWN BY FERNAND LUNGREN.   HALF-TONE PLATE ENGRAVED BY C. W. CHADWICK.

IN THE TUNNEL UNDER FORT GEORGE.

Miners at work in the heading; muckers wheeling spoil to cars on tracks in finished excavation. Temporary timbering to support dangerous roof until concrete arch can be built.

his Country spent the summer pointing majestically to a tool-shanty and a pile of steel columns, while the rear legs of his horse were standing on the brink of a forty-foot chasm.

From the dividing-line at One Hundred and Fourth street a two-track branch, tunneling some sixty feet below the surface through solid rock, swings off to the right,

of grass on the surface, and the way in which they have succeeded is suggested by the opening paragraphs of this article. Tunnels were started at each end and worked inward, and when the last wall was broken down, the plumb-lines of the two headings showed only a quarter of an inch divergence. The conservative citizen who ventured into this section during the summer was lowered

DRAWN BY FERNAND LUNGREN.   HALF-TONE PLATE ENGRAVED BY R. C. COLLINS.

EXPLORING THE BOTTOM OF THE EAST RIVER WITH
SOUNDINGS FOR THE BROOKLYN TUNNEL.

The working platform built on a cluster of piles in
deep, swift water was many times swept away. A
large steel pipe was sunk by a powerful water-jet
through mud and clay to rock, and the diamond drill
was lowered inside it, and the hole extended many
feet into the rock, bringing up solid cylindrical cores.

in a bucket into the sixty-foot pit at One
Hundred and Fourth street, and the donkey-
engine man had a way of letting this bucket
drop like a plummet to within a few feet of
the tunnel floor in a manner calculated to
accelerate the pulses of the rider. From the
bottom of this until one emerged, half a
mile or more away, just outside the greenery
of the Park, one was stumbling through
nothing more or less than a narrow mine.
But when this is completed, and the walls
are arched smooth with concrete and are
painted white, the subway passenger of the
future, returning to his Harlem home of an
evening, will probably never remember that
sixty feet of solid rock are between him and
daylight, unless he chances to look up from
his paper as his train swings round the curve
at One Hundred and Fourth street.

The main line, which, from One Hundred
and Fourth street, consists of three tracks,
proceeds by surface excavation to One Hundred and Twenty-second street, where a
viaduct leads it for half a mile across the
sudden depression of Manhattan valley, to
plunge underground again at One Hundred
and Thirty-third street. The contract as
first let for this part of the subway called
for a two-track road, but after the excavations had been partly made in some places,

the concrete bed and steel superstructure
had been built, and all was ready for the roof,
it was decided to have a three-track road.
The resulting labor and vexatious complica-
tions were almost as great as though the
work had never been started. One of the
contractors moved the walls of his tunnel
back bodily. Another moved the walls and
some two hundred feet of steel superstructure weighing over two thousand tons. Between One Hundred and Fourteenth and
One Hundred and Twenty-first streets the

DRAWN BY FERNAND LUNGREN.　HALF-TONE PLATE ENGRAVED BY R. C. COLLINS.

THE COLUMBUS MONUMENT HELD UP DURING EXCAVATIONS.

The foundations of the monument are supported on temporary steel girders and wooden posts while undermined for subway excavation under the monument and over sloping rock surface. The concrete floor of subway is shown finished and ready to receive the steel columns which will support its roof and the overhanging monument. The steel buckets containing excavated rock are hoisted by steam-derricks and dumped into wagons.

deepest surface excavation had to be made. There is an average depth of about forty feet down to the tunnel grade there. The material removed was solid rock lying in slanting strata, and overhead was a trolley-car line, the time-schedule of which could not be interfered with. Such are a few of the things that had to be reckoned with and overcome in a part of the subway which the ordinary down-town New-Yorker knows nothing about.

It is a strange land north of Manhattan valley and west of Washington Heights—

quite another country from the Harlem over the hill. Trinity Cemetery, smothered in verdure, rises on each side of the street beneath which the subway is laid, and the superstructure is set up where, only a few years ago, before the cut was made through the cemetery grounds, lay the graves of the dead. Here, too, was the fighting of Washington Heights, and the bronze memorial tablet marking the spot where breastworks were thrown up is not more than thirty feet from the tunnel walls. Everywhere are trees, —elms and soft maples,—arching in some places over the street, as they do over the main street of many an inland town. The coming of rapid transit will doubtless change all this, but if you should visit it now of a foggy afternoon when all out of sight is shrouded in mystery, it will give you a most extraordinary sensation of being in Manhattan and yet out of it—of being in dreamland or abroad.

The tunnel which dives into the solid rock at One Hundred and Twenty-eighth street is the longest on the line. At an average depth of one hundred feet below the surface it burrows through blackness for a distance of two miles with an unbroken roof, except at One Hundred and Sixty-ninth and One Hundred and Eighty-first streets, where elevators will carry passengers to and from the tracks. Except for the Hoosac Tunnel, there is no single tunnel so long in America. When I went down into the shaft at One Hundred and Sixty-ninth street it was difficult to fancy it looking as it will look, like the white and marbled station beneath the Circle, nearly six miles away. At the surface was a landing-stage from which every now and then emerged cars of broken rock. You stepped on the elevator platform, and down, down you went into the darkness and dampness of the pit, until, one hundred feet below, you struck bottom in a big cave with a few electric lamps glimmering against the walls and an air-pump forcing fresh air into the heavy atmosphere with slow, spasmodic coughs.

Along the tramway leading into the heading ambled the self-centered subterranean mule. When I ventured to make friendly overtures, he promptly swung about and decamped with all the adroitness which he would have used had he been nibbling thistles in the middle of a sunny meadow, and later, when the driver, in hitching him to the tram-car, gave the somewhat untechnical command, "Get in line, there!" he hopped to his place between the rails with just as much cheerfulness as though the command referred to a company drill and he had half a dozen team-mules to keep him from being lonesome.

It was in the tunnel just below One Hundred and Sixty-ninth street that another of those accidents occurred which is the price of every great achievement of engineering construction. Here again a slanting stratum became loosened, and slipping down, killed five of the men who were working beneath. I asked one of the workmen from just what part of the heading the rock had fallen.

"That chunk of work," said he, cheerfully, pointing straight at the roof above us, "fell out just over where you 're standing now."

From the end of the long tunnel to Fort George on the western line, and from the tunnel beneath the waters of the Harlem to Bronx Park on the eastern branch, the Rapid Transit road, as a railway, is scarcely enough advanced at this writing to require detailed description. These extreme northern sections are to be elevated structures, and passing as they do through what is now a comparatively sparsely settled part of the Greater City and not subject to the embarrassments of excavation through rock or beneath crowded streets, they can be, when once fairly started, rapidly pushed to completion. As yet little more than the foundations for the elevated pillars are laid. Already, however, the engines and generators, which will supply electric power for the vast traffic of the whole underground system, are being constructed, hundreds of cars similar to those used on the existing elevated, but heavier and of superior running qualities, have been ordered, and the general manager of the road is planning the automatic-signal system and arranging his time-schedules.

There are almost numberless details in this huge piece of work which cannot be touched on here. If you tell your friend Robinson that such-and-such a number of cigars are manufactured every year, he will forthwith begin to calculate how near they would reach to the planet Mars if they were placed end to end. You yourself, on the other hand, may be concerned more over the fact that, with a supply so great, the price is not cheaper, or that you do not get more of them. The opportunities for the Robinson point of view are quite unlimited in making a mental circuit from the City Hall to Fort George and the Bronx. The essential things for most of us to know, however, are what is going on to-day beneath our feet, and what, when the work is done, will be the result. Of the first of these we have here had a few glimpses. The other, the builders say, the town will know by next Christmas, almost a year ahead of contract time. A still more interesting question, perhaps,—that of the effect of this sudden increase in the ease and rapidity of transportation on the country at the city's edge, and of the other paths of rapid travel which are destined to honeycomb the underworld of our narrow Babylon,—the morrow, our all too precipitate to-morrow, will answer.

DIFFICULT ENGINEERING IN THE SUBWAY.

BY FRANK W. SKINNER, C.E.,

Author of "Triumphs of American Bridge-Building," in the June CENTURY, and Associate Editor of the "Engineering Record."

UNDER THE COLUMBUS MONUMENT.

NEAR where the subway swings around the southwest corner of Central Park it passes through and under the foundations of the Columbus monument. The slender stone shaft, surmounted by its heroic statue, is seated on a molded pedestal with extended base, which altogether rises seventy-five feet above the street and weighs nearly a million and a half pounds. It has a masonry foundation forty-five feet square and fourteen feet deep, which was built partly on rock, but mostly on earth. Its east corner overhangs the subway nearly forty feet, and the position of the latter is so near the surface that its walls and roof cut a wide and deep section out of the masonry.

This made it necessary to support the monument so that its tall shaft should neither lean nor settle a hair's-breadth, nor the thin, accurately fitted pedestal stones be cracked, or their polished joints open, under the great strains developed when the masonry was cut out to a mere shell and the support removed from under a third of its base and almost up to the center, reducing its stability to a slender margin. This would have been a delicate and hazardous task under any circumstances, but was made more difficult and dangerous by the unknown conditions and the known character of the soil.

It was uncertain whether the interior of the foundation masonry was sound and strong enough to resist the great strains which might be safely imposed on the best stonework, and great potential peril lay in the fact that only one corner of the foundation, that diagonally opposite to the subway, stood on the rock, the rest being built on earth and sand. The surface of the rock slopes down very steeply toward the subway and below it, so that when the excavation was made there the equilibrium of the com-

pressed earth was destroyed, the unbalanced pressures, especially in wet weather, might well cause the earth to slide out from under the foundation and produce a serious disaster. Safety alone was not sufficient: there could not be tolerated even a slight or harmless disturbance of the monument. The lofty shaft is like a sensitive needle, quick to quiver and diverge with an almost imperceptible displacement at the base, and to magnify many times the smallest unequal settlement, so as to deflect its graceful lines from the perfect vertical and emphasize even a trivial deviation to the appearance of an offensive blemish. These exacting conditions called for the work to be executed with an excess

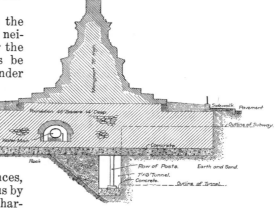

SUPPORTING THE COLUMBUS MONUMENT. (DIAGRAM 1.)

of solidity, and at the same time the commercial requirements demanded rapidity, simplicity, and economy.

It was determined first to extend the foundations under the center of the monument to a greater depth, so that they would reach below the subway excavation and beyond the base of the shaft, and thus carry most of the load directly and prevent any danger of slipping down the sloping rock surface. Afterward the wide corner of the

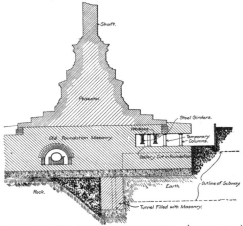

SUPPORTING THE COLUMBUS MONUMENT. (DIAGRAM 2.)

foundation was to be first supported, then
undercut and undermined, so as to allow the
excavation to be made under, through, and
alongside, and the subway to be built and
eventually carry the overhanging part of
the old foundation.

First, shafts fifty feet apart were sunk
about twenty-five feet deep on the north and
south sides of the old foundation, and their
bottoms were connected by a small tunnel
which was roofed by the base of the old
foundation and had its floor well below the
bottom of the subway, and its east wall
where the west wall of the subway was to
be built. A solid bed of concrete was laid
on the floor of the tunnel, and vertical timber
posts were set on it and wedged up against
the under side of the foundation to support
it. The tunnel was then filled solid with
stone masonry, beginning at the middle,
working out to
both ends, and
permanently in-
closing the tim-
ber posts. This
virtually made
a massive stone
beam support-

ing the foundation from side to side and
seated below the level which would be disturbed by the subway construction.

A trench ten feet deep was dug around
the east side of the monument, exposing
the upper part of the foundation where it
extended over the line of the subway. From
this trench a gallery, or slot, six feet high
was cut about twenty-five feet horizontally
into the face of the foundation masonry,
and as it advanced, vertical timber posts
were set on its floor and wedged up to support its roof. When the slot extended about
thirty feet through the corner of the foundation, two solid steel girders, like beams in
a railroad-bridge, were set in it between the
rows of posts.

A pit was dug close to the foundation at
each end of the slot, and the bottom was

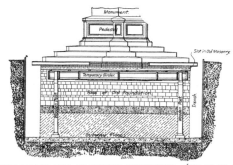

SUPPORTING THE COLUMBUS MONUMENT. (DIAGRAM 3.)

covered with concrete, which afterward
formed part of the subway floor. On this
concrete were set braced wooden posts to
carry the ends of the girders, which were
thus lifted clear of the floor of the slot.
Pairs of steel wedges were driven between
the tops of the girders and the roof of the
slot until they lifted the whole mass of masonry a fraction of an inch and transferred
the weight of the overhanging portion to
the girders. Then the roof posts were removed, and the outer edge of the foundation
and all that portion below the slot were cut
away, the excavation
completed, and the sub-
way built in it, under
the overhanging foun-
dation and around the
posts which supported
the girders.

Under the edge of the
overhanging foundation,
outside of the girders,
a wall was built on the
concrete roof of the sub-

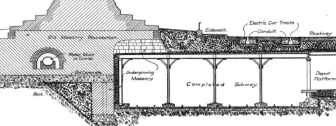

SUPPORTING THE COLUMBUS MONUMENT. (DIAGRAM 4.)

way which is very strong, with steel beams and columns. A course of cut stone was laid in the upper part of the wall, and on it many pairs of steel wedges supported a loose course of cut stone carefully fitted in under the overhanging masonry of the foundation. The wedges were driven up, and developed an enormous pressure, which lifted the monument again, transferred part of its weight to the new wall, and released the girders. They were removed, and the spaces they had occupied were filled in solid with masonry, built and wedged up from the center outward in the same manner as the wall. Liquid cement was forced into the interstices between the wedges, and solidifying as hard as flint, perfected the support of all the overhanging foundation on top of the finished subway.

In doing this work one portion had to be completed before another could be begun, and as but few men could work at once, and the operations were conducted with great care and accuracy, it took about six weeks to complete it in a manner which was highly creditable to the able engineers who designed and approved it and the experienced contractors who skilfully executed an undertaking unlike any previously recorded.

RELOCATING A LONG, THIN, HIGH WALL.

AN ordinary derrick will handle compact loads of three, five, or even ten tons; a hundred-ton load is about the limit of the capacity of the heaviest steel-ordnance cars drawn by powerful locomotives, or of the largest hydraulic jacks, which will lift it a few inches so slowly that the motion is scarcely perceptible. A building weighing five hundred tons may be carefully braced and lifted up or moved laterally with rollers on smooth level tracks by the help of scores of powerful jacks. It would require immense power to push along even a fifty-ton boulder resting on the ground, and be yet more difficult to move a long, thin, high wall several feet transversely without cracking, tipping, or twisting it.

Generally, when such a wall is to be relocated, it is taken down and rebuilt; but such was not the case on the subway above One Hundred and Thirty-fifth street, where, at the entrance to a tunnel section, walls nearly two hundred feet long retain the bank on each side of the cut. After the structure was completed it was decided to widen it eleven feet to receive a third track, and although it was at first intended to tear down

the masonry and build new, it was finally decided to move it bodily, and this was successfully accomplished at a saving of several thousand dollars.

The walls are of concrete and brick, thirteen feet high at one end, three feet thick on top, and weigh about four hundred thousand pounds each. The earth was dug away behind them for a width of six feet, and to a depth a little below their foundations. In the bottom of each trench a concrete floor was laid just below the level of the foot of the wall. Small holes were tunneled under the wall a few feet apart, and in them were laid transverse timbers reaching to the floor of the trench and having both ends supported on cross-sills. Narrow, thin, greased steel track-plates were inserted under the walls, on top of the timbers, and extended across the trench floors. Small steel bearing-plates were set on the track-plates under the front and rear edges of the walls, and pairs of oak wedges, driven between the cross-timbers and their sills, lifted the whole wall on the steel plates.

Horizontal five-ton jack-screws were set close together against the face of the wall at the base for its whole length, and being simultaneously operated, the wall in a few hours was moved back five and a half feet on to the floor in the trench. The projecting ends of the track-plates were cut off, and the spaces between the plates under the wall were filled with liquid cement. The work on each wall was done by twenty men in ten days, and the walls were not distorted the sixteenth of an inch.

MOVING A TUNNEL.

THE north ends of these walls join the tunnel section of the subway, which was a solid, rectangular concrete tube about twenty-eight feet wide, seventeen feet high, three hundred feet long, and weighed about six million pounds. It was built in an open trench, which had not yet been refilled with earth above the tunnel roof. It had a framework of steel columns and roof-beams five feet apart, which were bedded in the concrete, and, like the approach, had been built for two tracks. When it was determined to provide for a third track, it was decided to widen the old structure by moving its walls out both ways five and a half feet from the center, and building in between them new strips of roof and floor to complete a larger tube on the same center line.

A trench seven feet wide was dug down

to the bottom of the tunnel along each of its walls, and a concrete bed was laid in it to form a part of the new tunnel floor and side-wall foundation. As the tunnel had very little strength except to resist exterior pressure, it was thoroughly braced with timbers and wire ropes, inside and outside, to stiffen and bind it together to resist the temporary stresses and distortion of moving. Horizontal cuts were made from end to end of the tunnel through the bottom of the east wall and the top of the west wall, and the beams and columns were disconnected there so as to divide the structure into two nearly equal parts, one comprising the roof, east wall, and center columns, the other the west wall and floor.

The west ends of the roof-beams were lifted a few inches with jack-screws, tipping the roof and east wall about the foot of the east wall as a pivot, and raising the center columns enough to place steel track-plates under their bases. Then the east ends of the roof-beams were similarly lifted, rocking the roof back again around the feet of the center columns as pivots, and lifting the east wall and columns high enough to insert under them track-plates which extended across the concrete floor in the bottom of the east outside trench.

Fifty five-ton jack-screws were set against the ends of the horizontal cross-timbers in the bottom of the tunnel, bearing on the east wall and center columns, and twenty-five men, turning the alternate screws quarter revolutions simultaneously on signal, gradually pushed the roof, east wall, and center columns five and a half feet east in two days, although the speed was half an inch a minute when they were actually moving. In order to keep the motion regular, a piano wire was stretched from end to end of

the tunnel, one inch from the wall, and each man had a one-inch gage with which he tested this distance every time he turned his jack-screws.

A slot was cut from end to end of the west wall, separating it from the floor, stiffening-timbers were clamped to it, and horizontal cross-timbers were braced to the foot of it in such a manner as to project halfway across the tunnel, forming an extended base wide enough to give it great stability. Jack-screws under its braces lifted the wall enough to allow the insertion of track-plates under it and the base timbers; then it was pushed away from the undisturbed floor five and a half feet west on to the new floor in the trench by jack-screws set against horizontal braces from the inner face of the wall at its foot. Additional columns and roof-beams were set in the gap between the old parts of the tunnel, the extended roof and floor surfaces were closed up with concrete, the earth filled in on top of the roof up to the street surface, the braces removed, and the work successfully completed. The east wall and roof, as moved, weighed about three million pounds, and the west wall alone about seven hundred thousand pounds.

The work was done by forty men, at an estimated saving of six thousand dollars over the expense of tearing out the roof and walls, and is probably the first instance of moving a tunnel. The method was planned by the contractors, who executed it at their own risk, with the approval of the engineers. They were not tunnel-builders, but many years' experience in the erection of great bridges, roofs, and tall steel buildings had qualified them safely to undertake difficult and unusual heavy work requiring skill, ingenuity, and experienced judgment, and the safe handling of enormous forces and masses.

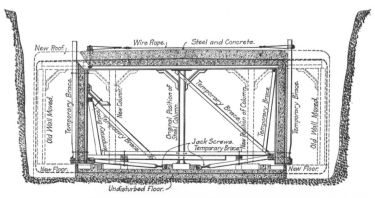

MOVING THE SUBWAY TUNNEL STRUCTURE.

13
Masters
of Their
Craft

McClure's Magazine

APRIL, *1903*

MASTERS OF THEIR CRAFT

BY ADRIAN KIRK

Illustrated by Corwin Knapp Linson

THE happiest men I know are those who get their chief pleasure in life out of the exercise of their own skill. They are "artists" in a broad sense, and artists in the narrow sense of the word like to admit the guild relationship of all mastercraftsmen.

We have cut society too much on the square. Perpendicular and horizontal lines do not make the only intelligent divisions. The relationship of Raphael with a pickpocket I talked to once is more intimate essentially than it is with some makers of "pictures" and moulders of "statuary." The thief had been arrested because, having obtained permission to live in New York provided he did not work there, he was caught stealing a watch.

"Why did you do it?" I asked him.

"Well, I'll tell you," he said. "I simply couldn't help it. I'm no kleptomaniac. It isn't the stealing I like, but the fun of doing a hard job prettily. This is the second turn I've made. The first was like this: I saw a rich, fat man in a crowd, and I noticed that his watch was hung in a new way, hard to break. My fingers itched, not for the watch, but to break it off. I moved up, lifted the watch, walked away with it, and then went back and hung the thing on the chain again. This second time was something like that. I saw a delicate job, tried it, got the watch, and just then the fellow happened to look for the time. He hollered, and a detective nearby pinched me. I don't think I'm what you'd call a natural thief, but I like to work with my fingers and I like the excitement of stealing."

My point is not a penal or even moral idea. We hear too much of the good and the bad, too little of the efficient and the inefficient; too much of the largest and the greatest, the richest and the poorest, too little of the beautiful and the ugly. The present contention is simply that just as there are leaders among men, whether of armies or gangs; and just as there are poets who sing and poets who only feel; so we have artists who realize in paint a religious ideal and artists who only steer a tug or wait on a table or lift your watch. The art instinct is a distinction among men of all ranks; "art for art's sake," a water-logged hulk of a phrase, carries a rich cargo of meaning for many a man who has never heard it.

Up and down Eighth Avenue in New York a certain chipper young motorman runs a cable-car, and though he has been at this job for eight years, he loves so much the art of his craft that he repeatedly has declined promotion. His superintendent told me about him. I described the type of man I was after, and the superintendent shook his head.

"Oh, they all work for the pay," he said.

"Of course," I said, "so do all of us, but there are some men who get their rewards in the doing of the thing."

161

" ' I like a clear track, but I like a crowded street, too ' "

The superintendent shook his head. He showed me a man who had studied the mechanics of his car, theoretical electricity, and read books on all subjects allied to his craft. I rode with this motorman.

"What are you after?" I asked him. "Do you like to run a car?"

"I hate it," he said. "I am studying for promotion."

A good man this, one of the American millions. I appealed again to the superintendent, and we waited beside the track watching the motormen go by.

".I know now what you want," he said. "I've been thinking it over. You want a blanked fool."

"Not at all," I answered. "Yes," I added, "yes, perhaps you're right."

On an Eighth Avenue Trolley

"Well," he said, "I've got one." And we went over on Eighth Avenue and found my motorman. It was a rainy day, but he was as happy as sunshine.

"Yes," he said, laughing, "I've passed up their promotions. I don't know why, exactly, except that I'd rather run a cable-car than eat. It's fun, yes; yet that isn't all. There's a knack to it. When you once get the feel of your car, and can lift her weight with a twist of the wrist, it's a pleasure to do just that. It's a pleasure to go full speed; it's a pleasure to stop her easy; it's a pleasure to start her easy. I like a clear track, but I like a crowded street, too. It's a pleasure to steal ground on the wagons. When a fellow's on the track ahead, it's fun to get him off; and a trick, too. You cuss and you jar the gong, and the driver'll keep you there till you're fighting mad; but you ring once, wait and that driver, ten to one, will get out of your way. If he don't I call out something friendly like. 'Break away, old man, it's dinner time for me,' and he'll clear out. If they fight that's fun, too. You can crawl up under a wagon, and push it up on the horse, or you can catch a mean cuss under the hub and turn him over into the street. I tell you it's all fun, but I've been a cigarmaker, too, and I tell you I've found out that the best fun in life is to do a neat job up neat. Now see that lady waiting to get on. Watch the rear step."

I looked back as he sailed slowly by the woman. He stopped the car so that she stepped on without moving up or down the track.

"Did she have to chase me?" the motorman asked confidently. "No, not on your life. I can stop on a chalk line. Now as to promotion, if they offer me a place with much more pay, say $20 a week, I'd have to take it. I've got a wife, and it's hard digging on $15, but do you know I hope they won't. I'd rather run a car than eat; rain or snow, sunshine or fog."

This is the spirit. And I have found it in all trades alike.

The Joys of 'Bus Driving

One of these artists was driving a 'bus down Fifth Avenue on a certain crowded morning. Secure in his skill, he had set himself a complicated problem: To keep behind him an automobile 'bus of his own company; to "head" a cabman who had

"sassed" him the day before; to pick up all the "fares" that hailed him, and keep up with the procession on his side of the street.

His half of the road was wide enough for two carriages to move abreast, and there were four columns of traffic in motion—two going up, two down. Had this condition been constant, the task would have been easy, but it wasn't. The up columns frequently thinned to one, so that the automobile had chances to shoot out and go by. The chauffeur plainly had his "dander" up, and, bound to get ahead, was overlooking some "fares" who let the horse-'bus pass to hail him. He hung out in the column farthest from his curb in readiness, black in the face, his lips moving as if he were saying things. My driver showed no sign of any feeling; he never turned his head (that seemed to be a self-imposed restriction of honor with him); he did not even look alert, and his horses moped along as if half asleep. Yet this wonderful man commanded the curb and the middle of the road, too. Spying a fare long before he approached a corner, he slowed up, jamming traffic a little behind him, swung out to turn the columns in to the curb, then bent sharply on himself, taking up the passengers before the tangle behind could clear and release the automobile. Moreover, he had to stop his back step exactly where the fare stood, to lose no time. Without seeming to hurry his horses, he yet had a way of pulling them down to business, and, once off, they loafed out into the middle of the road at a good rate, swinging back idly to keep any one from going by between them and the curb. The driver used everything to help him—a block, a cross-town car, a track, a driver off side; each checked in some way the automobile and sent my Jehu easily on his way.

The cabman ahead gained on the 'bus. He had every advantage—no stops, only two wheels, and a light vehicle, and he grinned back his triumph twice.

"Can you get him?" I asked.

"What?" asked the driver, as if he were caught stealing. He looked around shrewdly, saw I was on his side, and let a twinkle appear in his eye. "Yes; I've got him now—at Thirty-fourth Street."

That was two blocks away. Carriages

" One of these artists was driving a 'bus down Fifth Avenue on a certain crowded morning"

were thick there, crossing east and west, and north and south. A hundred feet lay between us and the tail of the double column ahead. We were free at both hubs ; my driver was in the middle of his half of the road. The cab was third from the rear of the curb column ahead of us, and the automobile next behind us. We closed up half our distance, rolling easily right and left to prevent passing, and I noticed that this was done so naturally that no driver behind complained except the chauffeur, and he had known of old. I could hear him muttering curses. A thin part of the column was coming. No doubt my driver meant to gain by it, but at Thirty-fourth Street he turned curbward and the strap pulled ; a passenger wanted to get out. Perhaps I looked vexed. At any rate, the driver said :

"Who-o, who-up. I knew that lady wanted to get down here. Always does. Watch the steam-engine."

The chauffeur was darting past at full speed, and he sailed out, leading his column, into the opening on past the cab. The lady was out. Our horses pulled up and we hurried out into the middle. The Jehu smiled vaguely. The automobile was stuck. It had met a coal wagon which would give not an inch, and the chauffeur was looking for a place to get into our column ahead, but the back pressure from Thirty-fourth Street had closed us in solid, and the "steam-engine" had to wait while we went by. As we passed, the chauffeur glared at me. I looked at our driver.

"That coal cart is the meanest cuss on the road," he said ; "regular hog. I seen him loading up at Thirty-fourth Street."

The cab driver remained ahead. He was in the curb column ; we were in the other. At a walk we all moved down on the tangle at the crossing, and I saw no way out. The Jehu, at perfect repose, held back half a length from the carriage in front. Two cars were allowed to cross, and, as they passed, the inner columns, both up and down, were started first, and we gained one place on the curb line. The cab was two places ahead, and up against a van. We still held an open space ahead. At the crossing one carriage in our column pulled out for the Waldorf-Astoria, and we crept up. I suspect my driver knew that was coming.

He closed up half-way again, and was occupied with the prospect across the street. Twice we were stopped and started, then I noticed the cabby trying to get out, not ahead of our leader, but of us ! My driver let him tuck his horses' heads in, then a break opened in the up column, our team lurched down on him, and, when an accident seemed imminent, we were trotting out in the opening, leaving the cabby behind us, hoarse with rage. We swung out, then back, and were bowling over the car tracks and down the avenue clear and free.

Cries arose behind, and I looked back. The chauffeur and the cabby were in collision—their wheels lightly, but their tempers violently. Each was venting on the other the rage aroused by my Jehu, who showed no feeling at all. They were blocking the road, and a policeman was going for them as we drew down where I couldn't see. The whole avenue on one side lay before us.

"Arrested ?" my driver asked.

"Oh, no," I said ; "it isn't so bad as that. The cop is between them."

"They'll get arrested yet, them two."

We tooled along in silence for a few blocks, my driver appearing to loaf, like his horses, though I saw that his hands worked slowly, gently, but constantly at the reins, while his eyes held the road and the curb.

"You seem to like your job," I remarked.

He did not answer right away. When he did he came back like this :

"I was delivered on this earth in '34. How old's that make me ?"

"Sixty-eight."

"Well, I've handled 'em ever since I was big enough." He nodded at the horses or the reins. "I've drove 'em always, better or worse, an' always will. They've offered me the stable in my day. 'Nope,' I says. I could 'a' had that steam thing back there. Not for your Uncle Willie—I'm a driver. I'd ruther drive 'n eat. If was younger I might like to drive somethin' else, but nowadays this is good enough for me—just t' tool 'em up an' tool 'em down again, makin' the most of th' road an' th' conditions o' th' way. I'd ruther drive 'n eat any day, an' always did."

Two or three of this driver's traits are characteristic of artists, as I use the word.

Besides the enjoyment of his skill, he has the ease and repose of the masters of their craft everywhere. There is concentration and intensity ; there is effort, but no nervousness, no waste of energy. The Jehu's face expressed perfect composure, his body sat squat, apparently at rest, yet his foot felt the brake and his hands handled the reins all the time ; but so gently did he control his team that his horses did not at any moment of that drive know that they were in a race.

In the Composing Room of a Big Daily

The most exciting time in a New York newspaper office is when the last edition of an evening paper goes to press. Five pages are "put to bed" between 2.56 P.M. and 3.16, some ten columns are set, five of them market reports. That isn't time enough, but the papers must get in the financial tables complete and correct between the close of the markets at 3 o'clock and 3.16 in order to catch the first brokers to leave their offices before they can reach their ferries and trains. The ticker doesn't stop till 3.11 or 3.12 o'clock, and the paper is in Wall Street by 3.28. In these few minutes a man can learn to respect skilled labor.

M. L. Frescoln, foreman of the composing room, "Commercial Advertiser"

At last everything concentrates upon the final page. Two groups of compositors are at work; one at the case setting by hand the "high low last" and the "bid and asked" of the stock market, as they get the quotations from the ticker boys who snip them with scissors from the rolling tape ; the other group at the machines setting late news. All the editors come up to the last form, the managing editor, the city editor, the telegraph, the financial, the real estate, the sporting editor, each with his "important" last item, edited down to the bones. All gather about the little table on rollers, and look over the form to see how much space will be left by the financial tables. There's rarely enough. The bank-man grabs the type, marks it for the place it is to go in the page, passes the type to the proof boy, who pulls three proofs for the managing editor, the department editor concerned, and the proof-readers, who have moved down *en masse* to be near the form. Corrections are marked on the proof, which is sent out to the machines, but the type goes in. The make-up men are receiving it with both hands and laying it in swiftly and gently.

"All over," cries the ticker boy, striking his scissors on the table. The ticker has stopped. All eyes look at the clock, all except those of the make-up man whose back is toward it ; he looks at the make-up man opposite, who says, "Half a minute late as usual."

A boy rushes upstairs with copy. The copy-cutter yells to the managing editor, "Copy, can't see it." The managing editor darts up and looks at it. "Must," he says, and it goes to No. 1 machine. No. 1 machine in my day was a red-headed young man who was over-worked because he could over-work, and he liked it. Late news went to him, late corrections went to him, and when I stole past the foreman and the copy-cutter to get in "a line" too late to have the consent of the managing editor, No. 1 would grin. "Give it here," he would say, and he'd pile his late news "line o' type" on one knee, his corrections on the other, put my copy in his lips and finish the job. Then my copy was set without apparent haste, with a word about the news itself and a shout for "boy" to carry the type to the form.

There the pressure is at its height.

"The most exciting time in a New York newspaper office is when the last edition of an evening paper goes to press"

Nervous men wriggle from foot to foot, or swear or lose time saying, "Can't do it," or "Oh, well —— it," or "See the time."

"I must get this in," says the telegraph editor.

"I should think this would go ahead of it," the city editor answers, showing his selected theme.

"Put them both in, throw out that Boston Copper item," the managing editor decides, and the make-up men hunch themselves. It breaks up two columns.

In a crisis like that, with eight hands at work on the form, four making corrections (pulling out bad lines and inserting good ones), weak nerves go to pieces. I have seen a make-up man throw up his hands and go back only at a sharp word of command. But I have seen two men prove their character. One was a little Scotchman who could feel the confusion wrecking the crew. By the time the last hands lifted and the tired nerves cursed, he'd say, in an irritating, comical way, "There's nothing to do but cheer up, *cheer-up, chirrup.*" He buckled in the harder, all the others grinned and steadied, and out they pulled the page, locked her, jammed, and half threw, half whirled her to the steam table.

But the best man was one who seemed to be slow. He never hurried, rarely spoke, never swore, never made a useless gesture or an expression, his eyes moved like his hands—deliberately, precisely, effectively. It was a beautiful sight to watch him doing his work so easily, and yet he was the quickest man in the shop. Not only did he place his type right, but he noticed errors, even in names, showing that his intelligence was wide awake; he asked questions which saved me many a mistake, and always he was willing to do more. Sometimes he smiled, or looked up at the clock, but if you were willing to risk being late, he'd try, and if he tried, you wouldn't be late, at least not more than once or twice in a season. He could lay out a page in his mind, lay it in all but a paragraph, and alter it to suit you without losing patience; I've seen his hand turn without a pause at a command and go at the changed arrangement, and though everybody had to bend to with doubled effort, he would finish in style, swing the locked form aside, and then go

at the next day's work without a rest or a pause. But that was only a way he had of slowing down after the high speed of the work. In two or three minutes he would quit, then go over to his coat, take out his pipe, sit and smoke. He was tired. He had put forth effort like the "hustlers," but none of his energy had been wasted. He and No. 1 and "Cheer Up" are artists as truly as Puvis de Chavannes or my 'bus-driver.

On the Empire State Express

As a final test I applied to the New York Central Railroad for permission to ride with the best engineer they had. The superintendent named three of the men who run the Empire State Express, giving me leave to ride up to Albany in the day time with one, down at night with another. I called on these three men before I made my choice. There was no choice, and it was almost enough simply to see them. The popular notion of a locomotive engineer is of a nerve-racked man who spends half his time under a fearful strain, cool, but aware of great danger, with one hand pulling open the throttle to the last notch, the other on the reverse lever, ready to back her, and, with a word to his fireman to jump, himself to stick to his post. If this were so, then all that I had been seeing elsewhere was exceptional. Well, it isn't so. These men were all very much alike; at bottom they were of one type. Slow of speech, composed in mind and body; intelligent, but not keen; ready, but not especially alert; they talked quietly, sensibly about their business. They don't know what "nerves" are, apparently. I found two at home on their "off day," and one was lying down, the other sitting idly, and it was plain they could rest; they could lie still, sit still, stand still. In other words, they had the repose I had noticed in other master craftsmen.

There is more true quietude in a locomotive cab than there is in the office of many an active bank president, much more than in a drawing-room, vastly more than in a Pullman dining-car. The engineer climbed into the cab about a minute before starting time, set away his oil can, wiped his hands carefully on a bunch of waste and took his place. "Ar-right," said the fireman, as he pulled his head in from his window. The engineer set his reverse and pulled the throttle a bit, and we started so gently you could hardly feel it. There was no slipping of the driver on the track, nor a pound too much steam turned into the cylinder. The train got under headway evenly. Slowly we rolled down the yard among the switches and ran into the tunnel. Both the fireman and the engineer kept their eyes out here, but this vigilance was not the fixed sort you read about. It was that which a good driver gives the road ahead—sure, known, steady (and, by the way, the smoke and gases which trouble passengers when a car isn't tight, are not noticeable on an engine; they pass overhead). Out under the clear sky the train moved faster, at about twenty-five miles an hour, till it turned off out of the yard switches; then, "We're off," said the fireman, and the engineer pulled the throttle a little wider. Out on the Hudson River full speed is made. Setting his lever

William Raymond, engineer of the Empire State Express

and pulling the throttle deliberately to a certain picked notch, the engineer let go and leaned back. That was the time of the greatest exhilaration. The great locomotive seemed to be reaching out. It moved like a snake, swaying in front from one side of the track to the other, and at each swing it took a better grip on the train, gathered more momentum. Rising at curves, it seemed to dive around them, and, once we were going full speed, behaved most like a huge buffalo driving ahead cumbrously, yet with a sense of power that made the motion easy; clumsy and stupid, but irresistible and effortless. We on its back were thrown

from side to side, towns passed with a bang, trains on the side track shrieked at us and rattled like tin pans, the air batted, cuffed, and slapped in on our faces.

Improving my grip, I looked over at the engineer. He was leaning on the window ledge, his throttle hand resting idly on the lever; and, though he was looking ahead, he seemed hardly interested. His whole attitude suggested a man at ease. For miles and miles the engine held the pace, the engineer the pose, and the Hudson River opened and closed, folded and unfolded beside us like a beautiful picture book in strong, old, slow hands. By and by we slowed for a town; then for water; then for another town; once to pass a place where men were repairing the track; then the engine slowed down, and rolled leisurely over the new bridge into Albany, just on time.

The engineer looked across at me. "Want to go back to the yard with us?" he asked.

"No, come and have lunch with me."

"Oh, I can't do that," he answered; "I've got to go to work now."

He meant that he had to oil and inspect and tighten this and that for his afternoon trip down; but he meant also that there hadn't been any work about running his train from New York to Albany, 144 miles in two hours and thirty-four minutes. There wasn't; at least no labor. There was responsibility, concentration, judgment, and a sure hand, but no conscious effort. Once during the trip he got down and told the fireman to "run her." The fireman sat like the engineer of the story books, his body leaning forward, one hand on the throttle, the other on the lever, and his eyes fixed ahead. *He* worked and he will work when he gets his first engine. But the old engineer, surer, with tried attention and a nicer, idler hand, so controlled that machine that, though he gave no sign of effort, physical or mental, we finished the last mile of our distance in the last minute of our time.

Well, perhaps the night trip would bear out the story teller. The darkness seemed to me to be absolute. "That makes the signals plain," the engineer said. It did, indeed; only I saw too many till he explained how to distinguish "ours" from the galaxies that confounded me. We rushed faster and faster into the dark. A light ahead floated across the track, back again, then seemed to shoot up into the air on the right; a white signal; another light on the right slid diagonally down across the track, and then headed, flying straight for my window. "Bang!" it struck, and I dodged —a passing up train. We seemed to be going twice as fast as at any time in the morning, and I asked the fireman what speed we were making. He spoke to the engineer, who leaned far over to see his watch in the light of the furnace. Sitting up again, he was still, till I forgot. By and by he bent over, again looked at his watch and spoke to the fireman, who reported : "We made that last seven miles in five minutes and twenty seconds." If this rough estimate was correct, it meant eighty miles an hour. The engineer was lying back, with his arm resting idly on the lever—his eyes not "glued to the track," but simply keeping him informed. For a while during the trip I stood up beside him, and we chatted quietly about lights and locomotives and runs, all in an easy conversational tone, and I noticed that his eyes, ready enough to turn into the cab to pull out a gauge or a screw, habitually turned back every other moment to the track. His vigilance was as subconscious as the movements of a man dressing in the morning. His mind could be on what he was saying to me, while his eyes were attending to their own business. He was not driving his machine by will-power, but machine-like, yet with his brain and senses so constantly on the lookout that they would react like clockwork to any sign meant for them. And

there were many he himself forgot to mention. Thus, while we were talking, when he was interested, he let her off a little, and I asked, as if by the way, whether we were on time. "Three-quarters of a minute ahead," he said; but he had already acted before I put his mind on it. Just as in any other art, it isn't industry, but inspiration, that counts.

As I climbed back on my seat and took the rush of air and the roar of sounds I looked across at the man who was doing it and thought how little of it was his doing—how much was his parents'. He was simply a well-made human being, perfectly adjusted to his craft —a part of his locomotive. He and the machine together were like a great man —a serene soul possessing a powerful body, and directing forces out of all proportion to his effort.

When we stopped in the station, our pilot three feet from the buffer, the clock stood 9.59. That was time, and I recalled what this man had said the first day I met him, when I asked what was the art, the trick, of running an engine.

"You've got so many miles to go in so many minutes. There are so many slow-downs, sure—so many clear streaks of track. You know your engine and your track; you know just what you can do— where, when, and how. Now, then, the trick is to keep your train up to a certain point. If you use too much speed here, she'll run down on you later, so you keep her balanced on a fine edge till you're near home; then you can draw her down all you want."

"That's the thing you feel then ?"

"Exactly ; and that's the fun of the job. It's easy when you do it by feeling, and a pleasure."

"And danger ?"

"Never think of it. There isn't any— not so much as there is walking along Broadway."

"But some engineers say there is."

"They've lost their nerve."

"What's that?"

"That's what I don't know."

The next day is the off day for those two engineers. They sit around, sleep, walk idly about, read a little. They don't talk much, but they like to listen to

" Though he was looking ahead, he seemed hardly interested "

Danny Cassin, Engineer of the Empire State Express

others' talk. Running the locomotive is their pleasure as well as their work. When they are busy they are happiest. They do not always know it, and that goes to prove the point : their joy is in their work, not a thing apart. Though they may stop for rest and recreation, their chiefest pleasure is in the doing of their job, whatever it may be, and, whether the reward for labor in their craft be wages or wealth, the compensation that keeps them at work is the delight of the craftsman in the exercise of his skill. If this is not the spirit of a man's labor he is not an artist—he is a painter or a merchant or a workingman. Artists don't work for money.

Not that money is a mean thing, and not that artists do not care for it. My motorman admitted the value of that, but money has simply nothing to do with the art, no matter how much it may influence artists. The same spirit manifests itself sometimes in a purely money-making business. I knew a merchant worth many millions who has it so highly developed that he grieves over it, and his expression of the feeling came out in the course of a warning to me to guard against it. He was advising me to take a post-graduate college course. "Take it," he said; "take all the education you can get. I had just enough to make me aware there were lots of sources of pleasure in the world—art, music, letters, the drama, sports—but I had to go to work before I had learned to enjoy these things—before I had acquired the need of them. This enabled me to work for the pleasure of work alone, and all my pleasure centered in my own particular business. Well, I did enjoy that; but when I tried to quit, and went abroad, I got no pleasure out of my travels. All the beautiful things that I knew were beautiful bored me. I had to come back, and, to this day, with more money than I know what to do with, I find satisfaction only in the details—the details, mind you—of my business, which piles up the money people think is all I'm working for."

This sort of man is rare, even among "artists," in the narrow sense. Think how many young painters draw until middle age—even all their lives—because they cannot resist the immediate money illustrating brings in. In business, money is usually the object of effort—money first, then the position and luxuries it brings; after that the excitement of the gambler, and, finally, the love of power which often furnishes a noble spectacle in finance, terrible, but magnificent. But I am not decrying any human motives. All I wish to recall—what we all know and forget—is that the art spirit thrives in commonplace surroundings, among all crafts alike, and that there are great men among the wage-earners, where we all can see and enjoy them.

14

New York:
Good Government
in Danger

NEW YORK: GOOD GOVERNMENT IN DANGER

BY

LINCOLN STEFFENS

AUTHOR OF ''THE SHAMELESSNESS OF ST. LOUIS''; ''CHICAGO: HALF FREE AND FIGHTING ON,'' ETC.

ILLUSTRATED WITH PORTRAITS

UST about the time this article will appear, Greater New York will be holding a local election on what has come to be a national question : good government. No doubt there will be other ''issues.'' At this writing (September 15th) the candidates were not named nor the platforms written, but the regular politicians hate the main issue, and they have a pretty trick of confusing the honest mind and splitting the honest vote by raising ''local issues'' which would settle themselves under prolonged honest government. So, too, there will probably be some talk about the effect this election might have upon the next presidential election ; another clever fraud which seldom fails to work to the advantage of rings and grafters, and to the humiliation and despair of good citizenship. We have nothing to do with these deceptions. They may count

175

in New York, they may determine the result, but let them. They are common moves in the corruptionist's game and, therefore, fair tests of citizenship, for honesty is not the sole qualification for an honest voter; intelligence has to play a part, too, and a little intelligence would defeat all such tricks. Anyhow, they cannot disturb us. I am writing too far ahead, and my readers, for the most part, will be reading too far away to know or care anything about them. We can grasp firmly the essential issues involved and then watch with equanimity the returns for the answer, plain yes or no, which New York will give to the only questions that concern us all:

Do we Americans really want good government? Do we know it when we see it? Are we capable of that sustained good citizenship which alone can make democracy a success? Or, to save our pride, one other: Is the New York way the right road to permanent reform?

For New York has a good government, or, to be more precise, it has a good administration. It is not a question there of turning the rascals out and putting the honest men into their places. The honest men are in, and this election is to decide whether they are to be kept in, which is a very different matter. Any people is capable of rising in wrath to overthrow bad rulers. Philadelphia has done that in its day. New York has done it several times. With fresh and present outrages to avenge, particular villains to punish, and the mob sense of common anger to excite, it is an emotional gratification to go out with the crowd and "smash something." This is nothing but revolt, and even monarchies have uprisings to the credit of their subjects. But revolt is not reform, and one revolutionary administration is not good government. That we free Americans are capable of such assertions of our sovereign power, we have proven; our lynchers are demonstrating it every day. That we can go forth singly also, and, without passion, with nothing but mild approval and dull duty to impel us, vote intelligently to sustain a fairly good municipal government, remains to be shown. And that is what New York has the chance to show; New York, the leading exponent of the great American anti-bad government movement for good government.

According to this, the standard course of municipal reform, the politicians are permitted to organize a party on national lines, take over the government, corrupt and deceive the people and run things for the private profit of the boss and his ring, till the corruption becomes rampant and a scandal. Then the reformers combine the opposition: the corrupt and unsatisfied minority, the disgruntled groups of the majority, the reform organizations; they nominate a mixed ticket, headed by a "good business man" for mayor, make a "hot campaign" against the government with "Stop thief" for the cry, and make a "clean sweep." Usually, this effects only the disciplining of the reckless grafters and the improvement of the graft system of corrupt government. The good mayor turns out to be weak or foolish or "not so good." The politicians "come it over him," as they did over the business mayors who followed the "Gas Ring" revolt in Philadelphia, or the people become disgusted as they did with Mayor Strong, who was carried into office by the anti-Tammany rebellion in New York after the Lexow exposures. Philadelphia gave up after its disappointment, and that is what most cities do. The repeated failures of revolutionary reform to accomplish more than the strengthening of the machine has so discredited this method that wide-awake reformers in several cities — Pittsburg, Cincinnati, Cleveland, Detroit, Minneapolis, and others — are following the lead of Chicago.

The Chicago plan does not depend for success upon any one man or any one year's work, nor upon excitement or any sort of bad government. The reformers there have no ward organizations, no machine at all; their appeal is solely to the intelligence of the voter and their power rests upon that. This is democratic and political, not bourgeois and business reform, and it is interesting to note that whereas reformers elsewhere are forever seeking to concentrate all the powers in the mayor, those of Chicago talk of stripping the mayor to a figurehead and giving his powers to the aldermen who directly represent the people, and who change year by year.

The Chicago way is but one way, however, and a new one, and it must be remembered that this plan has not yet produced a good administration. New

SETH LOW

An American mayor who is honest and efficient, too. Disliked in New York because he lacks the graces of the typical corrupt politicians.

for a good mayor? I think this election, which will answer this question, should decide other cities how to go about reform.

The administration of Mayor Seth Low may not have been perfect, not in the best European sense : not expert, not co-ordinated, certainly not wise. Nevertheless, for an American city, it has been not only honest but able, undeniably one of the best in the whole country. Some of the departments have been dishonest ; others have been so inefficient that they made the whole administration ridiculous. But what of that? Corruption also is clumsy and makes absurd mistakes when it is new and untrained. The "oaths" and ceremonies and much of the boodling of the St. Louis ring seemed laughable to my corrupt friends in Philadelphia and Tammany Hall, and New York's own Tweed regime was "no joke," only because it was so general, and so expensive—to New York. It took time to perfect the "Philadelphia plan" of misgovernment, and it took time to educate Croker and develop his Tammany Hall. It will take time to evolve masters of the (in America) unstudied art of municipal government—time and demand. So far there has been no market for municipal experts in this country. All we are clamoring for to-day in our meek, weak-hearted way, is that mean, rudimentary virtue miscalled "common honesty." Do we really want it? Certainly Mayor Low is pecuniarily honest. He is more ; he is conscientious and experienced and personally efficient. Bred to business, he rose above it, adding to the training he acquired in the conduct of an international commercial house, two terms as Mayor of Brooklyn, and to that again a very effective administration, as president, of the business of Columbia University. He began his mayoralty with a study of the affairs of New York ; he has said himself that he devoted eight months to its finances : and he mastered this department and is admitted to be the master in detail

York has that. Chicago, after seven years' steady work, has a body of aldermen honest enough and competent to defend the city's interests against boodle capital, but that is about all ; it has a wretched administration. New York has stuck to the old way. Provincial and self-centered, it hardly knows there is any other. Chicago laughs and other cities wonder, but never mind, New York, by persistence, has at last achieved a good administration. Will the New Yorkers continue it? That is the question. What Chicago has, it has secure. It's independent citizenship is trained to vote every time and to vote for uninteresting good aldermen. New York has an independent vote of 100,000, a decisive minority, but the voters have been taught to vote only once in a long while, only when excited by picturesque leadership and sensational exposures, only *against*. New York has been so far an anti-bad government, anti-Tammany, not a good government town. Can it vote, without Tammany in to incite it,

of every department which has engaged his attention. In other words, Mr. Low has learned the business of New York; he is just about competent now to become the mayor of a great city. Is there a demand for Mr. Low?

No. When I made my inquiries — before the lying had begun — the Fusion leaders of the anti-Tammany forces, who nominated Mr. Low, said they might renominate him; "who else was there?" they asked. And they thought he "might" be reëlected. The alternative was Richard Croker or Charles F. Murphy, his man, for no matter who Tammany's candidate for mayor was, if Tammany won, Tammany's boss would rule. The personal issue was plain enough. Yet was there no assurance for Mr. Low.

Why? There are many forms of the answer given, but they nearly all reduce themselves to one — the man's personality. It is not very engaging. Mr. Low has many

CHARLES F. MURPHY

Croker's successor as Tammany boss. The man who will rule New York if Tammany wins this year.

respectable qualities, but these never are amiable. "Did you ever see his smile?" said a politician who was trying to account for his instinctive dislike for the Mayor. I had; there is no laughter back of it, no humor, and no sense thereof. The appealing human element is lacking all through. His good abilities are self-sufficient; his dignity is smug; his courtesy seems not kind, his self-reliance is called obstinacy because, though he listens, he seems not to care; though he understands, he shows no sympathy, and when he decides, his reasoning is private. His most useful virtues — probity, intelligence, and conscientiousness — in action are often an irritation; they are so contented. Mr. Low is the bourgeois reformer type. Even where he compromises, he gets no credit; his concessions make the impression of surrenders. A politician can say "no" and make a friend, where Mr. Low will lose one by saying "yes." Cold and impersonal, he cools even his heads of departments. Loyal public service they give, because his taste is for men who would do their duty for their own sake,

not for his, and that excellent service the city has had. But members of Mr. Low's administration helped me to characterize him; they could not help it. Mr. Low's is not a lovable character.

But what of that? Why should his colleagues love him? Why should anybody like him? Why should he seek to charm, win affection, and make friends? He was elected to attend to the business of his office and to appoint subordinates who should attend to the business of their offices, not to make "political strength" and win elections. William Travers Jerome, the picturesque District Attorney, whose sincerity and intellectual honesty made sure the election of Mr. Low two years ago, detests him as a bourgeois, but the mayoralty is held in New York to be a bourgeois office. Mr. Low is the ideal product of the New York theory that municipal government is business, not politics, and that a business man who would manage the city as he would a business corporation, would solve for us all our troubles. Chicago reformers think we have got to solve our own problems ; that government is political business ; that men brought up in politics and experienced in public office will make the best administrators. They have refused to turn from their politician mayor, Carter H. Harrison, for the most ideal business candidate, and I have heard them say that when Chicago was ripe for a better mayor, they would prefer a candidate chosen from among their well-tried aldermen. Again, I say, however, that this is only one way, and New York has another, and this other is the standard American way.

But again I say, also, that the New York way is on trial, for New York has what the whole country has been looking for in all municipal crises — the non-political ruler. Mr. Low's very faults, which I have emphasized for the purpose, emphasize the point. They make it impossible for him to be a politician even if he should wish to be. As for his selfishness, his lack of tact, his coldness — these are of no consequence. He has done his duty all the better for them. Admit that he is uninteresting ; what does that matter? He has served the city. Will the city not vote for him because it does not like the way he smiles? Absurd as it sounds, that is what all I have heard against Low amounts to. But to reduce the situation to a further absurdity, let us eliminate altogether the personality of Mr. Low. Let us suppose he has no smile, no courtesy, no dignity, no efficiency, no personality at all ; suppose he were an It and had not given New York a good administration, but had only honestly tried. What then?

Tammany Hall? That is the alternative. The Tammany politicians see it just as clear as that, and they are not in the habit of deceiving themselves. They say "it is a Tammany year," "Tammany's turn." They say it and they believe it. They study the people, and they know it is all a matter of citizenship ; they admit that they cannot win unless a goodly part of the independent vote goes to them ; and still they say they can beat Mr. Low or any other man the anti-Tammany forces may nominate. So we are safe in eliminating Mr. Low and reducing the issue to plain Tammany.

Tammany is bad government ; not inefficient, but dishonest ; not a party, not a delusion and a snare, hardly known by its party name — Democracy ; having little standing in the national councils of the party and caring little for influence outside of the city. Tammany is Tammany, the embodiment of corruption. All the world knows and all the world may know what it is and what it is after. For hypocrisy is not a Tammany vice. Tammany is for Tammany, and the Tammany men say so. Other rings proclaim lies and make pretensions, other rogues talk about the tariff and imperialism. Tammany is honestly dishonest. Time and time again, in private and in public, the leaders, big and little, have said they are out for themselves and their own ; not for the public, but for "me and my friends" ; not for New York, but for Tammany. Richard Croker said under oath once that he worked for his own pockets all the time, and Tom Grady, the Tammany orator, has brought his crowds to their feet cheering sentiments as primitive, stated with candor as brutal.

The man from Mars would say that such an organization, so self-confessed, could not be very dangerous to an intelligent people. Foreigners marvel at it and at us, and even Americans — Pennsylvanians, for example — cannot understand why we New Yorkers regard Tammany as so formidable. I think I can explain it. Tammany is corruption with consent ; it is bad government founded on the suffrages of the people. The Philadelphia machine is more powerful. It rules Philadelphia by fraud and force and does not require the votes of the people. The Philadelphians do not vote for their machines ; their machines vote for them. Tammany used to stuff the ballot boxes and intimidate voters ; today there is practically none of that. Tammany rules, when it rules, by right of the votes of the people of New York.

Tammany corruption is democratic corruption. That of the Philadelphia ring is rooted in special interests. Tammany, too, is allied with "vested interests" — but Tammany labors under disadvantages not known in Philadelphia. The Philadelphia ring is of the same party that rules the State and the nation, and the local ring forms a living chain with the state and national rings. Tammany is a purely local concern. With a majority only in old New York, it has not only to buy what it wants from the Republican majority in the State, but must trade to get the whole city. Big business everywhere is the chief source of political corruption, and it is one source in New York; but most of the big businesses represented in New York have no plants there. Offices there are, and head offices, of many trusts and railways, for example, but that is all. There are but two railway terminals in the city, and but three railways use them. These have to do more with Albany than New York. So with Wall Street. Philadelphia's stock exchange deals largely in Pennsylvania securities, New York's in those of the whole United States. There is a small Wall Street group that specializes in local corporations, and they are active and give Tammany a Wall Street connection, but the biggest and the majority of our financial leaders, bribers though they may be in other cities and even in New York State, are independent of Tammany Hall and can be honest citizens at home. From this class, indeed, New York can and often does draw some of its reformers. Not so Philadelphia. That bourgeois opposition which has persisted for thirty years in the fight against Tammany corruption, was squelched in Philadelphia after its first great uprising. Matt Quay, through the banks, railways and other business interests, was able to reach it. A large part of his power is negative; there is no opposition. Tammany's power is positive. Tammany cannot reach all the largest interests and its hold is upon the people.

Tammany's democratic corruption rests upon the corruption of the people, the plain people, and there lies its great significance; its grafting system is one in which more individuals share than any I have studied. The people themselves get very little; they come cheap, but they are interested. Divided into districts, the organization subdivides them into precincts or neighborhoods, and their sovereign power, in the form of votes, is bought up by kindness and petty privileges. They are forced to a surrender, when necessary, by intimidation, but the leader and his captains have their hold because they take care of their own. They speak pleasant words, smile friendly smiles, notice the baby, give picnics up the River or the Sound, or a slap on the back; find jobs, most of them at the city's expense, but they have also news-stands, peddling privileges, railroad and other business places to dispense; they permit violations of the law, and, if a man has broken the law without permission, see him

through the court. Though a blow in the face is as readily given as a shake of the hand, Tammany kindness is real kindness, and will go far, remember long, and take infinite trouble for a friend.

The power that is gathered up thus cheaply, like garbage, in the districts is concentrated in the district leader who in turn passes it on through a general committee to the boss. This is a form of living government, extra-legal, but very actual, and, though the beginnings of it are purely democratic, it develops at each stage into an autocracy. In Philadelphia the boss appoints a district leader and gives him power. Tammany has done that in two or three notable instances, but never without causing a bitter fight which lasts often for years. In Philadelphia the State boss designates the city boss. In New York, Croker has failed signally to maintain vice-bosses whom he appointed. The boss of Tammany Hall is a growth, and just as Croker grew, so has Charles F. Murphy grown up to Croker's place. Again, whereas in Philadelphia the boss and his ring handle and keep almost all of the graft, leaving little to the district leaders, in New York the district leaders share handsomely in the spoils.

There is more to share in New York. It is impossible to estimate the amount of it, not only for me, but for anybody. No Tammany man knows it all. Police friends of mine say that the Tammany leaders never knew how rich police corruption was till the Lexow committee exposed it, and that the politicians who had been content with small presents, contributions, and influence, "did not butt in" for their share till they saw by the testimony of frightened police grafters that the department was worth from four to five millions a year. The items are so incredible that I hesitate to print them. Devery told a friend once that in one year the police graft was "something over $3,000,000." Afterward the syndicate which divided the graft under Devery took in for thirty-six months $400,000 a month from gambling and poolrooms alone. Saloon bribers, disorderly house blackmail, policy, etc., etc., bring this total up to amazing proportions.

Yet this was but one department, and a department that was overlooked by Tammany for years. The annual budget of the city is about $100,000,000, and though the powei that comes of the expenditure of that amount is enormous and the opportunities for rake-offs infinite, this sum is not one-half of the resources of Tammany when it is in power. Her resources are the resources of the city as a business, as a political, as a social power. If Tammany could be incorporated and all its earnings, both legitimate and illegitimate, gathered up and paid over in dividends, the stockholders would get more than the New York Central bond and stock holders, more than the Standard Oil stockholders, and the controlling clique would wield a power equal to that of the United States Steel Company. Tammany, when in control of New York, takes out of the city unbelievable millions of dollars a year.

No wonder the leaders are all rich; no wonder so many more Tammany men are rich than are the leaders in any other town; no wonder Tammany is liberal in its division of the graft. Croker took the best and the safest of it, and he accepted shares in others. He was "in on the Wall Street end," and the Tammany clique of financiers have knocked down and bought up at low prices Manhattan Railway stock by threats of the city's power over the road; they have been let in on Metropolitan deals and on the Third Avenue Railroad grab; the Ice Trust is a Tammany trust; they have banks and trust companies, and through the New York Realty Company are forcing alliances with such financial groups as that of the Standard Oil Company. Croker shared in these deals and businesses. He sold judgeships, taking his pay in the form of contributions to the Tammany campaign fund, of which he was treasurer, and he had the judges take from the regular real estate exchange all the enormous real estate business that passed through the courts, and give it to an exchange connected with the real estate business of his firm, Peter F. Meyer & Co. This alone would maintain a ducal estate in England. But his real estate business was greater than that. It had extraordinary legal facilities, the free advertising of abuse, the prestige of political privilege, all of which brought in trade; and it had advance information and followed with profitable deals, great public improvements.

Though Croker said he worked for his own pockets all the time, and did take the best of the graft, he was not "hoggish." One of the richest graft in the city is in the Department of Buildings. $100,000,000 a year goes into building operations in New York. All of this, from out-houses to skyscrapers, is subject to very precise laws and regulations, most of them wise, some impossible. The Building Department has the enforcement of these; it passes upon all construction, private and public, at all stages from plan-making to actual completion; and can cause not only "unavoidable delay" but can wink at most profitable violations. Architects and builders had to stand in with the department. They called on the right man and they settled on a scale which was not fixed, but which generally was on the basis of the department's estimate of a fair half of the value of the saving in time or bad material. This brought in at least a banker's percentage on one hundred millions a year. Croker, so far as I can make out, took none of this; it was let out to other leaders and was their own graft.

District Attorney William Travers Jerome has looked into the Dock Department, and he knows things which he yet may prove. This is an important investigation for two reasons. It is very large graft and the new Tammany leader, Charlie Murphy, had it. New York wants to know more about Murphy, and it should want to know about the management of its docks, since, just as other cities have their corrupt dealings with railways and their terminals, so New York's great terminal business is with steamships and docks. These docks should pay the city handsomely. Mr. Murphy says they shouldn't; he is wise, as Croker was before he became old and garrulous, and, as Tammany men put it, "keeps his mouth shut," but he did say that the docks should not be run for revenue to the city but for their own improvement. The Dock Board has exclusive and private and secret control of the expenditure of $10,000,000 a year. No wonder Murphy chose it.

It is impossible to follow all New York graft from its source to its final destination. It is impossible to follow here the course of that which is well known to New Yorkers. There are public works for Tammany contractors. There are private works for Tammany contractors, and corporations and individuals find it expedient to let it go to Tammany contractors. Tammany has a very good system of grafting on public works ; I mean that it is "good" from the criminal point of view — and so it has for the furnishing of supplies. Low bids and short deliveries, generally speaking (and that is the only way I can speak here), is the method. But the Tammany system, as a whole, is weak.

Tammany men as grafters have a confidence in their methods and system, which, in the light of such perfection as that of Philadelphia, is amusing, and the average New Yorker takes in "the organization" a queer sort of pride, which is ignorant and provincial. Tammany is 'way behind the times. It is growing; it has improved. In Tweed's day the politicians stole from the city treasury, divided the money on the steps of the City Hall, and, not only the leaders, big and little, but heelers and outsiders ; not only Tweed, but ward carpenters robbed the city ; not only politicians, but newspapers and citizens were "in on the divvy." New York, not Tammany alone, was corrupt. When the exposure came, and Tweed asked his famous question, "What are you going to do about it ?" the ring mayor, A. Oakey Hall, asked another as significant. It was reported that suit was to be brought against the ring to recover stolen funds. "Who is going to sue ?" said Mayor Hall, who could not think of anybody of importance sufficiently without sin to throw the first stone. Stealing was stopped and grafting was made more business-like, but still it was too general, and the boodling for the Broadway street railway franchise prompted a still closer grip on the business. The organization since then has been gradually concentrating the control of graft. Croker did not proceed so far along the line as the Philadelphia ring has, as the police scandals showed. After the Lexow exposures, Tammany took over that graft, but still let it go practically by districts, and the police captains still got a third. After the Mazet exposures, Devery became Chief and the police graft was so concentrated that the division was reduced to fourteen parts. Again, later, it was reduced to a syndicate of four or five men, with a dribble of miscellaneous graft for the police. In Philadelphia the police have nothing to do with the police graft ; a policeman may collect it, but he acts for a politician, who in turn passes it up to a small ring. That is the drift in New York. Under Devery the police officers got comparatively little, and the rank and file themselves were blackmailed for transfers and promotions, for remittances of fines, and in a dozen other petty ways.

Philadelphia is the end toward which New York under Tammany is driving as fast as the lower intelligence and higher conceit of its leaders will let it. In Philadelphia one very small ring gets everything, dividing the whole as it pleases, and not all those in the inner ring are politicians. Trusting few individuals, they are safe from exposure, more powerful, more deliberate, and they are wise as politicians. When, as in New York, the number of grafters is large, this delicate business is in some hands that are rapacious. The police grafters, for example, in Devery's day, were not content with the amounts collected from the big vices. They cultivated minor vices, like policy, to such an extent that the Policy King was caught and sent to prison, and Devery's wardman, Glennon, was pushed into so tight a hole that there was danger that District Attorney Jerome would get past Glennon to Devery and the syndicate. The murder of a witness the night he was in the Tenderloin police station served to save the day. But, worst of all, Tammany, the "friend of the people," permitted the organization of a band of so-called Cadets, who made a business, under the protection of the police, of ruining the daughters of the tenements and even of catching and imprisoning in disorderly houses the wives of poor men. This horrid traffic never was exposed ; it could not and cannot be. Vicious women were "planted" in tenement houses and (I know this personally) the children of decent parents counted the customers, witnessed their transactions with these creatures, and, as a father told with shame and tears, reported totals at the family table.

Tammany leaders are usually the natural leaders of the people in these districts, and they are originally good-natured, kindly men. No one has a more sincere liking than I for some of those common but generous fellows ; their charity is real, at first. But they sell out their own people. They do give them coal and help them in their private troubles, but, as they grow rich and powerful, the kindness goes out of the charity and they not only collect at their saloons or in rents — cash for their "goodness"; they not only ruin fathers and sons and cause the troubles they relieve; they sacrifice the children in the schools; let the Health Department neglect the tenements, and, worst of all, plant vice in neighborhood and in the homes of the poor.

This is not only bad; it is bad politics; it has defeated Tammany. Woe to New York when Tammany learns better. Honest fools talk of the reform of Tammany Hall. It is an old hope, this, and twice it has been disappointed, but it is not vain. That is the real danger ahead. The reform of a corrupt ring means, as I have said before, the reform of its system of grafting and a wise consideration of certain features of good government. Croker turned his "best chief of police," William S. Devery, out of Tammany Hall, and, slow and old as he was, Croker learned what clean streets were from Col. Waring, and gave them. Now there is a new boss, a young man, Charles F. Murphy, and unknown to New Yorkers. He looks dense, but he acts with force, decision, and skill. The new mayor will be his man. He may divide with Croker and leave to the "old man" all his accustomed graft, but Charlie Murphy will rule Tammany and, if Tammany is elected, New York also. Lewis Nixon is urging Murphy publicly, as I write, to declare against the police scandals and all the worst practices of Tammany. Lewis Nixon is an honest man, but he was one of the men Croker tried to appoint leader of Tammany Hall. And when he resigned Mr. Nixon said that he found that a man could not keep that leadership and his self-respect. Yet Mr. Nixon is a type of the man who thinks Tammany would be fit to rule New York if the organization would "reform."

As a New Yorker, I fear Murphy will prove sagacious enough to do just that: stop the scandals, put all the graft in the hands of a few tried and true men, and give the city what it would call good government. Murphy says he will nominate for mayor a man so "good" that his goodness will astonish New York. I don't fear a bad Tammany mayor; I dread the election of a good one. For I have been to Philadelphia.

Philadelphia had a bad ring mayor, a man who promoted the graft and caused scandal after scandal. The leaders there, the wisest political grafters in this country, learned a great lesson from that. As one of them said to me:

"The American people don't mind grafting, but they hate scandals. They don't kick so much on a jiggered public contract for a boulevard, but they want the boulevard and no fuss and no dust. We want to give them that. We want to give them what they really want, a quiet Sabbath, safe streets, orderly nights, and homes secure. They let us have the police graft. But this mayor was a hog. You see, he had but one term and he could get a share only on what was made in his term. He not only took a hog's share off what was coming, but he wanted everything to come in his term. So I'm down on grafting mayors and grafting office-holders. I tell you it's good politics to have honest men in office. I mean men that are personally honest."

So they got John Weaver for Mayor, and honest John Weaver is checking corruption, restoring order, and doing a great many good things, which it is "good politics" to do. For he is satisfying the people, soothing their ruffled pride, and reconciling them to machine rule. I have letters from friends of mine there, honest men, who wish me to bear witness to the goodness of Mayor Weaver. I do. And I believe that if the Philadelphia machine leaders are as careful with Mayor Weaver as they have been and let him continue to give to the end as good government as he has given so far, the "Philadelphia plan" of graft will last and Philadelphia will never again be a free American city.

Philadelphia and New York began about the same time, some thirty years ago, to reform their city governments. Philadelphia got "good government"—what the Philadelphians call good—from a corrupt ring and quit, satisfied to be a scandal to the nation and a disgrace to democracy. New York has gone on fighting, advancing and retreating, for thirty years till now it has achieved the beginnings, under Mayor Low, of a government for the people. Do the New Yorkers know it? Do they care? They are Americans, mixed and typical; do we Americans really want good government? Or, as I said at starting, have they worked for thirty years along the wrong road—crowded with unhappy American cities—the road to Philadelphia and despair?

15
The Kindergarten of the Streets

The Kindergarten of the Streets

By EDITH DAVIDS

Photographically Illustrated by Oscar Maurer

TO SPUR THE JEWISH BOYS ON BY STORIES OF OTHER BOYS WHO HAVE GROWN UP..

SCHOOL NO. — was tense with excitement. In the class-rooms work went quietly on, but one might have noticed that the quiet was bred of that hush of expectancy which momentarily awaits some vital intelligence. The Fifth Grammar boys were on a strike. The Fifth Grammar boys had been on a strike before, and the classroom had had to be temporarily closed. No. — lies in the section of the East Side district which skirts along the river front. The population of that section is a thing apart. It is not criminal; it is not poor to destitution, except in cases of extreme intemperance; it is not composed of an element conspicuously foreign in character, for most of the people down there are American born, of Irish extraction. But it is "tough"—consciously and gloriously "tough." The boys of No. — are the embodiment of the spirit of their community; the Fifth Grammar boys are the crystallization of that spirit. It is their boast that in any and every decision they carry the school with them. Just now they had decided that a strike was necessary to break the monotony of existence. They had disabled the class teacher and put an army of substitutes to flight. Desperate, the principal had put over them a man selected with a view entirely to pugilistic capacity rather than to pedagogy. But even six feet and two hundred avoirdupois went down before a hail of rotten apples and bricks. The iniquitous fame of the class had gone abroad, so that now no teacher could be induced to

enter into relations with it. In the absence of an instructor, the boys were passing the time pleasantly in their own fashion—vaulting over desks, engaging in bloody contests, and enjoying the discomfiture of the principal.

"I shall have to expel the whole class and close the room," that unfortunate man decided, wearily. "It will demoralize the school, but there is nothing else to be done."

It was an unpleasant decision to have to come to. The principal lingered in his office, reluctant to carry it into effect.

The door opened and a girl came into the room.

"You have a vacancy here for a substitute teacher?" she asked, hesitatingly.

The principal looked the speaker over abstractedly, as from force of long habit. She was small and slender, and looked scarcely

THE WORLD'S LOVELINESS IS A SEALED BOOK TO THEM.

CONSCIOUSLY AND GLOR-
IOUSLY "TOUGH."

eighteen years of age. The lines of weariness and perplexity about his mouth relaxed, and a slow grin crept over his face. He was an Irishman, and he saw the humor of the situation.

"Yes," he said, simply.

Then the grin broadened. He shot himself suddenly into an upright position in his chair. He had an inspiration. He knew that nearly every boy in the Fifth Grammar was of Irish extraction; knew that almost every boy in that class had a sense of humor as keen as his own. Perhaps this small girl was the very thing that would appeal to them.

"Boys," he said a moment later, "this is Miss ——." Then he left.

Sixty boys turned sixty grinning faces on the small teacher. Then from all over the room came softly and in concert the sound of humming to the tune of "There's Only One Girl in the World for Me." A tall boy with twinkling gray eyes and a delighted leer shot up from his seat in the back row and introduced himself.

"I'm Lovett," said he, "the boy that hit the last teacher over the head with a lead pipe. That's why she's absent."

After that the room was mysteriously silent while the teacher moved to the far side to take a book from the closet. When she turned round again, a diminutive youngster was holding up his hand demurely. He was by far the smallest boy in the class, and had a face like a cherub, languid eyelids drooping, curtain-like, over wide, innocent eyes. His little voice had a certain peculiar inflection, which might have been childish timidity and might have been tantalizing, elfish humor.

"Teacher," he announced, "teacher, the whole first section has gone out into the yard."

In the silence, while the teacher's back was turned, fourteen boys had dropped down on all fours and crept out.

The teacher had been initiated into the ways of the Fifth Grammar boys of No. ——.

Fortunately for herself, she possessed a keen sense of humor. It was that which won for her the first battle. During a reading lesson one day the larger boys were creating a disturbance. It was of no use to send them out to be whipped; their home training had been such as made any whipping they might receive at school a frivolous jest. The case seemed almost hopeless. She was only a slip of a girl herself, and some of these larger boys were fourteen and fifteen years old. But she was a keen observer, and noticed that whenever she chanced to touch one of them he would draw back shyly. This suggested the mode of punishment. Calling the largest boy to her, she said:

"Markham, I can't trust you out of my sight. So I'm going to take your arm, and you shall go with me as I move about the room."

The boy's face crimsoned as the teacher took his arm. A suppressed titter rippled through the class-room. A boy directly in front seemed particularly impressed with the humor of the situation. Markham watched his opportunity, and with his disengaged arm landed a punch that would have broken a nose less used to blows.

"Markham," exclaimed the teacher, sternly, "it appears that I can't even trust you

LITTLE MOTHERS.

TINY ITALIAN GIRLS DANCE TO TUNES PLAYED BY THE ORGAN MAN.

when you are at my side. You shall stand right in front of me."

And she placed the boy directly before her. Now the boy was about half as tall again and twice as broad as the girl. He completely concealed her from view. A howl went up from the class that could have been heard all over the school. The teacher collapsed in a chair, breathless with laughter. The noise brought the principal, and in this situation he found them. But he was a man who understood boys, and one glance at their faces told him that the girl had carried the day.

It was somewhat after this manner that one of the two worst boys in the class was vanquished. At first, of so desperate a character was the class, the teacher did not dare to keep any of the boys after school, as, in that event, those on the outside would have pelted the windows with stones. The majority of the boys won over, that obstacle to discipline was no longer to be feared. So she decided one day to keep Flaherty. When the others had all gone, Flaherty was called to a seat before the desk and, left alone, he

and the teacher faced each other. Obviously, the situation struck Flaherty as amusing. He had at all times a most infectious smirk, and now he sat quietly and with an air of bland contentment, twinkling and beaming on the girl. His delight and amusement seemed to increase with every moment. A long silence followed. Flaherty gave an extra beam and an extra twinkle. Then he chuckled softly and delightedly to himself, and asked, in a tone of urbane solicitude:

"Say, ain't you afraid your mother'll think you're lost?"

The teacher's sense of humor overcame her, and she laughed, first at the joke, then, being young, *with* the boy. They laughed together, and from that day they were friends.

The children of the East Side open their eyes to the light amid an environment of Old-World racial picturesqueness and wretchedness, their only heritage of birth fifty generations of foreign tradition and sentiment; for ninety-three per cent. of the dwellers in this district are of foreign parentage. Unlikeness to their small American neighbors of the north and west of town—unlikeness in tem-

A GENEROUS CITY PROVIDES FOR ITS WARDS.

perament, character, and in the attitude they assume toward life—is their distinguishing characteristic. They are born into a land, to begin with, as different from that in which the other children live as though it were beyond the seas. A glimpse of life in the foreign quarter—a mere walk through its streets at sunset—is like stepping into an Old-World scene. While the golden light of the afterglow is fading from the sky, along the streets the bizarre, picturesque life of a foreign people spreads its panorama. Pell-mell in its fantastic confusion, its blending of motley, vivid color, the teeming population of the tenements pours out. The national life of twenty-nine different lands is here in miniature. Hester Street swarms with Jews of a dozen fatherlands—Russians and Poles, Hungarians, Roumanians, Germans—a mosaic of humanity as foreign in garb and feature as if they had never left their outlandish homes. As the night comes down, and one by one the torchlights in the stalls along the curb flame into tongues of golden flame, the long street prospective melts into a sea of shifting light

and color which is the rival in foreignness of any of the street market scenes of Europe. Over in the Italian quarter, Mulberry Street, in its narrowness and its crookedness, might pass for a street in Old Italy were it not for the height and ugliness of its tall tenement rookeries. Italians with faces as beautifully brown, smiles as quick to show the gleam of white teeth, and garments as particolored as though they were at home in their own Naples, lounge in lazy dalliance about the little shops bright with garlands of red peppers, tomatoes, festoons of bologna salame, and clusters of great cheeses. Low stoops are thronged with swart-faced women clad in the purple and green beloved of the races of the South. In their ears are great hoops of gold, showing against black hair which gleams with oily smoothness. And all are gesticulating as gracefully, and talking as volubly, and nursing the children at their breasts as openly, as though they were still in their Neapolitan homes. From the cellars along the street —the eating-places of the quarter—comes the sound of the guitar, a strain of haunting melody, the scent of rose-leaves in its music, the windings of the river in the moonlight, the passion of the storm. In the twilight gloom of a hallway entrance a dark-eyed youth lounges, playing that oldest of old songs, "Santa Lucia." It is all as distinctively Old World as if Broadway, with its long glittering lines of electric illumination, its throngs of fashionable men and women, were three thousand miles away.

With rhythmic grace of movement the children flash in and out among the sombre shadows of East Side life. They have all the pretty graces, the gestures, bows, the little coquettish looks and smiles of Old-World children. The self-consciousness of the small, pert Anglo-Saxon is alien to their temperament. The motley pageant of the streets on a pleasant afternoon, when the children of so many lands are playing in the sunshine, has throughout a rare fascination. But if one

were asked to select the picture most replete with charm, I think it would be that presented by the group of tiny Italian girls who toss back their wealth of black curls as they dance to the tune of an old Spanish waltz played by the organ man. Or perhaps the picture of the old, white-haired priest of the Italian quarter, moving down the street, with a little band of children clinging to his cassock, would best please your fancy. Only over there you will witness the reverential Old-World custom observed by the children in kissing the hand of the parish priest. There, too, you may hear the children, in speaking of a gift bestowed in charity or a service freely rendered, describe it as given —in the beautiful Old-World phrase of the peasant class—" for the love of God."

The life of every child is lived, to a large extent, in a "make-believe" world of its own creation—a realm of the fantastic and the

IN SUMMER THE BAKED STREETS ARE COOLED BY FLUSHING.

SHARING A DAINTY.

when it was given into her small hands, all the wealth of fairy lore between its covers was for a moment forgotten in contemplation of the cover, a dainty design in gray and silver. All thought of the story vanished; the child stood there eying the book with a look that was a caress, her hands just touching the binding, tenderly, as something of fragile beauty. And then, very softly, as if to herself, she said: "I mustn't get it the least little bit dirty. It's *so* pretty."

The language of these foreign children has unique poignancy. Early in the term a teacher in an East Side school had distributed supplementary readers, out of which there had been, as yet, no time to read. She was taking an inventory of books, and desired each child to hand in his supply with "what the book was used for" written on the outside cover. Glancing over the class, she observed a small boy looking with a puzzled, indeterminate expression at his supplementary reader. At length, with a quaint air of finality, he took up his pen, and, "This is a book to have, but not to use," he summarized.

fairylike into which only a few rare grown-ups like Andersen and Lewis Carroll have ever been able to follow. But these Italian children possess a unique prodigality of that imaginative faculty which gives to childhood so many of its golden hours. It expresses itself quaintly in the East Side school-rooms. For example, upon being asked to solve the simple problem, "If a little boy's mamma gave him a penny, and by-and-by his papa gave him another, how many pennies would he have?" it would take the vivid imagination of an Italian child to insist that he had only "one penny."

LITTLE ITALIANS LOVE FORM AND COLOR.

"But what became of the first penny?" finally asks the teacher.

"He lost it," replied the small boy, with the absolute conviction of a highly imaginative child.

An instance of the Italian child's quick, poignant perception of the beautiful occurred the other day in one of the settlement libraries. A shy little maiden, with a world of dream-thoughts in the depths of her dark eyes, stood by the librarian's desk waiting for Andrew Lang's "Gray Fairy Book." But

MEAL-TIME ON THE CURB.

In pithiness the small boy's summary recalls an anecdote of Father Kearney, rector of the Pro-Cathedral on Mulberry Street.

"See that child over there?" said Father Kearney, pointing to a wisp of a "guinnie" seated on the curb across the street. "Well, that child is the pest of my life. He has the passion for collecting bright-colored holy pictures and medals, has Tony, and, since I

" 'Did you give *her* five cents?' he asked.

" 'Yes, Tony.'

" 'Well, my mamma says that she would like five cents.'

" 'Oh, Tony,' said I, 'I'm afraid your mamma is too old to get five cents for her birthday. Besides, I don't believe you know when your mamma's birthday is ; now do you?'

" 'Oh, yes, I do,' eagerly.

THE NATIONAL LIFE OF TWENTY-NINE DIFFERENT LANDS IS HERE.

can remember knowing him, he has never let me escape without giving him one. Oh, my, but the shrewdness of that child ! It's of that I started to tell you.

"I was coming down the street just now," he continued, "when a band of little girls beset me, and said one child meaningly, pointing to a little tot among them :

" 'It's her birthday.'

"The significance of which remark, interpreted, meant that I was to give the little one five cents ; which I did. Little Tony, watching from a distance for an opportune moment to descend upon me for his holy picture, saw this, and farther down the street he accosted me.

" 'Well, when is it, then?'

"Tony didn't have to stop an instant to think. Said he, demurely:

" 'Just now.' "

The hardships which devolve upon the little ones of the East Side are in but comparatively few cases the result of deliberate neglect or cruelty on the part of the parents. Indeed, it is usually the reverse, as in the case of four little girls who, one morning, came into school so thinly clad as to be almost frozen. The youngest had on nothing but a ragged calico dress. Although the snow was on the ground, her legs were bare and she was without a hat.

A CELESTIAL CHERUB.

They had been absent from school two days, and, when questioned, the little one innocently admitted that during that time they had had almost nothing to eat, that there had been no fire at home, and they had merely come to school "to get warm." Investigation showed that the mother, a widow, had struggled on through illness, dire poverty, and discouragement to keep the family together. They lived in an old rear house, and she was obliged to bring from the yard the water to do the washing which she took in to support them. One winter's day she had slipped on the ice while filling her pail at the hydrant. Her knee was badly injured, but the pail of water must be carried upstairs and money made by washing; so, for weeks, she stood on one foot, resting the injured limb on a chair. Immediately after this accident, blood poisoning attacked the fingers of her right hand, and for six weeks the washing was done with one hand. At length work was no longer possible. On the morning in question, there had been no fuel nor food in the house for several days, and the family was about to be turned out into the streets.

The first seven years of the life of the East Side child, before he is old enough to go to school, are lived practically upon the streets. In the most densely packed city quarter in all the world, life during the day is so crowded, so desperately busy with the sorting of rags and the making of garments, that there is no place for him within doors. When the stifling night-air brings no relief from the burning heat of the day, the barracks of the tenements are more like huge ovens than homes. And far into the midnight, hours after

The Rock-a-By Lady from Hush-a-By Street,
With poppies that hang from her head to her feet,
    Comes stealing, comes creeping

into the child-realm of the closely drawn white curtain and the shaded lamp, the little East Siders are kept up and out-of-doors because the rooms are unendurable. The tiny girl of four that I found on Monroe Street one night at two o'clock going round and round, with one arm encircling a barber's pole, and singing softly and happily to herself, "Ring around a Rosey," presents a picture not uncommon in the streets of the foreign quarter long after the midnight hour has rung out over the city. The streets are the only nursery these children know. They have no places for play within four picture-covered walls. Most of them never even hear of Central Park, where the little folk in smart frocks and gay sashes frolic on the green. I have seen a group of East Side youngsters hanging, open-mouthed, upon the descriptions of an adventure-loving, intrepid gamin who had travelled to that far-off wonderland as breathlessly as if he were a living Munchausen. Familiar only with the sights and sounds of the streets, the world's loveliness is a sealed book to them. A little band was waiting in the Grand Central Station for the train that was to bear them to the country home of one of the settlements. They were clad in their most brilliant finery for this gala occasion, and the small faces shone with the joy of anticipation. One solemn-looking little chap of seven, however, stood out in oddly grave relief against the radiant background. He gazed about him, with wide eyes, at the marble magnificence of the great depot, at the throng of well-dressed men and women, at the little gayly attired aristocrats. Then slowly he relaxed into an attitude of happy contentment, and two small hands were folded in demure satisfaction as he asked, softly, "Is this the country?"

It is often said of the older children of the

East Side that their worst trait is uncleanliness. But what can be expected when the early years of many have been absolutely unruffled by any disturbing element in the shape of soap and water, brushes and combs? This condition was forcibly evidenced when the good pastor of an uptown congregation, visiting a mission school, essayed to recite to the children the story of the prodigal son. Ardently he tried to contrast the condition of the prodigal when he left home arrayed in purple and fine linen and his condition when he returned. The children listened breathlessly to the recital of his glittering departure. "And when he came back home," queried the clergyman, running his hands over his clothing in a manner meant to be suggestive of rags, "he was all covered with—?" And out of the fulness of their experience of life, from all over the room came breathlessly the answer, "Bugs."

Long before they can possibly comprehend their meaning, the small East Siders are familiar with the form of words which stand for adversity. Just before the school season closed, a bright little fellow brought into his class-room a number of mud pies and two diminutive figures which he had modelled. "Here's a man and a woman," he said, "made out of dirt, just like Adam and Eve." Asked why he had made them so tiny, the little fellow explained, soberly: "Oh, I couldn't make 'em no bigger, 'cause times is hard."

Perhaps you have never stopped to realize that to the trimness and tranquillity about everything in the quiet house that stood in the midst of the old-fashioned garden of your own childhood; the little white bedroom with the fresh muslin curtains at the window parting to show the snowy blossoms of the pear tree in late April; the cool shadowy parlor with the shutters carefully bowed to keep out the bright sunlight; the well-kept garden where time, fragrance-laden, seemed to move so slowly that on warm June

afternoons it almost stood still; that to these early influences might be traced your love of a tranquil, well-ordered life. For inevitably the early familiar shapes one's ideals. Next to want and lack of privacy, the absence of tranquillity constitutes a prime factor in the East Side child's early familiar. This absence of tranquillity begets a restlessness which seeks an outlet in adventure. And as theft is the form of adventure most commonly known to the small East Sider, he becomes only too eager to enter the "Fagin" schools —by no means uncommon on the East Side —where boys, and sometimes girls, are trained as pickpockets. His story is already written, a story which will read like that of the young man of thirty rescued by Mrs. Booth of the Salvation Army. It was on Christmas-eve that he came to thank her. "To-morrow," he said, "will be my first Christmas outside of prison walls since I was a child of ten."

The little East Sider is pretty sure of at least a modicum of education; for the foreign parents realize that knowledge—especially knowledge of the language—is power. In the class-room, as on the street, the conflicting racial characteristics of the children of different nationalities, the influence of heredity, home-life, and environment, are all strikingly exemplified. The teachers soon come to

THE FIRST SEVEN YEARS . . . ARE LIVED PRACTICALLY UPON THE STREETS.

realize that the surest way to spur the Jewish boys on to renewed efforts in their studies is to tell them constantly stories of the positions of power and wealth which await boys who have the education to fill them, stories of other boys who have grown up to fill such positions. This method does not appeal at all to the dreamy, indolent Italian children. They can best be reached by an appeal to their love of pure scholarship, their appreciation of the artistic, of rhythm and music, of the beauty of form and color. With nothing in their unlovely lives to awaken a spark of artistic creativeness, once given a glimpse of artistic procedure in the modelling and drawing classes, they display that marvellous talent for creation which is their heritage of race, and which has outlived the degradation of fifty generations. The children of the East Side, and especially the Hungarians, have a

wonderful gift of language. They have, on the whole, a quicker, finer instinct of scholarship than have the children of the other side of town. The records of the settlement libraries show a remarkable love of books and reading among them. For one day the circulation of a certain library—and this is one of the very smallest settlements—numbered 424 volumes. Fairy tales, which are the delight of the young folk of every land, appeal especially to the romantic, imaginative foreign children. But these little people do a deal of reading in poetry and history; history being far more popular among them than with American or English children of corresponding age.

In the whole history of pathetic childhood, the saddest chapter is the story of the "Little Mothers" of the East Side. Scores of small girls, from five to twelve years old, are kept at home to assist their mothers in sweatshop work and to care for the babies. A scene in illustration of the premature sense of responsibility of these children was enacted one morning recently in an East Side court. It was when little May Corbett, aged twelve, came forward, leading her little brother Johnnie by the hand, and, approaching the magistrate, said she "wanted to put Johnnie in a home"; that her mamma was unable to come to court "because she is paralyzed. Johnnie," she added, "is getting to be a bad boy." It was ascertained that the commitment of the boy was the wish of the mother as well as of the little May.

If the babies are not too noisy, the "Little Mothers" sometimes bring their charges to the schoolroom. It is a touching picture that is presented by a child nine or ten years old supporting in her arms a sleeping brother or sister, and at the same time trying to write a lesson. One of these, a little girl of

"THEY HAVE ALL THE PRETTY GRACES . . . OF OLD-WORLD CHILDREN."

THE DANCING-SCHOOL OF THE TENEMENTS.

OUT-OF-DOORS BECAUSE THE ROOMS ARE UNENDURABLE.

cases, remain all their lives aliens in a strange land, among a strange people whose language they do not understand. There is something pathetically incongruous in the tender solicitude with which these young ones watch over their parents, endeavoring to shield them from the strange things all about. I witnessed a touching instance of this reversal of the natural relations between parent and child not long ago. It was in one of the great hospitals. A Yiddish man was being exhibited before a clinic. His shoulders were stooped with premature age, induced by hard and unremitting toil, and his face, showing above the dark beard, was white and haggard with suffering. Evidently the treatment hurt much, for he cried out in Yiddish in a heart-rending manner. He could speak no word of our language, and with him was his little daughter, who acted as interpreter. As her father's cries pierced the room, the child's lips quivered and her eyes sought mine in mute appeal. "He's never been sick before," she said, with a quaint touch of motherliness, "and he was always so good to us." "You cannot judge of this man's suffering by his outcries," the lecturer was saying; "generations of low breeding—" and there was a curl about the great physician's lips. But irresistibly my eyes were drawn back to the quivering lips, the white, drawn little face of the child who stood there, the central figure of a picture beneath which might fittingly have been written the words, "And He took a little child and set it in their midst."

ten, pleaded to be admitted to the cooking class. The teacher questioned the child as to why she wanted to learn to cook. She explained that she had no mother, and, being the eldest of the family, took care of the home. She did the washing and ironing, and looked after two younger children. Poor little girl! "She didn't know only a little bit how to cook," she said, and it was in order to learn how to better prepare the meals at home that she pleaded so hard to enter the class.

Often it is not only the younger brothers and sisters that they must care for. Picking up the language and the customs of the American people on the street and in the public schools, they come to exercise a sort of protection over their parents, who, in many

16
New York from the Flatiron

MUNSEY'S MAGAZINE.

JULY, 1905.

NEW YORK FROM THE FLATIRON.

BY EDGAR SALTUS.

THE MOST EXTRAORDINARY PANORAMA IN THE WORLD—A SURVEY
OF THE AMERICAN METROPOLIS FROM ITS FOCAL POINT AT THE
CROSSING OF ITS TWO MOST FAMOUS THOROUGHFARES,
BROADWAY AND FIFTH AVENUE.

"WHAT do you know of New York?"
said one wanderer to another.
"Only what I have read in Dante,"
was the bleak reply.

Dante told of the inferno. He told,
too, of paradise. Manhattan may typify
both. It represents other things also.
The latter, mainly, are superlatives.
From the top floors of the Flatiron you
get an idea of a few. On one side is

Madison Square Garden and Tower.　　　East River.　　　Long Island City.

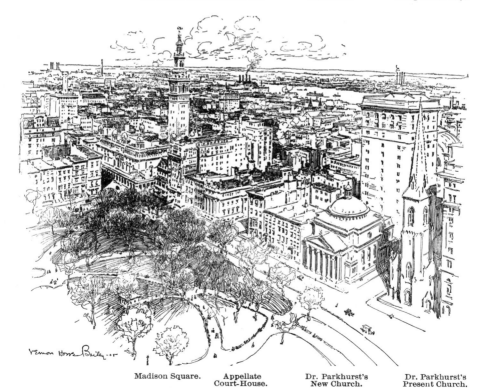

Madison Square.　　Appellate　　Dr. Parkhurst's　　Dr. Parkhurst's
　　　　　　　　　Court-House.　　New Church.　　Present Church.

VIEW FROM THE UPPER FLOORS OF THE FLATIRON BUILDING, LOOKING TO THE NORTHEAST ACROSS
MADISON SQUARE TO THE UPPER EAST SIDE OF NEW YORK AND THE EAST RIVER,
WITH LONG ISLAND IN THE DISTANCE.

Broadway. Barring trade routes, Broadway is the longest commercial stretch on the planet. On the other side is Fifth Avenue. Barring nothing, Fifth Avenue

The beetles are cabs; the ants are beings—primitive but human, full of soap-bubble loves and hates, of ephemeral cares and joys as insecure, hurrying

Greenpoint.　　　　　　　　　　East River.

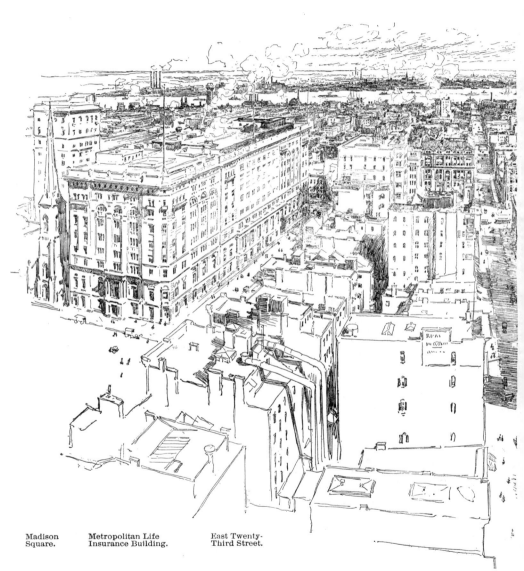

Madison Square.　　Metropolitan Life Insurance Building.　　East Twenty-Third Street.

VIEW FROM THE FLATIRON BUILDING, LOOKING TO THE EAST, AND ACROSS THE EAST RIVER TO GREENPOINT AND WILLIAMSBURG—

is the richest thoroughfare in the world. From the top floors of the Flatiron each looks meager, almost mean. In them are things that you would take for beetles, others that seem to you ants.

grotesquely over the most expensive spot on earth. They hurry because everybody hurries, because haste is in the air, in the effrontery of the impudent "step lively," in the hammers of the ceaseless skyscrapers ceaselessly going up, in the ambient neurosis, in the scudding motors, in the unending noise, the pervading scramble, the metallic roar of the city.

the west is a fourth. Beneath them are great ocher brutes of cars, herds of them, stampeding violently with grinding grunts, and, on the microbish pave-

Williamsburg. New East River Bridge. Brooklyn.

East Twenty-Second Street. All Souls' Church. American Lithograph Building.

—ON THE RIGHT, IN THE DISTANCE, IS THE LOWER EAST SIDE OF NEW YORK, A DENSELY CROWDED WILDERNESS OF SWARMING TENEMENTS.

Beyond is the slam-bang of the Sixth Avenue Elevated careering up-town and down, both ways at once. Parallelly is the Subway, rumbling relentlessly. Farther east are two additional slam-bangers. To

ments, swarms such as Dante may indeed have seen, but not in paradise.

In the morning they are there, scurrying to their toil; at high noon to their food; at evening to their homes; at night

Brooklyn   Skyscrapers of
Bridge.   lower New York.

VIEW FROM THE FLATIRON BUILDING, LOOKING TO THE SOUTHEAST, DOWN BROADWAY TO UNION
SQUARE AND BEYOND.

Skyscrapers of lower New York.   Staten Island.   Statue of Liberty.   Pennsylvania Station.   Jersey City.

VIEW FROM THE FLATIRON BUILDING, LOOKING TO THE SOUTHWEST, DOWN LOWER FIFTH AVENUE.

to amusements more laborious than their work. When they are not there you do not know it. Save at night, when the crowd moves elsewhere, always are there

rearing its knifish face with the same disdain of the ephemeral that the Sphinx displays, knowing that she has all time as we all have our day.

Jersey City.   Hoboken.   Castle Point.   Orange Mountain (in distance).

Sohmer Building.   West Twenty-Second Street.

VIEW FROM THE FLATIRON BUILDING, LOOKING WESTWARD TO THE HUDSON RIVER AND BEYOND IT TO THE NEW JERSEY SUBURBS—

compact throngs, always are there streams of incarnated preoccupations, pouring from whence you cannot say, to where you cannot tell; human streams which the Flatiron cleaves indifferently,

Ages ago the Sphinx was disinterred from beneath masses of sand under which it had brooded interminably. Yet in its simian paws, its avian wings, in its body which is that of animal, in its face which is that of a seer, there, before Darwin, before history, by a race that has left no other souvenir, in traits great and grave, the descent of man was told.

cisely as these huts were once regarded as supreme achievements, so, one of these days, from other and higher floors, the Flatiron may seem a hut itself.

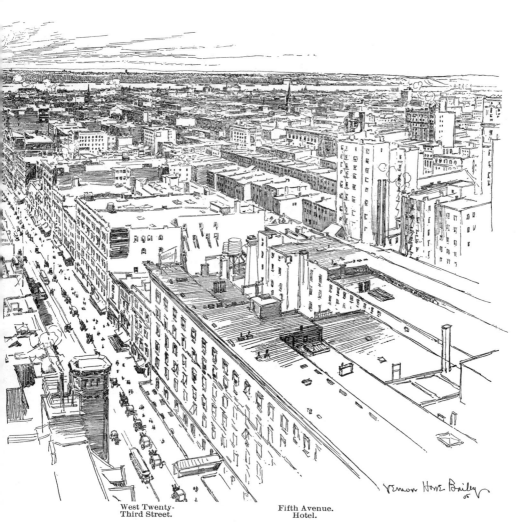

Weehawken. West Shore Station. The Palisades. Subway Power-House.

West Twenty-Third Street. Fifth Avenue. Hotel.

—THE RETAIL SHOPPING DISTRICT OF NEW YORK CENTERS AT ABOUT THIS POINT; IMMEDIATELY ABOVE IT (TO THE RIGHT) BEGINS THE REGION OF HOTELS AND THEATERS.

There remained his ascent. Ages hence the Flatiron may tell it. For as you lean and gaze from the toppest floors on houses below, which from those floors seem huts, it may occur to you that pre-

Evolution has not halted. Undiscernibly but indefatigably, always it is progressing. Its final term is not in existing buildings or in existing man. If humanity sprang from gorillas, from humanity

Upper
Broadway.

Victoria
Hotel.

Upper Fifth
Avenue.

Belmont
Hotel.

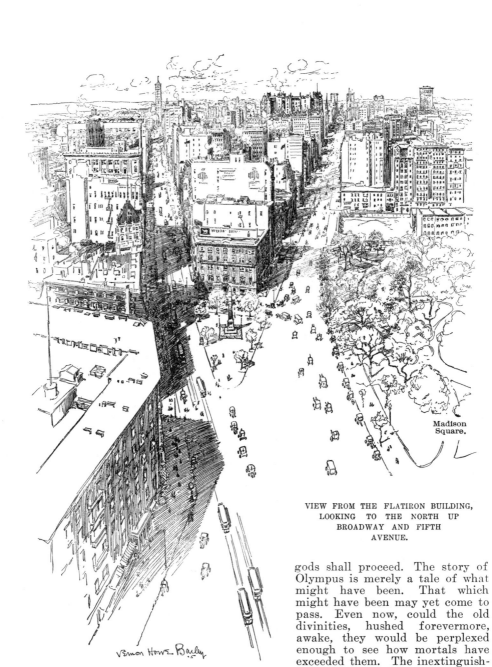

Madison
Square.

Fifth Avenue
Hotel.

Worth
Monument.

VIEW FROM THE FLATIRON BUILDING,
LOOKING TO THE NORTH UP
BROADWAY AND FIFTH
AVENUE.

gods shall proceed. The story of
Olympus is merely a tale of what
might have been. That which
might have been may yet come to
pass. Even now, could the old
divinities, hushed forevermore,
awake, they would be perplexed
enough to see how mortals have
exceeded them. The inextinguish-
able laughter which was theirs is
absent from the prose of life.
Commerce has alarmed their

afflatus away. But the telegraph is a better messenger than they had, the motor is surer than their chariots of dream. In Fifth Avenue inns they could get fairer fare than ambrosia, and behold women beside whom Venus would look provincial and Juno a frump. The spectacle of electricity tamed and domesticated would surprise them not a little, the Elevated quite as much, the Flatiron still more. At sight of the latter they would recall the Titans with whom once they warred, and slink to their sacred seas outfaced.

In the same measure that we have succeeded in exceeding them, so will posterity surpass what we have done. Evolution may be slow, but it is sure; yet, however slow, it achieved an unrecognized advance when it devised buildings such as this. It is demonstrable that small rooms breed small thoughts. It will be demonstrable that as buildings ascend so do ideas. It is mental progress that skyscrapers engender. From these parturitions gods may really proceed—beings, that is, who, could we remain long enough to see them, would regard us as we regard the apes.

Meanwhile, on those toppest floors, the eager sun, aslant, shuttles the mounting roar. In the noise and glare you need but a modicum of imagination to fancy yourself contemplating a volcano in active operation, one that is erupting gold, coining dollars in its depths, and tossing them in the crystalline air—whence they fall, as rain falls, on those who know enough not to come in, who get in the way, fight for a place, and hold it until they have made their pile. It is not of course from such as these that gods shall come, rather a race similar to the curious dwarfs of whom Pliny told, pygmies that passed their lives fighting with phantoms for coin. So, too, fight those that you behold from the toppest floors. The struggle is the impetus of their little lives, the substance of their loves and hates; it is the magnet that draws them from regions quasi-polar, wholly tropical, from zones remoter yet, from those nethermost planes where Dante went.

Above them, indifferently, the Flatiron looms. Semi-animate as the motor is, superhuman, vibrant with a life of its own, from its hundred eyes it stares. Below is Madison Square, circled with hotels, clubs, apartment houses, office-buildings, and a church. The church is that of Dr. Parkhurst. The vast building adjacent is an insurance company's—the Metropolitan Life. On the white

corner above is the Appellate Division of the State Supreme Court. On the next corner is the Madison Square Garden, the home of the horseshow, the circus, and the French ball. To the north and east gasp a few surviving huts. To the left, on Broadway, is the Fifth Avenue Hotel. In days gone by it was a great place for honeymoons. Now it is even a greater place for politicians of the Republican brand. A bit above is the Hoffman House, which the haunted Stokes made agreeable for everybody in general and for Democrats in particular. Higher up on Broadway are other hostelries either equally famous or with the future in which to accumulate renown, the old Gilsey for instance, the older Victoria, the new Astor, and the Breslin newer still. On Fifth Avenue are more, the Holland, the Waldorf, the St. Regis. There, too, is the Knickerbocker Trust Company, quite Greek in appearance, and Tiffany's, which is quite as French.

Of the two thoroughfares, Broadway is the older. Originally called the Breede Weg, it began with the beginning of things, when New York was Nieu Amsterdam and talked Dutch instead of slang. The incipiency of Fifth Avenue is more modern. It occurred a little prior to the Civil War. A bit later a residence thereon was endearingly regarded as quite equivalent to a title. As far as it went—and, until within relatively recent years, it did not straggle much above Forty-Second Street—it was a wholly residential stretch of brown-stone fronts.

The first to put a shop on the holy site was Mrs. Paran Stevens. The deed, highly radical, was regarded as sacrilege. The late Mr. Lorillard, a tobacco merchant, objected strenuously. Said Mrs. Stevens, who was quick with her tongue: "You would not mind, now, would you, if it were a tobacco shop?"

Then Mr. Lorillard shut up. But that which the lady began others continued, the result being that residentially Fifth Avenue has moved from Washington Square to the Plaza.

West of it is the river to which Hudson came, viewing from his little boat silent spaces crammed now with tooting craft, where dock liners leviathan as skyscrapers. Further up are the Palisades. Further down is Staten Island, between which and Manhattan the original Vanderbilt pursued, like Sappho's lover, the highly genteel avocation of ferryman, landing his fares where rises the Immigration Bureau to-day and where the primal skyscrapers began.

Thence upward with the stream of life the city flows, halting occasionally, occasionally too circumscribed, as in the lower East Side, which is a caldron, or in the Chinese quarter, which is a sewer. Over the way there is a glimpse of the nameless shames of architectural Long Island, the infinite horrors of Williamsburg. Yet with the glimpse comes the saving savor of the salt of the sea. There are compensating vistas also, the pillars of the Brooklyn Bridge, the statue of Liberty, the high Byzantine dome on Park Row, more distantly the roof of the Pennsylvania Railway station, a roof presently to be duplicated not far from the Grand Central, in front of which already rises the unfinished Belmont House, the tallest of tall hotels.

Intermediately, a half dozen streets to the rear of the Flatiron, lies Union Square, a bedlam of business and traffic, but which within the memory of the present writer was a sedate residential quarter, girdled with balconied houses that were festooned with honeysuckle bursting in the eager spring. The peace that was there survives still in New York, but only in Gramercy Park and lower Fifth Avenue, which latter, fusing at Fourteenth Street with the general pandemonium, knows no respite until it reaches the auriferous precincts above the St. Regis and the Plaza, where the newer plutocracy resides.

Indifferently on these things the Flatiron stares. Its front is lifted to the future. On the past its back is turned. Of what has gone before it is American in its unconcern. Monstrous yet infantile, it is a recent issue of the gigantic upheaval that is transforming the whole city, and which will end by making it a curiosity to which people will come and stare as they do at cataracts and big caves and great trees and fat women and whatever else is abnormal. Yet the changes, however disconcerting, are but tokens of others to be. In certain aspects New York still preserves its old colonial squalor. In others it presents the hasty hideousness of boom towns. In the lingering streets of brown-stone fronts it is embryonic still. Near the rivers it has thoroughfares and avenues which, in ruthless atrocity and shuddersome ugliness, are nightmares in stone. But these are as measles and mumps to a child. They are not definite conditions. Nor is there, nor will there be, anything definite here until, from the Battery to the Plaza, the buildings one and all are so huge that nothing huger is possible.

Existing department stores are, one might think, sufficient in dimensions. Not a bit of it. A new one is planned that is to cover an entire square from Fifth Avenue to Madison, and to approach the Flatiron's height. The massiveness of that will be duplicated, triplicated, multiplied over the town. Sooner or later there, where now are, say, eighty or a hundred buildings to a square there will be but one. After the fashion of a Broadway department store which, outgrowing the square it occupies, has reached out and subterraneously annexed a building across the way—after this suggestive fashion it is indicated that emporiums of the future will cover two squares—three, perhaps; that no hotel, no apartment house or office-building will be really content with less than one, and that however it may be elsewhere, on the thirty-five streets between Twenty-Third Street and the Plaza, Fifth Avenue will contain not many more than seventy structures, about one to each square, structures extending back on the west to Broadway or Sixth Avenue, on the east to Madison, with, on these arteries, similar structures, similarly extending, repeating themselves to the river fronts.

That is what people will come to see. It will be horrible; but analyze the horrible, and sometimes you find the sublime, again the unique, occasionally the commercial. The three derivatives present here will provide a spectacle shameful and superb, a congerie of temples for the deification of gold, a city of basilicas for the glory of greed. In somnolent Nieu Amsterdam, Nicholas was patron saint. These shall be the gods of Manhattan. Yet are not its deities now these divinities, whose worship is haste, whose incense is noise, and whose swarming suppliants you mistake, from those upper floors, for insects?

Tennyson compared humanity to so many gnats in the glare of a million million of suns. Insects they are. But they shall pass as Nieu Amsterdam passed, as passed the race unknown that left the Sphinx.

In their stead will be beings more august. In the mounting wonders of the city to be, humanity will mount also. It will deny its false gods, reverse their altars, and, on the pile it has made, reconstruct Olympus. From the toppest floors you get a vision of that in the significant sunsets and prophetic dawns. You see strange things from the Flatiron.

17
The New York Athletic Club

THE NEW YORK ATHLETIC CLUB.

BY MALCOLM W. FORD.

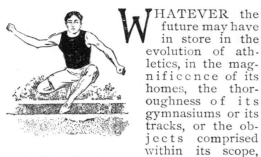

WHATEVER the future may have in store in the evolution of athletics, in the magnificence of its homes, the thoroughness of its gymnasiums or its tracks, or the objects comprised within its scope, the New York Athletic Club will forever hold the proud position of having been the pioneer organization of America. Indeed, its claim may be vastly widened, and, of a truth, it may be said to be the first club in the world that combined the preparation for and the performance of deeds of endurance with the social attributes of a club.

Man the world over, at least refined, cultivated, and educated man has the clubbable instinct. He is gregarious, and like will gather with like. In other lands this segregation had mainly been round politics or art or letters. True, the Alpine Club approached athletics as its raison, but it was left to America, and, in the result, to the New York Athletic Club, to gather together in a permanent home those whose motive of meeting was the cultivation of the human body for endurance, by healthful exercises and friendly competitions.

The magnificent pile facing New York's Central Park into which this oldest and largest athletic club in the world moved last spring compels the attention of the merest passer-by, and to those who for the first time pass within its portals, as well as for its thousands of members and a wider general public, the questions of how this tremendous organization originated, what started it, and how the promoters first managed to gain a material foothold in public favor, are of intense interest.

England has had her amateur athletes as far back as authentic history chronicles, although it has only been during the present century that athletic sport there has been correctly compiled; but in this country nothing in the way of amateur athletics was known of until the formation of the New York Athletic Club thirty years ago. It was not long after the civil war in America, which at the time of its progress engrossed all minds here, that the nation settled down and became ready for any form of pleasure which it had the inclination or time to engage in. The New York Athletic Club was conceived by a band of strong men who met in an off-hand way in their own various rooms, to contest in feats of strength.

EXTERIOR OF CLUB-HOUSE, FROM CENTRAL PARK.

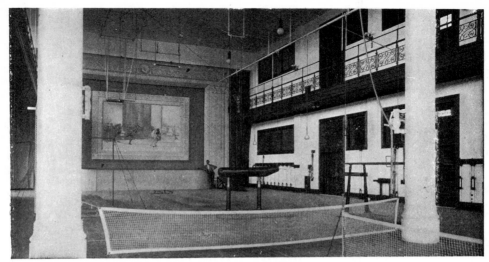

THE GYMNASIUM.

To be exact, it was on September 8, 1868, that the club was organized in the bachelor apartments of W. B. Curtis and John C. Babcock, who resided in what was then called the up-town district of New York, Fourteenth street, corner of Sixth avenue, now occupied by R. H. Macy & Co., a very busy part of the city of to-day, very much down-town for residential purposes.

A call had been sent around among a few intimate friends, and the regular organization was effected, when the following officers were elected: President, J. Edward Russell; Vice - President, John C. Babcock; Secretary, Henry A. Hires; Treasurer, Henry E. Buermeyer. The organization soon gave evidence of its vitality by deciding to hold an athletic meeting in the following November, in the building then standing at Third avenue and Sixty-

THE SWIMMING-POOL.

ALFRED H. CURTIS.

third street, known as the Empire Rink, and there the first athletic meeting ever held in America was in due course brought to the test. It was a very peculiar meeting compared with those of the modern day. The 100-yard run, and, in fact, all of the races, were started by the tap of a drum. The results were most satisfactory to the originators, and the club has never failed to hold annual games since then. In its thirty years of active life not a single year has passed when the club did not hold games and give other attractions in an athletic way. Other amateur athletic clubs have come and gone, some having only a meteoric career, while others have lasted long enough to show that in the vicinity where they lived there was more or less demand for an athletic rendezvous. But the N. Y. A. C has not a single failure in its life's existence scored against it, and it is doubtful if anything can now arise to retard its prosperous growth.

The first of the aggressive acts which mark like milestones the path of success which the club has ever marched, was taken when it added rowing to its subjects. With this object the club acquired a good boat-house on the Harlem River and concurrently leased a piece of property behind it on which to lay out a track. It was crude compared with present day-tracks, but it was handy to the boat-house, and in proportion to the

club's membership it was patronized a good deal. These grounds became the celebrated "Mott Haven" of amateur athletics and collegiate sports, and up to the time of the club's vacating them, when Travers Island was ready for occupancy, were considered the best grounds in this vicinity.

The club's first open games, where outsiders were allowed to compete, were held on grounds at 130th street and Third avenue, Saturday, May 27, 1871. The events were :

100-yard run, half-mile run, one-mile run, three-mile run and three-mile walk. The 100-yard run was won by Elliott Burris, no time. The half-mile run was won by F. H. Hyres in 2m. 23¼s., and the one-mile run by Francis S. Kinney in 5m. 25s. The three-mile walk was captured by Henry E. Buermeyer in 30m. 42½s., and the three-mile run was won by Francis S. Kinney, who covered the first mile in 5m. 47½s., and the two miles in 12m. 45s., the other contestants dropping out and the race not being finished. Among others who competed were B. E. Gafney, E. B. Gregory, D. D. Wylie, W. E. Van Wyck, C. Y. Rosevelt, Charles H. Cone, Paul A. Curtis, P. R. Stetson and H. S. Truax.

The ten oldest members of the club are as follows, with their numbers and dates of joining :

No.		
1. Paul Allan Curtis,	Sept.	8, 1868.
2. John H. Stead,	March	15, 1870.
3. Albert H. Wheeler,	Sept.	15, 1870.
4. William E. McCready,	Nov.	9, 1870.
5. R. Wm. Rathbone,	June	14, 1871.
6. Walter K. Collins,	Nov.	8, 1871.
7. Alfred H. Curtis,	March	15, 1872.
8. Waldo Sprague,	Sept.	4, 1872.
9. Daniel M. Stern,	Nov.	5, 1872.
10. James R. Curran,	Sept.	9, 1874.

Athletics were engaged in on the Mott Haven grounds in a very informal

HERMANN OELRICHS.

A MOTT HAVEN MEMORY.

1. William G. Morse.　2. George H. Taylor.　3. C. A. J. Queckberner.　4. Charles A. Reed.　5. Malcolm W. Ford.
6. Nelson A. Stewart.　7. S. T. Wainwright.　8. Herman E. Toussaint.

way, and the Saturday and Sunday crowds were very much of the same kind who now go to Travers Island, except that whoever visited Mott Haven was an athlete in some way or other. There was no other attraction besides the boat-houses, swimming, track and field. With no other class of men in the club than this it could be seen that the club was a purely athletic one, and it remained so up to 1882, hardly encouraging a feature outside of physical strength and activity. In other words, if a man did not take an active part in physical development, he would have very little use for the New York Athletic Club prior to 1882.

This condition was justifiable and perhaps necessary in the early stages of its existence, but in half a dozen years all around the eastern part of this country, but more especially in the vicinity of New York

SIX OF THE ANCIENTS.

1. Elliot Burris.　3. Wm. B. Curtis.　5. Chas. H. Cone.
2. George J. Brown.　4. Daniel M. Stern.　6. H. E. Buermeyer.

City, amateur athletic clubs came into existence, and athletic games were being held so often that dates conflicted, and there was more or less of a slack in the tide of the steady and rapid development of the New York Athletic Club.

The big club held its own through all this competition, but the leading spirits in it became restless over its condition. They would fain retain their original position as the first, and several of the more far-sighted members commenced promulgating plans which would make the club as impregnable during the days of great competition as it was when it had the field entirely to itself. It was not sufficient that it should be surrounded by the *éclat* which has always been connected with it; that its games were always good, its members were always looked upon as athletic experts, business men and gentlemen, who always figured largely as officials at other games ; it was felt that the club should grow and something had to be done to keep it from retrograding. Members had to be attracted, and how to do this was the great question.

The shrewd and fertile brain of one of the stanchest members, who is also among the ten oldest ones and the brother of the oldest one, came into play at this time, and to him credit must be given for starting the movement which has resulted in the club growing from 123 active members to 3,000, besides non-resident members and life members. Mr. Alfred H. Curtis had figured as the club's secretary and captain on a number of occasions, and had always been among the first to lend the club a helping hand in getting members, giving games, and creating general interest. He knew that the quarters occupied by the club, although all right for athletics, were entirely insufficient to attract members. To him, however,

W. R. TRAVERS, EX-PRESIDENT.

amateur sport was a noble subject, and he felt that average business men would become patrons of the sport if the subject were laid before them in a way that appealed to them.

At this time the club, outside of its athletic quarters, had so-called permanent rooms in the old Crescent Club, a political organization on West Twenty-third street. These rooms were small and dark, although there was a fairly well-equipped gymnasium, billiard tables and other club privileges. Everything was on a small scale. It was conceded by all interested in the club that the only way to get members interested

in athletics, but not competitors, was to build a suitable rendezvous. The question was asked : " How can we do it ? " " Such a few of us cannot float the scheme." " We have not financial standing enough." But a start had to be made.

The first prize captured was credited to Mr. Curtis, who succeeded in interesting Mr. Hermann Oelrichs, whom every one knew then as a patron of the highest kind of gentlemen's sport, and a man needing no description so far as his business and social standing is concerned. Mr. Oelrichs, with his large acquaintance and reputation as an unusually fine swimmer, boxer and polo player, was just the name that would surely attract others.

And so it transpired. The club took on a new lease of life almost from the day Mr. Oelrichs in 1882 became a member, and although the fact was not heralded, still the undercurrent commenced to form which drew in the club's ranks the most prominent and successful men in New York City and vicinity.

The next feather in Mr. Curtis's cap, after proposing Mr. Oelrichs, was in engaging the attention of Mr. William R. Travers, whose name in clubs, society and sport was identical with Mr. Oelrichs's, augmented, however, by many more years of age and experience. Although Mr. Curtis was the one who first spoke to Mr. Travers about joining,.and who eventually proposed his name, still he frankly admits that had it not been for Mr. Oelrichs the " old gentleman " never would have taken the interest he did. Any one familiar with the general life, characteristics and associations of Mr. Travers and Mr. Oelrichs can see that this may be so.

After Mr. Travers joined, then came another tug-of-war to get him to be president. Here again is where Mr. Oelrichs rendered invaluable service. The president at this time was Mr. D. Henry Knowlton, now deceased, much esteemed by the members, and who was ready to step out when a better man could be secured. Mr. Curtis laid the matter of the presidency before Mr. Travers and then rested on his oars. Mr. Oelrichs won the "old gentleman" around by talking to him for several hours about it in the Union Club one night, and several days after Mr. Curtis received the following letter, written from another club which Mr. Travers was president of :

RACQUET AND TENNIS COURT CLUB,
55 WEST TWENTY-SIXTH STREET,
April 27, 1882.

MY DEAR MR. CURTIS:

Your very kind and complimentary letter of the 13th, asking me to accept the honor of the presidency of the New York Athletic Club, only reached me yesterday afternoon.

While very sensible of the compliment paid me, I am not of the opinion that I can be of much service to the club. Still, as you and my friend, Mr. Hermann Oelrichs, both think so, and also assure me that this is the opinion of others, and as I am and always will be most anxious to aid and promote athletic exercises, I shall have great pleasure in accepting the position and in endeavoring to fulfill the duties of it to the best of my ability.   Yours very truly,
                                W. R. TRAVERS.

To A. H. CURTIS.

The effect of Mr. Travers' becoming president of the club commenced to be felt in a most material way. All the old workers for the club had a magnificent argument to present to their friends to join it. All they had to say was that " Hermann Oelrichs and Old Man Travers are members, and the latter is president," and any one who was in the least interested in club life and sport, and who could afford it, would sign an application for membership. The example was contagious and the roll of members increased as if by magic.

By the early part of 1883 propositions for a new club-house had assumed such shape that it resulted in negotiations being commenced for raising the money necessary for the purpose. Seventy-five thousand dollars was raised among the members on bonds, and a site was purchased, corner of Sixth avenue and Fifty-fifth street, seventy-five feet on the avenue and one hundred feet on the street. Then came the question of

BARTOW S. WEEKS, EX-PRESIDENT.

raising the money necessary to put up a building, and when, at a special meeting, it was announced that a large financial institution would advance one hundred and twenty-five thousand dollars, Mr. Travers, in his characteristic way, on hearing the news, said : " That's fine, boys, and if you need twenty or twenty-five thousand dollars more for incidentals, I will advance it." It is needless to describe how the feeling was at this meeting when it was decided

JAMES WHITELY, PRESIDENT.

to go ahead with the first permanent home of the club. No one saw anything but prosperity for the club, and the membership was soon raised to one thousand five hundred, so large was the waiting list.

When the club was getting ready to move into its first permanent home in the winter of 1885, an act of generosity was done by Mr. Oelrichs unparalleled in the club's history. Like all organizations engaged in building and equipping a new, large structure, this club had no more money than was actually needed to fulfill contracts, and yet it had had such a marvelous growth, and stood so high in the community,

the head of the club, and the whole affair attracted so much attention that applications for membership poured in faster than ever, and the limit of membership was raised, at a special meeting, from one thousand five hundred to two thousand. On the occasion of this special meeting the power of Mr. Travers was shown in a most forcible way. As is usual in all such cases, there was tremendous opposition on the part of many to increasing the membership. The arguments were that the club did not need more members, it had plenty of money and sufficient annual revenue to make its future assured, etc., and it looked, on the whole, as though the

SCENE FROM THE DINING-ROOM WINDOW, OVERLOOKING CENTRAL PARK.

that it was most fitting that a reception should be held on the doors being opened. Mr. Oelrichs was then a member of the Building Committee and Chairman of the House Committee, and so great was his interest in the success of the organization that he personally offered to foot the bills for the reception, and it was given in the name of the House Committee. The entertainment was an appropriate one for the occasion, and the six thousand dollars which it cost never found a place on the club's books.

This incident is mentioned to show what the general feeling was in those days by the class of men who were at

amendment increasing the membership would be lost, so great was the opposition to it on the part of the lucky ones who were safely in its ranks. A number of governors spoke earnestly and forcibly to the large gathering, showing that the club's expenses could not fail to be a great deal more than had been anticipated, for everything had to be the best, etc.; but all to no avail. The members were obdurate, and had the motion been put to a vote then it would surely have been lost. But Mr. Travers, who had been sitting quietly on the stage, arose, and, in his inimitable style of talking whenever he grew excited, won the whole one thousand members over in

THE DINING-ROOM.

a few minutes, put it to a vote, and adjourned the meeting in a way that made him more than ever established in deep-seated esteem.

After moving into this then grand building, the club's history consists merely in minding its own business, holding very successful athletic events and giving unusual privileges to its members. Several years then elapsed, and Mr. Travers died, he having been president from 1882 to 1887. His death occurred at Bermuda, where he had gone for his health in April, and the presidency of the club remained vacant the remainder of the year. When his

THE BILLIARD ROOM.

death was posted on the bulletin board, hardly a member entered the front door without visibly showing that he considered he had lost an intimate friend. It is generally conceded that even although the club's presidents have been men of unusual standing, not one has quite filled the gap made by the "old gentleman."

Being firmly and comfortably established in a city home where there was everything to make life as pleasant as it can be in the environments of brick walls and stone pavements, what remained to make life absolutely pleasant was the acquirement of a country home, and in 1888 the club purchased Travers Island in the Sound. Travers Island consists of a peninsula, jutting out into Long Island Sound, within easy access of the business portion of New York City. There is excellent water on the prominent sides of the island, and the lowland or marsh between the so-called main part of the island and the mainland can be filled in at the club's convenience and made just

THE BOXING-ROOM.

as useful and beautiful as the land now is where all the improvements have been built. The total acreage of the island and the unclaimed land is over thirty-three acres, and its natural beauty is remarkable. On it a fifth-of-a-mile track has been constructed, with a well-sodded infield. A feature in natural beauty of the track are the raised banks around certain parts of it, forming a natural amphitheatre. A fine view of everything going on in the field and on the track is obtained from the surrounding slopes.

The club-house on the island commands a good view of stretches of Long Island Sound, and is built in a low, rambling style, appropriate for the country. In it are all the accommodations found in the club's city quarters,

except on a plainer and smaller scale. The exterior architecture reminds one very much of the old English inns where additions have been made almost every decade. To the north or northeast of the club-house is the boat-house, in which are housed almost every kind of conceivable rowing craft. The club has the largest collection of boats for developing rowing of any organization in the world, exceeding even the number housed in the far-famed London Rowing Club. In front of the boat-house is a float, where oarsmen and swimmers may take turns in giving themselves sun and water baths, for right off the float there is eight feet of water.

Then there is the yachting department, more around to the west of the boat-house, where a number of such craft can be found in the water or up on shore in state of repairs at almost any time. Boats sail right in from the Sound, passing Glen Island and landing at the club dock, with as little concern and as much ease as though it were a public aquatic refuge. Passing further along, and more away from the general view, are quarters for attendants of the island, which, as can be imagined, number considerable during the summer season; but even in winter the club-house itself always is in charge of enough help to take care of members who visit it when forced to go over snow and ice. The tennis courts are on an elevation, and are much patronized. They are kept in as good repair as the running track, and, being made of clay, stand the wear and tear well. In fact, everything on the island is so constructed as to be thoroughly practicable and yet to embrace as much of the æsthetic side of the surrounding and beautiful country as possible.

The club life at Travers Island is very much of the same kind as is found in the club's city house, except that there is more country recreation than the more indolent pastimes associated with cities. Members ride out on their bicycles Friday and Saturday afternoons, and stay until Monday morning, as a rule. Very few of this kind engage in competitive athletics, but nearly all take up athletics in one way or another. There is so much to do when one gets there, in the shape of amusement, that the days go before one knows it, and when evening comes around, and visitors assemble in the club-house in their various groups and corners, it reminds one of a college dormitory.

The great new city home was decided on in 1892 when the retiring (1891) Board recommended to the incoming Board of Governors that steps should be taken to getting a new and larger building. Mr. Bartow S. Weeks succeeded Mr. Mills as president, and the first plan, a most conservative one, was in raising $100,000 by voluntary subscriptions or gifts. Sixty-one thousand dollars was subscribed with the condition that the whole should be raised, and in June, 1892, the present site was purchased for $260,000, and the limit of active membership was raised from 2,100 to, as it is at present, 2,500. Twenty-eight thousand dollars had been paid in by the members to the volunteer fund, and $7,000 extra was taken from the club profits, and those two amounts, $35,000 in all, was paid on account of the site, leaving the balance on mortgage.

Some bold yet delicate financiering was necessary to insure the flotation of the new club project, and the "man on the bridge" in this case was Mr. James Whitely, who was elected president in 1895, and who yet occupies this important post of honor. It is a curious coincidence that Mr. Whitely is more or less of a direct descendant in a financial way of Mr. Travers, for the latter was special partner in Mr. Whitely's firm up to his death, and he was the one who proposed Mr. Whitely for membership in 1885.

The club rested on its oars for some time, especially during 1893, the year which more or less disturbed all business of the country, but on the election of that year Mr. Whitely induced Mr. August Belmont to take the presidency, which he held for a year, and retired in favor of Mr. Weeks, with Mr. Whitely as Vice-President. Nothing was done by the club in that year except to make its usual $30,000 annual profit, for the books show that from January, 1892, to January, 1898, the net profits for the six years were $187,000.

Mr. Whitely was elected president in 1895, and Mr. August Belmont then wrote to him, saying that he considered the time had arrived when the club should build. A Building and Finance Committee, composed of the following members, was elected: James Whitely, Chairman; Thomas L. Watson, A. G. Mills, Bartow S. Weeks, August Belmont, John R. Van Wormer, W. D. Searles, Charles E. Goodhue, Charles T. Wills, Walter Stanton, and B. F. O'Connor, Secretary. This committee had full charge of the undertaking, which has just been put through so successfully, and it is all ready to be discharged, hardly the minutest detail in the whole affair remaining to be finished.

In March, 1895, prizes were offered for the best plans for a suitable building, and the financial plan was outlined for the raising of the funds. A first mortgage was put on the new site, with building, of $450,000, and a similar instrument was put on the Travers Island property of $50,000, in each case the old mortgages being paid off. Then the equity in both of these properties was mortgaged for fifteen years for $300,000, and these second mortgage bonds were taken very satisfactorily, almost entirely by members of the club, an example being set by Mr. August Belmont, Mr. Francis S. Kinney and Mr. George J. Gould, who took $20,000 apiece. As the building progressed, more money was wanted, and debenture bonds were issued to the extent of $150,000, running six years from November, 1897, this money being used chiefly to furnish the grand structure, which was then almost completed. Readers of the daily press will probably remember how, when the new building was opened last spring, it was announced that $47,000 of these debenture bonds had not yet been taken, and the total amount was sold in twenty minutes, conclusively showing what faith the members have in the stability of their property.

THE LOBBY.

During the process of the construction of the new building nothing happened to mar the way, except a slight mechanical one in laying the foundations, and work progressed steadily until it was completed. The corner-stone was laid November 28, 1896, by Mr. Whitely, the invocation being by Bishop Potter and the oration by Mr. Chauncey M. Depew.

The building stands on the southeast corner of Fifty-ninth street and Sixth avenue, with one hundred feet on each of those two thoroughfares and an L running back through to Fifty-eighth street. The building faces Central Park, and from its windows fine views of this citified oasis can be had. The entrance is by way of a broad staircase on Fifty-ninth street, and on entering one sees before him a huge hall, finished in white marble, with massive octagonal columns. To

THE PARLOR.

the east of the entrance is the library, a large, lofty room, forty feet square, containing several thousand books, mostly devoted to athletic subjects.

To the west of the main entrance, and running parallel with the Sixth avenue side, is the beautiful marble and white tile natatorium, ninety-six feet long and forty feet wide. This is surrounded by two balconies, from which visitors may get a good view. From the marble floor which surrounds the pool a broad hall-way leads to the Turkish bath, which occupies the northwest end of the building.

The wheel room of the club is one of

The third floor is given up exclusively to the living rooms for members. They are light, well ventilated, prettily furnished, and most of them command a fine view. On the fourth floor is the gymnasium, furnished with everything modern and improved in the line of gymnastic apparatus. Its light is unexcelled, and every afternoon scores of members can be found using the apparatus, mostly only as a means of building up bodily vigor. The running track is on the mezzanine floor.

To the south of the gymnasium is a large room used for boxing, with walls and projections padded wherever there

THE LOUNGE.

its best features. There is a storage room for five hundred wheels, a repair shop, and a wheel supply store. On this floor are also the six bowling alleys, and at one end of these there is a balcony with comfortable seats from which spectators may watch the bowling contests.

The parlor is at the east of the smoking-room. At one end is a large tile fireplace, over which is a decoration showing the winged foot. Cozy corners and comfortable chairs bid the visitor to remain in this handsome and well-lighted room. On the west of the smoking-room and occupying a space 100 feet by 40 feet, is the billiard room.

is danger of a participant coming in contact with them, and on the same floor is another room equally large for fencing.

The club dining-room is 120 feet long and 40 feet wide, and is on the sixth floor. It is furnished in quartered oak, and on the north side there is an unobstructed view of Central Park. This is the most used room of the club, and its general appearance, with its ornamentation of bronze, is one that the members can well be proud of.

The club's athletic history is so much public property that it suffices to say that it has had the great majority of the most prominent athletes in this country, and perhaps in the world, in its ranks.

Some of the best known of these, termed as they usually are by their intimates, are the following:

Bill Curtis, Harry Buermeyer, Dan Stern, Pete Burris, Benny Williams, Ernest and Rene La Montagne, Ed. Merrit, Craig Wilmer, Rege Sayre, Charlie Reed, Frank Kilpatrick, Hugh Baxter, Maxey More, "Queck" Jack Cory, "Rabore" Billy Morse, George Taylor, Arthur Schroeder, Evert Wendel, Wendel Baker, George Gray, Alec Jordan, Herman Touissant, Wilson Coudon, Charlie Sherrill, George Phillips, Walter Dohm, Eddie Carter, Roland Molineux, Bob and Tom Fisher, the former being the club's present captain ; Bob Stoll, Tommy Conneff, A. P. Schwaner, Dody Schwegler, Eddie Bloss, Tommy Lee, Mike Sweeny, Big Bill Barry, Jim Mitchell, Barney Wefers, Tom Burke, W. O. Hickok, Charlie Kilpatrick, "Count" Giannini, George Orton, J. H. Hurlbut, Steve Chase, John Flannagan, Maxey Long, Alva Nickerson, C. W. Stage, Alec Grant, "Tewk" I. K. Baxter, J. V. Crum, Mat. Halpin, W. P. and A. P. Remington, Harry Lyons, L. P. Sheldon.

The club's instructors have always been of the best, commencing with George Goldie, who was taken from Princeton University on the opening of the first club-house in 1885. No better tribute can be paid to this celebrated authority than to say that after being missed from Princeton a number of years, that university made him such a flattering offer to return that he did so, and he is now one of the faculty.

He was superseded by Eugene J. Giannini, who figured prominently in the club's athletic ranks previous to his receiving the offer to become its athletic director. He was known as the "Count," a title probably due to his physical idiosyncrasies. He is a splendid example of an all-round athlete, not only in looks but in records, and an expert oarsman, swimmer, weight-thrower and gymnast.

The well-known Mike Donovan, of boxing fame, has been with the club ever since 1885, coming at the time George Goldie did, and still rendering as good service as ever and enjoying the esteem of the members.

Gus Sundstrom, equally well known with Donovan, has charge of the swimming department, having been with the club since 1885.

Hugh Leonard, the wrestling instructor, is on an equal basis of knowledge as any of those who have been longer in their respective departments.

To sum up, all of the heads of these various departments, it can truthfully be said that their equal, as a whole, cannot be found anywhere in this country, and this assertion might just as well embrace the whole world, for there is no other place where athletics have been developed to such an extent as in the United States.

The great international athletic meeting, given under the club's auspices in 1895, will never be forgotten. It was the most wonderful athletic meeting ever held in the world, and the way the American athletes captured event after event conclusively showed their superiority, even though they had the best men in England, Scotland, and Ireland against them.

The club has had a number of handsome and valuable trophies presented to it for competition among the members. Chief among these was the Le Cato Cup, a large and massive piece of solid silverware given for a one-mile handicap run. It was won eventually three times by E. M. Yoemans, and became his property. Then there was the beautiful Travers diamond medal, a huge series of bars and pendant, with Mr. Travers' initials emblazoned in diamonds, a valuable and costly prize given for the one-hundred-yard handicap run, and won eventually for the third time by, and became the property of, myself. Mr. Oelrichs also gave a medal, second only in beauty and value to the one given by Mr. Travers, for the two-hundred-and-twenty-yard handicap run, and eventually won three times by H. Raborg, and which became his property. There are also two prizes which never can be won outright by members In those cases a medal is given whenever a win is made. These are the French silver cup for the one-mile run, donated by Mr. Seth B. French, and the Osborne one-mile single-scull diamond medal, donated by Mr. Charles J. Osborne to the Stock Exchange Rowing Club. By the amalgamation of this club and the New York Athletic Club it became the property of the latter.

18
Slumming
in New York's
Chinatown

SLUMMING IN NEW YORK'S CHINATOWN

A GLIMPSE INTO THE SORDID UNDERWORLD OF THE MOTT STREET QUARTER, WHERE ELSIE SIGEL FORMED HER FATAL ASSOCIATIONS

BY WILLIAM BROWN MELONEY

ON the morning of June 18 last, New York was horrified by the discovery of the body of a murdered girl hidden in a trunk in a Chinese waiter's room over a chop suey restaurant in Eighth Avenue. Within a couple of hours, detectives and newspaper men had established the girl's identity, and the news of the crime went ringing to the ends of the world.

The girl was Elsie Sigel, a nineteen-year-old Sunday-school teacher, and a granddaughter of the famous Civil War general, Franz Sigel. Letters of an astounding nature, which were found in the room of death, led the police before nightfall to telegraph the authorities of every community on the North American continent to arrest, as her murderer, one Leung Lim, known also as William Leon, a "Christianized" Chinese, who had been one of her Sunday-school pupils for nearly two years. The police also telegraphed to arrest, as a "material witness," Chung Sin, another waiter of the "Christianized" type, who had occupied a room across the hall from Leung Lim's, and of whom, as of the accused, there was no trace.

Three days afterward, Chung Sin was caught in Amsterdam, New York. After a day and night of "sweating," he made a confession to the police, fastening the murder of Elsie Sigel on Leung Lim. Chung Sin said that the girl had been killed on the morning of June 9. He told how he had peeped through a key-hole and watched Leung Lim first chloroform his victim then strangle her to death with a cord, and put her body in the trunk. He explained his flight by saying that he feared, if he had remained, or had informed the police, they would have accused him of the murder.

Investigation disclosed that Elsie Sigel must have been slain within two hours after leaving her home on Washington Heights to answer a secret summons from Leung Lim. During the first few days of her absence, her family's apprehension as to her safety was allayed by a telegram signed "Elsie," which her mother received from Washington on the night of June 9, and which said that the girl had gone to the capital in connection with her church work. This forged telegram was sent and prepaid by a Chinese, who was either Leung Lim or one of his agents.

Mrs. Sigel and her daughter had been frequenters of New York's Chinese quarter for several years. The mother, in the beginning, was dominated by an obsession to save "heathen souls" from the burning. Under such an influence this obsession was quickly communicated to Elsie — an impressionable character, who, with all her girlish ardor of innocence, plunged headlong into an unguarded association with Chinese of the cueless, "Americanized" sort, like Leung Lim.

It was in a Chinatown restaurant called the Port Arthur, and owned by Chu Gain, cueless and well-to-do, that Elsie Sigel met Leung Lim, who was employed there. The girl accepted the two Chinese on a footing of equality.

They visited her home, they pretended faith in her Man of the Cross, and they attended her church — to the end revealed by the letters discovered in Leung Lim's room, which the commissioner of police suppressed in the interest of public policy.

CHINATOWN AT NIGHT

Night has come, and it is the time when we may view and examine the sur-

A five-minute walk northward from where the great presses of Park Row are forever booming, or eastward from the Tombs and the Criminal Courts Building, or southward from Police Headquarters, and the acrid odors of New York's Chinatown are stinging one's nostrils and palate. There it lies, unfathomed and unknown, in the very ear of the city where all things come to be known — where a pin dropped on the

THE INTERIOR OF A TYPICAL STORE IN CHINATOWN, WHERE VISITORS TO THE QUARTER MAY PURCHASE CHINESE PORCELAIN, BRASSWORK, FANS, GONGS, PURSES, SLIPPERS, AND THE LIKE

roundings in which the soul of Elsie Sigel was throttled a year before a cord and Leung Lim's yellow fingers choked her girlish form into the stillness of death.

It is at night only that you may see the Mongol quarter of New York in its quickened phases, for there the people come to life with darkness and disappear with the dawn. In keeping with this law, as it were, the murderer of Elsie Sigel chose a morning when all the normal world was awake and glad with early June to send her into eternity.

other side of the world is heard an instant afterward — contemptuous, blandly mysterious, serene, foul-smelling, Oriental, and implacable behind that indefinable barrier which has kept the West and the East apart since the centuries began. Within the boundaries of the three acres which it occupies, five thousand slant-eyed children of Cathay and three or four hundred whites, who have cast their lot with them, order their existence like rabbits in a warren.

There is a shack in the Bowery, near the lower end of Mott Street—it is now occupied as a saloon—which is responsible for the location of New York's Chinatown. A Chinaman opened a small cigar-shop there in 1878 or 1879. He did a good business. Presently one of his countless " kah-sans " became aware of this, and settled near him. Then another and another cousin followed, until the old-fashioned Irish population of the neighborhood was com-

trail, until, with a sudden turn northward, it runs full tilt into Pell. Pell keeps on for a block and ends in Mott, while Bayard holds its way to the westward, into Little Italy and Mulberry Bend, crossing Mott at right angles.

A TYPICAL SLUMMING-PARTY

Here is a typical party of slummers going into the quarter. None is a New

THE INSCRUTABLE AND IMPERTURBABLE ORIENTAL—DENIZENS OF CHINATOWN WATCHING A
SLUMMING-PARTY ENTERING THE QUARTER

pelled to give way before the yellow influx. Such was the beginning of the quarter.

Let us enter Chinatown from Chatham Square, at Mott Street. This is where the big sight-seeing automobiles disembark their cargoes of slummers, and raucous-voiced guides begin their pilotage. The automobiles are too large for the narrow streets of the quarter. Two standard vehicles can barely pass between the sidewalks.

Mott, Pell, Doyers, and Bayard— those are the names of the principal streets. They dart at crazy angles out of the Bowery and Chatham Square. Doyers winds tortuously like a cattle-

Yorker, except the Semitic-faced youth in the lead, whose flaunting banners and " spieling " netted them along upper Broadway and in the hotel districts. They are people who belong beyond the city's gates — eager, curious, prurient even, to know the worst that lies hidden within. Let us follow them.

Listen! The guide is talking; but see, few of his followers are listening to him. They are bewildered, uncertain. They feel they are on the threshold of a mystery. The women are clinging timidly to their escorts, or holding one another's hands. The men are trying to look unconcerned and as if it were an old story to them. The guide says:

" Ladies and gents, on th' spot wher-r-re ye're standin' at this instant, a short time ago th' warr-rin' highbinder tongs got busy, an' when th' smoke cleared away th' street on which ye're standin' wuz runnin' r-red with b-l-lood. There was ten dead men layin' all around here!"

His sanguinary tale is designed to catch the interest of just such people as are following him for a dollar or two dollars a head. It is successful.

As the barker finishes the highbinder part of his declamation, he swings in his tracks and points upward to the left.

" Now, ladies and gents, followin' th' point of me finger, yer can be-hold th' famyus Port Arthur. It was right in there that Elsie Sigel useter go with her little prayer-book an' eat chop suey. But more a-non!"

The slummers are studying the exterior of the garish hole avidly. They turn with lingering steps from the place where Elsie Sigel became enthralled in the tragic lure of Leung Lim's and Chu Gain's jealous attachment. The three-storied building, with its iron porticoes and fanciful awnings, is blazing from sidewalk to roof with electric lights and fish-bladder lanterns. " Port Arthur " is lettered in incandescents as large as a Broadway star's in the zenith of a successful season. But the bulbs do not shine with the brilliancy that they have up-town. A bluish haze enshrouds them. It is the same everywhere in Chinatown. Its lights, like its life, must be seen through this haze of punk and opium, and the noisome outpourings of its greasy chop-suey joints and its swarming tenements. That sickening, dominating peanut odor is the smell of opium.

OPIUM—A SHOW FOR THE SLUMMERS

The slummers move on. The pilot halts at the door of a forbidding tenement, and beckons them to pass inside and climb an ill-smelling, creaking flight of stairs which leads to Georgie Yee's.

THE TWO-ROOM APARTMENT ON PELL STREET IN WHICH A WHITE WOMAN—THE " HAZEL " OF
THE ACCOMPANYING ARTICLE—LIVES WITH HER HUSBAND, A CHINESE
RESTAURANT-PROPRIETOR

THE INTERIOR OF ONE OF THE LARGEST AND MOST SHOWY RESTAURANTS IN THE CHINESE
QUARTER OF NEW YORK—IT WAS IN A PLACE LIKE THIS THAT ELSIE SIGEL
MET LEUNG LIM, WHO WAS EMPLOYED THERE AS A WAITER

Now the peanut odor is strong. The building reeks with it. The pilot accounts for all of his crew and hurries ahead, leading the way into a low-ceilinged kennel of a room. There is no light save a flicker from a tiny, sputtering flame in a glass globe with a hole in the top. The light is in the middle of a matting-covered platform.

Something moves on the platform. Some of the more timid slummers hesitate, but the guide's "spiel" on the horrors of opium-smoking reassures them. As he goes on, their eyes adjust themselves to the dim light and the fume-laden atmosphere. They know what it is that is moving on the platform. A Chinaman is lying to the left of the sputtering lights, and to the right is a shell of a white woman, with hollow cheeks and bare, bony arms. The eyes of the Chinaman and the woman—she is his wife—seem ready to burst from their heads.

The pair go through the motions of opium-smoking—the twisting of a wire in a tiny box made of horn, the twirling of the molasses-like stuff, which the wire catches on its point, over the flame at their side until it sputters greasily; the manipulation of the "cooked" opium into a pill, the placing of the pill over a needle opening in the bowl of the pipe, the holding of the canted bowl against the flame; and then the long, guttural inhalations and a burst of smoke from the nostrils.

The two go through this performance anywhere from ten to twenty times a night, for pay. It is their "turn" on the slummers' stage. They were players on a real stage once. The Chinaman was a member of a theatrical troupe; his wife had a place in polite vaudeville under a name which has been forgotten.

On the wall of the den is an outline drawing of the implements of an opium-layout. Opposite this is placarded:

One half of the world doesn't know how the other half lives.

The eyes of the slummers, as they step into the street, are brilliant, dancing, excited, eager. The women have lost their timidity. They do not cling so closely to their escorts as they did when they went into Georgie Yee's. They no longer miss the clean, fresh air of the wide streets and open spaces to which they are used. The taint of the drugged and poisoned atmosphere of the quarter is in their lungs, but they do not realize it. They talk loudly; they laugh without occasion. Most of them fail to pull in their skirts now as the Chinese go jostling by them on the narrow sidewalk. They no longer turn their eyes away from the impudent glances of the slant-eyed yellow men staring at them from the shop doors and the dark openings of the noisome tenements. They give back stare for stare.

TEMPTERS AND TEMPTED

See those two young women — fresh-faced country lasses — who have fallen behind the slummers, and who are looking in a shop window at a display of lingerie. A sleek Chinaman, smiling and deferential, is inviting them within. They return his smile, declining, but not resenting the invitation.

"Listen to them!" whispers Mike Galvin, the police captain in command of the precinct, as we sidle close to the window.

"How muchee?" asks one of the girls, pointing unashamed at an article of feminine finery, and unconsciously using "pidgin English," to which, half an hour ago, her tongue and ears were alien.

The Chinaman's answer is a repetition of his invitation, and the naming of a

A CHINESE WITH HIS TWO SONS, THE CHILDREN OF A WHITE MOTHER

ridiculously low price. The girls look at each other hesitantly, and then around them, to discover themselves alone and the other slummers half a block ahead.

"No can buy now, John," says the girl who spoke first. "Bimeby. Maybe to-morrow;" and the two hurry off, laughing inordinately, to rejoin their companions.

"That's the way and that's the kind," says Galvin, looking after the girls. "There is always a to-morrow for one or two of every slumming party, who have not seen enough the night before. Did you catch the pidgin English? I'll bet those girls were never in a Chinatown in all their lives before to-night!"

The captain was right. He later found a way of engaging the two in conversation. They told him they were only a few months out of high school. Their home was in Rochester. Their big brother and a married sister were among the slummers. Galvin pointed the girls out to one of his plain-clothes men, with instructions to keep an eye out on the morrow and "fan 'em" —that is, drive them away — if they appeared in the quarter without a proper escort.

Next in the slummer's itinerary is a glimpse into the Chinese theater. They issue from the playhouse with their ears buzzing from the crash of gongs and cymbals of brass, the squeaking of one-stringed fiddles, and the falsetto voices of the actors, to hurry in and out of a mission for white wrecks of the Bowery, where a hymn is sung for the visitors' benefit, and for whatever coins they have to spare.

Then there comes a dash into a joss-house, where taloned fingers make sacrifice with punk-burning and then seek to trace the fortunes which slant eyes pretend to see in the clean, white hands of the women. There is nobody to tell the monly made of an *olla podrida* of pork, onions, rice, rice-sprouts, bamboo-sprouts, beef, and chicken, served with much gravy. There are many kinds of chop suey, the ingredients varying according

A WOMAN WHO WORKS AS A MISSIONARY IN CHINATOWN (ON THE RIGHT),
WITH TWO OF THE WHITE WIVES OF THE QUARTER

slummers of the saying set down in the "Ming Hsien Chi," a book of Chinese proverbs, which runs thus:

No image-maker worships the gods. He knows what stuff they are made of.

Let us leave the slummers in the Port Arthur, eating chop suey—a dish com-

to the initiation and the taste of the eaters.

The women are in ecstasies over the heavily carved ebony tables, with their inset tops of dull onyx marble; the carved unbacked stools, the dainty teacups and brewing-pots, the rice-bowls and the dinner-plates. The banners of

ONE OF THE SMALL CHOP-SUEY RESTAURANTS OF CHINATOWN, WHICH ARE KEPT OPEN ALL
NIGHT FOR THE BENEFIT OF SLUMMING-PARTIES—THESE PLACES HAVE MULTIPLIED
GREATLY DURING THE LAST FEW YEARS, AND THERE ARE NOW SCORES
OF THEM IN MANY PARTS OF NEW YORK

A ROOM ON THE SECOND FLOOR OF A TENEMENT-HOUSE ON PELL STREET—"A COOP WITH
A WIRE-MESHED WINDOW"—IN WHICH LULU SHU, ONE OF THE WHITE WIVES
OF CHINATOWN, HAS LIVED FOR EIGHTEEN YEARS

rich embroideries, with always a dragon rampant dominating the scheme of decoration, hold their eyes. They do not notice the floor, covered with linoleum or sawdust; the cheap wall-paper, against which the embroideries are hanging; the thinness and tawdriness and staginess of it all.

The two Rochester girls who stopped

seers happened to look up, but all she saw was a bamboo screen moving slightly and a silhouette behind it. Hazel lives there, one flight up, in the front, behind an oaken door with strong bars and spring locks.

Nammock, one of the precinct plainclothes men, led me to Hazel's. As we entered the dimly lighted hallway, I

A TYPICAL PARTY OF SLUMMERS COMING OUT OF A CHINATOWN RESTAURANT AFTER A
MIDNIGHT BANQUET OF CHOP SUEY AND CHOW MEIN

to look into the Mott Street shop window, are at a table in a corner where Elsie Sigel and her mother used to sit, and where Elsie finally came to sit alone with Leung Lim and Chu Gain, believing foolishly that by such equality she was making it easier for them to enter a religion of which the world was not even dreaming when Confucius had shaped the tenets of a true Chinaman's moral code.

THE WHITE WIFE OF A CHINESE

There was an open window in Pell Street, at which the face of a white girl appeared for a second as the slummers passed below. One of the women sight-

heard a woman's pleasant voice reading aloud a newspaper report of the Sigel tragedy. I stumbled over a garbage-can, which, with true Chinese disregard for the fitness of appearances, had been left standing in the middle of the stairs, and it went crashing down into the entryway. The reading stopped, and there came a shuffling of slippered feet on the landings overhead, a slamming of doors, a shooting of bolts, and snapping of locks.

Hazel's door is painted a pea-green, and opens with a brass knob. It was locked when we reached it, and all was still on the other side, but a word and a knock from Nammock brought a whispered "Who is it?"

His answer was a key which swung it open. There stood Hazel, young, round-faced, and fresh, in a sweeping robe of fine, thin yellow silk with iris-blossoms scattered through its weave. She was smiling, curious, but unembarrassed. I thought of a woman who once lived on the wall of an old city, and about whom a tremendous story has been written; but I was wrong. For eight years Hazel has been the wife of a well-to-do chop - suey restaurant proprietor named Chu Man, bound to him by the laws of the sovereign State of New Jersey.

"I was out in the hall, reading about the Sigel case to one of my white neighbors," Hazel explained to us. "I would not have run away if I had known who was coming up the stairs." She smiled, sensing the inquiry to which her explanation gave rise, and added: "One who lives in Chinatown never knows what may happen; and if one owns a strong door, one should use it."

Hazel's speech was softened by the broad "a" of the Boston native, and before we left her she told us that she had been born and reared in the Yankee capital, and that her family still had their home there.

"IF MY GRANDMOTHER KNEW!"

"I go home to see my people as often as I please, but only one of my sisters knows I am here," said the girl. "La, la, if my dear old grandmother—she is eighty-nine now — knew that I am a Chinaman's wife, she would have me hanged!"

Hazel laughed, but I thought there was a note of sadness in her sally.

"Regret?" she repeated, answering an inquiry. "Regret what?"

As elusively as the yellow folk to whom she now belongs, she turned the conversation to a framed embroidery— a treasure of China's strange crafts— which reached half-way from the low ceiling to the floor.

"There are one hundred and sixty different birds in that embroidery," she said. "Isn't it beautifully done?"

She laughed like a pleased child when I agreed with her estimate.

The reference to the embroidery made it easy to study without embarrassment the rest of the room. It was about ten feet square, electrically lighted by a heavy, low-hanging brass chandelier. Along the wall toward which the door opened was an upright piano, half hiding a common iron sink in the opposite corner. The furniture, like the piano, was modern mahogany. It consisted of four chairs, a settee, and a table in the center of the room. A collection of massive Chinese vases on a cheap marble mantel, a brass-bugled phonograph, ivories, embroideries, an electric fan, and a photograph of Chu Man completed the ensemble. It suggested a play-room in which a pettish child had littered its toys. A small door leading from this room disclosed a cubby-hole so full of a brass bed and a bird's - eye maple dresser as to leave little space for anything else.

Hazel interrupted the survey of her abode with one of her sudden laughs.

"I am trying to think where I shall go for a vacation—the White Mountains or Atlantic City," she said. "I like both places. Take my husband?" Again she laughed. "No, indeed! My husband is a Chinaman. He stays home. No, they are not docile any more than white men. They would rule you with a rod of iron if you would let them. Yet a woman may rule them so long as they are sure of her affection, and nothing she may ask will be denied.

"I come and go when I please. I know nothing of the quarter save these four walls. If you will let the people here alone, they will let you alone. A Chinaman will never make the first advance. When I step out of Chinatown, I become a white woman again. When I come back, I become yellow and mind my own business. If a Chinaman were to see me away from here, do you think he would let on that he knew me? Never would he give a sign, no matter how good friends we might be, unless I wished it. A white man would never be so forbearing.

"When my husband and I go out of Chinatown in company, you would never know we were together. He either walks ahead of me or behind. That is the Chinese way. I have traveled all over the country with him, and few have ever commented on it.

" Let me tell you that the Chinese need nobody to teach them charity or humility; and if the missionaries would let them alone, there would be no Elsie Sigel tragedies to stir hatred against the yellow people."

We left Hazel seated at the window of the bamboo screen, her thick braid of golden hair falling carelessly over one shoulder, and the diamonds on her fingers glistening in the rays of the chandelier.

DENIZENS OF THE QUARTER

As we emerged from Hazel's, a Chinaman with a vertical streak of red painted between his eyebrows moved into the shadow of the adjoining building. That was the sign of a candidate for admission to the Lone Gee Tong—the order of Chinese Free Masons—worn on the forehead so that he might be known to those whose secrets he wished to bind to himself.

Crossing the street, we climbed the stairs of a building crazy with age and dust and smells. We groped down a narrow hall on the second floor, and in a coop with a wire-meshed window we found Lulu Shu lying on the floor. Her layout was spread before her on a pallet, and a big gray cat was cuddled in the nape of her neck, drinking in the fumes of the drug as they escaped over her shoulder. Lulu Shu has lived in Chinatown for eighteen years, and during the past three years she has not stirred from her room.

Much has been written about the " white slaves " of Chinatown. That is all fiction. No bars or strong doors keep them there. They are slaves only in the sense in which Lulu Shu is one. Addiction to opium is their only warder.

Leaving Lulu Shu's, and now led by Brickley, one of Nammock's partners, we entered a building on the opposite side of the street, and felt our way through a black hallway which led into a small court. After several seconds in this hidden enclosure I traced the outline of a three-decked tenement, with blurred lights in its open windows. Standing in the street, one would never suspect that building to be there.

When I had become accustomed to the darkness of the court I saw through the wire coverings on the cellar windows a white woman, and a white boy of nine or ten, sitting against a cooking-range, which took up most of the space in a room about eight feet square. A lamp flickered on a small table. Soon I distinguished English and Chinese voices in conversation.

" That's Margaret with the boy," whispered Brickley, pointing toward the woman. " She's the second white wife of that boy's foster father, Charley Wing. The boy's mother drifted into Chinatown one day ten years ago. She was sick and starving. Wing took her in, nursed her, and gave her food; and in a few weeks that boy was born. Wing married the mother and took care of them both. When the mother died, a couple of years ago, he adopted the boy."

At that moment two white women emerged from the cellar and melted into the night. Margaret Wing followed shortly, and, finding us there, said to Brickley, with a chuckle:

" That was my mother and sister. They came over from Jersey to see whether I had been killed. All this stuff in the newspapers has made them nervous."

Across the courtyard from Margaret Wing's is Chu Hin's opium-joint, where white men and yellow foregather and set sail for Poppyland. First, however, they must pay the price of the journey to Chu Hin's white wife, who sits at a little desk just inside the door, tallying and casting accounts of the dreams her husband sells. Chu Hin was once, according to Chinese standards, a great comedian. He was the first actor of note to appear in the Chinese theater in New York, but he has long since forsaken the stage. Chu consented to having his place and its occupants photographed, but not until after he had been permitted to doff negligee for more formal attire.

Three flights of narrow stairs to the top of a tenement in another street carried us to the abode of Mrs. Chu Wing. Mrs. Chu Wing's name is Elsie. In the quarter, the white women are generally known by Christian names—their own or adopted ones—and it is the familiar etiquette of their scheme of things to address them so. Elsie's husband is the proprietor of a number of laundries in

Hudson River towns like Peekskill and Poughkeepsie. They were married in St. Louis, she told me, in 1902. We found her home the familiar one-room establishment of the quarter, but with an incongruity all its own. A gilded plaster bust of Shakespeare stood on the inevitable marble mantel between two exquisite Chinese glazed vases. Around the bard's neck hung a purple ribbon, and I could not help but smile.

"Oh, I know Shakespeare!" Elsie smiled back with a challenging perk of her head. Seeing that I would not accept her challenge, she turned to Nammock and said: "Have you heard that the excursion planned for to-morrow is off?" Catching my look of inquiry, she went on: "There are to be no more missionary excursions this year. It has been the custom for the Sunday-school societies to hire a steamer three or four times every summer and go on picnic excursions. I attended three last year. First I went because I felt that I could go in company with my husband without being subjected to criticism or comment. I went the second time to confirm my observations of the previous occasion, and the third time I went to strike an average and round out the experience. It was unique. I discovered that the white wives of the quarter were somewhat out of the scheme of the missionaries. To the fresh-faced girl Sunday-school teachers, the chief attraction was the cueless Chinks in American clothes."

Elsie's blue eyes twinkled with a cynical mirth.

"Soon after the third excursion, a young Chinaman came to me with a letter from one of the Sunday-school teachers who had turned her nose up at me. When I had fixed her identity I consented to do what he asked. He could not write English, and I composed him an answer. And after that— well, I played *Cyrano* to his *Christian* for nearly two months, and—now they are married, ha, ha, ha!"

I started forward, shocked, but Elsie misunderstood, or pretended to do so.

"Surprised?" she laughed. "I know Rostand. 'At the envoy's end I touch.' Or should I say 'touched' in this instance? Ha, ha, ha! Oh, if I were a

man, I should love to play that part. But, tell me, don't you think that it was rather droll of me to write that Chinaman's love-letters?"

I was silent.

"Bah!" she exclaimed.

A firecracker exploded loudly in the street below, and Elsie leaned out of the window and looked down. Keeping her eyes averted, and seeming to be watching something on the roofs of the buildings opposite, she said in a changed and bitter voice:

"THERE IS A WALL!"

"I am ashamed! Every white woman in Chinatown who has not deadened her senses with drugs is ashamed!" Then, turning round, with her features drawn and her eyelids narrowed to conceal the tears, she went on in an impassioned tone: "No chains, no barred doors hold us here! But there is a wall! You cannot see it; you cannot even imagine it; but it is there! I can see it! I have dashed myself against it and been hurled back!"

There was a pause, and again Elsie's eyes went drifting out into the blue haze. Presently she turned back. Her eyes were dry, and she spoke calmly:

"I have never known but one white woman to get over that wall and back to our own kind. She and I were graduated from—no, that is another story. I will say that she was well bred and well educated. In fact, she took honors over me, and I was among the first ten in my class. No, never mind where it was. That's in the past. How she came here or why she came does not matter, either. How she got out and over the wall is what I want to tell you.

"Three years after coming here this girl was rainbow-chasing in poppyland. You would have turned her over to the first policeman you met if she had dared to speak to you in the street. But when she was herself, and there were no rainbows in her brain, she could charm you with her mind.

"One day a newspaper man came drifting through the quarter. She was herself that day, and she interested him. After many weeks he persuaded her to go away from New York where once in a while she could see real rainbows and green trees and grass. In three or four months she came back to the city. In that short time she had once more become the girl I had known in the beginning. She had been studying typewriting and stenography, and the newspaper man found her a position in an office.

"No, they didn't marry and live happily ever afterward. This isn't that kind of a story. It couldn't be with that sort of a man. Once he was certain that she was on her feet, he let her go her own way. The most he ever said to me about it was to call what he had done for her ' just an experiment.' He died in a little while, but his experiment has outlived him. She runs the office where she works. She could marry well, but there's a grave in Greenwood. The experimenter doesn't know, but that's her anchorage, and—' at the envoy's end I touch.' "

"SLIGEL CLASE VELLY UNFLORTUNATE"

As Nammock and I descended to the street, little clusters of punks were burning in the keyholes or in the jambs of most of the doors on the different landings. That is the way they " sport their oak " in Chinatown.

"Here's the president of the Chinese Sunday-school outfit," said Nammock as we stepped out of Elsie's door.

He hailed a cueless young Chinese in his shirt-sleeves who was standing in the middle of the street smoking a big black cigar.

"This Sligel clase velly unfortunate flor Chinese," said he. "To-day I am held up by blig Ilish p'leeceman, who take me flor Willum Leon. Chinese got be velly clareful now. I glive up the ples-see-dencee of Chinese Sunday-school to-day. I tell 'um not advlisable to hold exclursion to-mollah. I person-al-lee want nothing to do with exclursion just now. This Sligel clase velly, velly sad. It glieve me deeply."

"Humph!" said Nammock as we turned away. "The whole outfit was on one of their excursions three days before Elsie Sigel's body was discovered in Leon's flat. This'll put a kink in 'em for a little while."

A white man passed us in the shadows, a low-crowned derby pulled down over his bullet-shaped head, accentuating a ponderous, bony jaw. His eyes were cast upon the gutter. It was "Chuck" Connors, famous among the Bowery's characters and sometimes called "the mayor of Chinatown."

A census taken by missionaries in 1908 showed one hundred and ninety-five white women living in Chinatown; but a count made a few months later by Captain Galvin, of the police, showed only one hundred and thirty. Galvin's first command—he is one of the youngest captains on the New York force—was the Elizabeth Street precinct, which includes Chinatown. At the outset he inaugurated a war on the whites of the yellow quarter by enforcing the sanitary provisions of the tenement-house law. He closed the gambling-houses, too—something which none of his predecessors had even attempted to do, for were not these dens of pi gow and fan tan worth from five thousand to ten thousand dollars a week in tolls to "the system"? Galvin was in the full swing of his campaign for cleanliness when the Sigel tragedy startled the world, furnishing proof of the need of such work.

It was dawn as Galvin and I walked out of Chinatown and into the Bowery.

"I'd like to pile all of it on a barge and sink it in the East River," he said, looking backward through Doyers Street.

I followed his gaze and saw a candle in a fish-bladder lantern flickering out. The people behind Elsie Chu's wall were going to sleep, and these lines from a Chinese poem, written many centuries ago, came to me:

The very wax sheds sympathetic tears,
And gutters sadly down till dawn appears.

19
Romances
of New Americans

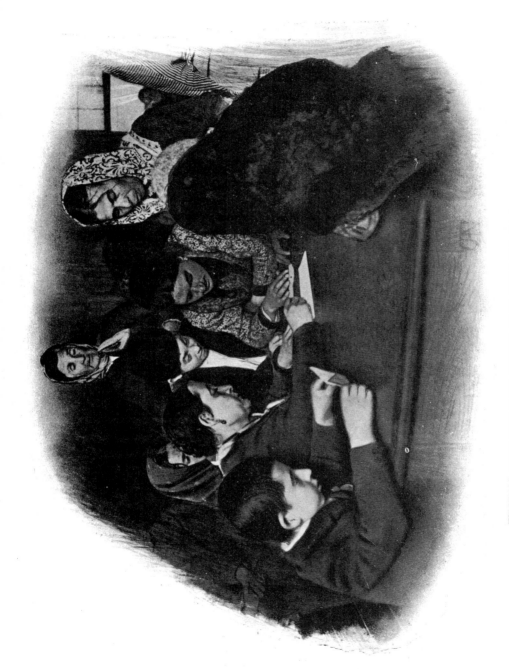

WRITING HOME THE FIRST LETTER FROM THE LAND OF THE FREE.

ROMANCES OF NEW AMERICANS

By ELEANOR HOYT.

PHOTOGRAPHS BY J. H. ADAMS.

DESERTED BY HER
LOVER.

THERE is comedy on the Ellis Island stage, though hardly enough to feed a healthy sense of humor. There are immigrants by the thousands who pass all examinations quickly and successfully, are hailed by friends in the Hall of Joyous Meetings—which the immigration authorities wouldn't recognize under that name—and plunge happily, confidently into the great new world. But there are other immigrants who are cast for roles in detention and separation, and these are pathetic, even tragic plays—just how tragic even the actor himself hardly knows while the curtain is up and the action progressing.

It is no place for the sentimentalist, is Ellis Island, unless he be in search of sensations or of copy. The immigrant official who does his work well must be a patriot, a philosopher and a man of business; otherwise his nerves will wear to fiddle strings or he will harden into unfeeling brutality. He must realize that the restriction of immigration is necessary to the welfare of the country, and that such restriction can be made effective only by inflexible rules; but even with such moral and mental panoply to fortify him, this immigrant official possibly will not sleep well o' nights during his novitiate.

They are so optimistic, these hordes of foreigners who are pouring into their promised land, so confident of flowing milk and honey, so glad that the wandering is over. They swarm off the boats and are met by loud-voiced, impatient men who have seen shoals of immigrants come and go and who have lost their dramatic sense in the development of an executive ability that would rouse envious admiration in the breast of an expert cattle herder.

The nervous, excited, deprecatory crowd must be handled quickly, for more are coming—and more—and more. A large percentage of the immigrants are dirty, ill-smelling, repulsive. Bewilderment and confusion make them appear hopelessly stupid. Dumb brutes they are in outward seeming, dumb brutes with appealing, frightened eyes, and the ordinary under official takes them at that valuation. If they don't understand, he shouts at them. That is an infallible recipe for making oneself understood by foreigners. If shouting doesn't move them, he shoves them, hustles them into line.

The flood pours through the doors, up the stairs, and into the big examination room.

At the end of a narrow passageway, hemmed in by iron railings, waits an alert, keen-eyed doctor with a watchful matron by his side. He does his duty swiftly, automatically, uncompromisingly; looks for contagious scalp disease and eye disease, notes every

GENIAL ITALIANS WHO CAN'T LIE SUCCESSFULLY ENOUGH TO CONCEAL THEIR LABOR CONTRACTS.

sign of physical weakness. A motley crew passes through his hands. Men, women and children in the garb of all nations, old and young, strong and feeble, terrified, curious, defiant, indifferent. Sallow, emaciated men, with the marks of ill-health written on their dull faces, try pitiably to brace themselves into vigor before the doctor or to slink by him unnoticed. Sturdy, yellow-haired Scandinavians square their broad shoulders and look the inquisitor

defiantly in the eyes, serenely conscious of their splendid physiques. Homely women scuttle past. Pretty girls bridle and blush. Bewildered children cling tightly to their mothers' skirts and stare with great, frightened eyes at the man who pulls off their caps and tilts back their heads to look into their faces.

All found wanting are turned aside into the detention pen. The others, safely past the doctor, fall into the hands of other men who examine their papers, find out how much money they have, and ask questions enough to make the best-intentioned foreigner lie from sheer confusion. Rescued from this Scylla, the immigrant is swept into an appalling Charybdis where contract labor examiners lie in wait. If, hurled from reef to reef, he finally reaches smooth water and is tossed ashore, dazed, breathless, uncertain of his fate, he is then taken in hand by agents who resuscitate him and send him on his way to American citizenship.

If fault has been found with him, he joins the "S. I.'s" and awaits the pleasure of the Board.

The second act of the drama takes place before the Board of Special Inquiry. The room is a pleasant one. The mild-mannered men grouped around the big desk do not appear formidable, but he who has tried to stand up before them and lie consistently finds them appalling; and, scattered over Europe, are hundreds of poor wretches who, when they picture the devil, give him the face of a member of the Ellis Island Special Inquiry Board.

The function of these amateur St. Peters is to separate sheep and goats, and all day long detained immigrants file before them and undergo a fire of cross-questionings. Major Sempsey does the talking for the Board, and apparently has no preference in the matter of tongues. He's ready to talk any language, any dialect the immigrant chooses; and the foreigners cling pathetically to this big man with the kind eyes and the gruff voice who speaks to them in the vernacular of their homes. He handles them considerately, though he doesn't spare them; and, with the women and children, his brusquerie softens into something like gentleness. A woman's a woman, even when she is dirty and ill-favored, and when the truth is not in her; and the women who come before the S. I. Board are usually pitiful cases.

A TYPE FROM THE MOUNTAINS OF ITALY.

"Giuletta Racchochini," calls the secretary. The summons is passed on into outer darkness, and a nervous little Italian woman, in the dress of a Savoyard peasant, scurries into the room, her black eyes roving from face to face, a rising stream of protest and exclamation dammed insecurely behind closed lips. She has a child— yes; and Tomaso has sent for her. He has work on the big ditch—yes; and he can take care of her. Mother of God, why is it that one is not allowed to go to the home that is waiting over the grocery shop, in the street of the Mulberry? The little Giacomo is ill? But no; of a surety he has the strength of an ox. That he should

A SWEDISH GIRL SENT FOR BY HER PROSPEROUS LOVER.

have a disease of the head! Name of a cabbage, what child has not a disease of the head? Send him back to Italy? The signors are jesting. It is impossible. He is but a bambino. How could he go alone? Go with him! The flood of volubility breaks loose and surges through the Board room, but the Major checks it.

Tomaso is not on hand, but a neighbor has come in his place and is called in. The bambino has a bad case of favus and cannot be admitted. The mother or some responsible person must go back with him; and, as the truth filters slowly through the brain of the woman, she drops her persuasive Italian smile, her honeyed voice, and storms, sobs, denounces, until taken away to await word from the absent Tomaso. A home on the street of the Mulberry will be to let.

"Anna Nelsen."

The matron comes with her, and the Major blows his nose savagely. This case has been up before.

The fair-haired Norwegian girl stands quietly beside the matron, her blue eyes staring vaguely at the faces in the room.

"No word from the sweetheart?"

The matron shakes her head.

"She wrote she was coming?"

"Yes, but he hadn't sent for her. It had been understood she would come when her mother died. She thought it would be all right."

"No money? No other friends?"

"No."

"The doctor thinks the thing has unbalanced her mind permanently?"

The matron nodded.

The girl was smiling now, in a puzzled fashion, but at every sound she turned swiftly toward the door.

The St. Peters looked uncomfortable.

"Three weeks since she came?"

to the footsteps in the corridor, and again the Major blew a trumpet blast.

Love stories are a drug in the Special Inquiry market, and sometimes they have happy endings, in witness whereof stands the Ellis Island Marriage Bureau, but in real

A TYPICAL GROUP OF ITALIANS WAITING FOR ADMISSION.

"Yes."

"Excluded," said one member of the Board quietly. The others nodded. The girl was led away, still smiling, still listening

life love stories are not formed to suit the prejudices of the readers, and the Ellis Island officials often close the book when pathos and tragedy are at flood-tide.

INMATES OF
THE DETENTION ROOM AT DINNER.

When the lover does not meet the penniless sweetheart who has come across the seas to him, when he cannot be found, or, being found, disclaims all responsibility, what can the S. I. Board do?

If the girl has other friends who will provide for her, or if she be strong, able to work, willing to stay in a strange land alone and earn her living, she may be admitted. If not, she must go back, shamed, heartsick, wretched.

There was one lovers' tangle which some of the employees on the Island still remember with a twinge in the region of the heart.

A Swedish girl came over to be married to a sweetheart who had come on before to prepare a home for her. She had waited, but now the home was ready. Olaf had sent for her, would meet her in New York, and they would go home together — to the farm. Yes, he had a farm—in three years—all his own. It was wonderful—but then, Olaf was so remarkable—and in America one has the chance.

All the steerage heard the story, and listened patiently. She was so pretty, so happy. Even the immigrant women whose

EXCLUDED ITALIANS MUST SURRENDER ALL WEAPONS
BEFORE ENTERING THE DETENTION ROOM.

ITALIANS PASSING THE FIRST MEDICAL INSPECTION FOR FAVUS AND TRACHOMA.

views on domesticity had lost their rose color hadn't the heart to air those views before Christina. They compared matrimonial notes and shook their heads behind her back, but they accepted Olaf's halo without question.

And when the Island was reached, every one kept an eye out for Olaf. He would be the handsomest man one had ever seen. There couldn't be the slightest difficulty about recognizing him. Christina had assured them of that.

As for Christina, she was all eyes.

From the moment the boat anchored she expected him to appear; but when it was explained to her that she must go through the examination before she could see any friends, she tried to be reasonable. After all, it was perhaps even harder on Olaf than on her.

But when the examination was over and she needed only to be claimed, and no Olaf was forthcoming, her smiles became a trifle uncertain. The matron was kind. Doubtless the tardy sweetheart had been delayed by the trains, since he was coming from Minnesota. Once more the smiles were beaming. That was it, surely. It was very far, this Minnesota, and he would have to be on the steam cars all night. She would wait. Poor Olaf!

So she waited, but the next day came, and the next, and no Olaf. Inquiries were made. The man had a farm at the address given, but he was away. No one knew where. It was the old story; and when a week had gone by and no news had come, a return steamer sailed and a wretched little Swedish girl sailed on it. The matron was glad the matter was ended. She wore upon one, that broken-hearted little Christina who did not cry.

Two days later a strapping young Swede stormed Ellis Island. His name was Olaf Ericson, and he had been lying sick in a little western town where the railroad accident had occurred. Telegraph? How could he when he was out of his head? Gone back? Christina gone back! And then the officials had an object lesson in Berserker wrath.

He calmed down at last and was utterly miserable. Poor little Christina! And she thought he had forgotten! He would cable. She could come back on the next boat. Money? Of course he had money—and he proved it by ocular demonstration.

The cable was sent off, and then it was Olaf's turn to wait. In time an answer came. She knew. She was coming back. Everybody celebrated, and then there was more waiting. At last the day came round, and the boat came with it. Every one had a smile ready for Christina and Olaf—had ready more than smiles.

But she didn't come in the first rush, as

1. HAPPY IMMIGRANTS WAITING FOR THE TRANSPORT BOAT.   2. A TYPICAL RUSSIAN WITH HIS PACK-HORSE WIFE.
3. A FAMILY OF PAUPERS WHO CANNOT BE ADMITTED, SOME OF THE CHILDREN HAVING EYE AND SCALP DISEASE.

was expected. The crowd dwindled to a thin stream—still no pink-cheeked, yellow-haired girl with radiant face. The matron began to feel vaguely disturbed. A man with papers in his hand touched her on the arm.

"Death in the steerage," he whispered. "Christina Jansen."

the proof of their unfaithfulness during the separation is beyond hiding; other wives who have come in search of husbands grown careless in matters of writing and money-sending. The immigrant officials assisting at stormy scenes, at emotional crises, have a chance to study human nature in the raw, and with the help of the clergymen and

DRIVEN FROM FINLAND TO SEEK NEW HOMES IN THE LAND OF PLENTY.

Here the story ended, for of final happenings Ellis Island keeps no record.

Olaf went back to his farm.

There are women in the detention room whose love stories tell of shame as well as grief, girls who have left the homes they have disgraced and in blind hope followed the lovers who loved and sailed away; wives who were left behind by husbands, and now sent for, have come in abject fear because

missionaries they adjust moral issues as best they may, but the tangle is bad enough when all is said.

There are many causes for which an immigrant may be turned away from our shores, but pauperism, ill-health and violation of the contract labor laws bar more foreigners than do all other causes together. During 1902, 4,479 paupers, 274 contract labor violators and 711 diseased persons

dumped upon foreign soil, possibly without money or provision for reaching his native place, which may be across half the continent from the port. The German Government has a contract with German steamship companies by which the latter are pledged to send all returned emigrants to their native places; but even under this wise dispensation the situation is bad enough. Many of the deported have before leaving home sold everything they owned, converting it all into money to pay their passage. No homes are waiting for them; their hopes are dead; they are shut out from the life of which they dreamed, and cannot even take up the old life where they left off with it.

There is the real consummation of the deportation tragedy, but it is played out far from the Ellis Island stage.

The ship company's responsibility does not end even when an immigrant has successfully passed immigration examinations. If, at any time within a year, he becomes a public charge from causes existing at the

AN ITALIAN RELEASED FROM THE DETENTION ROOM AT THE ELEVENTH HOUR.

were sent straight back to Europe at the cost of the steamship companies. The steamship authorities are required to examine every immigrant before he is taken on board ship, and if he is ineligible to admission at New York to refuse passage to him. This being the case, if on being examined at Ellis Island the immigrant is found ineligible, the steamship company is held responsible and gives him free passage upon a return steamer. When the boat reaches the other side the outcast is

DISAPPOINTED IMMIGRANTS WATCHING THE DEPARTURE OF THE RELEASED ITALIAN.

TYPICAL ITALIANS.

time of his shipping, the company is still liable and must carry him back to Europe; and many poor mortals, after safely passing through the storm and stress and joyfully turning their backs upon Ellis Island drift there again after weeks or months, disillusioned, despondent, helpless. Some of them are brought by relatives or acquaintances who are unwilling to support them, some come of their own accord, some come through the city's charity department, which will not provide for foreigners who have been in the country less than a year.

Several months ago an old Russian Jew, weak, emaciated, helpless, was turned over to the Island authorities by the Department for Relief of the Outdoor Poor.

He had been picked up, half starved, half frozen, wholly unconscious, in an East Side doorway, one bitter night. The authorities would have sent him to Blackwell's, but found when he was able to talk that he had been in America only two months. So they forwarded him to the Immigration Bureau with their compliments. There his case was looked up and various officials remembered him. He had been detained because he was old, feeble, had incipient pulmonary trouble, and was without money. But two buxom daughters appeared to plead his cause. They were enthusiastic, garrulous, all affection and devotion. It would be their privilege to provide for dear papa. One was married to a man whose business was worth $9,000. The other was single, but earned $15 a week in a factory. Their filial affection was an object lesson to all beholders, and the little old father with the mute lips and the tragic Slav eyes stood in his rough peasant clothes and watched his talkative, elaborately dressed children with

something between pride and awe. Finally they carried him off triumphantly, and the judges made remarks to each other about the strong family affection among the lower classes in general and the Hebrews in particular.

The sequel to the story came out when the old man was brought before the Board two months later. Yet he shrank from telling it and it had to be pieced out from monosyllabic answers.

The married daughter had taken charge of him first, but her husband soon grew tired of the burden, and she adored her husband. They wanted him to work, and he tried. He had been a tailor, but the climate was different, and he was old, and the work would not go. They sent him to the other daughter then. She did not like it, but she was kind at first. When she found how much she must give up in order to provide for him, she stopped being kind, and always she was wondering why God allowed old people to live when they were but burdens. She believed he could work, and he tried again, but it only made him ill. He tried to eat little; he needed no fires. But the daughter was angry always. At last one night she turned him into the street. The report of the Charities Department told the rest of the pitiful tale.

"There should be some way of forcing the children to keep their promises, and some adequate punishment for perjury before the Immigration Board," said the Commissioner, "but there is neither. There's nothing to do but send him back to Russia, and Heaven knows what will become of him there."

Such cases of unfilial brutality are fortunately rare, but many an unhappy old father or mother passes the Board and finds temporary lodging in the detention room; and the mothers whose children have failed them win the sympathy of even the burly doorkeeper, who has an old mother of his own in Ireland.

A ROSY-CHEEKED IRISH IMMIGRANT.

One old Italian woman, who lingered for two weeks in the detention room, had three sons in America, "all good boys." When the father died, she sold the little house—why should she stay now that she was alone?—and set out to join her boys. There was money enough for the passage, and it would cost but little to keep her. She would cook and mend and clean—she could save them money. Two of the boys were married, yes; but Carlo was not. He was the

A RUSSIAN FAMILY.

youngest. Perhaps the others would not be glad, after all, but Carlo would. No one had met her, but there were many things that might explain. She waited for "the children" while the Immigration Bureau set its machinery at work to find the dutiful ones. After a time she gave up the two older boys, but of Carlo she was sure. The married sons in Pittsburg declined to make any promises of support. Carlo was not to be found. He was working somewhere on a

THE AMERICANIZED SYRIAN INQUIRING FOR NEWS OF HER SISTER WHO HAS JUST ARRIVED.

A POOR OLD WOMAN WHOSE HEARTLESS CHILDREN ARE SENDING HER BACK WITHIN THE YEAR LIMIT.

Jewish.   Syrian.   Polack.

IMMIGRANT TYPES OF YOUNG WOMEN.

western railroad bed. The little old mother in her short, stuff skirts, her gay kerchief and bodice, her white headdress, went back to Italy, where there was no home waiting, no child to greet her.

All this is not sentimentality. It is fact—fact hard enough, cold enough to satisfy the veriest Gradgrind, and the mills of the Immigration Bureau grind out such facts in liberal measure, but all the exclusions are not set to so plaintive a tune.

There are men by the score who know that they have come in violation of the law and are primed with lies which usually work their undoing through lack of consistency. Some of them have come to fill promised jobs. Some have unsavory European records and perhaps bear the convict brands. Some are mere human flotsam, paupers, loafers, incapables, drifting with the crowd because lacking force to swim in any direction.

A few are clever enough to escape suspicion. More are held up by the examiners and given short shift. There is a right of appeal from the decision of the Board to the Secretary of the Treasury at Washington; and in the course of such an appeal comes an examination by the Commissioners, who recommend the case or set the seal of their disapproval upon it.

Day after day all the year round the play goes on in the Board room over on the north side of the building: the detained are hoping against hope; the excluded are waiting for the beginning of the last act.

The women of the two classes are kept together, and the rooms are swarming with women and children on any day of the year, although in summer there is an overflow to the roof garden. There are sick and sad faces in the crowd, yet the atmosphere is not particularly gloomy. The children take the curse off and stir up some merriment, and the women themselves, as a class, find a certain pleasure in such a supply of neighbors, such an opportunity for gossip. There is always some one to whom one can talk, and topics for conversation are as the sands of the sea. The quarters are more comfortable than the homes many of the women have left. One has three square meals a day—and some of the immigrants taste meat for the first time at those long, bare, wooden tables. Some individual women are desperately unhappy, but the crowds of ignorant femininity display a pervasive cheerfulness.

On the men's side of the corridor things are more somber, and it is a queer impression a visitor receives as an employee throws open the door of the deportation room.

The air of the long, narrow room is blue with tobacco smoke. Listless figures huddle on the benches and are grouped about the windows, through which one sees the Goddess of Liberty holding her torch high against the background of sky. Through the thick haze, dull faces, chiefly Slavic, stare at the visitor, but with no trace of special interest. They are expecting nothing, these men whom the wonderful land has rejected.

Arabian.

Irish.

Hungarian.

IMMIGRANT TYPES OF OLD WOMEN.

Bitter faces, sullen faces, unhappy faces, indifferent faces, all tell the same story—excluded!

From the consumptive Italian actor to the English convict, from the mournful-eyed, hollow-chested Hebrew patriarch to the half-blind German musician, they are failures all; and even when the door is closed upon them an imaginative brain still sees the dreary faces peering through the smoke clouds like a Dantesque vision of lost souls.

The detention room is another story. There one finds no lack of lively interest in chance callers. When the door is opened the on-rush fairly sweeps visitor and employee from their feet. A babel of tongues arises that makes the historic Babel of one's tradition seem tranquil as an Ollendorf exercise.

Every one is demanding tidings. Every one is handing out fresh telegrams. Every one is clutching at hand-luggage, and ready to respond to the awaited call.

Has son or father or brother or uncle or friend come, written, sent money? Is the waiting over? Is one free to go? The man

JUST ARRIVED FROM FINLAND.

in uniform is seized from every side. Appeals deluge him. Papers are shown him. He laughs good-naturedly, shakes his head, talks a dozen different varieties of pigeon English, backs away and the door closes.

As the two free-born American citizens go down the corridor, past the room where the haunting faces lurk in the curling smoke, the door is flung open and a man shoots out like a projectile. In one hand he carries a carpetbag, in the other a big bundle. His face is quivering with excitement, half incredulous, half rapturous, and he stumbles from sheer nervous haste as he walks. A broad-faced, genial Irish agent follows him and tosses a word to his fellow employee in passing.

"Old uncle in Chicago anted up at the last minute. Chap was to sail to-morrow."

So there are eleventh-hour salvations even when one has joined the faces in the smoke, and that is a comfort to the sentimentalist. But then, as has been said before, the sentimentalist has no business on Ellis Island. He would make an uncommonly inefficient guardian of the public welfare.

20
The Walk
Up-town

THE WALK UP-TOWN

IN NEW YORK

By Jesse Lynch Williams

THE walk up-town reaches from the bottom of the buzzing region where money is made to the bright zone where it is spent and displayed ; and the walk is a delight all the way. It is full of variety, color, charm, exhilaration—almost intoxication, on its best days.

Indeed, there are connoisseurs in cities who say that of all walks of this sort in the world New York's is the best. The walk in London from the city to the West End by way of Fleet Street, the Strand and Piccadilly, is teeming with interest to the tourist—Temple Bar, St. Clement's, Trafalgar Square and all—but, for a walk up-town, a walk home to be taken daily, it is apt to be oppressive and saddening, even without the fog ; so say many of those who know it best. Paris, with her boulevards, undoubtedly has unapproachable opportunities for the *flaneur*, but, like Rome and Vienna and most of the other European capitals, she has no one main artery for a homeward stream of working humanity at close of day; and that is what "the walk up-town" means.

And yet so few, comparatively, of those whose physique and office hours permit, take this appetizing, worry-dispelling walk of ours ; this is made obvious every afternoon, from three o'clock on,

by the surface and elevated cars, into which the bulk of scowling New York seems to prefer to push itself (after a day spent mostly in-doors) ; here to get bumped and ill-tempered, snatching an occasional glimpse of the afternoon paper held in the hand which does not clutch the strap overhead. It seems a great pity. The walk is just the right length to take before dressing for dinner. A line drawn eastward from the park plaza at Fifty-eighth Street will almost strike an old mile-stone still standing in Third Avenue, which says, " 4 miles from City Hall, New York." The City Hall was in Wall Street when those old-fashioned letters were cut, and Third Avenue was the Post Road.

I

MANY good New Yorkers (chiefly, however, of that small per cent. born in New York, who generally know rather little about their town except that they love it) have not been so remotely far down the island as Battery Park for a decade, unless to engage passage at the steamship offices which have usurped until recently all of the sturdy houses of the good old Row (though once called " Mushroom Row ") opposite the oval of the ancient Bowling Green, where now the oddly placed statue of Abram de Peyster sits and stares all day. (These old gable windows and broad chimneys are now to be pulled down, and I wonder how he will like the new Custom-house.)

Now, the grandmothers of these same New Yorkers, long ago, before there were any steamships, when Castle Garden was a separate island and Battery Park was a

. . . opposite the oval of the ancient Bowling Green.

fashionable esplanade from which to watch the shipping in the bay and the sunsets over the Jersey hills—their grandmothers, dressed in tight pelisses and carrying reticules, were wont to take a brisk walk, in their very low-cut shoes, along the sea-wall before breakfast and breathe the early morning air. They did not have so far to go in those days, and it was a fashionable thing to do. To-day you can see almost every variety of humanity on the cement paths from Pier A to Castle Garden, except that known as fashionable. But the sunsets are just as good and the lights on the gentle hills of Staten Island quite as soft, and there are more varieties of water-craft to gaze at in the bristling bay. I should think more people would come to look at it all.

I mean of those even who do not like to mingle with other species than their own and yet want fresh air and exercise. On a Sunday in winter if they were to come down here for their afternoon stroll they would find (after a pleasant trip on nearly empty elevated cars) less " objectionable " people and fewer of them than on the crowded up-town walks.

What there are of strollers down here—in winter—are representatives of the various sets of eminently respectable janitors' families (of which there are almost as many grades as there are heights of the roofs from which they have descended), and modest young jackies, with flapping trousers, and open-mouthed emigrants, though more of the latter are to be seen on those flimsy, one-horsed express wagons coming from the Barge Office, seated on piles of dirty baggage—with steerage tags still fresh—whole families of them, bright-colored head-gear and squalling children, bound for the foreign-named immigrant hotels and homes which are as interesting as the immigrants. Some of these latter are right opposite there on State Street, including one with " pillared balcony rising from the second floor to the roof," which is said to be the earlier home of Jacob Dolph in Bunner's novel—a better fate surely than that of the other New York house for which the book was named.

Across the park and up around West Street are more of these immigrant places, some with foreign lettering and some plain Raines's law hotels with mirrored bars.

. . . immigrant hotels and homes.

No. 1 Broadway.

Lower Broadway during a parade.

One of them, perhaps the smallest and lowest-ceiled of all, is where Stevenson slept, or tried to, in his amateur emigranting.

These are among the few older houses in New York used for the same purposes as from the beginning. They seem to have been left stranded down around this earliest part of the town by an eddy in the commercial current which sweeps nearly everything else to the northward from its original moorings. . . . But this is not what is commonly meant by " down-town," though it is the farthest down you can go, nor is it where the walk up-town properly begins.

The Walk Up-town begins where the real Broadway begins, somewhat above the bend, past the foreign consulates, away from the old houses and the early century atmosphere. Crowded sidewalks, a continuous roar, intent passers-by, jammed streets, clanging cable-cars with down-towners dodging them automatically ; the region of the modern high business building.

Above are stories uncountable (unless you are willing to be bumped into) ; beside you, hurried-looking people gazing straight ahead or dashing in and out of these large doors which are kept swinging back and forth all day ; very heavy doors to push, especially in winter, when there are sometimes three sets of them.   Within is the vestibule bulletin-board with hundreds of men's names and office-numbers on it ; near by stands a judicial-looking person in uniform who knows them all, and starts the various elevators by exclaiming " Up ! " in a resonant voice. While outside, the crowd still hums and hurries on ; it never gets tired ; it seems to pay no attention to anything.   It is a matter of wonder how a living is made by all the newsstands on the corners ; all the dealers in pencils and pipe-cleaners and shoe-strings and rubber faces who are thick between the corners, to whom as little heed is given as to the clatter of trucks or the wrangling of the now-blocked cable-cars, or the cursing truck-drivers, or the echoing hammering of the iron-workers on the huge girders of that new office building across the way.

But that is simply because the crowd is accustomed to all these common phenomena of the city street.   As a matter of fact, half of them are not so terrifically busy and important as they consider themselves.   They seem to be in a great hurry, but they do not move very fast, as all know who try to take the walk up-town at a brisk pace, and most of them wear that intent, troubled expression of countenance simply from imitation or a habit generated by the spirit of the place.   But it gives a quaking sensation to the poor young man from the country who has been walking the streets for weeks looking for a job; and it makes the visiting foreigner take out his note-book and write a stereotyped phrase or two about Americans—next to his note about our "Quick Lunch" signs which never fail to astonish him, and behind which may be seen lunchers lingering for the space of two cigars.

An ambulance, with its nervous, arrogant bell, comes scudding down the street. A very important young interne is on the rear keeping his balance with arrogant ease. His youthful, spectacled face is set in stony indifference to all possible human suffering. The police clear the way for him. And now see your rushing "busy throng" forget itself and stop rushing. It blocks the sidewalk in five seconds, and still stays there, growing larger, after those walking up-town have passed on.

The beautiful spire of Trinity, with its soft, brown stone and the green trees and quaintly lettered historic tombs beneath and the damp monument to Revolutionary martyrs over in one corner—no longer looks down benignly on all about it, because, for the most part, it has to look up. On all sides men have reared their marts of commerce higher than the house of God.

The beautiful spire of Trinity . . .

It seems perfectly proper that they should, for they must build in some direction and see what valuable real estate they have given up to those dead people who cannot even appreciate it. Here among the quiet graves the thoughtful stranger is accustomed to moralize tritely on how thoughtless of death and eternity is "the hurrying throng" just outside the iron fence, who, by the way, have to pass that church every day, in many cases three or four times, and so can't very well keep on being impressed by the nearness of death, etc., about which, perhaps, it is just as well not to worry during the hours God meant for work. Even though one cannot get much of a view from the steeple, except down Wall Street, which looks harmless and disappointingly narrow and quiet at first sight, Trinity is still one of the show-places of New York, and it makes a pleasing and restful landmark in the walk up Broadway. It deserves to be starred in Baedeker.

Now comes the most rushing section of

. . . clattering, crowded, typical Broadway.

. . . City Hall with its grateful lack of height . . .

What's the matter?

In the wake of a fire-engine.

all down-town : from Trinity to St. Paul's, clattering, crowded, typical Down-Town. So much in a hurry is it that at Cedar Street it skips in twenty or thirty feet a whole section of numbers from 119 to 135. The east side of the street is not so capricious ; it skips merely from No. 120 to 128.

The people that cover the sidewalks up and down this section, occasionally overflowing into the streets, would probably be pronounced a typical New York crowd, although half of them never spend an entire day in New York City from one end of the month to the other, and half of that half sleep and eat two of their meals in another State of the Union. The proportion might seem even greater than that, perhaps it is, if at the usual hour the up-town walker should, instead, try to wade up Cortlandt Street or any of the ferry streets down which the solid streams of commuters pour.

Up near St. Paul's the sky-scrapers again become thick, so that the occasional old-fashioned five or six story buildings of solid walls with steep steps leading up to the door, seem like playthings beside which the modern building shoots up—on up, as if just beginning where the old ones left off. More like towers are many of these new edifices, or magnified obelisks, as seen from the ferries, the windows and lettering for hieroglyphics. Others are shaped like plain goods-boxes on end, or suggest, the ornate ones, pieces of carefully cut cake standing alone and ready to fall over at any moment and damage the icing.

Good old St. Paul's, which is really old and, to some of us, more lovable than ornate, Anglican Trinity, has also been made to look insignificant in size by its overpowering commercial neighbors, especially as seen from the Sixth Avenue Elevated cars against the new, ridiculous, high building on Park Row. But St. Paul's turns its plain, broad, Colonial back upon busy Broadway and does not seem to care so much as Trinity. This churchyard is not so old nor so large as Trinity's, but somehow it always seems to me more rural and churchyardish and feels as sunny and sequestered as though miles instead of a few feet from Broadway and business.

Now, off to the right-oblique from St.
Paul's, marches Park Row with its very
mixed crowd, which overflows the sidewalks, not only now at going-home time,
but at all hours of the day and most of
the night ; and on up, under the bridge
conduit, black just now with home-hurry-
ing Brooklynites and Long Islanders, we
know we could soon come to the Bowery
and all that the Bowery means, and that,
of course, is a walk worth taking. But The
Walk Up-town, as such, lies straight up
Broadway, between the substantial old
Astor House, the last large hotel remaining down-town, and the huge, obtrusive
post-office building, as hideous as a badly
tied bundle, but which leads us on because
we know—or, if strangers, because we do
not know—that when once we get beyond
it we shall see the calm, unstrenuous beauty of the City Hall with its grateful lack
of height, in its restful bit of park. Here,
under the first trees, is the unconventional
statue of Nathan Hale, and there, under
those other trees—up near the court-house,
I suppose—is where certain memorable
boy stories used to begin, with a poor, pathetic newsboy who did noble deeds and
in the last chapter always married the
daughter of his former employer, now his
partner.

By this time some of the regular walkers up-town have settled down to a steady
pace ; others are just falling in at this point
—just falling in here where once (not so
very many years ago) the city fathers
thought that few would pass but farmers
on the way to market, and so put cheap red
sandstone in the back of the City Hall.

Over there, on the west side of the street,
still stands a complete row of early buildings—one of the very few remaining along
Broadway—with gable windows and wide
chimneys. Lawyers' offices and insurance
signs are very prominent for a time. Then
comes a block or two chiefly of sporting-
goods stores with windows crowded full
of hammerless guns, smokeless cartridges,
portable canoes and other delights which
from morning to night draw sighs out of
little boys who press their faces against the
glass awhile and then run on. Next is a
thin stratum composed chiefly of ticket-
scalpers, then suddenly you find yourself
in the heart of the wholesale district, with
millions of brazen signs, one over another,

No longer to be thrilled .   .   .   will mean to be old.

.   .   .   Grace Church spire becomes nearer.

Instead of buyers . . . mostly shoppers.

Through Union Square.

. . . windows which draw women's heads around.

with names "like a list of Rhine wines;" block after block of it, a long, unbroken stretch.

II

THIS comes nearer to being monotonous than any part of the walk. But even here, to lure the walker on, far ahead, almost exactly in the centre of the cañon of commercial Broadway, can be seen the pure white spire of Grace Church, planted there at the bend of the thoroughfare, as if purposely to stand out like a beacon and signal to those below that Broadway changes at last and that up there are some Christians.

But there are always plenty of people to look at, nor are they all black-mustached, black-cigared merchants talking dollars; at six o'clock women and girls pour down the stairs and elevators, and out upon the street with a look of relief; stenographers, cloak inspectors, forewomen, and little girls of all ages. Then you hear "Good-night, Mame." "Good-night, Rachel." "What's your hurry? Got a date?" And off they go, mostly to the eastward, looking exceedingly happy and not invariably overworked.

Others are emissaries from the sweat-shops, men with long beards and large bundles and very sober eyes, patriarchal-looking sometimes when the beard is white, who go upstairs with their loads and come down again and trudge off down the side-street once more to go on where they left off, by gaslight now.

And all this was once the great Broad-way where not many years ago the prom-

. . . crossing Fifth Avenue at Twenty-third Street.

enaders strutted up and down in the afternoon, women in low neck and India
shawls ; dandies, as they were then called,
in tremendous trousers with huge checks.
Occasionally even now you see a few
strollers here by mistake, elderly people
from a distance revisiting New York after many years and bringing their families with them. " Now, children, you are
on Broadway !" the fatherly smile seems
to say. " Look at everything." They
probably stop at the Astor House.

As the wholesale dry-goods district is
left behind and the realm of the jobbers
in "notions" is reached, and the handlers
of artificial flowers and patent buttons and
all sorts of specialties, Grace Church spire
becomes nearer and plainer, so that the
base of it can be seen. Here, as below,
and farther below and above and everywhere along Broadway, are the stoop and
sidewalk sellers of candies, dogs, combs,
chewing-gum, pipes, looking-glasses, and
horrible burning smells. They seem especially to love the neighborhood of what
all walkers up-town detest, a new building
in the course of erection—with sidewalks
blocked, and a set of steep steps to mount
—only, your true walker up-town always
prefers to go around by way of the street
where he is almost run down by a cab,
perhaps, which he forgets entirely a moment later when he suddenly hears a stirring bell, an approaching roar, and a shriek-
ing whistle growing louder.

Across Broadway flashes a fire-engine,
with the horses at a gallop, the earth trem-
bling, the hatless driver leaning forward
with arms out straight, and a trail of sparks
and smoke behind. Another whizz, and

. . . Madison Square with the sparkle of a clear . . .
October morning.

In front of the Fifth Avenue Hotel.

· · · Diana on top, glistening in the sun.

Seeing the Avenue from a stage top.

the long ladder-wagon shoots across with firemen slinging on their flapping coats, while behind in its wake are borne many small, crazed boys, who could no more keep from running than the alarm-bell at the engine-house could keep from ringing when the policeman turned on the circuit. And young boys are not the only ones. No more to be thrilled by this delight—it will mean to be old.

III

AT last Grace Church, with its clean light stone, is reached ; and the green grass and shrubbery in front of the interesting-looking Gothic rectory. It is a glad relief. And now—in fact, a little before this point—about where stands that melancholic building still bearing the plaintive sign " Old London Streets "—which has been used for church services and prize-fights and has never apparently been a great success at anything—about here, the up-town walkers notice (unless lured off to the left by the thick tree-tops of Washington Square to look at the goodliest row of houses in all the island) that the character of Broadway has changed even more than the direction of the street changes. A short distance below the bend all the stores were wholesale, now they are becoming solidly retail. Instead of buyers

the people along the street are mostly shoppers. Down there were very few women ; up here are very few men. This is especially noticeable when Union Square is reached, with cable - cars clanging around Dead Man's Curve in front of Lafayette's statue. Here, down Fourteenth Street, may be seen shops and shoppers of the most virulent type ; windows which draw women's heads around whether they want to look or not, causing them to run you down and making them deaf to your apologies for it. Big dry-goods stores and small millinery shops ; general stores and department stores, and the places where the sidewalks are crowded with what is known to the trade as " Louis Fourteenth Street furniture." All this accounts for there being more restaurants now and different smells and another feeling in the air.

From the upper corner of Union Square, with its glittering jewellery-shops and music-stores and publishers' buildings, and its somewhat pathetic-looking hotels, once fashionable but now fast becoming out-of-date and landmarky (though they seem fine enough to those who sit and wait on park benches all day), the open spaciousness of Madison Square comes into view, the next green oasis for the up-town traveller. This will help him up the intervening blocks if he is not interested in the stretch of stores, though these are a dif-

. . . people go to the right, up Fifth Avenue.

A seller of pencils.

ferent sort of shop, and they seem to say, with their large, impressive windows, their footmen, their buttons at the door, "We are very superior and fashionable, are we not?"

The shoppers, too, are not so rapacious along here, because they have more time; and the clatter is not so great, because there are more rubber-tired carriages in the street. Nor are all these people shoppers by any means, for along this bit of Broadway mingle types of all the different sorts of men and women who use Broadway at all : nuns, actors, pickpockets, detectives, sandwich-men, little girls going to Huyler's, artists on the way to the Players'—the best people and the worst people, the most mixed crowd in town may be seen here of a bright afternoon.

When they get up to Madison Square the crowd divides and, as some would have us think, all the "nice" people go to the right, up Fifth Avenue, while all the rest go to the left, up the Broadway Rialto and the typical part of the tenderloin.

But when Madison Square is reached you have come to one of the Places of New York. It is the picture so many confirmed New Yorkers see when homesick, Madison Square with the sparkle of a clear, bracing October morning, the creamy Garden Tower over the trees, standing out clear-cut against the sky, Diana on top glistening in the sun ; a soft,

purple light under the branches in the park, a long, decorative row of cabs waiting for "fares," over toward the statue of Farragut, and lithe New York women wearing clothes as they alone know how to wear them, crossing Fifth avenue at Twenty-third Street while a tall Tammany policeman holds the carriages back with a wave of his little finger.

It is all so typically New York. Over on the north side by the Worth monument I have heard people exclaim, "Oh, Paris!" because, I suppose, there is a broad open expanse of asphalt and the street-lights are in a cluster, but it seems to me to be as New Yorkish as New York can be. It has an atmosphere distinctively its own— so distinctly its own that many people, as I tried to say in a former article, miss it entirely, simply because they are looking for and failing to find the atmosphere of some other place.

IV

Now this last lap of the walk—from green Madison Square and the old Delmonico's up the sparkling avenue to the broad, bright Plaza at the Park entrance, where the brightly polished hotels look down at the driving, with their awnings flapping and flags out straight—makes the most popular part of all the walk.

This is the land of liveried servants and

It is also better walking up here.

. . . those who walk for the sake of walking.

At the lower corner of the Waldorf-Astoria.

jangling harness, far away, or pretending to be, from work and worry; this is where enjoyment is sought and vanity let loose—and that, with the accompanying glitter and glamour, is always more interesting to the great bulk of humanity.

It is also better walking up here. The pavements are cleaner now and there is more room upon them. A man could stand still in the middle of the broad, smooth walk and look up in the air without collecting a crowd instantaneously. You can talk to your companion and hear the reply since the welcome relief of asphalt.

Here can be seen hundreds of those who walk for the sake of walking, not only at this hour but all day long. In the morning, large, prosperous-looking New Yorkers with side-whiskers and well-fed bodies—and, unintentionally, such amusing expressions, sometimes—walking part way, at least, down to business, with partly read newspapers under their arms; while in the opposite direction go young girls, slender, erect, with hair in a braid and school-books under their arms and well-prepared lessons.

Then come those that walk at the convenience of dogs, attractive or kickable, and a little later the close-ranked boarding-school-squads and the cohorts of nurse-maids with baby-carriages four abreast, charging everyone off the sidewalk. Next come the mothers of the babies and their aunts, setting out for shopping, unless they have gone to ride in the Park, and for Guild Meetings and Reading Clubs and Political Economy Classes and Heaven knows what other important morning engagements, ending, perhaps, with a visit to the nerve-specialist.

And so on throughout the morning and afternoon and evening hours, each with its characteristic phase, until the last late theatre-party has gone home, laughing and talking, from supper at Delmonico's or the Waldorf-Astoria, the last late bachelor has left the now quiet club; the rapping of his cane along the silent avenue dies away down an echoing side-street; and a lonely policeman nods in the shadow of the church gate-post. Suddenly the earliest milk-wagon comes jangling up from the ferry; then dawn comes up over the gas-houses along East River and it all begins over again.

But the most popular and populous time of all is the regular walking-home hour, not only for those who have spent the day down toward the end of the island at work, but for those who have no more serious business to look after than wandering from club to club drinking cocktails, or from house to house drinking tea.

All who take the walk regularly meet many of the same ones every day, not only acquaintances, but others whom we somehow never see in any other place, but learn to know quite well, and we wonder who they are—and they wonder who we are, I suppose. Pairs of pink-faced old gentlemen, walking arm-in-arm and talking vigorously. Contented young couples who look at the old furniture in the antique-shop windows and who are evidently married, and other younger couples who evidently soon will be, and see nothing, not even their friends. Intent-browed young business men with newspapers under their arms ; governesses out with their charges ; bevies of fluffy girls with woodcock eyes, especially on matinée day with Lyceum programmes in their hands, talking gushingly.

It is a sort of a club, this walking-up-the-avenue crowd ; and each member grows to expect certain other members at particular points in the walk and is rather disappointed when, for instance, the old gentleman with the large nose is not with his daughter this evening. " What can be the matter ? " the rest of us ask each other, seeing her alone.

There is one man, the disagreeable member of the club, a bull-frog-looking man of middle age with a Germanic face and beard, a long stride, and a tightly buttoned walking-coat (I'm sure he's proud of his chest), who comes down when we are on the way up and gets very indignant every time we happen to be late. His scowl says, as plainly as this type, " What are you doing way down here by the Reform Club ? You know you ought to be up by the Cathedral by this time ! " And the worst of it is, we always do feel ashamed and I'm afraid he sees it.

This mile and a half from where Flora McFlimsey lived to the beginning of the driving in the Park is not the staid, sombre, provincial old Fifth Avenue which

. . . with baby carriages.

This is the region of clubs. (The Union League.)

. . . close-ranked boarding-school squads

. . . the coachmen and footmen flock there.

The Church of the Heavenly Rest.

Flora McFlimsey knew. Up Fifth Avenue to the Park New York is a world-city.

Not merely have so many of the brownstone dwellings, with their high stoops and unattractive impressiveness, been turned over to business or pulled down altogether to make room for huge, hyphenated hotels, but the old spirit of the place itself has been turned out; the atmosphere is different.

The imported smartness of the shops, breeches makers to His Royal Highness So-and-So, and millinery establishments with the same Madame Luciles and Mademoiselle Lusettes and high prices, that have previously risen to fame in Paris and London, together with the numerous clubs and picture-galleries, all furnish local color; but it is the people themselves that you see along the streets, the various languages they speak, their expression of countenance, the way they hold themselves, the manner of their servants—in a word, it is the atmosphere of the spot that makes you feel that it is not a mere metropolis, but along this one strip at least our New York is a cosmopolis.

And the Walk-Up-town hour is the best time to observe it, when all the world is driving or walking home from various duties and pleasures.

There, on that four-in-hand down from Westchester County comes a group of those New Yorkers who, unwillingly or otherwise, get their names so often in the papers. The lackey stands up and blows the horn and they manage very well to endure the staring of those on the sidewalks.

Here, in the victoria behind them, is a woman who worships them. She would give many of her husband's new dollars to be up there too, though pretending not to see the drag. See how she leans back in the cushions and tries to prop her eyebrows up, after the manner of the Duchess she once saw in the Row. She succeeds fairly well, too, if only her husband wouldn't spoil it by crossing his legs and exposing his socks.

Here are other women with sweet, artless faces who do not seem to be strenuous or spoiled (as yet) by the world they move in, and these are the most beautiful women in all the world; some in broughams (as one popular story-writer invariably puts his heroines), or else walking independently with an interesting gait.

Here, in that landau, comes the latest foreign-titled visitor, urbane and thoughtfully attentive to all that his friends are saying and pointing out to him. And here is a bit of color, some world-examining, tired-eyed Maharajah, with silk clothes— or was it only one of the foreign consuls who drive along here every day?

There goes a fashionable city doctor, who has a high gig, and correspondingly high prices, hurrying home for his office hours. Surely, it would be more comfortable to get in and out of a low phaëton; this vehicle is as high as that loud, conspicuous,

Approaching St. Thomas's.

advertising florist's wagon—but not for the same reason, surely not.

Here in that grinding automobile come a man and two women on their way to the Martin *table d'hôte*, to see Bohemia, as they think ; see how reckless and devilish they look by anticipation ! Up there on that 'bus are some people from the country, real people from the real country, and their mouths are open and they don't care. They are having much more pleasure out of their trip than the self-conscious family group entering that big gilded hotel, whose windows are constructed for seeing in as well as out (and that is another way of advertising).

Here comes a prominent citizen outlining his speech on his way home to dress for the great banquet to-night, for he is a well-known after-dinner orator, and during certain months of the year never has a chance to dine at home with his family. Suppose, after all, he fails of being nominated !

Here come a man and his wife walking down to a well-known restaurant—early, so that he will have plenty of time to smoke at the restaurant and she to get comfortably settled at the theatre with the programme folded before the curtain rises ; such a sensible way. He is not prominent at all, but they have a great deal of quiet happiness out of living, these two.

And there goes the very English comedian these two are to see in Pinero's new piece after dinner, though they did not ob-serve him, to his disappointment. It is rather late for an actor to be walking down to his club to dine, but he is the star and doesn't come on until the second act, and his costume is merely that same broad-shouldered English-cut frock coat he now has on. We, however, must hurry on.

Because it keeps the eyes so busy, seeing all the people that pass, one block of buildings seems very much like another the first few times the new-comer takes this walk, except, of course, for conspicuous landmarks like that of the late reservoir (it seems a pity its grimness and greenness has to go), or the late Windsor Hotel, with its ghastly memories ; but after awhile all the blocks begin to seem very different ; not only the one where you saw a boy on a bicycle run down and killed, or where certain well-known people live, but the blocks formerly considered monotonous. There are volumes of stories along the way. Down Twenty-ninth Street can be seen, so near the avenue and yet so sequestered, the Church of the Transfiguration, as quaint and low and toy-like as a stage-setting, ever blessed by stage-people for the act which made the Little Church Around the Corner known to everyone, and by which certain pharisees were taught the lesson they should have learned from the parable in their New Testament.

Farther up is a church of another sort, where Europeans of more or less noble

274

"Olympia" Jackies on shore leave.

The new University Club . . . with college coats-of-arms.

blood marry American daughters of acknowledged solvency, while the crowd covers the sidewalks and neighboring house-steps. Here, consequently, other people's children come to be married, though neither, perhaps, attended this church before the rehearsal, and get quite a good deal about it in the society column too, though, to tell the truth, they had hoped that the solemn union of these two souls would appropriately call forth more publicity. Shed a tear for them in passing. There are many similar disappointments in life along this thoroughfare.

Farther back we passed what a famous old rich man intended for the finest house in New York, and it has thus far served chiefly as a marble moral. Its brilliance is dingy now, its impressiveness is gone, and its grandeur is something like that of a Swiss *châlet* at the base of a mountain since the erection across the street of an overpowering, glittering hotel.

This is the region of clubs; they are more numerous than drug-stores, as thick as florists' shops. But it seems only yesterday that a certain club, in moving up beyond Fortieth Street, was said to be going ruinously far up-town. Now nearly all the well-known clubs are creeping farther and farther along, except the old Union Club, which still stands in its cheerless exclusiveness down at the corner of Twenty-first Street, stranded among piano-makers and publishers. Soon the new, beautiful University Club at Fifty-fourth

Street, with the various college coats of arms on its walls, which never fail to draw attention from the out-of-town visitors on 'bus-tops, will not seem to be very far up-town, and by and by even the great, white Metropolitan will not be so much like a lonely iceberg opposite the Park entrance. I wonder if anyone knows the names of them all; there always seem to be others to learn about. Also one learns in time that two or three houses which for a long time were thought to be clubs are really the homes of former mayors, receiving, according to the old Dutch custom, free from the city the two lighted lamps for their doorways. This section of the avenue where, in former years, were well-known rural road-houses along the drive, is once more becoming, since the residence *régime* is over, the region of famous hostelries of another sort.

There is just one of the old variety left, and it, strangely enough, is within a few feet of the two most famous restaurants in this hemisphere—the somewhat quaint and quite dirty old Willow Tree Cottage; named presumably for the tough old willow-tree which still persistently stands out in front, not seeming to mind the glare and stare of the tall electric lights any more than the complacent old tumble-down frame tavern itself resents the proximity of Delmonico's and Sherry's, with whom it seems to fancy itself to be in bitter but successful rivalry—for do not all the coachmen and footmen flock there during the long, wet waits of winter nights, while the dances are going on across at Sherry's and Delmonico's ? Business is better than it has been for years.

Nearing Forty-second Street I always look at the narrow, little, sad gray house pushed a rod or so back from the pavement, with a small, damp grass-plot in front. It is always for sale but never bought. There are three or four real-estate signs there at once, and as soon as one is worn out another is put up ; but the sad little house still stands there unoccupied, squeezed in between two modern buildings so chokingly tight that a bow-window protrudes from the second floor like a tongue lolling forth. It is a remnant of what was once a large, impressive place —a house with a past. I wish someone would buy it and tear it down and put it out of its misery.

In time, even the inconspicuous houses that formerly seemed so much alike become differentiated and, like the separate blocks, gain individualities of their own, though you may never know who are the owners. They mean something to you, just as do so many of the regular up-town walkers whose names you do not know ; fine old comfortable places many of them are, even though the architects of their day did try hard to make them uncomfortable with high, steep steps and other absurdities. When a " For Sale " sign comes to one of these you feel sorry, and when one day in your walk up-town you see it finally irrevocably going the way of all brick, with a contractor's sign out in front blatantly boasting of his wickedness, you resent it as a personal loss. It seems all wrong to be pulling down those thick walls, exposing the privacy of the inside of the house, its arrangement of rooms and fire-places, and the occupant's taste in color and wall-decorations. Two young

women who take the walk up-town always look the other way when they pass this sad display ; they say it's unfair to take advantage of the house. Soon there will be a deep pit there with puffing derricks, the sidewalk closed, and show-bills boldly screaming. And by the time we have returned from the next sojourn out of town there will be an office-building of ever-so-many stories or another great hotel. Already the sign there will tell about it.

You quicken your pace as you draw near the Park ; some of the up-town walkers who live along here have already reached the end of their journey and are running up the steps taking out door-keys. The little thirteen-year-old boy in knicker-bockers who always lights up Fifth Avenue has already begun his zigzag trip along the street ; soon the long double rows of lights will seem to meet in perspective. A few belated children are being hurried home by their maids from dancing-school ; their white frocks sticking out beneath their coats gleam in the half light. Cabs and carriages with diners in them go spinning by, the coachmen whip up to pass ahead of you at the street-crossing ; you catch a gleam of men's shirt-bosoms within and the light fluffiness of women, with the perfume of gloves. Fewer people are left on the sidewalks now—those that are look at their watches. The sun is well set by the time you reach the Plaza, but down Fifty-ninth Street you can see long bars of after-glow across the Hudson.

In the half-dark, under the Park trees, comes a group of Italian laborers ; their hob-nailed shoes clatter on the cement-walk, their blue blouses and red necker-chiefs stand out against the almost black of the trees ; they, too, are walking home for the night. The Walk Up-town is finished and the show is over for to-day.

21
Fighting
the Hudson

FIGHTING THE HUDSON

AN UNRECORDED ADVENTURE IN THE CONSTRUCTION OF THE HUDSON RIVER TUNNEL

BY H. ADDINGTON BRUCE

ONTHS have passed since one of the most difficult and daring engineering feats that the world has known was conceived and successfully carried into execution in the tunnel still in process of construction beneath the Hudson River; up to the present, however, not the slightest hint as to its nature or magnitude, or even its occurrence, has crept into the public prints. True, the conditions which necessitated it made a huge commotion for the time being, for it was currently reported that the long tubeway upon which so much thought, labor, and money had been expended had been flooded by the waters of the giant stream, resulting in great loss of life. The newspapers of New York sought to obtain details, to procure photographs, to present their readers with authoritative statements. It was in vain that they plied the officials, their questions receiving no answer save a categorical denial that there was any foundation for the alarmist reports. Those in charge of the work not only believed that they were within their rights in maintaining silence, but were convinced that to make public the conditions confronting them would seriously embarrass their future operations. The tunnel had not been flooded, but had been invaded; and for a distance of more than eighty feet, denuded of its natural protection of mud, it was undergoing a constant battering by the powerful river.

The Hudson had thrown down the gauntlet in such a way that the challenge could not be declined. The story of how human ingenuity and human pluck flung back the glove is one of the most thrilling chapters in the annals of engineering, culminating as it does in the never before attempted feat of tunneling not under, but *through*, water.

In order to understand how this perilous situation arose it is necessary to explain the methods of subaqueous tunnel construction, which differ materially from those employed in ordinary tunnel work. In forcing their way through the rock and silt of a river the engineers are obliged to devise a means of overcoming the natural pressure of the water and mud, else it would be impossible to keep the tubeway intact long enough to put the metal lining in place. For this purpose recourse is had to compressed air, which is pumped from the engine-house to the "heading," as that part of the tunnel where work is in progress is technically called, and pressure maintained sufficient to offset the natural pressure of the elements. The "cutting" of the tunnel also presents peculiar difficulties, which are surmounted by the use of what is known as a shield.

The shield employed in the Hudson River tunnel is a cylinder, thirteen feet long and twenty feet in diameter, with a hardened-steel "cutting edge," fifteen inches in length and three inches in circumference. Behind the cutting edge comes the outside "diaphragm," with several openings to admit the mud displaced by the shield's advance. Back of these openings are chambers four feet in length, one chamber for each opening, and through these the mud is admitted by means of hinged doors, to be taken by small cars to the entrance. The hinged doors are always in operation, regulating the quantity of mud passing through the chambers into the tunnel.

Behind the chambers are fourteen jacks, or hydraulic rams, which are used to push the shield forward. These jacks work at

place by hydraulic pressure, and bolted and calked to insure against possible leakage.

Between the lining and the tail-end of the shield there is always an unprotected space of an inch and a half. This small opening would, under ordinary circumstances, be insignificant, but it is of great moment in subaqueous work, owing to the fact that the mud pressure at the top of

FIRST AIR-LOCK, FROM THE NEW JERSEY SIDE

The small door beside which the men are standing is the entrance to the first of the tunnel air-locks. Without these air-locks it would be impossible for the tunnel laborers to accustom themselves to the great air pressure at the heading. On each side of the tunnel run the pipes through which the air is forced into the heading and the pipes whereby the hydraulic pressure is applied to the shield. In that portion of the tunnel visible in the picture the air pressure is normal.

a pressure of five thousand pounds to the square inch. The remainder of the thirteen-foot cylinder is known as the "tail-end," its function being to afford a protection to the unfinished section of the tunnel during each "shove"—the vernacular equivalent for the operation of advancing the shield. In making a shove, the mud doors are opened, the power is turned on, and the gigantic cylinder moves slowly forward until it has advanced twenty-five inches, that being the distance which it is deemed safe to gain before putting in a ring of the permanent lining of the tunnel. The lining is composed of cast-iron plates, forced into

the twenty-foot shield is eight and a half pounds less than the pressure at the bottom of the shield, because the pressure varies according to the depth. In the compressed air, however, such a variation is impossible, since there is no means of pumping the air into the tunnel so that the pressure will vary as the mud pressure varies. As a result, the necessity of maintaining an air pressure sufficient to offset the mud pressure at the bottom may cause the disintegration of the silt above the small opening, in which case it will be " blown away " and the tunnel exposed to the action of the river. The danger is greatest, of course,

SECTION OF TUNNEL SHOWING MANNER OF LIGHTING THE HEADING

when for any reason progress is delayed, because the air is then directed constantly against the same spot.

Things went smoothly beneath the Hudson until work had been finished for a distance of about forty-three hundred feet. The constructors knew, however, that they might thereafter expect trouble, for their charts showed them that they were liable at any moment to strike rock. Finally the day came when the shield refused to move despite the enormous pressure behind it, and investigation showed that it had struck against a ledge and that the cutting edge had been badly turned. Nothing could be done until this was repaired, and to make repairs it was necessary to go outside the tunnel and into the bed of the river.

In order to get beyond the shield a bulkhead had to be built. This in itself is a delicate and interesting piece of work, and it becomes doubly so when carried out in the depths of a river's bed. The tunnel workers, or "Sand Hogs," enter the lower chambers of the shield and force out into the mud what are known as "polling-boards." These extend about eight feet from the shield, and when in position give a serviceable overhead covering while the task of "breastboarding" is in progress. By breastboarding is meant the gradual advance of small upright boards from the shield, the intervening mud being taken out little by little and passed through the chambers. A small room is thus constructed in front of the shield, and the work of repairing may then begin.

The building of the bulkhead took about seven days. Further delay resulted from the substitution of an "apron" for the polling-boards, the apron being an overhead sheet of steel attached to the shield and designed to provide a permanent shelter for any further bulkhead work. Meanwhile, in order to maintain the integrity of the tunnel, the compressors were kept constantly in action. As a result, the mud covering, or "blanket," which at this particular spot was very soft and of a thickness not exceeding ten feet, while the depth of the river was sixty-five, gradually became disorganized, and finally yielded to the air pressure. As fast as it was blown into the river, fresh silt appeared in the opening, to be in turn dislodged by the air, until a cup-like depression extending for a distance of eighty-five feet along the line of the tunnel was eventually hollowed in the bed of the Hudson. At once the river, infuriated, began to bombard the unprotected roof with boulders, ice, and the force of its own waves, until the tunnel rang with a perfect fusillade of marine ammunition. Heroic measures were necessary.

Charles M. Jacobs, the engineer, had been kept advised of the situation by the works manager, George B. Fry, who had been quick to foresee the danger. Mr. Jacobs, to whom has also been intrusted the building of the great subaqueous tunnels for the Pennsylvania Railroad, stands at the head of his profession and has had a wide and varied experience in under-river engineering, but never before had he been called upon to cope with the problem that then presented itself. The question was how to continue work without flooding the tunnel. So long as the shield remained where it was this danger was not immediate, for although compressed air does not of itself keep out water, it holds in position anything that will, and for this purpose a quantity of small bags filled with sawdust is kept in the heading, ready for an emergency like the present one. With an attempt to advance the shield, however, the packing would be dislodged and the situation completely changed.

The logical method of procedure was to make a false covering for the tunnel by dropping barge-loads of clay into the depression; but the time was midwinter, the clay-banks were frozen fast, and the vagrant ice would, in any event, render extremely difficult the task of alining the barges in the river. For a time Mr. Jacobs seriously considered the advisability of deferring further operations until clay could be obtained; but, realizing that the greater the delay the greater the risk of losing the tunnel, he ultimately resolved on a bold stroke, and gave orders that so soon as the

IN THE HEADING: CLEANING UP AFTER A SHOVE

Subaqueous tunnel workers are never busier than immediately after a "shove," for things must be made shipshape before the work of lining the tunnel can be resumed. The camera has caught a group of "Sand Hogs" hard at work. Some are shoveling the river mud into the little cars. One laborer is already upon the "erector" examining the new section of tunnel. The disk in the background is the end of the shield, the huge boring-machine that pierces the silt of the river-bed.

repairs on the cutting edge were completed a shove was to be attempted.

The works manager at once began to marshal his forces. He provided an extra number of the invaluable sawdust-bags; gave directions that the men in the engine-room should stand prepared, on receiving a hurry telephone call from the heading, to force the compressors to manufacture their limit of air, so that every available ounce might be utilized at the seat of hostilities; and dropped a hint to the tunnel foremen to the effect that some delicate work was on foot and they must keep a close eye on their men. With the dawning of the day when the supreme test was to be made the officials felt that they were well prepared for what they deemed the inevitable struggle.

Barely had the first, almost imperceptible movement of the shield been made when that struggle began. The river, as though taken by surprise, hesitatingly

trickled through the displaced packing, but, as the gap around the huge circle grew wider, soon hurled itself forward in one continuous flood. For a moment the working force wavered. Some recovered themselves in an instant, and leaped to join issue with the enemy. Others there were who fled for their lives, until their foreman, in tones that rose above the roaring of the waters and the hissing of the air, stormed out words of command that rallied them and made them remember that they owed it to their pluckier comrades and to their employers to face the foe shoulder to shoulder. Now the battle was on in earnest: air against water, muscle and brain against the cruelest of elements.

Never did the huge light that glows unceasingly in the heading cast its rays upon a wilder scene. Knee-deep in water, the men forced old clothes, jute sacks, and the magic sawdust-bags into the open gap around the shield. Even these proved unavailing, and off came coats and shirts, to be whipped into position by the Sand Hogs, desperate with death staring them in the face. Not a voice was heard save that of the foreman, demoniacally urging his men to renewed efforts. Whenever the air pressure weakened until it became less than the hydrostatic head of the water, the sacks and clothes would vanish, to be replaced in a second by new packing. One yawning vent defied every effort until, savage from fear, the defenders lifted a comrade from his feet and held him against the opening. It took twenty minutes to advance the shield far enough to permit the emplacement of a new ring of lining, and every second was a battle for life. The end came with a suddenness that startled even the most optimistic. Upon the completion of the shove, the river, baffled, slunk away, while the workers hurriedly put the iron plates in place, thus erecting a strong barricade against the devouring waters. Upon the next shove, however, and for two more shoves, the battle was renewed, and on every occasion the Sand Hogs were victorious. By that time the tunnel had been advanced into ground beyond the confines of the deadly void, and the danger was at an end.

It should be noted that the direct cause and cure of the trouble was compressed air. Without this artificial aid it would be impossible to carry the work to a successful termination; but at the same time it is compressed air which makes the task so arduous to the toilers of the deep. The normal air pressure is only fifteen pounds to the square inch, whereas the pressure at the heading is anywhere from thirty to forty pounds above normal, a pressure which the human organism could not withstand unless properly prepared. The needed preparation is secured by an elaborate system of "locks," whereby the change from one atmosphere to another is gradual.

A tunnel lock is a cylindrical, boiler-like chamber with doors at each end. The workman en route from the shaft to the heading enters the first lock from the normal atmosphere, the door by which he has entered is immediately closed, and a valve is opened, admitting air from the next section of the tunnel, where the pressure is in the neighborhood of fifteen pounds above normal. The door giving the workman

entrance into the farther section cannot be opened, however, until the air in the lock is of the same pressure as that in the tubeway beyond. But there is no lengthy delay, the air rushing in very rapidly and with a noise that resembles nothing so much as a distant waterfall. As soon as the required pressure is obtained, the valve is closed, the far door opens, and the toiler proceeds to the next lock, where he accustoms himself to a still rarer atmosphere. When he arrives at the heading he will find, among other odd things, that, although he can breathe as freely and naturally as in the open air, it is impossible for him to whistle. Purse his lips as he may, he cannot utter a sound.

Experience has shown that it is not advisable to remain in the heading more than four hours at a time. Further delay may bring on an attack of the "bends," the colloquial name given to a disease peculiar to compressed-air work. Under certain conditions the bends may attack a man who has been in the heading a comparatively short time, and before a Sand Hog is allowed to enter the air he must undergo a rigid medical examination. If he is suffering from a cold, has poor heart-action, or is accustomed to the use of liquor, he is at once debarred, for he might fall a speedy victim. For those affected by the air a hospital in the form of a big lock is provided in the office quarters, where the patient is treated by the company physician, the treatment consisting chiefly in the pumping in of air until the pressure is the same as that in which the Sand Hog has been working. Slowly the terrific pains that have been shooting through every joint of the patient's body pass away, and as they pass, the pressure is reduced little by little until it descends to the normal fifteen pounds.

These toilers of the deep are now busily engaged upon not only the tunnel in which they won their great victory, but upon a twin tunnel, immediately to the south, work on which will not be completed for several months. This second tunnel, or "South Tunnel," as it is termed in contradistinction to the tubeway in which the conflict took place, runs parallel to its mate, both entering the river at the foot of Fifteenth street in Jersey City and emerging at the foot of Morton street in New York, between the piers of two steamship com-

IN THE RIVER-BED BEYOND THE TUNNEL

The illustration shows the "apron," which has played an important part in the building of the tunnel. The apron is the overhead sheet of steel extending from the shield, a section of which is to be seen on the left. By means of the apron the tunnel workers are enabled to pass beyond the shield into the bed of the river and blast the rock impeding their progress, or make any necessary repairs to the shield. The men to the left are busily drilling preparatory to a blast. The rock has to be broken into small pieces to allow it to pass through the doors of the shield into the heading whence, as shown by a previous illustration, it will be taken out of the tunnel.

panies. William G. McAdoo, president of the New York and New Jersey Railroad Company and head of the syndicate which is financing the tunnels, is hopeful that within a year both will be available for the purpose for which they are being built — trolley-car transit between Jersey City and New York; but it would appear probable that he is over-sanguine, for subaqueous engineering is something that cannot often be carried through according to schedule. In submarine tunneling the truth of the old adage is daily apparent: "More haste, less speed."

The idea of tunneling the Hudson is by no means of recent birth. Several attempts in this direction have been made since 1874, when the first company to undertake the construction of a sub-Hudson tunnel came into being. Little progress had been made, however, when, through an accident to the door of an air-lock at a critical moment, the tunnel was flooded and a number of laborers were drowned. The water was pumped out and work resumed, but a bad leak once more caused a long delay. By this time something had been accomplished in both tunnels, but the company had now come to the end of its financial resources and was obliged to order a permanent cessation of work. The years passed, and eventually an English syndicate undertook to complete the tunnel. In their turn they found the task beyond their powers. Finally Mr. Jacobs declared his willingness to begin where the others, defeated, had withdrawn. He and his associates are now satisfied that they have solved the most difficult problem likely to arise in this or future subaqueous tunnel work. They have assuredly proved that air, if properly reinforced, will serve to stem the most powerful of torrents, and the demonstration of this must be said to mark a milestone in the march of engineering science.

285

22
The Delusion of the Race-track

THE COSMOPOLITAN

From every man according to his ability: to every one according to his needs

JANUARY, 1905.

BOOK-MAKERS AT SHEEPSHEAD BAY, NEW YORK, WATCHING THE FINISH OF AN IMPORTANT RACE

THE DELUSION OF THE RACE-TRACK

By DAVID GRAHAM PHILLIPS

MR. JEROME, District Attorney of New York County, was making one of his impressive and most important demonstrations that there are short cuts to justice as lawful as, and vastly more effective than, those devious, bog- and pit-beset paths which the lawyers have invented. He burst into a gambling-house; he burst into its safe. Among several curious exhibits was a huge roll of paper money, about as thick as a fire-plug. It contained, in bills of all denominations, no less than three-quarters of a million dollars. It was the "roll" of a well-known book-maker, used each day at the track and deposited with the keeper of the gambling-house each night.

During the racing-season there are always a score such "rolls," and several hundred smaller ones. They constitute the most important factor in the state-protected, society-patronized, fashionable and respectable industry of "improving the breed of thoroughbreds." Not in artistically laid-out tracks, not in strings of beautiful horses, not in any other of the attractive accompaniments of racing, do its true nature and purpose so clearly appear as in these "rolls," not a bill in a single one of them got by any but dishonest and unlawful means, most of them got by means which, as we shall presently see, are not short of infamous.

There are less than thirty race-tracks in the United States, less than ten thousand horses kept in readiness for the track, less than fifty thousand persons directly interested in tracks and horses; probably the total investment of capital is considerably less than seventy-five millions. But in results, in dividends, no other activity, not even the liquor traffic, compares with racing. For, as a judge recently pointed out, the race-track is directly the largest agent, and the most successful, in recruiting for the criminal class. It makes more thieves, more murderers, more moral wrecks, than any other. And to deprave and debauch is its chief object.

It has three objects—the object alleged in the law; the object alleged by its emi-

distances—rarely more than a mile and a quarter, oftenest for about seven-eighths of a mile. The horses are so trained that staying power is absolutely sacrificed for speed. With an occasional, most rare exception, the thoroughbreds of the racing-stables can be beaten, certainly in a course of five miles, probably in a course of three and a half or four miles, by horses which have no especial pretensions to blood or to speed. Further, these raced thoroughbreds are used by their owners in reckless fashion, are entered

IN THE BETTING-RING AT THE MORRIS PARK RACE-TRACK, NEW YORK

nent and most respectable patrons; the real object.

The legal object always means the one put forward by the projectors of any questionable enterprise, to fool the moral sense of the people or to enable the people themselves to fool their moral sense. In the case of horse-racing the legal object is, to quote again the New York law, "to improve the breed of the thoroughbred." That this is not the real object, that it is not even a part of the object, is patent upon the surface of the facts. The most of the contests are for short

and run in race after race as long as they can stand the killing pace, and then are discarded. A few owners put humaneness to the horses before money-making; but these are few indeed. The test of a stable is its winnings, and the way to win is to speed the horses in it that show ability, and to speed them as often as they will respond.

There is a movement in this country toward improving the breed of thoroughbreds; but it has only an incidental, practically an accidental, connection with racing. If there were not a race-track,

BOOK-MAKERS AT JAMAICA, NEW YORK, WHILE A RACE IS BEING RUN

not a racing-stable, not a "patron of the turf," in the country, the demand for fine horses for riding and driving would continue the improvement of the breed of the thoroughbred, for which that demand alone is thus far responsible. To say that racing is the cause of fine and finer horses is like saying that the consumption of milk-punches is responsible for the improved breed of cows, and that if no more milk-punches were made, we should soon have only the cow that gives the pale-blue milk.

If we had to look for the development of our breed of horses to the race-track, with its killing speed and its merciless sacrifices of two-year-olds, we should soon have a retrograde breed, weak, deformed, short-lived.

The second of the admitted objects of racing, unlike the first, has reality in it. Ever since the world has had idle rich, with a fondness for spectacular ways of wasting money in

E. R. THOMAS (AT THE LEFT) AND CLARENCE MACKEY (IN THE CENTER) FIGURING ON THE ODDS

BETTING-RING AT GRAVESEND, NEW YORK, ON THE DAY OF THE
BROOKLYN HANDICAP

amusements too costly for the ordinary man to initiate, there have been horse-races. And our own idle rich of our fledgling but ambitious aristocracy of commerce, aspiring to be in all respects like the "gentlemen" of the Old World, have lifted racing out of the oblivion into which it was sinking, and have made it respectable and fashionable and have glozed it with what some people call a moral tone. There was a time when we had racing in this country under the patronage of "gentlemen"— the antebellum, slavery days. But with the spread of intelligence, with the development of public moral sense, with the rise of the idea of the dignity of honest labor, ra-

J. H. ALEXANDRE
Steward of the National Steeplechase Association, discussing a race

cing swiftly went down, until it was almost wholly in the hands of the criminal class where it belongs; the prospect was for an end of it. Then, along came our new crop of idle rich, with the passion for aping the aristocracy of Europe. And we have racing "rehabilitated"—that is, its hideous reality covered with the mantle of social respectability.

This brings us to the third, the chief, the real object of the race-track. That real object is gambling. Not at all for the improvement of the breed of the thoroughbred horse. Partly for the improvement of the breed of the thoroughbred "gentleman"—in the unmanly, un-American, European sense of the word. And chiefly for the improvement of the breed of the thoroughbred rascal—for, of the many breeds of rascals your gambler is the most thorough. In his nature all vices breed as naturally as maggots in a rotten cheese. In his heart all the virtues inherent in mankind are swiftly stifled. A practitioner of any other vice may retain some virtues, may make them flourish even. But the gambler becomes wholly debauched. And the worst of it is that because the outward and visible signs of the utter rottenness within are often lacking, his fellow men who do not gamble or gamble only "for fun" do not realize the ravages this lust for gain without toil has made in him. And we hear human hyenas, cheats, procurers, debauchers, spoken of as "Honest Johns" and ''Square Dicks!" And book-makers who hide under an air of prodigality the instincts and practices that would shame the pawnbrokers of fiction, are called "good fellows," men with the "highest sense of honor."

A few of the owners of race-horses are rich men of character, with a more or less amiable weakness for imitating dukes and earls and princes. And some of them, through custom or carelessness or selfishness, blind themselves to the infamy they aid and abet. The most of the owners are men whose secret thoughts would make daylight shudder. They use their horses as the proprietor of a sweat-shop uses his slaves. They are coldly, mercilessly, unscrupulously "on the make." Of course, being shrewd and calculating, they have the showy kind of honesty that is the necessary part of their business assets—they pay what they owe, pay it without written bond, since their entire business is unlawful. But to praise this, to call it real honesty, is like eulogizing a merchant for not employing highwaymen and pickpockets to ply upon the customers that enter his shop. And, aside from that compulsory virtue, they have none that ever exhibits itself. Their talk and their habits are low and coarse; they are false friends, false husbands and false lovers, and their society is seduction to depravity; their very charities, on analysis, are seen to be a propaganda of the vices they boast as virtues — vices which dazzle the innocent, allure the young and cause the weak to fall.

JAMES R. KEENE (AT THE LEFT)

How could it be otherwise when they make their livelihood and their career by creating and by trafficking with profligates and thieves? How could it be otherwise when they are engaged in a business whose most respectable patrons are of necessity law-breakers and law-defiers, bribers of police and legislators?

Also, there are connected with race-tracks as officials under directors and stewards a few men of sound character

JOE VENDIG

A typical successful book-maker (at the right), watching
the progress of a race

whose large pay — from five thousand dollars to forty thousand and more a year—ought to make them reputable, are, with a few notable and by contrast brilliant exceptions, rascals whom the owners of horses and the stewards of jockey-clubs watch incessantly—but, only too often, in vain.

To gamble is the great, the fundamental, the real object of the race-track. Without gambling, there would not be a race-track or a racing-stable in the country. With gambling, racing would thrive and flourish were there not a single thoroughbred from Maine to Texas.

In the neighborhood of one or more large cities in every section of the country there are one or more of these great gambling-plants—near New York and Buffalo and Washington, near Chicago and Louisville and St. Louis and Cincinnati and Memphis and Little Rock and New Orleans, near Detroit and Denver and San Francisco, et cetera, et cetera. Over four circuits— the Eastern, the Southern, the Western and the Pacific Slope— the horses are sped into premature decrepitude that thousands of persons may be ruined and tens of thousands totter along the line between crime and the longing and dread to commit crime. The horses go round and round, and out at the hopper of the swift machine come the dissolute life, the blunted moral sense, the defaulter, the thief, the suicide, the murderer.

The schemes for inducing public sentiment to tolerate this public debauchery vary with the section in hypocrisy and criminality. Let us take New York state, for example. For it has more race-tracks than any other state; there the dividends in crime and degradation are largest; and there the pretense of respectability is most slimily hypocritical.

If you will read New York's racing-laws, you will find that the sole object of racing is the improvement of the

—decent, honorable, straight fellows whose love of sport blinds them to the true nature of the enterprise to which they lend their names and their powerful support. Without these men, not even the determination of the idle rich to maintain the "royal sport" could keep the race-tracks open. For it is under the cover of the real honesty and sporting enthusiasm of many fine fellows of the racing-associations that the rascality is able to keep itself alive. They are the ten just men who save Sodom from destruction. How tiny and frayed a fringe of the mantle of virtue will completely cloak a very behemoth of evil. Most of the people round race-tracks and racing-stables are of the criminal class—and no one denies it. Touts and tipsters, rail-birds and jockeys and all the rest of them, are, for the most part, of the scourings of society. Even the jockeys,

"PITTSBURG PHIL" (ON THE RIGHT) DISCUSSING THE BETTING

breed of horses. The laws carefully eliminate every feature that could possibly be objected to. As for gambling, either at the tracks or anywhere else, it is classed as a crime and severely and rigidly prohibited. To make sure that racing shall be nothing but a cold matter of science and progress, racing-clubs are

AUGUST BELMONT ON THE RACE-COURSE AT MORRIS PARK RECEIVING CONGRATULATIONS AFTER WINNING THE TREMONT STAKES

A NUN BEGGING AT THE TRACK

Above her is a "Notice to the Public" which the public
does not notice. It reads: "The public is hereby notified that
disorderly conduct of any kind, pool-selling, book-making or
gambling of any character is prohibited on these grounds.
"Per Order of the
                              "Board of Directors"

incorporated under the most upright and
stiff of rules; and to make assurance
doubly sure, a State Racing Commission
is established to supervise associations
and tracks and to see that only lawful
things are done. Reading the law, you
would say the purposes of an incorporated church could not be more innocent than the purposes of a jockey-club
in the state of New York. And, if you
went on to discover that the governor,
in the faithful discharge of the duty imposed upon him by the law, had appointed as the unsalaried, public-spirited
members of the State Racing Commis-

sion three as respectable, as
substantial, as reputable citizens as were contained within
the state's borders, you would
feel that whatever racing
might be elsewhere, in New
York state it must be an honest and single-minded, if
misguided and foolish, attempt to "improve the breed
of the thoroughbred."

But in reading the law you
would come upon one clause
which might rouse your sus-
picions. You would note that
five per cent. of the gross
receipts of the racing-associations was to be taken by the
State Racing Commission and
paid over to the various agricultural fair associations of
the state.

If you were in the habit of
examining the laws passed by
our ingenuous and devoted
public servants at state capi-
tals, you would catch upon this phrase the
stealthy grin of the familiar "joker."
And you would pause if necessary and reflect. If these races are to be so innocent,
if gambling is to be prohibited, how will
there be any "receipts"? How will the
public, which knows nothing of the points
of thoroughbreds and cares less, be
induced to attend, to make the journey,
to pay the large admission-fee? And
why, oh, why this proffer of a bribe to
the honest farmers banded together in
county fair associations? Why should
it have been necessary to put into the
law something which would enable

PARADE OF ENTRIES TO THE STARTING-POST AT THE BRIGHTON BEACH
RACE-TRACK

legislators from the "moral" rural districts to go back home with a defense of their votes for this innocent and praiseworthy measure? Why does the farmer have to be cozened with a "rake-off" to let benevolent, public-spirited rich men provide better breeds of horses for him?

With this suspicion, or wonder, in your mind, you go to the offices of the fashionable and exclusive Jockey Club under whose auspices and supervision are all the ten tracks in the state of New York, and you ask there whether gambling is somehow permitted at the race-tracks. "We know of no gambling," will be the

where a rumor which would start you to a race-track. You would see in person how these good men were being slandered. At the track you see in every conspicuous place a copy of the law forbidding gambling, forbidding it with all the majesty of the mighty and sovereign state of New York. You presently drift with the vast crowd into a vast shed, as conspicuous as the adjoining grandstand.

A "betting-shed"! Why does the honorable management provide a "betting-shed" when there must be no betting?

AT THE LEFT, SHOWING PROFILE, LARRY WATERBURY; THE TALLEST MAN IS HARRY PAYNE WHITNEY

reply. "The law forbids gambling; we are an organization composed of honorable men and law-abiding citizens; our president is a member of the State Racing Commission, an official of the state, and has therefore taken an oath to maintain the laws of the state. There can be no open gambling at any of the race-tracks; for if there were, he would know it and would therefore be a lawbreaker, a criminal, a violator of his oath of office."

And you would go away, humbled. How unjust your suspicion!

But perhaps you might hear some-

On many of the pillars of that shed you see copies of that same anti-gambling law. Between these pillars and set in a frame of copies of the anti-gambling law you see the stands of the book-makers, men upon platforms in front of them shouting out the odds; you see the wagertakers and the sheet-writers and crowds surging about each stand, handing in money; and after each race, you see crowds about the rear ends of these stands receiving money.

Possibly you would be stunned by this shameless, this impudent defiance of the solemn enactments of the people of a

HERMAN DURYEA (WITH MOURNING BAND), SUC-
CESSOR OF W. C. WHITNEY

great state, by this proof that there were
reputable men in the community brazenly
flouting the laws, brazenly violating their
solemn oaths of office. And this that a
horde of scoundrels who never did an
honest day's work may fleece the public,
may tempt the young and the weak to
crime!

Unable to believe your own eyes, you
go up and proffer a wager. It is accepted;
the only difference between the old
and the new procedure is that, instead of
giving you a ticket, the book-maker takes
the number of your badge—and pays on
its showing, if your horse wins.

But, you might say to yourself, the
officials of this racing-association, the
officials of the Jockey Club, the members
of the State Racing Commission, do not
know of this. They quiet their con-
sciences, they save themselves from the
open shame of collusion with criminals
in crime, by refusing to see what their

eyes reveal, by refusing to
hear what is dinned into
their ears by these loud-
mouthed rascals. And then
you learn:

First. That each of these
book-makers pays the ra-
cing association for the
privilege of setting up his
gambling-stand; that book-
makers in the "big ring"
pay fifty-seven dollars a
day each, book-makers in
the back line thirty-seven
dollars a day each, book-
makers in the "stand-up"
line seventeen dollars and
a half a day each, book-
makers in the so-called
"free field" thirty-seven
dollars a day each. And to
make the matter more
shameful, they are com-
pelled to minister to the
hypocrisy of the "gentle-
men" in the criminal con-
spiracy by paying the
money in the form of
purchases of admission-
tickets, the tickets being
not taken or even offered,
and additional and real
admission-tickets being purchased by
each book-maker and each of his
clerks. In all, the money taken by
the "gentlemen," the law-abiding citizens of the racing-associations, from
their frankly disreputable pals, is between seven thousand and eight thousand dollars a day for each racing-
day.

Second. Whenever the stewards of
the Jockey Club suspect that a jockey
has pulled a horse in collusion with a
book-maker, they send for and examine the betting-sheets of that book-
maker!

Thus these honorable and reputable
"gentlemen," social leaders, business
leaders, political leaders, become law-
breakers not that their families may
have a little better incomes, not for
higher wages, not for bread, but that they
may indulge a selfish, showy passion at
the expense of the characters and the

careers of tens of thousands of the young men of their country!

But the real perfidy of the whole transaction does not appear until you look beneath the surface and see the contrivance by which these "gentle-men" are enabled to be lawless yet un-molested. Under the state constitu-tion in force until 1895, gambling was prohibited, but in terms so general that the "gentlemen" amateurs and the criminal professionals of the race-track were able to concoct a law in evasion. It is unnecessary to say how this was got through the Legislature. But at the Constitutional Convention of 1894 the Constitution was revised to read, in Section 9 of Article I, "Nor shall any lottery, or the sale of lottery tickets, pool-selling, book-making, or any other kind of gambling hereafter be authorized or allowed within the state, and the Legislature shall pass appropriate laws to prevent offenses against any of the pro-visions of this section." This sounds specific enough. But it is not specific enough to prevent legislators and police officers from turning a dishonest penny by tolerating gambling at race-tracks.

The eminently respectable amateurs and the pariah professionals of racing joined forces, bought the Legislature and got it to pass the racing-law of 1895 (Chapter 570). Under this astounding statute, perhaps the most insulting piece of lawlessness that ever bore the name of law, the crime of gambling at the race-track is made punishable only by a civil action on the part of the loser of a wager to recover the amount lost.

And the highest courts of the state of New York, in sympathy with the eminent gentlemen who "patronize" racing, and enamored of the hair-split-tings which bring justice into contempt, have sustained that preposterous law-to-defeat-law! Legislators bribed, po-lice officers subsidized, courts cajoled —all this that a loathsome disease may be perpetuated!

Each racing-day the attendance is from ten to thirty or forty thousand. There is in the crowd a sprinkling of really respectable people, lovers of out-door sport; there is a sprinkling of more or less reputable people directly and indirectly connected with racing. But also, all the jungles of vice and crime have been emptied of their cowardly beasts of prey—the keepers and patrons

WEARING THE DARK OVERCOAT, IN THE RIGHT FOREGROUND, IS FRANK
FARRELL, LARGELY INSTRUMENTAL IN THE POLITICAL SITUATION
FAVORABLE TO THE RACE-TRACKS

of dives and dens, the political heelers, the thieving police officers, the most offensive elements in the city. And then, there is the crowd—thousands of young and youngish men, neglecting their work, wasting their small earnings, preparing themselves for that desperate state of mind in which accounts are falsified, tills tapped, pockets picked and the black-jack of the highwayman wielded.

But this is not all, not half, not a small fraction, of the scandal and the shame. The results of each race are telegraphed to pool-rooms in every city. There are several hundred of these pool-rooms in New York, almost as many in Chicago, scores in such cities as Boston, New Orleans, Cincinnati and San Francisco. And who are the patrons of these places? For the most part, the young men on small salaries throughout the country. And each and every one of them is headed straight for disgrace and ruin; and not a few thousands will arrive there. The pool-room—that is, the race-track; that is, the jockey-clubs; that is, the few reputable gentlemen who maintain in a vile hypocrisy of respectability the "royal sport"—is responsible for the most of the downfalls among the class of young men on which our future depends.

The Western Union Telegraph Company a short time ago bowed to public indignation which happened to penetrate to some of its directors of pious repute. But as soon as the storm passed, the company resumed its service to these pool-rooms, these trap-doors into hell. The profit—about five million dollars a year—was too great a temptation for the company's pious directors. Religion and morality that call for such enormous material sacrifices are far too dear.

When "leading-light" citizens have palms that thus itch for dirty dollars, when other "leading-light" citizens amuse their leisure by setting snares for the souls of the young, is it not amazing how morality and steadiness and respect for law persist?

To sum up:

There is not a horse that is the better for any purpose but short-speed spurts because of race-tracks; there is not a penitentiary anywhere that is not the fuller by from thirty to seventy per cent. because of race-tracks and pool-rooms. There is not a man anywhere who owes or attributes any part of that in him which is honorable or reputable to racing.

Racing does not "improve the breed of the thoroughbred."

Its whole root is gambling; its whole flower and fruit, crime.

From the "gentlemen" perjurers and violators of their oaths of office and of the laws who promote and protect it, down to the book-makers and pool-room-keepers and touts and tipsters and thieves who live by it, there is only difference in shading of crime. And its baneful influence, its poison, permeates everywhere into office and into home.

What bloody butcheries of characters and careers to make the race-track's smiling holidays!

BOOK-MAKERS FIGURING OUT THEIR SLATES BEFORE THE DAY'S RACING BEGINS

23
Human Need
of Coney Island

"So near to the simple life of the sea"

HUMAN NEED OF CONEY ISLAND

By RICHARD LE GALLIENNE

TO call Coney Island one of the wonders of the world is not for me.
I think it has been already said. When
Assistant District Attorney Rand, in a
recent case, said and said again, with
a certain childlike melodramatic effect,
"I wonder! I wonder!" I am sure that
he was thinking of Coney Island. One
of the wonders of the world! One!
Why, surely, Coney is all the wonders
of the world in one pyrotechnic master-
piece of coruscating concentration. I
write—or try to write—in this style on
purpose—for am I not writing of Coney

Island?—and it was not till I went down
to Coney Island, on a brief duck-shooting expedition, that I realized why the
word "pyrotechnic" had been invented.
I had often fondled the word in diction-
aries, or on those circus-posters which,
to my mind, are the masterpieces of a
certain kind of literary style, but I had
never hoped to meet with anything
equal to the word. One so seldom meets
with anything equal to a word. A word
like "pyrotechnic" is like the name of
some beautiful woman whom we never
expect to meet except in dreams. But

303

interesting, such as, say, the Human Pin-Cushion, the Balloon-Headed Baby or the Six-Tailed Bull-Terrier, and there is no limit to its gaping astonishment. Forlorn horrors of abortion, animals tortured into talent, or feats of fantastic daring, these win the respect and thrill the exorbitant imagination of man. Nothing pleases him better than to see some skilled human being, with ghastly courage, risking a horrible death for the sake of his entertainment. Death, or at least the fear of it, as always, still holds a foremost place in popular amusements; though we are, I suppose, a little less cruel than they were in ancient Rome.

But I must not write as though I felt

SLIDING DOWN THE HELTER-SKELTER

at last I have met my beautiful lady-love Pyrotechnic—in Coney Island. Her sister, too—whose name is "Coruscating." Arm in arm with Pyrotechnic and Coruscating, you and I, if you have a mind, may see all the wonders of the world in this million-faceted false diamond known as Coney Island.

All the wonders, I say, and I use the plural advisedly; for, have you noticed how men and women flock to wonders —but how little they know, or care, of Wonder? That, of all things, most struck me in Coney Island—man's voracity for wonders, and his ignorance of Wonder.

Mankind will not give a second look at the rising moon, but present it with some disagreeable monstrosity, something that nature ought never to have allowed, something also essentially un-

superior to Coney Island. Indeed not. The human appetite for fairs has been implanted in my bosom also, and Coney, of course, is just the village fair in excelsis, catering to the undying demand for green spectacles and gilded ginger-bread and quaint absurdities of amusement, and, generally speaking, man's desperate need of entertainment, and his pathetic incapacity for entertaining himself. Really, it is strange, when you think of it, that in a world with so many interesting things to do, so many, so to say, ready-made fascinations and mar-vels—that man should find it necessary to loop-the-loop for distraction, or ride wooden horses to the sound of savage music, or ascend a circle in the air in lighted carriages slung on a revolving wheel, or hurl itself with splashing laughter down chutes into the sea. When one might be reading Plato—ever so much more amusing.

And yet so man has been made, and there come moments when it is necessary for him to shy sticks at a mark in the hope of winning a cigar or a coconut, or divert himself with the antics of cynical mountebanks, or look at animals in cages, menagerie marvels which are interesting chiefly from being caged, or gaze upon gymnasts and athletes performing feats of skill and strength which would be really astonishing if they were not the tricks of so old a trade, professional astonishments handed down, like the craft of shoemaking, from immemorial time. There is nothing especially marvelous about snake-charming. It is a business, like any other; and to swallow knives, or "eat-'em-alive," for a living is, no doubt, hard work, yet what modes of working for a living are not? Sword-swallowing is scarcely so arduous as bricklaying, and, though one is as essentially interesting as the other, the humble bricklayer draws but small audiences for his exhibitions of skill.

But, as I said, man has been made with an appetite for eccentricities of diversion rather than the love of more normal pleasures. Personally, I am the last to blame him, and he who can look upon a merry-go-round without longing to ride the wooden horse once more before he dies, for all the maturity of his middle age, can hardly be a human being.

I said that I went down to Coney on a duck-shooting expedition. I should, of course, have explained that it was a tin-duck-shooting expedition, and even when I say that, you will hardly understand if you have not fallen under the strange spell of that perpetual progression of tin ducks which invites the tin sportsman hard by the Dreamland gates of Coney Island. If you haven't shot at those tin ducks, or if you disdain

THE WATER-TOBOGGAN

to shoot at them, you may as well not visit Coney Island. The Congressional Library you might find congenial, or you might go on a pious pilgrimage to Grant's Tomb, but I fear you will never understand Coney Island. Besides, Coney Island might misunderstand you, and to be misunderstood in Coney Island is no laughing matter—for to misunderstand you is one of the many serious interests of that "happy isle set in the silver sea."

Tin ducks remind me of tin-types. If you are not a friend of the Gipsy photographer, the Daguerre of the highways and byways, in the little tents pitched by the roadside, the only photographer that never calls himself an artist, but,

A PYRAMID ON THE BEACH

Coney Island. My friend Pyrotechnic and I, being simple souls, bathing in all the pristine hallucinations of the place, sat together hand in hand with a heavenly expression under a very real electric light, and a moment after saw our faces fried over a little stove, another moment we were in gilt frames, another moment we were out again on the Broadway, with our eyes on Dreamland —but just as we were about to enter, a stout old crone of the American - Italian species beckoned us into her enchanted cave, and proposed to tell our fortunes.

Again, if you are too superior to have your fortune told by some peasant woman who knows nothing about it, and knows

nine times out of ten, gives you the best picture you ever had—again, don't go to that you know that she doesn't—don't go to Coney Island.

THE STEEPLE-CHASE

AN IDEA OF THE ORIENT OBTAINED AT CONEY ISLAND

The great charm of Coney is just there. It not only knows itself a fake, but, so to speak, it makes so little bones about the matter. It knows that you know, and it expects you to pretend to be taken in, as it pretends to think that it is taking you in. And yet, as Mr. Rand would say, "I wonder." I wonder if, perhaps, Coney Island, like all similar institutions in all times and in all lands, does not regard the public as a big baby in need of a noisy, electric-lighted rattle.

Or, on the other hand, do the magicians of "Dreamland" and "Luna Park" persuade themselves that their domes and minarets of fairy fire are really anything more than, so to speak, shareholders lit by electric light, the capitalistic torches of modern Neroism? Do they really think that "Dreamland" is dreamland, or that any one but a lunatic would look for the moon in "Luna Park"?

Yet, after all, whatever the mind and meaning of this strange congregation of showmen may be, whether they merely cater in cynical fashion to the paying needs of a contemptible uncomprehended multitude, or whether they gratify their own pyrotechnic and coruscating tastes, this much is true: that Coney Island, more than any other showman in the world, has heard and answered man's cry for the Furies of Light and Noise. Whatever else the speculators back of Coney Island don't know, they understand the—Zulu. Coney Island is the Tom-Tom of America. Every nation has, and needs—and loves—its Tom-Tom. It has its needs of orgiastic escape from respectability—that is, from the world of What-we-have-to-do into the world of What-we-would-like-to-do, from the world of duty that endureth forever into the world of joy that is graciously permitted for a moment. Some escape by one way and some by another—some by the ivory gate, and some by the gate of horn—or gold. The thing is to escape.

STARTING FOR A JINRIKISHA RIDE

It is of no use to criticize humanity. Like all creations, it—survives its critics. The only interesting thing is to try to understand it, or, at least, appreciate. Perhaps Coney Island is the most human thing that God ever made, or permitted the devil to make.

Of course, the real reason of its existence in our day has nothing to do with its modern appliances, electric and otherwise. The real reason is that it is as old as the hills. Nothing younger than the hills is alive to-day. The flowers look younger—on account

RESTING BETWEEN DIPS IN THE SURF

of their complexions—but perhaps they are even older than the hills. Coney Island is so alive with light and noise every night because it is so old-established an institution. Man needs Coney Island to-day, because he has always needed Coney Island. A scholar I knew once told me the name of Coney Island in Babylon; but he died recently, and I know no one else to ask.

rich seeking pleasures so very different— —or even the refined gentlemen who write books and paint pictures and criticize them?

No, Coney Island exists, and will go on existing, because into all men, gentle and simple, poor and rich—including women—by some mysterious corybantic instinct in their blood, has been born a tragic need of coarse excitement, a

RESUSCITATING A BATHER OVERCOME IN THE SURF

I wish that I could remember the name, but never mind—of course, it was not the name of the place where the most fine and subtle and distinguished fugitives from humdrum Babylon made their refuge—and yet I am not so sure that it was not, for, after all, if a place like Coney Island is a Palace of Poor Pleasures for Poor Men, do we find the

craving to be taken in by some illusion however palpable.

So, following the example of those old nations, whose place she has so vigorously taken, America has builded for herself a Palace of Illusion, and filled it with every species of talented attractive monster, every misbegotten fancy of the frenzied nerves, every fantastic

310

PICNIC-GIRLS AT BRIGHTON BEACH

marvel of the moonstruck brain—and she has called it Coney Island. Ironic name—a place lonely with rabbits, a spit of sandy beach so near to the simple life of the sea, and watched over by the summer night; strange Isle of Monsters, Preposterous Palace of Illusion, gigantic Parody of Pleasure—Coney Island.

24

The Tenements
of Trinity Church

The Tenements of Trinity Church

By CHARLES EDWARD RUSSELL

Author of "Soldiers of the Common Good," "Where Did You Get It, Gentlemen?" etc.

EDITOR'S NOTE—The Corporation of Trinity Church, New York City, a very large and wealthy landowner, possesses many tenement-houses that by reformers, philanthropists, and health-officers have often been made the subject of bitter criticism. This article aims to describe the actual condition of some of these Trinity tenements and to give an idea of their relation to the health and security of the city It also raises a very great and interesting question: whether the good wrought by the charitable and philanthropic enterprises of Trinity equals the evil wrought by the tenements that finance the charities.

ON the lower West Side of New York City, in the old Eighth Ward and not far from the docks, is a place called Hudson Park, where in certain poor piles of sand the little children of the tenements sometimes come to play.

It is not much of a park; a little slice of rescued city space, a mere glimpse of open sky, a part of a city block without the usual hideous city houses and set with weary trees, uncertain grass, some rigid benches—no more than that. In the center, a curious and unreasonable depression adorned with some doubtful classicism, and at the rear the sand piles where the chalk-faced children play. That is all.

And yet you, looking upon it, poor and forlorn as it is, feel in your heart an impulse to fall upon your knees there in the reek of the filthy street and utter gratitude for even so much. All about you to the south blink the frowsy, scaly, slatternly, bleary, decayed, and crumbling old houses, leering from dirty windows like old drunkards through bloodshot eyes; the broken shutters awry like deformities, the doors agape like old, toothless mouths. All about is the hell of the West Side tenement-house

region, and compared with its outward and visible signs, this maidenhood of Hudson Park, albeit ill-clad and gawky, is something sweet. You think back upon the years of dreary struggle and contest and argument and travail that were required to secure this little island of sanity in the mad region around you, and wonder to yourself if we are all perfectly crazy that we tolerate such things.

Drunken, disreputable, decayed, topsy-turvy old houses, the homes of thousands of families and the breeding-places for so many children that are to carry on the world's work —who owns these terrible places? Who draws the wretched profit of their existence?

Trinity Church, holder of one of the greatest estates in New York or in the country, owns many of them. This is the heart of her possessions: street after street is lined with her properties. Here is Clarkson Street, on the south of the tiny park—she owns a dozen tenement properties there; Varick Street, crossing Clarkson at right angles—she owns sixty-six tenement properties there; West Houston, noisome and dilapidated—she owns fifty-one tenement properties there; upper Greenwich Street— she owns sixty-five tenement properties there; Charlton Street, a dreary place—she owns twenty-six tenement properties there; Canal Street toward the North River—she owns forty-seven tenement properties there; Hudson Street—she owns 138 tenement properties there. You do not think well of the appearance of Vandam Street; Trinity owns forty-one tenement properties there. You think Barrow Street down here looks ancient and seedy; Trinity owns twenty-two tenement properties there. Wherever you walk in this dreadful region, you find something that Trinity owns, and, as a rule, it is something that you know she ought not to own.

For this is the state to which have come

313

certain cabbage-fields and swamp-lands once (in the earliest days of New York) bestowed upon the church by the careless hand of the good Queen Anne; this is the Jans farm of the ancient days; this is the wealth that the sheer growth of New York has made for Trinity; and this is the fortune that by the managers of this remarkable church is guarded with a strange secrecy and care. It owns in the city property worth, according to different estimators, from $39,000,000 to $100,000,000, from which it draws an enormous revenue, the amount of which is never made public. For many years no investigator has been able to obtain any more definite knowledge of these matters than that this is the wealth of Trinity which she holds for good purposes.

What? Expressed in wretched, rotten, old tenement-houses? Yes. Expressed in hundreds of such tenement-houses.

I have before me the testimony of a very eminent authority about tenement-houses, and she says that confirmed tenement-house dwellers are as a class sickly, anemic, iethargic, and show unmistakable tendencies toward constitutional weakness. Tuberculosis has a strong hold upon them; the effect of tenement-house life is such that the third generation of tenement-house dwellers (if you can conceive of a third generation) is usually of an inferior mentality, without intelligent interest in anything, leads dull and vacant lives, and furnishes recruits for the reformatory and the state prison.

It appears, therefore, that while the charities established by Trinity since 1857* are trying to lead men upward, the Trinity tenements, with an irresistible force, are crushing men downward; and we are therefore presented at once with a very memorable spectacle of the contradictions and inconsistencies of this our mortal state.

Because if the tenement, speaking generally, works ill, Trinity's tenements must be a matter of grave concern to us all, Trinity's tenements must work more than common ill, for they are the worst tenements in New York.

One reason why they are the worst is that they were never designed for tenements at all.

They are the residences that a century ago began to show from St. John's Park northward the growth of the young city. Two-story and basement houses, most of them, they were planned in every case to be the homes each of a single family. You can imagine, then, the results when, with an amazing parsimony in repairs and alterations, these same houses are made to shelter five or six families. But unless you have been there, you cannot possibly imagine the horrible dirt and neglect and slovenliness that are spread over so many of these places.

Is it not strange? No, it is not strange; it is only a part of a yellow wizardry that in many ways gives to the management of Trinity Corporation an aspect furtive and mysterious, that seems to impel it to many courses inconsistent with candor and to bewitch many good men engaged in the conduct of its affairs. Profit, much profit, very great profit, lies in property of this sort; it yields much to the golden stream. These are houses that old-time tenants built on land had from Trinity on short leases. When the leases expired, Trinity, following a consistent and profitable policy, refused to grant renewals—to the late tenants. It also refused to purchase the house that the tenant had built. The tenant, therefore, was confronted with this situation: he could tear his house down brick by brick and cart it away to the dump or the river; or he could abandon it (as it stood) to Trinity, sometimes for nothing, sometimes for a nominal sum. These are houses, therefore, in which the investment of Trinity was almost nothing, possibly an average of $200 each, and now from these same houses she gathers $40 or $50 a month for rent, paying out nothing for repairs.

Some of these houses are brick, some are wooden. Very few of them are fit under any circumstances for any human habitation. Not one of them is fit for human habitation as at present it is inhabited.

Tastes differ. I know that the vestry of Trinity would be terribly shocked at a suggestion that the corporation should make money by administering arsenic to people, or carbolic acid, or deadly nightshade. But the vestry or the standing committee that represents it in these matters has no objection whatever to making money for the corporation by maintaining poisonous tenements.

As between tuberculosis and arsenic, where lies the choice?

Suppose now we turn us from these reflections (which may be supposed to threaten the sacred basis of the social edifice) and see how the facts stand. We will imagine

---

*Trinity was investigated in 1857 by a Committee of the State Senate. One result was a report severely condemning the church for its apparent indifference to charitable enterprises and religious benevolence.

that we guide a party of inquiring and well-fed tourists to whom the tenement-house is merely a name, comfortable and genial tourists, that sleep o' nights. We take you first into one of the tenement-houses that blink out disreputably about the little park and gather much income for Trinity, a tenement-house in Clarkson Street near Hudson. It presents to the street a dirty brick front, scaly, like its fellows, and long demanding paint. Come inside and see how you like it. Four floors there are, three of them made into dwellings for families, two dwellings on a floor. An old house, very old, very poorly built, very flimsy, very ramshackle. Everything about it seems going to decay. The halls are narrow, dark, dirty, and smell abominably. The stairways are narrow, wooden, and insecure. On the second and third floors are interior bedrooms that have no natural light nor ventilation, and must therefore, according to the Board of Health, be a prolific breeding-place for the germs of tuberculosis. A horrible, mephitic odor and the dampness that clings about old

cellars and sunless courts seem to strike against you with a physical impact. You know that in this heavy and sickly air is no place to rear men and women.*

The only sanitation for the families dwelling in this dreadful house is to be found in wooden sheds in the back yard. It is of a nature that one might expect to see in Chinese cities, but never in the foremost city of America. The back yard is a horror into which you set your foot with an uncontrollable physical revulsion against the loathsome contamination. It has much rubbish, it is vilely unkempt, it seems to exude vileness. The water-supply in the house consists of one common tap for each floor, placed in the hall. Formerly even these primitive conveniences did not exist, and the overwrought women that live in these houses were obliged to carry in pails up the steep stairs the water-supply, each for her household. The water-tap on each floor was commanded by the new Tene-

*I am pleased to state that this particular building has now been sold to the city and is about to be demolished.

HUDSON PARK—A LITTLE BREATHING-PLACE FOR WEST SIDE CHILDREN,
WON AFTER A LONG CONTEST.

A VACANT LOT WHERE THE OWNER TORE DOWN HIS HOUSE RATHER THAN LET IT PASS INTO THE HANDS OF TRINITY.

ment-House Law, and it was this feature of the law that Trinity most opposed.

In the rear, reached by a narrow passage, is another tenement-house, a four-story brick building, occupied, when I was there, by seven families. If the front tenement is bad, what shall we say of the tenement in the rear? Whatever is abominable in the one is more abominable in the other. The gloom is worse, the ventilation is worse, the aspect of dreary decay and neglect is worse. Some of the dwellers in the front house can get air and light; most of the dwellers in the rear house can get very little of either. When the building was new and clean, it might have been a tolerable place in which to house horses— temporarily; say for a day. It was never, at any time, a tolerable place in which to house human beings. For fifty or sixty years it has been unfit for anything except burning. How would you like to draw an income from the maintaining of such a place? You would want to have the money disinfected before it touched your hand, would you not? Lest into your presence it bear some odor of the rear tenement, or some bacteria from the interior bedrooms, or from the filthy courts.

Come, then, into the filthy little back yards

at the rear of No. 20 Clarkson Street, and, looking over the rotting fences, you may discover a peculiarity of many of the houses in this region. The front walls are of brick; the rear and side walls are wooden. On the wooden walls the clapboards sag and sway and are falling off, the ancient laths and plaster are exposed beneath. Window panes are broken out. On one of the days when I was there, a bitter day in December, an icy wind blew through these apertures. I went into some of the living-rooms. There were women and children around the fire in the one stove that cooked for them and gave them heat. They were trying to keep warm—with coal they bought by the pailful at the rate of $16 a ton. They paid $5.50 a month for the two miserable rooms—one with light, the other without.

And what kind of people are these that dwell in such quarters? "Foreigners, likely, only lately recruited from the hives of Naples or Palermo, and finding even these habitations not much worse than those to which they have been accustomed." So you think. But these are not foreigners. These are Americans; respectable and industrious Americans. They are old-time residents of the

Eighth Ward, most of them; their fathers lived there, they were born there; with that fatuity that is so common and still so hard to explain, they cling to the familiar regions of their youth. And not the least pathetic part of the unfortunate situation is the struggle they make against their environment, the painful effort to keep their poor little rooms neat and tidy; the cherished old pictures on the dismal walls, and the handful of ornaments on the shelf. You cannot crush out the instincts of the race by two decades in a tenement-house; but you can in four, or five, good gentlemen of the vestry.

The good gentlemen of the vestry have strong and steady nerves; they are not easily worried; they are not likely ever to die of heart-failure. I know that they have large and well-grounded philosophies and rest steadfastly upon the belief that a Special Providence watches over the tenement-house region. I know this must be so because otherwise they would never be able to sleep, under the terror that the condition of their tenement-houses must inspire. Of all the tinder-boxes in New York these houses are the worst. If some of them had been designed for the express purpose of trapping and destroying human beings, by no possibility could they

have been more ably arranged to that end.

The old wooden walls, the old wooden stairways, the old wooden floors, dry as powder, inflammable as oil, are only a part of the peril. The one access to, the one exit from, the rear tenement is usually through a narrow passage, or a tunnel, maybe three feet wide, sometimes with wooden sides and top; sometimes above it is part of the front house.

In the event of a fire, these tunnels would become almost at once impassable. Thereupon the people in the overcrowded rear tenements would have no conceivable chance to escape. Many of them could not even get down to the ground floor, because some of the houses have no fire-escapes. Yes, I know the law provides that there shall be such things, but here are houses on Trinity property to which this law seems never to have been applied. There are no fire-escapes on the houses at Nos. 32, 34, and 36 Clarkson Street, for instance. I suppose that technically this is not Trinity's fault; but narrow old wooden stairs, dry old tinder walls, an overcrowded building, and no fire-escapes! Yes, I think the vestrymen have good nerves; they cannot be susceptible to carking care.

And how about the rest of us that are not obliged to lead our lives in such sur-

REAR OF 593 GREENWICH STREET, A FAIR SAMPLE OF A TRINITY BACK YARD.

roundings, but are still our brothers' keepers? I know that there is a belief more or less widespread among us that tenement-house dwellers do not have feelings like ours. They are differently constituted, their fibers are different, their ganglia are of another material; so by a merciful provision they do not feel the pangs of poverty nor mind dirt, darkness, and squalor. We should mind such things, but these people do not, because of some great difference in their physical and mental make-up. In fact, they are said to be very happy in the station to which Providence has assigned them, and we really should let them live on in their cellars and back rooms so long as tuberculosis and typhoid will allow.

I know this view must be correct, because I have heard it urged by very learned and wise persons, and I make a point of not disputing eminent authority. Still, I should think that even to persons of a very different fiber indeed the sensation of burning to death would be painful, and most of us would prefer not to derive an income from tinder-box houses that are without fire-escapes.

I can only suppose, therefore, that about this matter Trinity Corporation has implicit faith in the idea of a Special Providence.

The Special Providence went off watch on the night of March 29, 1896, and the tinder-box at No. 374 Hudson Street exploded into flame; for it seems an inaccuracy of speech to say that one of these places merely takes fire. Of course the wooden stairway was unusable, and the unfortunate and trapped inhabitants were driven to throw themselves from the windows. Four of them, two men and two women, were killed; about a dozen were badly injured. I gather from this that while the fiber of people that live in tenements is different from the fiber of the rest of us, it is not sufficiently different to prevent such people from being burned, nor from having their bones broken if they fall far enough.

It was also not different enough to prevent some of the survivors from grieving over the loss of their relatives and from suing Trinity as the responsible cause of that loss. So the whole story was turned up in the courts. But I have been unable to find that anything ever came of these actions. Somehow, nothing usually comes of a suit against Trinity.

Bearing in mind what happened at No. 374 Hudson Street, I should think the vestry might at times feel a slight uneasiness. No. 374 Hudson Street was a fire-proof structure compared with some of the other properties. At Nos. 192½ and 192¾ Varick Street, for instance, is an ancient, sorry-looking structure of wood, three stories high, and there is no fire-escape at either number. What the inmates would do in case that tinder-box were fired, I do not know; burn with the tinder, I suppose. The fire-escapes that exist on some of the other houses are makeshifts. Perhaps an adult man or a woman of average weight could get upon one without fetching the whole thing away, but I do not see how. Why worry? The houses have never burned. Hence let us conclude that they never will burn.

But we tourists of the well-fed and bett orders resume our excursion among tl habitations of the lowly, and here are son of the places we enter; no better and no worse than others. Human beings actually live in these places; many human beings; and pay for the privilege.

No. 265 West Houston Street. Brick, three stories and basement, four families, rear fire-escape, dirty back yard, sanitation in two wooden sheds in the yard, water in halls. An interior bedroom on top floor, where an old woman says, "That's all right; we get too much air in the winter."

No. 368 Hudson Street. Brick, three stories, fire-escapes in rear, small yard, sanitation in wooden sheds, interior bedroom.

No. 342 Hudson Street. Three stories, rotten wood in front, half wood, half brick in rear; a dilapidated old shack. Fire-escape in front, house occupied by three families and two stores. Dirty little yard heaped with rubbish, sanitation in old wooden sheds.

No. 344 Hudson Street, corner of Charlton. Three stories, wooden, old, side fire-escapes, three families, water in halls.

No. 85 King Street. Two and a half stories and basement, brick front, wooden rear, eight families, including one in basement, fire-escapes, wooden sheds for sanitation, water in halls, no gas in halls, law being thereby violated. Tenant says halls are very dark and that because of the darkness an old woman fell down the stairs and died of fractured skull. In basement is interior bedroom, also one on first floor. Very dirty and repulsive place.

No. 84 Charlton Street. Two and a half stories with basement, wooden, very old, fire-escape, four families, water in halls, wooden sheds in yard for sanitation, much rubbish. The basement is at present unoccupied.

No. 196 Varick Street. Two and a half

stories with basement, frame, front fire-escape, four families, one family in the basement consisting of ten members. Interior bedrooms of worst kind on first and second floors. Two wooden sheds in back yard for sanitation.

No. 198 Varick Street. Same as above. Four families, front fire-escape.

No. 200 Varick Street. No fire-escape.

No. 202 Varick Street. Same as No. 196, four families, fire escapes.

No. 204 Varick Street. Similar to No. 198, but yard taken up with sheds.

Nos. 192½ and 192¾ Varick Street. Three stories, wooden, very old, in last stages of disrepair, no fire-escapes. Old, rotting, wooden porch hanging out from rear of second floor. House most unsafe in case of fire. Three families in No. 192¾, two families in No. 192½, one old wooden shed for sanitation in rear of each house, dirty little yards, water in halls.

No. 190 Varick Street. Two and a half stories, wooden with brick front, no fire-escape.

No. 39 Clarkson Street. Brick front, remainder of wood, three stories, three families. In rear, wooden tenement, three stories, three families, dirty yard, four rotten sheds for sanitation. This house is very old and rotten, stairway is out of plumb and looks as if it might fall. No gas in rear tenement, no fire-escapes. Owner of the buildings says, "Oh, yes, there are fire-escapes. There is a wire ladder kept on each floor." She pays Trinity $400 a year ground-rent.

No. 41 Clarkson Street. Brick, three stories and basement. No gas. Interior bedrooms on second and third floors. Yard in very bad state, sanitation sheds very bad. Another tenement in rear, very old and dilapidated. Both have fire-escapes.

No. 32 Clarkson Street. Brick, three stories and basement, no fire-escapes. A tenant says that the hatch on the roof was nailed down, so that there was no possible escape that way. Tenants, therefore, neatly trapped. One wooden shed in yard.

No. 38 Clarkson Street. Brick, sheathed in wood, three stories, wooden extension in

ALL ABOUT IS THE HELL OF THE WEST SIDE TENEMENT-HOUSE REGION.

ROTTEN STAIRS IN THE REAR OF 591 GREENWICH STREET, SHOWING TYPICAL ALLEY BY WHICH A REAR TENEMENT IS REACHED.

rear, seven families, no gas, rusty old ladders in rear for fire-escapes, dirty yard, sheds.

Almost indefinitely I might extend this gruesome list. Indeed, decay and neglect, misery and squalor seem to brood wherever Trinity is an owner. Gladly I would give to such a charitable and benevolent institution all possible credit for a spirit of improvement manifested anywhere, but I can find no such manifestation. I have tramped the Eighth Ward day after day with a list of Trinity properties in my hand, and of all the tenement-houses that stand there on Trinity land I have not found one that is not a disgrace to civilization and to the city of New York.

I need not be told, as with much virtuous indignation I shall be told, that of the instances I have cited not all the buildings are technically owned by Trinity. I know that well enough. And I need not be told that according to the Trinity leases the lessee is responsible for repairs upon the property. I know that well enough. And I need not be told that Trinity is not technically responsible for the dirt and the misery, the poverty and squalor. I know that well enough. But the land is owned by Trinity, wherever the bricks in the building are not, and from the moral responsibility for these conditions there is no escape on any plea I have been able to think of. To rent property and permit it to become a breeding-place for tuberculosis is exactly as bad as to rent it for immoral purposes. Whatever distinction, therefore, the good vestrymen may draw between the buildings that stand in the name of Trinity and the buildings that stand on Trinity's ground in the name of this person or that, is a technical, and no moral, defense. For, however the title deeds may say, it is from this property so conducted and so crying out against civilization that there is drawn the income that year after year pours into the mysterious coffers of the corporation.

It seemed to me after a time that I had no need for the list of Trinity holdings; I could pick them out unaided, I could tell them as far as I could see them, tell them by indubitable signs. Whenever I saw a house that looked as if it were about to fall down, one that looked in every way rotten and weary and dirty and disreputable, I found that it was owned by Trinity or stood upon Trinity ground. Frequently other owners

AN INSIDE ROOM AT 12 CLARKSON STREET—NO LIGHT, NO AIR.

seemed to make some effort to improve their property, or at least to keep it from desperate decay. Trinity seemed to make none. You can see side by side in some of these streets a tumbling and forlorn old hovel and a modern apartment-house, and if you have any familiarity with the ward, you know at once that the hovel has something to do with Trinity and the apartment-house is owned by some one that is struggling hard against the conditions that Trinity fosters.

To be sure, all tenement-houses are bad, I know that; all tenement-houses are terrific indictments of the conditions of grab and gain and splendor and shame that we tolerate. But how comes it that on the East Side of New York have been built in recent years all these bright, clean, fire-proof, and sanitary flats, in such numbers that certain regions have been transformed by them, and life for those that dwell in them has been changed from direst misery to something almost suggestive of decency, while Trinity has done nothing of the kind?

How comes it that the Astor Estate, owner of hundreds of tenements, has pursued for years one settled policy of improvement for the benefit of the tenants, and the Trinity tenants have been left to shift for themselves?

The Astor Estate maintains no charities; it has no missions, no hospitals, no beds, and no Sunday-school excursions; yet I am perfectly certain that the balance of actual good in the world is in its favor; I am perfectly certain that to obliterate one court that breeds tuberculosis is better than to spend $70,000 a year on organ music, and that to provide a tenement with fire-escapes is better than to preach a sermon of remote and genteel theology. The management of the Astor tenements indicates what even a small measure of civilization can do in the midst of barbarous conditions; the management of the Trinity tenements shows what callous neglect can do to further and aggravate barbarous conditions.

But the owners of the Astor property can see at any time every book and every document or paper that relates to any part of their property. They know what the property is, and what it yields, and what is done with the revenue, and who is in charge of it. For ninety-four years the owners of Trinity have known nothing whatever about it. There is no growth from secrecy except some form of trouble, and the crop of trouble in the case of Trinity is large and various enough to overflow into all our seed-lands.

Yet I do not see why the crop should be reaped by the tenants of Trinity. What have they done? It is not their fault that the houses are damp and dark and old, that the stairways fall from the walls, that bacteria thrive in the unlighted rooms, that the hallways are rank and reeking, that the basements are full of horrible smells, that they dwell exposed to the most frightful forms of death. What have they done? They are not responsible for the vestry and standing committee of Trinity Church; they have not created the mysterious methods of Trinity once investigated and denounced by a Committee of the Senate of the State of New York; it is not their fault that Trinity is a bad citizen, and will not improve its property.

You say, why don't they move elsewhere? Yes, to Staten Island maybe, or to Yonkers or Poughkeepsie, all admirably adapted to be places of residence. Dear soul, so long as Trinity offers a tenement at $5.50 a month somebody (in the conditions of life that we create and maintain) is certain to live in it. But how does that excuse Trinity? In what way does that clear her of the moral responsibility for the chalk-faced children that are growing up in the terrible places she owns?

The children! Ah, well, I was coming to them. I have now in mind some pictures that stand out above the others of the horrible things I saw in my wanderings here. I remember one place: a tiny and scantily stocked store in front, the living-room of the family next, and beyond that a wretched wooden shed used as a bedroom. A little girl lay sick on a bed against the further side of the shed. The old mattress she lay upon was filthy, the old blanket that covered her was filthy, the floor was filthy, the walls were bare, the room was a cold, cheerless hole, almost dark, for the one window that

REAR OF A TUMBLE-DOWN HOUSE IN
VANDAM STREET.

opened upon the filthy back yard admitted hardly any light. The child lay close by the thin wooden wall of that shed, and on the other side of that wall were the reeking back yard and things I must not speak about. She lay there in that choking and fetid atmosphere, and a constitution enfeebled by years of such existence was still battling for her life.

What kind of children do you think will develop in such an atmosphere, supposing them to escape the mercy of death? The only times in their lives when they can breathe anything but mephitis is when they can get into the roaring streets, and when they get into the roaring streets the trucks and cabs run them down or the police chase them off the block. Imagine the eighteen growing years of a life spent among the damp and dripping walls of some of these places, with the nauseating rubbish of the neglected back yard for a prospect and the darkness of filthy halls and stairways for a companion. Do you think it in any way wonderful that some lives thus led and thus trained should turn to crime? If you wished to rear a criminal, do you think you could devise a better training place?

Five children, two boys and three girls, came out of one of these rear tenement halls as I entered the dirty court that separates the front building from the other. They were not going out to play—the children in this perdition do not play very much—they were going out on various errands. Of the five there was not one that did not bear some sure stamp of the tenement-house curse. One of the girls had a running sore at her ear; all of them looked unwholesome and abnormal. They were dirty, for how could you expect them to be clean in the midst of all this filth? They were pale, of course, for they slept in rear rooms and inhaled poison; they were dull, for they reflected a dreary environment; and they were obviously of an inferior vitality, for they had been stupefied by the crushing misery in which they lived.

What do you think the five will be twenty years hence, providing they escape the tinder-box, tuberculosis, and cholera infantum?

But is Trinity, which draws hence so much mysterious revenue and disposes of it as mysteriously, indifferent to its duty as a benevolent institution? Not at all. Look in the year-book of the parish. You will see there that Trinity maintains trade-schools, parochial schools, Sunday-schools, missions, many kinds of philanthropy. It teaches girls to cook and sew and gives military training to boys. Every summer it gives to the children of its Sunday-school an excursion, up the Hudson, for instance, and I am assured that these excursions are delightful occasions, and the children are very happy, and it would do one good to see how they enjoy the fresh air and the sunshine. Every chapel in the Trinity organization has its guilds and associations for charitable work; every one of its clergy is thoroughly impressed with the idea of doing good in the world. But the fact from which I have found no escape is that the money for these excellent excursions is produced from a living inferno, and the greatest of all the mysteries seems to be this: that even for the religious and benevolent purposes specified by Trinity's charter the means should come in this way.

The crushing influence of the tenement-house! I saw its perfect product in one old woman that came to the door in answer to my knock. She was sixty-five or seventy, with silver hair, and she looked respectable and decent in spite of her surroundings; but the last vestige of the human spirit had long been crushed out of her. She looked about her with a vague, senseless terror, and she cringed and fawned so pitiably at every question it would have made you sorry and ashamed to see her.

In her vision there was nothing left but dis-aster; the coming of some stranger, the asking of the simplest question, foreboded trouble. She would not believe that anyone could come to her except with evil intent, and yet she had no idea of resenting anything, but only of trying in some blind way to propitiate misfortune. She had lived in tenement-houses all her life, and not being of the kind that finds refuge in drink, the utter dreariness of her surroundings had shriveled away the soul of humanity in her until there was nothing left but this shape of perpetual fear. Grand triumph of our civilization! You should see her; she would make you feel so comfortable and warm and full of content. She was dressed in rags, she was gaunt and bent, and in her eyes was an unspeakable terror of you and of me and of all the world that had brought her down to this.

Ah, yes, blessings on the Sunday-school excursions, blessings on the trade-schools blessings on the parochial schools, blessings on the fruit and flower missions, blessings on the organ music, blessings on the chapel guilds, blessings on the contributions for the poor of St. John's. Beautiful, indeed, are all these things. But while they keep their wonted way, the mill of the tenement-house goes on crushing, and the products of the crushing stare us in the face with ugly questions, not to be answered with Sunday-school excursions.

So runs this extraordinary story. Many strange features pertain to it. The managing forces of Trinity control a very great property. The real owners of that property are the communicants of the church. For ninety-four years none of the owners has known the extent of the property, nor the amount of the revenue therefrom, nor what is done with the money. Every attempt to learn even the simplest fact about these matters has been baffled. The management is a self-perpetuating body, without responsibility and without supervision. All these are strange conditions. But stranger than all is this: that a Christian church should be willing to take money from such tenements as Trinity owns in the old Eighth Ward.

25
The New York Plan for Zoological Parks

The concourse, and north end of Baird Court.
New administration building on left, Italian garden in centre, large bird-house on right.

THE NEW YORK PLAN FOR ZOOLOGICAL PARKS

By William T. Hornaday
Director of the New York Zoological Park

VERY large American city in which the masses are intelligent and proud, desires a good zoological park; but for all that, a city can be very proud and boastful without having sufficient energy to make one. The New York Zoological Park is an object lesson of which many American cities may well take heed. It points the way by which every city, large or small, may create and maintain a zoological park of a size suitable to its population and resources. That end is to be attained by a judicious union of private effort, and municipal support at the expense of the taxpayers. New York has clearly demonstrated the fact that the taxpayer is willing to be taxed in a

reasonable way for something that will furnish free and perpetual entertainment both to his wife and children and to himself, and at the same time be a credit to his home city. Give the taxpayer a fair chance, and he will support the zoological park idea, willingly and even gladly.

The prime essentials to success in the creation and maintenance of a joint-effort zoological park are few in number, but the demand for them is inexorable. There must be (1) a free site in a public park; (2) permanence of control; (3) absolute freedom from "politics" and "graft" of every description; (4) wise but energetic management by a zoological society; (5) a general plan of development based on the best expert knowledge; (6) the merit sys-

tem in choosing employees; (7) all collections must be furnished by the Society, (8)
and all improvements and costs of maintenance must be paid for by the taxpayers.
Finally, the park must be free on five days
of the week, but two week-days should be
pay-days, unless the population of the city
concerned is under 500,000.

The European plan for the creation and
maintenance of live-animal collections differs from the above, in several important

nicipal support, and the very poor never see
the inside of the establishment, because
they cannot afford the price. I think it may
truly be said that, even with occasional days
of admission for the equivalent of ten cents,
the zoological gardens of Europe chiefly
benefit the rich and the well-to-do classes,
to the exclusion of the very poor masses.

New York City builds no public institutions from which the Man-Without-A-
Quarter is shut out. In a liberality of spirit

The den and swimming pool of the polar bears.

particulars. Rarely does the municipality
furnish a free site, or even free water. Usually the creating society is compelled to purchase ground, and it is usually selected as
near as possible to the heart of the city concerned, so as to be very easily accessible.
The result is a zoological *garden*, of from
twenty to sixty acres, surrounded by dwellings, and sadly limited in space for the
animals. A huge and costly restaurant and
concert hall provides entertainment that
draws society members, and strangers, also,
many times each year; and there is no admission for non-members without the pay-
ment of a fee at the gate. There is no mu-

entirely surpassing that of the American
nation, at least as it is represented at Washington, and with not one pennyworth of aid
from the State of New York, this city has
created and to-day maintains for her citizens and the world at large six great institutions for public betterment, all of them of
national importance. I refer to the Metropolitan Museum of Art, the New York
Public Library, the American Museum of
Natural History, the New York Zoological Park, the Botanical Gardens, and the
Aquarium. In this field of high-class educational endeavor there are only three other
cities that are in New York's class—Lon-

don, Paris and Berlin; but I think that New York clearly is entitled to first place.

Through a combination of private generosity and municipal support, wise provisions of Nature and good management, imperial New York has created in ten years time, and now presents to her people and to the world, an institution that three distin-

the nerve-weary business and professional men of New York, how many are there who know that during the whole forenoon of every day in the year, and all day on paydays, the Jungle Walk in the Zoological Park offers nerve balm of rare quality?

On Sunday afternoons, even the sight of the crowd is inspiring. It is good to see,

The elephant house, and surrounding yards.

guished foreign critics have openly declared to be the foremost vivarium of the world. Those critics were Lord Northcliffe, Sir Harry Johnston, the African explorer, and Mr. F. G. Aflalo, a qualified expert on zoological gardens, and author of out-door books. It is for the purpose of furnishing a bill of particulars that the writer has been editorially coerced into writing at this time.

Every perfectly appointed zoological garden is a haven of rest to overwrought nerves, with the gentle and healthful stimulus of restful interest in new and different lines of thought. At ten o'clock in the forenoon, when the housekeeping of the day has been finished, and before the daily crowd has begun to arrive, a well-appointed zoological garden—with a good showing of flowers—comes as near to being an earthly paradise as the skill of man ever can produce within reach of the busy haunts of men. Of all

at one sweep of the eyes over Baird Court and the region below it on the west, fully twenty thousand well dressed people, one-third of whom are well behaved and attractive children, busily enjoying the beauties of the place, and the band music. It is good to see, on every Monday morning in summer, from the records of the turnstiles, that on the previous day between 30,000 and 40,000 people have enjoyed the temples and shrines of Nature that God and man together have created for the benefit of the working millions in South Bronx Park.

The correct building of zoological gardens and parks is an exact science, just as much so as is astronomy, and the building of observatories. In formulating principles, and in working out the general design of the New York Zoological Park, we diligently studied nearly all existing zoological gardens, partly to ascertain what errors to avoid, and partly to acquire ideas of

practical use. Know-
ing well what all the
world had done previ-
ously, and having in
hand the ideal site of all
the world, is it then any
cause for surprise that
the last built institution
for living wild animals
is the best one for the
health and comfort of its
occupants? The writer
has been persuaded that
it is no violation of the
proprieties frankly to
state, for the information
of the American public,

Hippopotamus cage in elephant house.

Interior of elephant house.

just wherein we think we have improved
upon the work of our predecessors.

It must be counted as actually providen-
tial that the New York Zoological Society
was founded in 1895 by Madison Grant;
that it immediately attracted the support
of Dr. Henry Fairfield Osborn; that for
twelve years both those gentlemen have
dedicated an important portion of their
lives to the Society's work; that South
Bronx Park was acquired by New York
City in 1884 and had remained an un-
spoiled wilderness; that the administration

of Mayor Strong accepted in good faith
the partnership proposal of the Zoological Society; and that every Mayor and
Comptroller and Board of Estimate since
1897 has faithfully *and generously* supported the Zoological Park undertaking.

The Zoological Park represents a perfectly harmonious joint effort on the part
of a powerful philanthropic organization
and the taxpayers of the City of New
York. By reason of the first large financial sacrifice of the Zoological Society,
justly regarded as a pledge of good faith,
from the inception of the undertaking,
the city government has relied absolutely
upon the men and methods of that organization. In the plans and their execution, and in the selection of a permanent working force of 145 persons, there
never has been even a hint of interference, or pressure, "political" or otherwise. In working out its own systems
of economy in money, and in the saving
of time, the Zoological Society has been
permitted a degree of freedom of action
that is probably without precedent in such
matters.

In "maintenance" and in "construction" combined—our two grand divisions
of all labor and expenditure—the Zoological Society has paid out at least $2,000,000
of public money, so far as we know without
even a whisper of a charge of "graft," or
"favoritism," "mismanagement," or even
"extravagance."

The zoological park idea.
About one-half the American bison herd, in the breeding ranges.

We mention thus prominently the confidence of the city government in the Zoological Society, because that confidence has been a factor of tremendous importance in securing for New York, in eleven years of active work, a Zoological Park which represents high-water mark for such institutions.

We began under the Reform Administration of Mayor Strong and City Chamberlain McCook and Comptroller Fitch; and we were generously prospered under Mayors Van Wyck and Low, and Comptrollers Coler and Grout. Then there followed eight glorious years under Mayor McClellan and Comptroller Metz; and thus have we been enabled to achieve in eleven years of actual labor the goal of our heart's desire —practical *completion!* And what has been the price paid by the Zoological Society for the confidence of the highest officers of this city—the Mayor, the Board of Estimate and the Board of Aldermen?

In actual money expended it has cost about $475,000; but in comparison with the unpurchasable time and services of the members of the Executive Committee, the half million of money is not the most important item. Without having seen it, I would not have believed it possible that such men as Henry Fairfield Osborn, Charles T. Barney, Samuel Thorne, Levi P. Morton, John L. Cadwalader, John S. Barnes, Percy R. Pyne, Philip Schuyler, Madison Grant and William White Niles would give time and services without limit, not only cheerfully but even joyously, for twelve busy years, to any undertaking of this kind. It requires a great many fine men, as well as a great many fine animals, to make a great Zoological Park.

The past eleven years have been years of intense, unremitting, and at times exhausting effort; but they have produced a succession of triumphs. Even the " hard times" did not stay the Society's progress by more than a few months on our two final improvements for animals. We say to-day that the Park is practically "complete," because, for such an institution as ours, that term is accepted by all sensible persons in a comparative sense. We do not say that the Park is no longer open to improvement, or that further beautification is impossible. It is entirely possible that, during the next ten or twenty years, some other animal buildings may be found desirable.

Prior to 1898, many persons outside of New York wondered why the metropolis of the American continent remained for so many years without a zoological establishment for live animals in keeping with her municipal rank. Even when the men of New York were asked, they could not answer; but now we know.

The event was waiting for South Bronx Park and the Zoological Society!

The former came through the splendid wisdom and foresight of the Municipal Park Commission of 1880–84, which contained, among others, William W. Niles (Sr.) and Charles L. Tiffany. And how many men of New York are there to-day who know that the passage of the act so

own hands, and said to the trees, the rocks, the valleys and the meadows—"Be thou here!"—I am sure we could not have produced the ideal result that the cunning hand of Nature fashioned for us in that marvellous site. Our total area is 264 acres; and it is all that we desire.

Fate graciously so ordered events that the pleasure of discovering South Bronx Park and revealing its beauties to the Zoological Society was reserved wholly

The zoological park idea.
Herd of American elk in their range.

opportunely creating that commission was due to the hard work of Assemblyman Theodore Roosevelt, or that he was specially chosen for that service by Matthew P. Breen?

As the stranger passes through one of our turnstiles, there spreads before him the most magnificent composition of land and water that ever was dedicated to zoology. Its qualities were well summed up in one sentence by an English critic, F. G. Aflalo, when he described it as being "at once the envy and the despair of all European makers of zoological gardens."

If we could have modeled a site with our

for me. The day was a sunny afternoon in February, 1896.

"—when comes the calm mild day as still such
      days will come
To call the squirrel and the bee from out their
      winter homes ;
When the sound of dropping nuts is heard, though
      all the trees are still,
And twinkle in the smoky light the waters of the
      rill."

I entered Bronx Park by way of West Farms, alone and unguided; went along the eastern bank of Bronx Lake up to Pelham Avenue, crossed the old iron bridge and zigzagged back through the wilderness

The small-deer house and corrals.

and the glades wherein our animal buildings now stand. I saw everything.

My first sensation was of almost paralyzing astonishment. It seemed incredible that such *virgin forest*, of huge, *old* oaks and chestnuts, tulips, sweet-gums and beeches, had been spared in the City of New York until 1896! But there they were, waiting for us. And then the beautiful ridges and valleys, the open woods, the meadows, the Rocking Stone, and the basins for ponds!

The magnificent possibilities of the place as an ideal home for wild animals in comfortable captivity—*freedom in security*—unrolled before me like a panorama. At the end of two hours I saw a great New York Zoological Park. But I did not dare to hope that even imperial New York would be willing to spend the money to make it in ten short years.

First, then, of all our advantages we must place our marvellous grounds, which, for such purposes as ours, are in a class by themselves, and incomparable. Because of the tremendous advantage they gave us at the outset, it is hardly fair to compare our establishment with others that are handicapped by small grounds, on a dead level.

Second in line we place our open-air animal dens, aviaries and ranges, generally. Opportunities for out-door life are available to *about seven-tenths* of all our vertebrates. It is only the serpents and a

few other reptiles, some of the smaller monkeys, and about three-fourths of the birds in the Large Bird-house that in summer are not quartered out-doors. The open-air ranges for our hoofed and horned animals are from two to eight times as spacious as such animals can be allowed in even the largest Old World zoological garden.

As an important item under the above heading, consider our series of Bear Dens, that has only one rival—in the National Zoological Park at Washington.

The bear dens of Europe annoy me greatly; for, in general, they are quite inexcusable. Evidently some of them have been designed by men who never hunted bears. By reason of the improved conditions that surround them—space, open view of the world, sunlight, abundance of water, rocks and companionship—our bears are the jolliest, happiest and most amusing of any in captivity, or out of it! They are more playful than so many monkeys, and although very troublesome on account of their vigor, they are assuredly one of the chief attractions of the Park.

The third feature in this enumeration is our House of Primates, unofficially called the Monkey House. It is notable because it is a house in which apes and monkeys can live long and happily, and because it is free from sickening monkey odors. The undenied success of our Monkey House is due to its new and practically perfect

The large bird-house and sea-lion pool, on Baird Court.

schemes of heating, ventilation, cage arrangements, lighting and sanitation.

Rotterdam has paid us the compliment of building, with the aid of our plans and specifications, an understudy of our Primate House, about as complete as it was possible to erect, even to the wire netting on the guard rails, only the roof and walls being of different materials.

Our Lion House is the only lion house in the world that employs wire netting for cage fronts instead of heavy prison bars; that has balconies in its cages, and beautiful green tiles on its cage walls instead of whitewash or paint. It is also the only animal building that contains a studio for painters and sculptors.

The Large Bird-House is the only one of which we know that is filled with great flocks of birds flying about in large cages, and with a huge flying cage in the centre of its main hall. Our fundamental idea of large communal cages is, I think, new in our bird-houses. It is also our belief that nowhere else in the world is there to be found such a splendid collection of rare and beautiful tropical birds living in such freedom and comfort under one roof.

There are several great out-door flying cages in other zoological establishments, both in Europe and America. That ours is the most spacious of all is nothing particularly commendable; for all of the others—at Rotterdam, London, Paris, Wash-

ington, St. Louis and San Francisco—are amply large to render their feathered occupants supremely contented and happy. But in one respect we have made a great advance over our colleagues. Our Flying Cage (150 feet long, 75 feet wide, and 55 feet high) has been provided with a concrete pool, of running water, 100 feet long by nearly 30 feet wide, and so deep that it is a constant delight to the diving pelicans, cormorants, ducks, gulls, herons and flamingoes for which it was designed. Visitors like activity among the birds and mammals they come to see, and this spacious pool provokes it, to a delightful extent.

Our Antelope House is the equal of the best elsewhere, and thus far it has preserved its living inhabitants in remarkably good health. Its outside yards are about three times as spacious as those around any other antelope house that we know. They have a total frontage of 1,200 feet and an average depth of 90 feet.

The Small-Deer House is the first of its kind. It houses a great number of species of small deer, gazelles, wild goats and sheep that cannot endure our wet New York winters in the open; and it keeps on exhibition a fine selection of animals that otherwise would have to be taken from their ranges in November or December, and kept in storage until May.

The only rivals of our Reptile House are

334

in the zoological gardens of London, Philadelphia, Rotterdam, Amsterdam, Frankfort and Paris; but we know that our alligator pools, and the systematic collection of turtles and terrapins, are not matched elsewhere.

Our Mountain Sheep Hill is unique, in that it is the only fine, *natural* outcrop of rocks in a zoological garden or park that is available for a systematic collection of wild sheep and goats. Between this and manufactured rocks there is a wide difference. But, after all, this feature has brought some disappointments. While other species do well, for some reason as yet unknown the White Mountain Goat and Chamois do not thrive upon it, and require quarters elsewhere.

Let all those who are interested in making comparative studies of the zoological gardens and parks spend a few moments in considering our provisions for bison. The "zoological park idea" is well illustrated by our herd of 36 American Bison, roaming over two spacious ranges with a total area of about 20 acres. There are some zoological gardens that *as a whole* contain only that area! When you see the breeding herd —about 25 head of cows and "young stock" —either grazing contentedly on the knoll in the centre of the main range, or galloping toward the corrals at feeding time, you are thrilled by the feeling that this is an adequate representation of the great American Bison as he lived and throve on his native plains. It was from this herd that the Zoological Society founded the Wichita National Bison Herd, as a contribution to the perpetual preservation of the species by our government. The nucleus herd was taken out of our ranges in October, 1907.

After all is said, it is not alone the fine buildings of brick and stone, or the fine corrals and ranges, that make a zoological establishment great or commanding. It is the living creatures themselves. I have seen some fine animal buildings that were poorly filled with animals, and others that were fully filled with poor animals. If the exhibits do not frequently compel visitors to exclaim, "*How fine your animals look!*" you may know that something is wrong.

If the animals of the "zoo" are not round and sleek and shiny; if their eyes are not bright and their heads erect; if there are no cases of assault and battery on the fences and gates, there is a lack of the glowing vigor that rightly belongs in every well-conditioned wild animal. Our latest Park sensation was caused by the great Alaskan Brown Bear, "Ivan," who, in order to gain access to a hated rival and his lady love, bodily tore out a large and heavy panel of woven steel bars from the partition between his corral and the next, and trampled it down upon the floor as if it had been a sheet of tin. It would have required at least six men with two heavy sets of blocks and tackles to have done in an hour what that bear did with his naked claws in ten minutes. The exhibition of ursine strength was astounding; and a little later the battle of the two Alaskan giants was a fearsome sight. They stood up on their hind legs, more than seven feet high, and chewed each other in silence until separated.

One word here regarding the personnel of our bear collection, by way of an impression of its zoological value. I think that all of the bears of Europe added together would not make a collection *zoologically* equal to this one; and the reason is—seventeen species in fine condition.

Of the very remarkable yet little known giant Brown Bears of Alaska there is *not one in all Europe;* but we have a collection of seven individuals, representing four good species (and possibly five), as follows: 1 *Ursus eulophus* ("Admiral"), from Admiralty Island; 2 *Ursus dalli*, from Hudson Lake; 1 *Ursus merriami* from the Alaska Peninsula; 2 *Ursus middendorffi*, from Kadiak Island (the famous Kadiak Bear). Last, and most valuable of all, we have recently acquired an undetermined new Alaskan Brown Bear from the Kobuk River, *north of the Arctic Circle*, and only 300 miles south of Point Barrow!

There are also four grizzlies—from Yukon Territory, Wyoming, Colorado, and Mexico. There is a huge Yezo Bear (*Ursus ferox*), from Yezo Island, Japan; a regulation Japanese Black Bear (*U. japonicus*), and a fine side-whiskered Himalayan Black Bear (*Ursus torquatus*), also from Japan! Central Asia is represented by two beautiful golden-yellow Hairy-eared Bears from Kuldcha (*Ursus piscator*) · and from Trebizond, Asia Minor, there has come a very satisfactory Syrian Bear. The queer Sloth Bear of India and the ugly and mean Malay Sun Bear have not been ignored. Of the American

Alaskan brown bears.

Black Bears we have specimens from eight different localties, scattered all the way from Prince William Sound, Alaska, to Chui-huahu, Mexico, and finally, after ten years of constant effort, we have at last secured a good, healthy black cub from the Andes of Colombia, which represents the relative of the Spectacled Bear, recently described as *Ursus ornatus majori*.

By reason of the work that Nature has done on our Polar Bear Den, it is, in my opinion, the finest bear den in the world; and it contains a pair of white bears that are up to the standard fixed by the den itself.

Our Elephant House and its adjacent yards represents high-water mark in wild-animal buildings. It is the crowning feature of the Zoological Park—spacious, beautifully designed, well built, perfectly lighted, heated and ventilated, and generously provided with open-air yards for all its animals. The keepers say that the elephants, rhinoceroses and hippo greatly enjoy their fine quarters, winter and summer; and where has New York City ever acquired elsewhere so fine a building for so little money as $157,000?

But the finest Elephant and Rhinoceros House is of small interest unless the collection under its roof is also of commanding importance. We are extremely fortunate in being able to exhibit a collection of elephants and rhinoceroses in every way worthy of the new building. It contains five elephants, representing three species— the Sudan African, West African Pigmy, and the Indian; three rhinoceroses of two species—Great Indian and African Black Rhinoceros; the Hippopotamus, and two species of Tapir.

Of the animals in the Elephant House, the Indian Rhinoceros is the greatest prize. Our lusty young male specimen is the only one of its kind that has come to America in fifteen years, and it cost the Society $6,000. The Sudan African Elephants, from the Blue Nile country, are young, but by 1915 each one will be so huge that a stall which now serves well for both animals will be none too large for one. The tusks of this species are said to be smaller than those of the African elephants of Uganda and British East Africa, but in height and bulk the Blue Nile ani-

mals grow as large as the largest; which means eleven feet at the shoulders.

Consider the collection of antelopes, and other animals, also, in the Antelope House; and ask how many of the world's zoological gardens and parks contain such a showing of rare species. Certainly not more than two or three. We find there a pair of Sudan Three-Horned Giraffes, a Greater Kudu, a pair of Elands, a Sable Antelope, Baker Roan Antelope, the Addax of the Sahara, and the Beatrix Antelope. of the Arabian desert (three), the Beisa, the Sing-Sing Waterbuck, the Leucoryx, the Nylgai, the Bontebok and two species of Sitatunga, the White-tailed Gnu and the Brindled Gnu, the Reedbuck, Indian Black Buck (a herd), the Grevy Zebra, Mountain Zebra, Grant Zebra, Chapman Zebra (just arrived), Tibetan Kyang and Persian Wild Ass. The Zebras and wild asses will shortly make room for hartebeests, gazelles and bushbucks.

Of the above, the following species have bred here: Eland, Beatrix Antelope, Leucoryx, Nylgai, Black Buck and Grant Zebra. Since our Giraffes arrived, in October, 1903, they have not been sick for a day, and the male has grown from 10 feet 3 inches, to 14 feet 3 inches. With the wild equines named above we should mention the Prejevalsky Wild Horses (a pair), from the Gobi Desert, Mongolia, to whom a fine colt was born in May, 1909—the first birth for that species in America.

Our Asiatic deer (eleven species) are breeding at a rate so rapid that the young animals have become a serious embarrassment. Of all our Asiatic deer, the most satisfactory are the Axis, or Spotted Deer, from the jungles of India. They are surpassingly beautiful, they do not fight (much), they are "easy keepers," and they breed persistently.

No sketch of the New York Zoological Park can be complete without a reference to the only herd of Rocky Mountain Goats in captivity, and besides which only two (one died recently) other individuals exist on exhibition. Of the five kids brought from the mountains of British Columbia by the writer in October, 1905, four are alive and in perfect health. The fifth one gave her life to the first kid ever bred or born in captivity. The latter, now eighteen months old, is a lusty male, large for his age, very vigorous, and so free with his horns that it has been necessary to saw off their sharp and dangerous tips.

We find it rather strange that the Mountain Goat can live, and thrive, and even breed on the Atlantic Coast, where the Rocky Mountain Sheep cannot survive longer than about eighteen months. Thus far not one specimen of the latter has ever reached maturity in the eastern United States. But, after all, is not our success with the Goat more surprising than our failures with the Big-Horn? Think of abruptly transplanting a herd of animals from the summit of the Canadian Rockies, 10,-000 feet up, above timber-line, and from *dry* cold in winter down to tide-level, 3,000 miles away, hot in summer, horribly rainy in winter, humid at all times, and salty besides. At the same time, we make an entire change in food and drinking water. To ask animals of the summits of the continental divide to endure such a change, and live, surely is °asking much.

Of the bewildering variety of zoological varieties in the small Mammal House, there is space to mention only such distinguished foreigners as the Hyrax, Hyæna Dog, Caracal, Thibetan Fox, Suricate, Kusimanse, Spotted Genet, Binturong, Patagonian Cavy, Kinkajou, Clouded Leopard, Yaguarundi, Paca, Hutia, Golden Agouti, and the Giant Malabar Squirrel.

The Lion, the Tiger, the Jaguar, the Leopard and the Puma are common-place, and even *passé*. Every collection of live animals has them; but one can count on the fingers of one hand all the zoological gardens and parks that exhibit specimens of the rare and beautiful Snow Leopard, or Ounce of Tibet, the Clouded Leopard of Borneo, and the Cheetah of Africa.

Our finest lion, old "Sultan," is well beloved of the animal painters and sculptors, and I think he has been painted and modelled about one hundred times. His countenance is refined,

Markhor.

Rocky Mountain goat.

Snow leopard.

Sable antelope.

Sudan African elephants.

The Tegu lizard.

Florida crocodile.

Elephant tortoise.

Reticulated python.

Boa constrictor. (Black phase.)

dignified, imposing and beautiful, and his form is about perfect.

Our herd of Elk is to be viewed with unalloyed complacence. The stock is fine and robust, and the four males are as heavily antlered as any elk-hunter could possibly desire.

The Caribou, Moose and Big-Horn sheep we have given up as impossibilities; at least for acclimatization in New York. The salty humidity of the climate, the low altitude and the wet weather of every winter is hopelessly against those species.

And all this time we have not found space for a word concerning our wonderful bird collection, to which we have devoted the Aquatic Bird-House, the Large Bird-House, the great Flying Cage, the Duck Aviary, Pheasant Aviary, Ostrich House, Crane Paddock, and Wild-Fowl Pond. The great Eagle and Vulture Aviary will come in the near future, as the finish of the final plan that we laid down eleven years ago. The total number of species to be seen on July 15, 1909, was 644, and the whole number of specimens then on exhibition in good health was 2,816.

The Large Bird-House shelters, within and without, a glorious array of rare, odd and beautiful feathered forms. Of all birds, no species is more immaculate than the green and crimson Touracou, or Plantain-Eater, with his jaunty crest, and wings of flame that contain in their primaries ten per cent. of metallic *copper!* Structurally, no bird is more interesting than that odd mixture of characters, the Seriema, from South America, a composite stork-plover-bird-of-prey-without-talons. The South American Sun Bittern beside it, with a glorious sunburst painted on each wing, is equally rare. The Laughing Jackass from Australia is really a giant kingfisher. The long row of queer but pleasing Toucans of several species instantly arrest the eye, and the Toco Toucan would excite admiration anywhere. Close beside the Victoria Crown Pigeons of New Guinea, the odd and erratic Roadrunners from southern Arizona cheerfully hop and jerk through the day, watching the visitor with eyes that suggest practical jokes and mischief.

In the great main hall of the Large Bird-House about 75 species of birds, perhaps the queerest *omnium gatherum* ever peacefully harmonized in one apartment, disport joyously in the huge indoor flying-cage. There are gaudy Mandarin Ducks, Wood Ducks, Patagonian Plovers, Ruffs, Sandpipers, Quails of various species, Golden Pheasants, Bleeding-Heart Pigeons from the Philippines, a few Terns and Skimmers, and song birds in great variety of color and song.

The Parrot's Hall is teeming and screaming with Parrots, Macaws, and Parakeets; but there also will be found a large collection of tropical Pigeons, Doves, and Quail. When the visitors have had enough of the noisiest birds on earth, it is pleasant to drift out into the Glass Court, where the American song-birds have almost exclusive possession. There you will find twelve species of our warblers living most happily in one big cage; and near by there are other and more vigorous songsters in goodly numbers.

The Ostrich House was built for the ostriches, rheas, emeus and cassowaries, and while it contains good examples of all these groups, many other rare feathered folk have crept into that comfortable haven of refuge. It is an odd gathering, scattered somewhat in summer, but in winter embracing such zoological prizes as the California Condor (now nearly extinct), the Harpy Eagle of South America, the odd Bateleur Eagle of Africa, the gorgeous King Vulture, the Paradise Crane, Java Peacock, and others.

Our Pheasant Aviary is 240 feet long, and its 48 runways and shelter houses are all 8 feet in height. It is a two-story installation. The pheasants live upon the ground; and aloft, on the perches and in the bush-tops, live many species of hardy song-birds, pigeons and doves. Each bird in the place can exercise the following options provided for the promotion of its comfort: a sandy bed in the sun, a perch in the sun, a shelter open on the front only, or a closed shelter with only one small door. It is here that the pheasant fancier will find the gorgeous Golden, Reeves, Amherst, and

California condor.

Frigate bird.

Black-footed penguin.

Crested screamer.

Whooping crane.

The lion house, showing open-air cages.

Impeyan pheasants; the Silver, Japanese Ring-neck, English, Fire-back, Elliott, Eared, and many others.

The Reptile House was the first building erected in the Park, and it was dedicated at the formal opening on November 9, 1899. It was built by the Zoological Society, and, with about 20 other installations, was presented to the city on the date mentioned. It was given a leading position in the pro-gramme because of the universal ignorance of the public regarding reptiles generally; and it is safe to say that it has cured a greater amount of ignorance and folly than any other collection of the Park.

Under this broad roof, in comfortable captivity, is gathered the world's greatest collection of poisonous and other serpents, crocodilians, turtles, terrapins, tortoises, and lizards.

Entrance to the lion house.

Our alligator pool in the Reptile House is far in advance of every other crocodilian pool, and represents one of the most com-

and view the world whenever it suits him to do so. Our crocodiles and alligators eat as greedily as pigs, and they grow with a

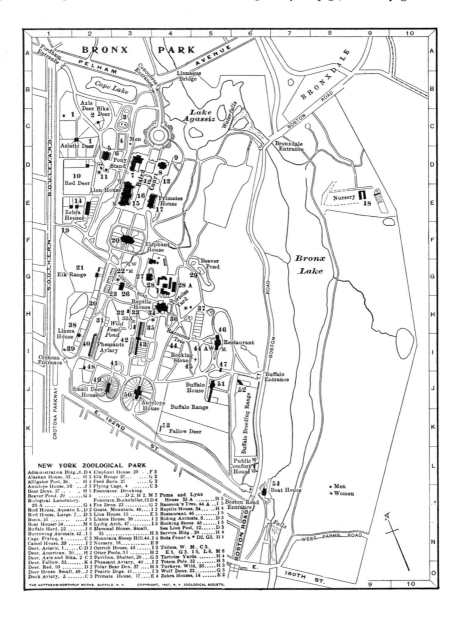

NEW YORK ZOOLOGICAL PARK

plete "hits"—in a small way—that we have made. It is beautifully lighted, it has a living jungle background, it is deep and wide, its water is properly warmed, and each habitant can crawl out upon the bank

degree of rapidity that has completely up-set all previous ideas and records of the growth of such reptiles.

We have been at much pains to establish in the centre of the main hall of reptiles an elaborate turtle crawl, with a deep pool at one end, in which to make comfortable a systematic collection of fresh-water turtles and terrapins. The eastern wing of the building is our Tortoise and Lizard House, heated in winter like a bake-oven, and in summer opening upon a series of sanded yards, in which the reptiles can roast themselves in the hot sun until they feel "fine."

Iguanas and monitors do not thrive in small cages, but put them in a sanded yard that is hot enough to roast eggs, and straightway they begin to run, and jump fences, fight and eat in a manner that is at first fairly bewildering! It seems odd to think of Iguanas fighting, but in our yards they are much given to it, greatly to the annoyance of their keepers.

If we are to be fair to ourselves, we must call attention to the labeling of the Zoological Park collections, particularly the descriptive labels, the maps of distribution, the charts, keys and picture-labels in endless profusion, to inform and entertain the visitor, and render the collections of the utmost value.

Naturally, the public will desire to know something of the number of specimens living in the various great zoological gardens of the world. Very few institutions publish their statistics annually, but we will offer all that are available at the present date. The latest general census was that for January 1, 1907, when the figures were as shown below, drawn chiefly from the official report made by Dr. Gustave Loisel, of Paris, to the French Government. All are as of January 1, 1907, except New York and London, which are for 1908:

Institution.	Mammals.	Birds.	Reptiles and Amphibians.	Total.
New York Zoological Park	607	2530	897	4034
Berlin	946	2176	27	3149
London	873	1621	478	2972
Philadelphia	487	952	1087	2526
Hamburg	473	1665	251	2389
Schoenbrunn	593	1351	171	2085
Cologne	424	1479	98	2001
Breslau	592	1067	184	1843
Frankfort	644	1002	158	1804

And how do our collections stand to-day in number of species and of individuals? The animal accommodations of the Park are crowded full, to the overflowing point. On July 15, 1909, a careful census revealed the following:

LIVING ANIMALS NOW IN THE NEW YORK ZOOLOGICAL PARK.

Mammals	246	species	743	specimens
Birds	644	"	2816	"
Reptiles	256	"	1969	"
Total,	1146	"	5530	"

The tale is told. The Zoological Park and its collections must now speak for themselves. Last year they spoke to 1,413,739 visitors. The common people hear them gladly, but as yet the scientists of America, as a mass, do not seem to know that the New York Zoological Park has arrived. They are, as a rule, too much interested in soarings after the infinite and divings after the unfathomable to care for such trivial things as living animals drawn from strange places. But the unscientific millions, whom we specially desire to instruct and entertain, are with us, in ever-increasing numbers; and for them we will continue to strive.

26
In Up-town New York

In Up-town New York

BY CHARLES HENRY WHITE

WHEN in the middle of the eighteenth century a man settled on the northern end of Manhattan Island, then gradually being reclaimed from the wilderness, he had every reason to be proud of the fact, even though this was Harlem. His neighbors, though not numerous, were distinguished; Harlem had become the rural retreat of the aristocratic New-Yorker, and the social significance of residing there caused a man to enter this rugged country in the same buoyant spirit which at a later date characterized his departure from it. This suburban life, however, had its inconveniences; access to the old Welvers Tavern in New York was not easy, and a glance at the rocky, uneven formation of Harlem to-day—its granite eminences and deep, unexpected embankments—would imply that the homeward journey of the jocose element was a particularly hazardous performance after nightfall. When once a man's midnight yodling has suddenly been interrupted by a twenty-foot drop down an embankment, it is apt to shake him up and make him sceptical. One may assume, then, that the old resident was good in spite of himself; made sacrifices and retired early.

But the chief charm of old Harlem—its well-bred seclusion—was destined to be transitory. Later, when New York's business centre moved steadily up-town, greatly increasing the value of real estate and the cost of living, a horde of New-Yorkers moved to the north, and Harlem soon became a haven for the clerks and small merchants, the family man and the newly married couple and the young professional man, who all flocked thither; and there came into existence in its logical sequence the Harlem flat: a frail, angular, overelaborated structure, which at the advent of spring occasionally showed strange crevices in its sides, preparatory to descending in a cataract of bricks.

With this influx of humanity a wise and humane administration caused railings or bumpers to be erected along the embankments and gullies, making access to one's home, at night, easy for the normal and possible for the abnormal. This was only a few years prior to the pre-digested breakfast-food era, and all were content and merry in Harlem—and might have continued so had not a certain individual with an undeveloped sense of propriety (whom many to-day denounce as a myth) thrown the bone of contention.

It was at 125th Street—or was it at 120th Street? (opinions differ)—that this ostentatious person, who presumably had made money more rapidly and ingeniously than the law even to-day allows, drew an imaginary boundary-line for Harlem, with the unfortunate remark, " Thank the Lord, I'm out of it!" and forthwith moved to 115th Street. The seeds of discord had been sown. Our latent perversity makes us resent being told by a casual stranger just exactly where we are; it embarrasses a man and makes him feel cramped. Indeed, in this particular case it even went so far as to cast aspersions on one's social position, and has since been the means of much unnecessary bitterness in determining Harlem's exact boundary-line. Those who hitherto had been content—nay, even anxious—to live in Harlem soon began to speculate upon the possibility of there being a grain of wisdom in the stranger's exultation on leaving it. In short, a random remark had been the means of suddenly stimulating the Harlemite's critical sense at the expense of his happiness.

Thus, to-day, it is extremely difficult to get a Harlem resident with the correct mental attitude to answer you as to where New York ends and Harlem begins. He is rarely impersonal.

" Do you like Harlem?" you unwittingly ask your friend who resides at 120th Street.

HARLEM'S ARCADY
Etched on copper by C. H. White

"I'm not in Harlem," he replies, with considerable bitterness. "Oh no! Don't fool yourself . . . it's not as bad as *that!* Harlem begins at 125th Street!"

"Cheer up!" you say; "it's only temporary." And with this you leave him in Harlem, to grope about for a motive in this wilderness of asphalt and tomblike houses; to wander through interminable vistas of glaring white pavement and geometrical brick; to dodge trolley-cars and elevated structures; to pass beneath windows bulging with ill-assorted humanity in pink and blue undershirts, gazing vacantly across the street; or to tumble against a throng of perspiring rooters grouped about the corner baseball game—until his nerves reach a supreme crisis: he pauses deliberately to listen with a morbid interest to the hoarse metallic raspings of the distant phonograph in one of the local palaces of artificial merriment!

On such an occasion, after having formally cursed Harlem, should you catch a glimpse of a dim strip of silver fringed with green, with here and there a faint suggestion of distant shipping and still more distant hills, faintly outlined at the vanishing-point of some great brick and plaster vista,—follow it, and presently the obvious side of Harlem,

the appalling monotony of her streets, the tin mouldings and venomous rococo, are left behind. A gentle breeze laden with fern and earthy forest odors reaches you from somewhere beyond the lofty masses of patriarchal oak and elm, like a distant call from Vagabondia which must be answered. You press on; here scaling steep embankments and rocky promontories, scarred and weather-beaten, thickly carpeted with velvety green lichen; now wandering through drowsy vales of moss and fern, beneath a lofty canopy of soaring branch and leafy foliage, until confused murmurs—perhaps the distant whistle of some river tug signalling for the drawbridge, or the low muffled tremolo of a passing motor-boat—reach the ear faintly. You hurry along, expectant, emerging from the woods to find yourself in Harlem's Arcady.

At your feet stretches a shimmering sheet of water, winding its way placidly in long graceful curves about the distant points, or losing itself in a rare vista of sky and water spanned by a silver network of innumerable swinging bridges. A distant tug and its train of barges steal lazily down the river, looking not unlike some mammoth eel in the odd perspective; and in the valley far

IN THE LEE OF THE ONE-HUNDRED-AND-TWENTY-FIFTH STREET BULKHEAD
Etched on copper by C. H. White

below, seen through a veil of mist, the apartment-hotel, with its French towers and steep mansard roofs, rears itself defiantly in its girdle of heavy foliage, like some medieval stronghold. And this is Harlem! Not the barren, naked, obvious side with its strange anomalies, but unobtrusive Harlem, refined upon, jealously revealing itself in one of those rare moods when a monastic grayness steals imperceptibly over the river, lending to the most prosaic thing a new significance.

First blithe and debonair, mirroring in her depths great rocky highlands, this whimsical river drifts capriciously into a minor vein through the Harlem

Bad Lands — a barren tract hemmed in by raw, vacant tenements and the still remoter fringe of factories half veiled in smoke. The desolation here is so complete that it commands admiration. The stranded wreck of a canal-boat imbedded in the mud, its clawlike ribs overgrown with moss and barnacles, and perhaps a stray naked urchin besmirched with mud, alone in this city wilderness — knee-deep in the stagnant filth — only heighten the deserted, forbidding aspect of the place. This is a superannuated public dumping-ground. At the approach of night one may see here, on rare occasions, a few isolated black spots detach-

ing themselves against the uniform grayness of the uneven ground; moving with
painful uncertainty, and stopping from
time to time to hover restlessly about the
numerous pyramids of refuse. These are
the local ragpickers — miserable, half-
starved humanity — who occasionally
haunt the scrap-heaps in a vain hope of
sweating a few cents out of these thrice-
sifted scavengerings.

To what extent Harlem is appreciated
can only be fully realized after having
seen the throngs of votaries in easy
sprawl along her shores, who toil not,
neither do they spin; or by a visit to
Bill Conlin's—a derelict of a boat-house
tucked away snugly in the lee of the
125th Street bulkhead, and dotted pro-
fusely by robust fellows in faded undershirts, contentedly watching the distant
train of golden clouds roll past and tower
into new formations; noting with unceasing interest the flood and ebb tide
with its wake of stranded pleasure-craft,
shaking with unfeigned good humor when
the gasoline-launch runs foul of the
sunken reef, or when the yachtsman, in
immaculate white duck suit, slips with
much throaty gurgling, amid a flood of
bubbles, from the treacherous slime of
the gangway into the river.

A fine old pensioner who fought with
Farragut, an army veteran who went to
Custer's relief, an ex-plumber and alleged gas-fitter, an involuntary tailor, a
man of temperament who makes bromide
enlargements that are never understood,
and to this heterogeneous collection add
Mike Dorlan, watchman of the dock, and
"Fog Eye," an Italian junkman with a
glass optic, and you have the little coterie
of boat-house loungers that I stumbled
upon by some happy accident one fine
summer's day. They say little, these
dreamers of the river, and when the
spirit moves them to converse (which
is seldom), it is usually a hoarse mono-
syllable spoken between clenched teeth
—sideways through the corner of the
mouth. Their infallible good humor and
natural primitive buoyancy have been acquired in many cases by the liquidation
of business interests; while others have
sacrificed home and mother—at times
even a wife and child—to answer the
call of the river.

Bill Conlin calls this the "boat-house

fever," and Bill is a close observer; but
Cauliflower Jim's testimony, while hardly impersonal, is not without value. "It
gits on me nerves," he explained, "to
sit round the house with the wimmen,
and hear talk o' feathers and the like,
and the new shape o' corsets." Howbeit,
year in and year out they are there, basking in the sunshine and ripening into a
mature old age waiting for the final har-
vesting. Save for an involuntary trip
or two to the Island, little, it seems,
intrudes upon the even tenor of their
existence. So secluded is this little niche
that few outsiders ever gain access to
it. Occasionally, it is true, a stray
Italian laborer in quest of work may
pass through the low doorway into the
mysterious gloom within and timorous-
ly approach the ponderous carcass of
Mike Dorlan, watchman and inspector
of the dock, in easy sprawl on the narrow balcony.

"Gota job? . . . Gota work?" Mike
will repeat after him in pidgin-English;
and then the sunburnt face of the
dock-inspector wrinkles in a philanthropic smile.

"See that bridge over there, and those
hills 'way off 'n the east?" he will begin,
softly. "Walk straight down the dock,
turn to yer right and beat it acrost the
bridge, and keep right on movin'," and,
his simple duties accomplished, the felt
hat descends once more over the broad
good-natured face, and with a deep sigh
he relapses into a blissful silence.

Bill Conlin tells me that with the exception of myself industry has only
prompted one man to visit the boat-
house. He was a newspaper reporter
who appeared one day with elaborate
photographic paraphernalia during the
coal strike, three years ago, just after
the boys had borrowed enough coal from
the freight-yards across the river to last
them the whole winter.

"He give us each fifty cents to git
out on the float and have our pictures
took sawin' wood," Bill explained, with
a significant wink. "'It's just to show
the people of New York what the poor
is doin' durin' the coal famine,' sez the
rayporter, winkin' and trainin' the camera
on us." Bill chuckled softly. "We did-
n't say nawthin', but kept right on sawin'—see?"

In spite of the apparent lack of anything approaching industry in these river loungers, if the occasion seems to warrant it they can bestir themselves into feverish activity. When the Harlem River refuses to give up its dead, and the family of the deceased offers a handsome remuneration for the recovery of a suicide, the sporting element latent in the river's floating population comes to life.

Fishy - eyed, thick - necked dreamers, upon whose ponderous boots can be seen embryonic forms of vegetation, and who for months have lain by the river's edge in a state of alcoholic coma, promptly awake from their lethargy and seem to take a new lease on life, rising with the dawn, when the grotesque flotilla sets forth with its strange débris of dragging paraphernalia. Crowbars with hooks attached, drag-nets heavily weighted, lead pipes with newfangled wire attachments —anything with clawlike properties—are eagerly pressed into service. Men whose hands show everything but the signs of honest labor scour the wrecking-yards of the neighborhood for water-logged dories capable of floating, with vigorous bailing, one or two men; and Tony the barber and Angelo the peanut-vender, haunted by dreams of untold treasure and touched with the craze for speculation, draw out their hoard of pennies and strike for the river.

Meanwhile the cannons blaze away over the placid waters of the stream; here a boat-load of plumbers of an adventurous turn shout hoarse orders at one another as they pass in a derelict of a sloop, propelled at uncertain moments by the second-hand motor but lately rescued from the junk-yard; while behind them comes the pale, anæmic man who, after three sleepless days and nights, has just rescued a pair of archaic stays from the river-bed, and proffers, as he rows along, a string of foul and blasphemous oaths. Bill Conlin, too, laid aside his sandworm industry to search the river. "Every guy in the bunch was fer settin' himself up in business with the proceeds," he explained to me later, half-apologetically. "And late one afternoon when old man Duggan from Highbridge pulls him up, the crowd went ravin' mad. The cop was fer nailin' the stiff himself and fadin' away with the

proceeds; but, 'No,' says old man Duggan. 'I'll take care of *him* meself—see? Hands off!' sez he, with a wild look in his eye, 'or I'll have the law on ye,' sez he, tremblin' with excitement. 'It's my stiff and I seen him first,' and sez he, 'you can play with him all ye like after I've cashed in,' sez he. And with that he froze on to him like a lobster, and now he's retired entirely."

"What are the chances for floaters around this season?" I asked, after he had relapsed into silence again.

"*Nawthin'* doin'," he replied, derisively. "I tell you the river ain't what it was."

On a fine midsummer Sabbath afternoon all Harlem appears to have reunited along the river's edge in one great *fête champêtre*. Outing parties in their Sunday's best line the shores, and it would seem, in loitering along its banks, watching the innumerable pleasure-craft ply back and forth, and the distant train of restless tilted sails slowly beating their way across the treacherous channels of the "Kills," that along this stream pleasure surely plays as important a part as commerce. A warm, genial atmosphere envelops everything; and when this subtle influence takes hold of one, a strange metamorphosis takes place.

Jim the iceman, "Aulie" the plumber, and Fritz of the milk-wagon, resplendent in Third Avenue "Admiral Dewey" suits —a mass of gorgeous braid interlacing their ample bosoms, topped with white yachting-caps—issue forth and shape an uncertain course down the river in their improvised "power - boat"; power that comes when one least expects it—at half-minute intervals, preceded by violent explosions. Along the docks loiter the less fortunate—the workmen with their wives and children, a fluctuating mass of color relieved against the uniform gray and salmon of the houses. The throaty anthem of the perspiring Sängerbund, crowded together in the Casino, reaches the ear in fragments above the confused noises of the river; and in the hush which at times unexpectedly falls upon this Harlem Kermess the distant brassy strains of a band playing rag-time to the lunatics in the asylum on the Island steals softly across the river.

It takes the Harlemite to appreciate

A DERELICT OF A BOAT-HOUSE, WITH ITS HANGERS-ON

Etched on copper by C. H. White

THE "KILLS," SEEN FROM THE GOUVERNEUR MORRIS MANSION
Etched on copper by C. H. White

the real significance—the rare possibilities—of Sunday. Theirs is a Continental, a healthy German, Sabbath; a day of leisure, evoking long, shimmering stretches of water fringed with heather, bathed in genial delight, and racing clouds aloft, and untold wealth of beer and pretzels.

Concerning Harlem's former history little interest is manifested; crowds daily ply back and forth across the "Kills" almost in the shadow of "Morrisania," the romantic Morris mansion, without so much as a glance at this splendid Revolutionary relic, nor a thought of the significance of its destruction. To wander through its spacious halls that once echoed to the tread of a high-heeled Revolutionary pageant, to loiter in the grand reception-room where perhaps Washington and Lafayette trod a measure, or to pause within the sombre precincts of the library, panelled with mahogany, where the first rough draft of the Declaration of Independence came to light, and then return to see these panels rent asunder by the workmen engaged in demolishing it, is to

fully appreciate the capacities of a miserable thin-skinned patriotism. As the work of vandalism progressed, curious things came to light: a few old French coins, an antiquated tea-chest inlaid with ivory, and a dainty eighteenth-century flat-iron for the frills and ruffles of former gallants—things of another epoch—recalling the Reign of Terror with its hasty departures, its deserted palaces and deserted lawns run wild with hyacinth and daisy.

If the down-town New-Yorker takes but little interest in the significance of his landmarks, his brother in Harlem cares still less, for neither is imaginative. The latter's temperament craves something more vital, more tangible; and when the conversation turns to local legend and bizarre incidents, he shows an intense appreciation. Late one cloudy afternoon last summer Bill Conlin rowed me through the "Kills" past Morrisania and cheerfully dismissed it with, "It's an old castle; they're goin' to tear it down." But when we had entered the treacherous currents that sweep in dangerous eddies past the almost unnavigable channels in the rear of Blackwells Island, he showed signs of animation, the direct cause of which I perceived to be the long point stretching out before us, upon whose green turf were frequent ochre-colored furrows—the scars of recent excavating—and along whose shores walked sundry listless figures in blue overalls.

"Those are the dopes from the funny-house takin' an airin'," he observed, indicating the distant blue spots that moved aimlessly about the turf. Then he became visibly irritated.

"It's a pity the day ain't fine or they'd be out diggin' their canal," he mused.

I was somewhat in the dark, when he enlightened me.

"You see, it's this way," he went on. "Even a guy who's nutty gits tired o' talkin' it all over with himself. It's wearin' on him to have to give all the answers; so one o' the doctors over there hits on a new idea, and next day has all the dopes lined up—guys wot thought they was bank presidents side by side with others wot simply stood and picked at things—all looked alike to him; and that there doctor was chuck full o' brains, and could hand it out in a line o' talk with the best o' the lawyers.

"MORRISANIA," THE GOUVERNEUR MORRIS MANSION
Etched on copper by C. H. White

A BOAT CLUB ON THE HARLEM
Etched on copper by C. H. White

"'Friends,' sez he, after he had them all bunched together, 'we're goin' to dig a canal to cut off that there point,' sez he. 'Are ye on?' sez he, and some o' them waved at him and grinned and almost understood him. 'Fall to!' yells the doctor, 'and let's see how fast you can do it.' And when the warden give them spades and wheelbarrows you should have seen the dirt fly! They no sooner gits the canal dug, when the doctor comes down agin and steps behind a tree to wipe the smile off his face, and starts in again. 'Friends,' sez he, 'the administration has changed their minds,' sez he, 'and have decided to have the canal run through in the opposite direction; so you'll oblige me by fillin' this wan up and beginnin' th' other. It's a good job you've made, boys, and accept me compliments; it's a *very* nice little canal,' sez he, pattin' a couple o' them over the head. 'Ta, ta!' sez he, fadin' away.

"Year in and year out they keep on diggin' that there canal, and I only heard tell of one guy in the bunch who ever had the brains to see that somethin' must be wrong; and when the doctor begun givin' his little song and dance about the administration changin' their minds again and movin' the canal four points to the west, a lad named Leary, from County Cork, Ireland, who was out there on trial, butted in with, 'Say—will you tell me who the blazes voted fer this administration?' And they thrun him out of the funny-house next day . . . a sane man, fer fear he'd contaminate the rest."

27
The Hugeness of New York

THE HUGENESS OF NEW YORK

BY

RENÉ BACHE

Author of "The National Ravages of Alcohol", "America's Race Suicide", etc.

TEN years from now New York will be the largest city in the world. It has at the present time, according to the latest estimate, 4,285,435 inhabitants—a population one-fourth greater than that of Paris. London, it is true, is still ahead by nearly six hundred thousand; but New York is growing seven times as fast as the British metropolis, having shown an increase for the last decade of no less than thirty-seven per cent., against five per cent. for greater London.

When we come to make a comparison between the two cities, however, the most striking fact has to do with density of population. Ever so much has been written about the crowding of the people in the slums of London, where, as reliable statistics show, the unfortunate inhabitants are so thickly packed that in some quarters there are as many as two hundred for each acre of land. Think of crowding that many human beings into such a space! Why, it is like packing sardines in a box.

And yet, when one looks the matter up, it is found that densest London is less thickly populated than densest New York. There are, in fact, in the great American metropolis two thousand, six hundred and twenty-six acres with over two hundred persons to the acre! To put the case differently, and even more strikingly, nearly three-quarters of a million persons (in exact figures, 739,470) in New York are housed more densely than the residents of the most thickly packed districts of London. Indeed, considerable areas in our most congested districts have two occupants for every one in the most crowded parts of London; and even this statement does not fully express the truth, inasmuch as New York has seven hundred and three acres with over four hundred and forty-seven persons to the acre!

In the whole of Manhattan and the Bronx, if all of the inhabitants of these two boroughs were equally distributed relatively to area, there would be ninety for each acre. Of course, however, some districts are comparatively sparsely settled (leaving out of consideration 6836 acres of parks) and this means a proportionate overcrowding in other sections. The lower east side of Manhattan is notoriously a congested region; but in the Sixteenth Ward of Brooklyn, human beings are packed almost twice as thickly as in the worst slums of London.

In the slums of the West Central district

359

BROAD STREET, LOOKING NORTH, THE HEART OF THE CITY'S FINANCIAL DISTRICT. THE MASS OF PEDESTRIANS
ON THE SIDEWALKS MAKES THE USE OF THE STREET NECESSARY ALSO

Photographed by Brown Brothers

FIFTY THOUSAND PERSONS, IT IS ESTIMATED, ARE SHOWN HERE IN LONGACRE SQUARE, NORTH OF THE "TIMES" BUILDING. THE SEARCH LIGHT ON TOP OF THE BUILDING IS FLASHING THE NEWS OF HUGHES'S ELECTION AS GOVERNOR. THE STREAK OF WHITE ALONG BROADWAY IS CAUSED BY THE IMPRESSION MADE ON THE CAMERA BY THE HEADLIGHTS OF THE TROLLEY-CARS

Photographed by Brown Brothers

VIEW NEAR SOUTH FERRY, THE EXTREME SOUTHERN END OF MANHATTAN; THE BEGINNING OF THE CONGESTED BUSINESS DISTRICT WITH ITS HUGE OFFICE BUILDINGS

of London there are eleven and a half people for each house. For each dwelling in the whole of Brooklyn the average number of inmates is almost as great—that is to say, ten and a half. Thus it would seem that congestion of population is far more intense in New York than in any other city of the world—a very unfortunate circumstance,

RESIDENCE OF CHARLES M. SCHWAB ON RIVERSIDE DRIVE. THIS BUILDING WITH ITS CONTENTS REPRESENTS AN OUTLAY OF ABOUT SIX MILLION DOLLARS. ITS ARCHITECTURE IS A COMBINATION OF FOUR OF THE MOST FAMOUS FRENCH CHATEAUS— BLOIS, CHENANCEAU, CHAMBORD AND AZAY-LE-RIDEAU. A STAFF OF EXPERT MECHANICS IS NEEDED TO HANDLE THE HEATING AND ELECTRICAL APPARATUS

one must admit, inasmuch as experience shows that crime in communities increases in direct ratio with density of population. Where human beings are thickly herded together there is always a tendency to the multiplication of degenerate specimens of the race who make a business of preying upon society.

It is interesting to consider the fact that a density of two hundred persons to the acre signifies a distribution over that area of the occupants (if they were arranged equidistantly and after the manner of pieces on a chessboard) with spaces of less than fifteen feet between person and person. At ninety to the acre (representing Manhattan and the Bronx) they would be twenty-two feet apart. Considering the most congested districts of New York, the inhabitants (four hundred and forty-seven of them to the acre) would be separated from one another by distances of less than ten feet. This is rather instructive, and may explain in some measure why, as was found by recent investigation, two thousand five hundred and sixty-three tenement families enjoyed the use of only thirty-six bathtubs!

Another melancholy fact is that in New York, relatively to the size of the population, fewer people own homes than in any other city of the world. There dwell on the island of Manhattan 391,687 families, only 16,316 of which hold title to the houses they occupy. Ninety-four out of every hundred families pay rent—one result of which circumstance is that the population of the American metropolis shifts in a more kaleidoscopic fashion than any other known. On the other hand, we observe the singular spectacle of ownership by one family (the Astors) of an immense multitude of dwellings, its property having a number of tenants greater than the entire population of Hartford or of Troy.

The construction of huge communal dwellings, called apartment houses, has a tendency to assemble large numbers of persons within relatively small areas. There are now on the island of Manhattan two thousand one hundred and twelve first-class "flat" buildings, the average number of families in each being twenty, and the average number of persons per family, four. This means forty-two thousand, two hundred and forty families (comprising 168,960 individuals), who are sheltered in such houses. It is estimated, however, that twenty-five years from now there will be in Manhattan ten thousand buildings of the kind, affording homes for a million persons.

Of first-class hotels in Manhattan there are to-day one hundred and thirty-six, with an average of four hundred rooms apiece —making in all fifty-four thousand, four hundred rooms. It is easily seen, then, where at least a part of New York's vast "floating population" find bed and board. Twenty-five years hence there will be at least four hundred such hotels on the island, nearly all of them "sky-scrapers"—a mode of construction no longer condemned, as erstwhile, by popular prejudice—and quarters will thus be afforded for one hundred and sixty thousand visitors all the year 'round.

An ingenious statistician, by the way, has reckoned that if a flat house were built covering one entire block, with fifty apartments on each floor and five persons to each family, it would have to be sixteen thousand stories high in order to accommodate the entire population of Greater New York. Such a thing being obviously an impossibility, it may be more interesting to consider this imaginary structure as being cut slicewise into one thousand apartment houses of sixteen stories apiece, each of them occupying a whole block. These would contain very comfortably all the inhabitants of the metropolis.

Before leaving the subject of houses it may be worth while to refer to the fact that many of the private residences of New York are unequaled in point of magnificence by any to be found elsewhere in the world. One may say that in its newest development the rich man's dwelling has ceased to be merely a home, and has taken on the aspect of a palace, with departments devoted to fine art, music, in-door sports, hygiene, and even religion. Mr. Charles M. Schwab's residence has a swimming pool and a bowling alley; but the house of Senator William A. Clark is in a class by itself. It has one hundred and twenty-one rooms (without counting twenty bathrooms), a Turkish bath plant, and an art gallery; and, with its contents, it will cost, when completed, fifteen millions of dollars.

In the year 1790, the population of New York was only 33,131. By 1830 it was 202,589. Twenty years later, in 1850, it was 515,547, and by 1870 it had reached 942,295. During the next ten years it passed the million mark, being reckoned in 1880 at 1,206,299. But these figures, of course, were only for Manhattan Island. With the inclusion of Brooklyn and three other boroughs, the Greater New York of to-day, as already stated, has considerably over four million inhabitants. Of females there are thirty-two thousand more than males.

Photographed by Brown Brothers

TWO OR THREE MINUTES ONLY WERE NEEDED TO COLLECT THIS CROWD AROUND AN OPEN-AIR EVANGELIST

Photographed by Brown Brothers

BROADWAY, LOOKING NORTH TOWARD THE "TIMES" BUILDING.   THE CROWD OF SHOPPERS IS AN EVERYDAY ONE

Photographed by Brown Brothers

THE BOWERY: NOTE THE SURFACE LINES, THE OVERHEAD RAILROADS, THE CROWDING OF THE SIGNS ALL ALONG THE THOROUGHFARE

On the other hand there are in New York at the present time seventy-five thousand, six hundred and eighty more bachelors than spinsters of twenty years and over. In the population of the city there are, of ages from twenty up, 357,986 single men, 626,603 married men, 48,272 widowers, and 1189 divorced men. Of women of like age there are 282,306 spinsters, 610,321 wives, 147,386 widows, and 2040 divorced. The widows and widowers alone of the metropolis would make a city bigger than Providence, Rhode Island.

Just about one out of every three inhabitants of New York City was born in a foreign country. Manhattan alone has 789,342 residents of foreign birth, and Brooklyn 355,697. The total number of foreigners domesticated in the metropolis is, in precise figures, 1,297,080. They would alone compose a city as big as Philadelphia, considerably larger than Constantinople, or more than twice as big as Boston.

Half of the population of the State of New York is located within the limits of the great American metropolis, which has more inhabitants than Switzerland by one-fifth, and more by one-third than Denmark, or Servia, or Greece. The population of New York City is more than equal to that of nine sovereign states of the Union combined— Maine, Connecticut, Delaware, Florida, North Dakota, South Dakota, Colorado, Montana and Nevada. To this total Arizona and Alaska would have to be added in order to furnish as many Americans as are to be found within the precincts of the five boroughs.

To get a notion of the magnitude of this population, which the mind is hardly able to grasp off-hand, let us imagine all the people of New York formed in procession and marching down Broadway, ten abreast and with lines six feet apart. Regulate their speed of progress so that they will pass a given point at a uniform rate of fifty thousand an hour; and conceive, if you can, that you are sitting on a grand stand at a convenient place for observation on the route of the parade. It will be an entertaining spectacle, exhibiting to view after the manner of a diorama all classes of New Yorkers, from richest to poorest, and from the very young to the very old, and you can afford to devote a little of your valuable time to watching them.

The foremost files of this imaginary procession go by, let us say, at ten o'clock in the morning. At ten in the evening the people are still marching on, and you are beginning to be rather tired; but, on making a brief reckoning with pencil and paper, you find that in all those hours only six hundred thousand have passed. By ten o'clock the next morning 1,200,000 in all have gone by—less than one-third of the parade. If you persist in your determination to see it out, you will have to make some arrangements for incidental meals; and even thus, unless you take a good many cat-naps from time to time, you are likely to succumb to exhaustion before the affair is over. At the end of three days and three nights the procession is still going by, and on top of this there will still be eight hours of it before the rear guard has brought up the tail of the mighty host.

Now, if it were supposed that all of these persons took the subway as a means of getting back to their starting point, and each car accommodated one hundred of them, it is easily figured out that they would require for their transportation five thousand trains of eight cars each—or forty thousand cars in all. These trains, placed end to end, would extend for a distance of over six hundred miles, and the fares to be paid (supposing infants in this case to be charged full price) would exceed $200,000 just for this one ride.

The subway in New York at the present time carries on an ordinary week day four hundred and seventy thousand people. In a year it transports one hundred and fifty million persons, or thereabouts. Plans for several more subways running the whole length of the island, however, have already been approved, and it is understood that five years will be required to build them and for the construction of two crosstown lines, which will pass beneath the up-and-down-town roads. One of these latter will run under Chambers Street and beneath the North River to Jersey City, connecting with the Jersey City and Newark surface lines. The other, under Thirty-fourth Street, will pass beneath the East River and connect the surface roads converging in Long Island City with the subway system of Manhattan. All the longitudinal subways will unite at the Battery, and arrangements will be such that passengers via the cross-town tunnels can be transferred readily and comfortably to them.

IN THE MOST CONGESTED DISTRICT OF NEW YORK TWO THOUSAND FIVE HUNDRED AND SIXTY-THREE TENEMENT FAMILIES
WERE FOUND WITH BUT THIRTY-SIX BATH-TUBS AMONG THEM ALL

This will give a notion of the extent to which underground traffic in New York will be expanded within the next few years. There are already in the metropolis more than thirteen hundred miles of surface and elevated trackage; but the expectation is that the elevated roads, which are already regarded as an out-of-date expedient for urban traffic, will be entirely done away with in the non-distant future.

The year 1907 will see Manhattan Island connected with Long Island and with New Jersey by tunnels. We are now, indeed, at the beginning of a new era—the era of river tubes. Three double-tube tunnels passing under the North River are now building to connect Manhattan with Jersey City, and two more are projected. Beneath the East River two similar double-tubes are in process of construction, and two additional ones are planned. To a great extent, these tunnels will take the place of bridges in future traffic between the boroughs—a duty which, it may be supposed, they are well able to perform, inasmuch as John B. McDonald, architect of the present subway system of Manhattan, declares that a bridge costing $30,000,000 has a traffic capacity no greater than a $15,000,000 tube.

SENATOR CLARK'S HOUSE HAS TWENTY BATH-
ROOMS

The theaters of New York, all of them together, hold about one hundred and twenty thousand persons. If it be supposed that at an average performance they are only two-thirds full, it follows that eighty thousand persons in the metropolis must go to the play every week-day night—a number equal to the population of Savannah, Georgia.

To maintain the peace in the five boroughs, seven thousand, eight hundred and fifty-four policemen are required, without counting twelve hundred and forty "specials" and watchmen. For keeping under proper subjugation the treacherous "fire fiend," about three thousand firemen are hired, the apparatus they employ comprising one hundred and sixty steam-engines (besides chemical and hand-engines), twenty-four thousand feet of ladders, and nearly half a million feet of hose. Eleven hundred horses are used by the Fire Department, notwithstanding whose efforts some seven million dollars' worth of property goes up in smoke every year in the city of New York.

What might be called "one day of trouble in New York" is represented by a few figures recently obtained by a person curious about such matters, who, taking a chance twenty-four hours of life in the metropolis, discovered that in that length of time there were twenty-six fires and thirty-five serious accidents; five persons were found dead, two attempted suicide, and three hundred and ninety-two individuals were arrested for various offenses more or less important.

It is more interesting, however, to review

THE POPULATION OF NEW YORK IS EQUAL TO MANY, FRANCE, ITALY, AUSTRO-HUNGARY, RUS-

THE COMBINED ARMIES OF GREAT BRITAIN, GER-SIA, JAPAN, AND TURKEY, ON A PEACE FOOTING

such occurrences by the year. Careful inquiry has elicited the fact that on every day of the twelvemonth, taking an average, ten fatal accidents are reported to the police in the metropolis. Two persons commit suicide every day, and one man or woman is murdered every three days. In Greater New York twelve human beings meet violent deaths in one form or another every day of the year. During the year 1905, the total number of violent deaths was 4425, out of which number 162 were homicides, 648 suicides, and 3642 accidental.

During the last year in New York City one person was born about every four minutes; there was a death every seven minutes, and a marriage was solemnized every twelve minutes. One-third of the persons who died were under five years of age, and 16,526 of these children did not survive long enough to reach the age of one year. On the other hand, six hundred and ninety-five died of old age. The number of deaths during the twelve months was exactly 73,714. Every death is certain to be known by the Department of Health. But the records of that office are very incomplete in regard to births, many of which are not reported. Thus, though the number of births for 1905 is put down at 103,875, it was in reality not less in all likelihood than 120,000.

There are in New York five hundred and twenty schools, with six hundred and seventy-five thousand pupils, who undergo instruction in nearly eleven thousand school-rooms. This means that the number of boys and girls who are seeking an education in the metropolis is greater by seventy-five thousand than the population of St. Louis. There are thirteen thousand, five hundred teachers,

who, if they formed a community, would make a town equal in size to Ansonia, the clock-making center of Connecticut. It is reckoned that twenty-five years from now New York will have a school enrollment of one million, five hundred thousand pupils, and a corps of teachers numbering fifty thousand.

To help both young and old to study and to learn, New York has libraries which contain in the aggregate two millions of books. Counting each time of use as one book, six million volumes are withdrawn by citizens during a twelvemonth for home use, and three million are read or consulted in the reading rooms.

There are in Greater New York eighteen hundred and fifty miles of paved streets, the mere cleaning of which requires the services of twenty-nine hundred persons all the year 'round. Out-door illumination is supplied by 3,300,000 electric lights, all of which, except sixty thousand, are of the incandescent kind. These represent a total lighting power of 173,000,000 candles, which, if they were real candles, and were stood in line six inches apart, would stretch more than two-thirds of the way around the world —or, to speak in exact terms, sixteen thousand, four hundred miles.

New York will soon be the greatest commercial port in the world, her trade for the last year amounting to considerably over nine millions of tons. She is still behind London, but within ten years from the present time she will have passed the British metropolis in this respect, assuming a supremacy which she seems likely to maintain for all future time.

If its ash pile be regarded as an indication of a city's size, New York has undeniable reason to boast of the fact that she produced during a twelvemonth 2,121,319 tons of ashes. Think what a mountain such a quantity would make if thrown into one heap!

During the last year over seventy thousand persons in the metropolis died. There were in the same period forty thousand marriages, and ninety thousand babies were born. Of divorces there were eleven hundred.

Of all occupations pursued by New Yorkers the most important seems to be that of domestic service. There are in the metropolis 103,963 women servants and 31,211 men servants—a total greater than the entire population of New Haven, Connecticut. Next come the building trades, which employ ninety-eight thousand persons; and after these, in point of numbers engaged, the tailors. To dress four millions of souls a lot of workers in the clothing line are needed —no fewer, in fact, than 56,094 tailors and 15,069 tailoresses.

New York, of course, is a big shop, and to dispose of the wares it has to sell 45,740 salesmen and 22,705 saleswomen are required. There are 13,451 errand and office boys, and nearly two thousand girls employed in similar capacities. More than ten thousand persons are engaged in agricultural pursuits (including gardeners and florists); and it is odd to learn that the much-mixed population of the city includes 1993 farmers and one hundred and sixteen lumbermen.

This is the greatest publishing center in the world, bar none, and the printers and press operators number 26,414, of whom eight hundred and ninety-three are women. To shave the men and cut and care for the hair of both sexes, there are 12,022 barbers and hairdressers of male persuasion and eight hundred and fifty-two female tonsorial artists. It is no small task to attend to the health of so huge a community, and this business alone keeps busy nearly sixty-seven hundred doctors, five hundred and ten of whom wear petticoats.

It is an exceedingly thirsty population, too, and nearly thirteen thousand bartenders are required to mix and serve drinks. On the other hand, three thousand clergymen are enough to attend to the work of saving souls. There are slightly fewer than eight thousand lawyers, rather more than eleven thousand nurses and midwives (thirteen hundred and forty-two of them men), over thirteen thousand professional peddlers,

4733 actors, 2629 actresses, about four thousand artists and teachers of art, approximately ten thousand musicians and teachers of music, forty-four hundred candy-makers, fourteen thousand stenographers and typewriters, and fifteen hundred and seventy-two undertakers.

In this classification of occupations most interest naturally attaches to curious and out-of-the-way feminine employments. There are in New York, for example, seventy-three women clergymen, seventy-eight women dentists, three women street-car conductors, forty-eight women carpenters, sixteen women keepers of livery stables, thirty-seven women masons in brick and stone, five women paper-hangers, forty-five women plumbers, sixteen women blacksmiths, and two hundred and fifty-one women painters and glaziers.

Women, in this age of intense industrial activity, are invading on an extensive scale handicrafts hitherto regarded as belonging exclusively to the sex male. Nevertheless, though this fact has become in a general way familiar, it seems surprising to discover that there are at the present time in New York four women fishermen and oystermen, ninety-seven women officials of banks and corporations, sixty-seven women bankers and brokers, seventy-eight women lawyers, sixty-six women electricians, and thirty women boatmen.

It has been said with truth that the greatest of all the wonders of the world is a big city like New York. Here all races are brought together into a single cosmopolitan community. Everything that is produced anywhere on the earth is for sale in the metropolis and to be bought for a price. It is the commercial heart of the nation, and to it flows through a multitude of veins and arteries of trade all the money of the country —to be thrown out again through the channels of industry and traffic, giving life to the body politic and spreading business prosperity far and wide. For, in the last analysis, a metropolis like this is a mighty and wonderful market, to which all the peoples of the world bring their goods, and where the cleverest trader—whether he has merchandise or brains to sell—secures the universally-desired reward of riches. Nowhere else is the struggle for existence so intense (in some of its aspects painfully so), and nowhere else is life so keenly interesting and enjoyable to those who are fortunate enough to be winners in the strife.

28
The Most Valuable Ten-acre Lot in the World

LOOKING NORTHWARD FROM THE ROOF OF THE NEW YORK PRODUCE EXCHANGE, WITH THE
SKYSCRAPERS OF LOWER BROADWAY ON THE LEFT AND THOSE OF
BROAD AND WALL STREETS ON THE RIGHT

THE MOST VALUABLE TEN-ACRE
LOT IN THE WORLD

BY EUGENE SANDS WILLARD

THE FINANCIAL DISTRICT OF NEW YORK, PART OF THE TRACT
WHICH PETER MINUIT BOUGHT FOR TWENTY-FOUR DOLLARS
THREE CENTURIES AGO — THE TREMENDOUS PRICES NOW
PAID FOR LAND IN THIS REGION OF COSTLY SKYSCRAPERS

PROBABLY the best real estate investment on record was made by Peter Minuit in 1626, when that sturdy Dutch burgher bought the whole of Manhattan Island—estimated to contain some twenty-two thousand acres—for a few beads, baubles, and some rum, to the value of twenty-four dollars. Minuit has often been criticized for driving a sharp bargain, but we must remember that in his day the purchasing power of gold was five times as great as it is now, so that he really gave the equivalent of one hundred and twenty dollars. He could hardly have been expected to pay the present valuation of the island, and no doubt the Indians were better satisfied with the toys and the firewater than they would have been with money. At the present time, just two hundred and eighty years after Minuit's purchase, the island is worth, as real estate, at least four billion dollars—which may be called a nice profit for a shrewd investor.

It has been calculated that this same time, would now amount to about fifteen million dollars. It seems safe to infer that it is more profitable, on the whole,

LOOKING DOWN WALL STREET FROM BROADWAY—THE PROPERTY AT THE CORNER, NOW OCCUPIED BY A ONE-STORY CIGAR-STORE, RECENTLY CHANGED HANDS AT A PRICE EQUAL TO NEARLY SIX HUNDRED DOLLARS PER SQUARE FOOT

twenty-four dollars, put out at compound interest at the various rates prevailing between 1626 and the present to invest money in New York land than to put it into a savings-bank.

To-day, twenty-four dollars would

buy only one twenty-fifth of a square foot—less than six square inches—of land at the southeast corner of Wall Street and Broadway, at the rate of six hundred dollars a square foot, which was the published price of the recent sale of the property. The building that stood there, an old four-story structure numbered as 86 Broadway, was not counted as of any value, and was promptly torn down. Plans have been completed for a tall building to go on the site, and the ground floor is offered for rent, in advance, for thirty-five thousand dollars a year.

We publish with this article a sketch map of the district where real estate has soared higher than anywhere else in the world. Whatever its future may be, its record of advancement in value will probably never be surpassed, in America or Europe. Three centuries ago it lay in the outskirts of an isolated trading-post; to-day it is the financial center of America. It will, beyond peradventure, remain for generations the commercial barometer of a vast, teeming land whose terrific, restless energy it but reflects.

Let us glance at the various buildings which challenge attention here, and pay some slight attention to their history.

The most valuable single holding in America, of its size, is undoubtedly the Equitable Life Building, comprising the block bounded by Broadway, Nassau, Pine, and Cedar Streets. In 1721, two lots on this part of Broadway, measuring fifty by a hundred and sixty feet, brought a little less than three hundred dollars. The latest assessed value of the

BROAD STREET, FROM THE CORNER OF WALL, WITH THE MAIN FRONT OF THE STOCK EXCHANGE ON THE RIGHT AND THE OFFICE OF J. PIERPONT MORGAN & COMPANY ON THE LEFT

BROAD STREET TWO HUNDRED AND FIFTY YEARS AGO

LOOKING DOWN BROAD STREET FROM THE
ROOF OF THE SUB-TREASURY—THE DARK
MASS IN THE STREET IS THE CROWD
OF CURBSTONE BROKERS

Equitable Building is eleven millions,
the land alone being worth more than
eight millions. The most interesting
of its historical associations is the fact
that Aaron Burr's law-office was on the
Nassau Street side, where is now the entrance to the famous Belmont banking-
house.

Across Broadway stands the Trinity
Building, with its twenty-two stories, the
topmost of which is higher than Old
Trinity's spire. Adjoining, on the north,
a large site has recently been cleared of
its "encumbrance"—a good eight-story
structure, taxed by the city at three hundred thousand dollars, but mowed down
to make way for a huge addition to the
Trinity Building. The land for this addition was bought by the first John Jacob
Astor in 1828 for about one hundred and

twenty thousand dollars, and given
by him to his daughter as a marriage-
portion in 1842. Its last transfer was in
1902, at the rate of two hundred dollars
a square foot.

Next to this is Trinity Church—the
grand old Gothic edifice which has done
so much to uplift and ennoble New York,
both architecturally and morally. Its
steeple rises to-day amidst all the noise
and bustle, like a finger pointing to
things above money and stocks and mere
commercial enterprise. Its quiet churchyard is worth many millions to-day,
though its first seven years' lease was
for the nominal rental of fifty bushels of
wheat a year. Later, under good Queen
Anne, Trinity succeeded to the ownership of the King's Farm, which made it
the wealthiest parish in America.

THE TWENTY-STORY EMPIRE BUILDING TOWER-
ING ABOVE THE GRAVE OF ALEXANDER
HAMILTON, THE FATHER OF
AMERICAN FINANCE

TRINITY CHURCHYARD, WITH THE TRINITY BUILDING ON THE LEFT AND THE AMERICAN
SURETY BUILDING ON THE RIGHT—THE COMPARATIVELY LOW STRUCTURE
BETWEEN THE TWO SKYSCRAPERS IS THE EQUITABLE BUILDING

The big Empire Building, twin sister to the Trinity, and sharing its watch over the old graveyard, houses the executive offices of the United States Steel Corporation and other interests with estimated assets of four billions of dollars. The land it covers is valued at more than two million dollars.

Let us stop a moment to look at that ridiculous little lane called at different times by all sorts of names, from Flatten Barrick Alley to Tin Pot Alley and its

LOOKING UP BROADWAY FROM THE
BOWLING GREEN—ON THE LEFT
IS THE BOWLING GREEN BUILDING,
THE THIRD LARGEST OFFICE-
BUILDING IN NEW YORK

present title of Exchange Alley. It had its origin in a little path leading to the old Dutch battery on the bank of the North River. On the north side of it is the home of the famous Pinkerton Detective Agency, while across the way is the fine Astor Court Building. Property here is now worth a hundred and fifty dollars a square foot, while in 1737 a lot on this same corner brought eighteen cents a square foot.

Below, on the west side of Broadway, is Aldrich Court. Four little huts, the first habitations of white men on Manhattan Island, were built on this spot by Adriaen Block, the Dutch navigator, who stopped here in 1612. On the other side of the famous street towers the enormous cliff dwelling at 42 Broadway. This is New York's second largest office-building, with more than a quarter of a million square feet of floor space.

A few doors farther down Broadway —passing No. 34, where Commodore Vanderbilt had his steamboat office —we reach the home of the Standard Oil Company and its multitude of affiliated enterprises, at No. 26. It stands upon the site of an old burying-ground, and the remains of the old Dutch burghers were relentlessly dug up to make way for the headquarters of the modern financial magnates. Next, on our way southward, we pass by the old Stevens House, and the crouching lions of stone which still mark the site of Delmonico's original restaurant and of Daniel Webster's one-time residence. The last two structures on Broadway are the massive Bowling Green Building, the third largest office-building in New York, and the Washington Building, built by the late Cyrus Field of Atlantic cable fame.

These overlook the Bowling Green, the drill-ground, battle-ground, play-ground, and business-ground of Dutch, English, and American colonists. On the other side of the tiny open space is the great red-brick Produce Exchange, which covers an area of forty-six thousand feet, and which cost more than three million dollars to build, in 1884. Its elevators carry nearly thirty thousand passengers a day, or more than three times the city's population two centuries ago.

Here let us turn and find our way northward to the Broad Exchange Building, at the southeast corner of Broad Street and Exchange Place. The former thoroughfare owes its width, and consequently its name, to the canal—the Heere Graft, or chief channel—which in Dutch days extended along its middle and ended at this same corner. The great office-building that stands there now is the largest in New York, with a total floor space of nearly five hundred thousand square feet, or ten acres. Its assessed value to-day is five and a quarter millions. A

A STEEL-RIBBED NEW YORK CAÑON—LOOKING DOWN EXCHANGE PLACE FROM BROADWAY

little farther north, on the other side of Broad Street, is the imposing white marble façade of the Stock Exchange, the institution that rules supreme in the world of American finance.

Wall Street took its name from the early stockade—the chief landward defense of the little Dutch settlement—which ran along its length. In 1653, when the wall was built, it was but a common pasture; later, the north side became Abraham De Peyster's garden. In 1718 De Peyster and a citizen named Bayard divided the whole of the street into lots, and sold them. The former gave to the city the site of the present Sub-Treasury, facing Broad Street. This building has been the scene of many stirring events in New York's history, including the reading of the Declaration of Independence and Washington's inaugural and farewell addresses. To-day it stands the solid guardian of the Federal government's gold, while Washington's statue on the steps reminds us of its early association with the First President.

The visitor, after strolling through this teeming and

wonderful district, may very well be struck by two extraordinary facts in connection with it. First, why are its values and rents so high? Second, why are its buildings so tall?

The first phenomenon is due to various causes, the principal reason being that the center of American finance is the New York Stock Exchange. Bankers and financial institutions of all sorts do their utmost to secure offices close to the Exchange and the Clearing-House, and competition among these wealthy bidders has driven prices up to enormous figures. The skyscraper is a natural consequence. If land is exceedingly costly, a landlord who erects a building must figure on receiving a correspondingly large return for his money. With a limited floor space or rental area—let us say four or five stories—it would be impossible for him to do this, unless he charged a rate so exorbitant that few people would care to rent from him. If, however, he puts up a twenty-story building, his floor space is at once quadrupled or quintupled.

Such structures, however, have only recently become possible. Fifty years ago the average height of buildings in New York was three or four stories, with six as the practical limit. The city authorities required that the thickness of the sustaining walls should be in proportion to their height; so that if a building was to be of more than half a dozen stories the lower floors would be obstructed with vast masses of masonry, limiting the floor space, restricting the light, and rendering the question of a foundation increasingly difficult. The invention of the steel frame construction and the development of the swift passenger elevator changed all this; and now the practicable height of an office-building is only limited by the question of a sufficient elevator service. If the structure rises much above twenty-five floors, the "lifts" needed by its tenants and their visitors use up as much valuable space as was formerly occupied by the heavy sustaining walls.

The Broad Exchange Building, for instance, with twenty floors, has eighteen elevators, each of which is calculated to "feed" twenty-six thousand square feet of floor area. In the Park Row Building each elevator feeds thirty-one thousand

THE CURBSTONE BROKERS IN BROAD STREET — ON THE RIGHT IS THE BROAD EXCHANGE
BUILDING, THE LARGEST OFFICE-BUILDING IN THE WORLD

square feet. As the service is now no more than sufficient, it is obvious that if the buildings were twice as tall, twice as many elevators would be needed; so that the added area of the top floors would be offset by the wasted space given to extra elevators.

Notwithstanding this, the Singer Company is about to build on Broadway an office tower taller than the Washington Monument, and the tallest building in America. The plans are already filed, and soon New York will boast of a business structure five hundred and eighty feet high.

It seems hard to believe that the high steel building is only twenty years old. In spite of its critics, it is now a demonstrated success, and has come to stay. In the upper portions the offices are light; they are cool in summer and easily heated in winter; they usually command fresh, pure air and a fine view; there is little dust or dirt, and practically no noise from the street.

In Boston and Chicago, where the height of buildings has been limited, the values in the financial districts are greatest at about eighty or ninety dollars per square foot. If we wish to find any real estate as valuable as that of the Wall Street district of New York, we must turn to London, where land at certain points fetches almost as much as in New York. In one instance the Bank of England paid three hundred and seventy-five

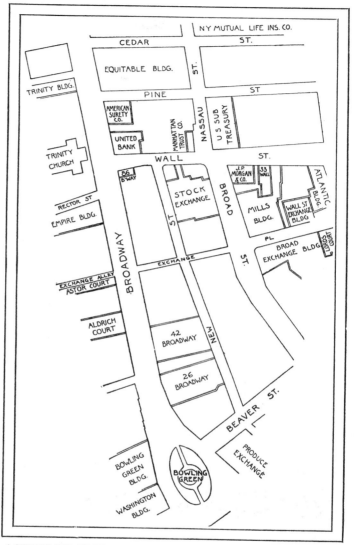

A SKETCH MAP OF THE FINANCIAL DISTRICT OF NEW YORK, WHICH MAY BE CALLED THE MOST VALUABLE TEN-ACRE LOT IN THE WORLD

dollars a square foot for a small parcel of land—the highest recorded price for land in England. On the whole, however, New York leads the world in real estate values, and this is all the more surprising when we remember that the present year rounds out just three centuries since a white man's eye first beheld Manhattan Island, while London has two thousand years of history to back her prestige as the metropolis of the British Empire and the largest city in the world.

29
The Doorways of New York

The Doorways of New York.

BY FRANK S. ARNETT.

ONE OF THE BEST FEATURES OF NEW YORK ARCHITECTURE—
THE ARTISTIC EXCELLENCE AND GREAT COST OF THE ENTRANCES
OF MANY METROPOLITAN RESIDENCES, CLUB HOUSES, AND
BUSINESS BUILDINGS.

THE crudity to which New York pleads guilty is not altogether the crime of youth. That well worn excuse for our artistic shortcomings does not here suffice. The responsibility is not that of the present generation. It rests upon those who laid out the city. This service they performed seemingly with an undertaker's conception of the expression, their plans dead to any hope of general beauty. They held the future in contempt. The creation of Central Park was a miracle. Older than Washington, older still than Russia's proud capital, New York in appearance is inferior to both. To bring forth today a city of beauty would require nothing less heroic than the Cæsarean operation.

We have not one completed and stately avenue, no square of real magnificence, few splendid monuments or statues. What, then, have we of art

THE DOORWAY OF THE RESIDENCE OF THE LATE C. P. HUNTINGTON'S RESIDENCE AT FIFTH AVENUE AND
FIFTY SEVENTH STREET, NEW YORK—A RICH AND DIGNIFIED ENTRANCE, SIMPLE IN DESIGN,
AND APPROPRIATE FOR A LARGE BUILDING OF ROUGH STONE.

THE ARTISTIC OUTER DOORS OF A RESIDENCE ON MADISON
AVENUE, NEW YORK.

ways, unostentatious, appreciable only by close inspection, when Ruskin, after that superb, blood quickening description of St. Mark's, rising " like a vision out of the earth," was forced to add:

And what effect has this splendor on those who pass beneath it? You may walk from sunrise to sunset, to and fro before the gateway . . . and you will not see an eye lifted to it, nor a countenance brightened by it. Priest and layman, soldier and civilian, rich and poor, pass it by alike regardless.

And so in New York the Madison Avenue car carries thousands past doors and gates that are marvels of loveliness in wrought iron, in perfect glass, in priceless bronze, and not an eye is lifted from the daily paper. And on pleasant Sundays, when Fifth Avenue is thronged by those that see it on no other day, ever and anon you will hear the awe inflected whisper of one that points out to his open mouthed companions the home of some famous millionaire; but there is none to stop and note the grandeur of the bronze or of the iron that has been beaten into beauty.

This richness, which every passer by may enjoy, is the more notable because, while there still exist in London and the cities of Europe many quaintly attractive, splendidly carved, and heavily hinged entrances, all are those of long ago centuries. In New York age and the elements have darkened few of our doors; no old time extinguishers are at entrances where once the link boys guided our guests; few are the knockers that have known the artist's hammer. Skyscrapers mark the place where once the old Dutch homestead stood, and only in out of the way corners of Long Island can now be found the porches and doorways of such old time families as the Garretsons and the Vandeveers.

THE MODERN INTEREST IN DOORWAYS.

Between colonial days and the recent past there was little praiseworthy in our entrances. With sudden wealth, we treated huge blocks of stone as though

that is not labeled in some deserted museum? Stroll the length of Fifth and Madison Avenues and through the connecting streets from the Thirties upward. Excluding all else, seek for our picturesque doors and doorways. Take this walk, note these features in houses you have thought prosaic, monotonous, a cramped succession of swardless homes little removed from tenements, and, whether stranger or New Yorker, never again will you pass through these streets unimpressed, pleasureless, eager for your destination. That so many have done so is understandable. What could be expected of New York's door-

they were of lace; gave fragile glass the air of protecting a fortress; erected towering pillars that guarded doll's house doors. Disdainful of harmony and proportion, we employed material in

worthy their highest efforts. In this they follow the great masters of old. The doors of the Villa Grimani at Rome were the creation of Michelangelo. Giotto executed those in bronze adjoin-

MAIN ENTRANCE AND BASEMENT DOORWAY OF THE HARRAGH RESIDENCE—AN EFFECTIVE TREAT-
MENT OF THE "HIGH STOOP" WHICH IS SO TYPICAL OF NEW YORK HOUSES.

a way that was in itself a lie. With a wealth and a culture that have attained to their second and third generation, we have partly recovered from this hideous epidemic.

Today New York artists and architects find the long neglected door

ing the baptistry of Florence. Donatello competed in designs for others. Our American homes could not properly absorb Michelangelo's sublimity any more than they could fittingly be entered through the mammoth edifices that served as doorways to ancient Egypt's temples. But with such predecessors it is not surprising that living artists of repute do not disdain to design a hinge or grille, or that workmen of high ideals should now busy themselves with doors in bronze and wrought iron.

An encouraging sign of advancement is it that the doors of the majority of our palatial homes and public edifices now come from New York workshops. One appreciates their great cost only after visiting the places whence many of

PORTE COCHÈRE OF THE RESIDENCE OF THE LATE CORNELIUS VANDERBILT, AT FIFTH AVENUE
AND FIFTY EIGHTH STREET. THIS IS PROBABLY THE MOST ELABORATE
AND COSTLY ENTRANCEWAY IN NEW YORK.

ORNAMENTAL IRON GATEWAYS OF THE RESIDENCE OF THE LATE THEODORE A. HAVEMEYER, ON MADISON AVENUE, NEW YORK.

them emanate. Here he sees drawn from the earth those pots of molten copper, tin, and lead from which the bronze takes life in liquid fire. Here he realizes that each iron leaf is worked into graceful form by a hand that creates its model as it labors. Here, too, he learns that from a single seemingly inexhaustible deposit in France comes all the sand used in molding bronze in whatsoever part of the world.

THE MEANING OF THE DOORWAY.

Yet in making a tour of the streets you will not be amazed by magnificence. True, occasionally you will find it. But in one instance it will have nothing of hearty welcome; you will carry away the impression that the doors are seldom opened by hands that ache to clasp those of the guest in honest greeting. Near by, perhaps, if you know the story of the owner, a doorway will sadden you by its expression of dramatic solitude over-shadowing that of stately frankness.

Here and there you may see a garden court framed by towering, richly heavy gates; in the distance oak doors that will last for generations, given further dignity by cloister-like stone columns. A few such, in the simplicity of their classicism, seem entrances to the palaces of cardinals or princes of the blood. But, in general, our doorways are as miniatures in architectural art.

And, too, while seeking and not finding magnificence, you may be shocked at noting how our architecture has long been a matter of changing fashion— hence the reincarnation of architectures that should have been allowed to remain forgotten, the utter lack of unity, the continuous lines of quarreling styles and heights. Numerous, also, are individual incongruities and inharmonious proportions. Despite all this, seldom will you fail to find one perfect detail. Almost always a portcullis, a gateway, or a door will amend the hideousness of the rest.

The old doorways facing Washington

THE OUTER DOORS OF THE MILLIKEN RESIDENCE,
ON MADISON AVENUE, NEW YORK.

Civic Art, with invitations to partici-
pate in which but two other American
cities have been honored—Philadelphia,
which has jealously and wisely preserved the beauties of her past; and
Washington, which, more elaborately
than any municipality in the world, has
planned for future beauty.

Surely invitations such as this have
much of promise, for we are receptive
even though we have little to give in
return; and with equal certainty the
artistic entrances we already have may
be looked upon as entrances to a future
of more wide spread worth in our civic
architecture. We Americans are so accustomed to venerate the architecture
of Italy, believing it all to be that of
the Italy of romance, that it comes with
something of a shock when Ruskin reminds us that if Dandolo and Foscari
" could be summoned from their tombs,

THE OUTER DOORS OF THE BOWNE RESIDENCE,
NEW YORK.

Square are notable for the simplicity of
their perfection. Many cross streets
east of Central Park show more modern,
though admirable and unpretentious,
doors and doorways. Riverside Drive,
too, is worthy. Here, where the massive
stone wall already shows signs of inclosing one of the most beautiful avenues in the world, broken here and there
by monuments and stately, vista giving,
granite canopied seats; here, where an
irregularly circling line of oddly en-
tranced houses zigzags in and out for
blocks, is a succession of excellent creations in brass, bronze, wrought iron, and
beautiful glass.

THE PROMISE OF NEW YORK'S FUTURE.

All, therefore, is not ugliness. And
perhaps even at Dresden next year New
York will not have cause to blush for
her representation in the Exhibition of

and stood each on the deck of his galley at the entrance of the Grand Canal, . . . the Doges would not know in what spot of the world they stood, would literally not recognize one stone of the great city." but because of its increased beauty; around its artistic entrances arising a complete architecture, not, as now, wonderful in cast and size, but in true loveliness and dignity. For in these

THE DOORWAY OF THE NEW YORK YACHT CLUB'S HOUSE ON WEST FORTY FOURTH STREET—
AN ARTISTIC DESIGN, THOUGH SOMEWHAT "SQUATTY" IN EFFECT.

But if the magic beauty of the Venice of today is a thousand fold less gorgeous than that the Doges knew, and if, to the cosmopolitan American, this fact is disheartening, the antithetic picture, even if a prophetic one, shown in his own metropolis, is heart strengthening.

For here already may be found signs indicating that if the elders of the present generation could be placed, even fifty years hence, on the pinnacle of the spire of St. John's, they, too, "would not recognize one stone of the great city." Not because of its decadence,

doors and doorways, in these grilles and gates and fences, is there not promise of the time when the American architect will have realized that his is indeed "the art which so disposes and adorns the edifices raised by man for whatsoever uses, that the sight of them contributes to his mental health, power, and pleasure"?

OUR BEST ARCHITECTURAL EXHIBITS.

True, it may be another century before the imposing doorway of the Cathedral of St. John the Divine will give entrance to the completed structure; perhaps also a century before the mighty portico of the Institute of Arts and Sciences leads to what is hoped to prove the most marvelous building in the world. But on every side is progress. In the residential district are

night the way to the magnificent bronze entrance doors of New York's costliest apartment house. Turn in the opposite direction, to the region where men toil that beautiful women may enter their palaces through almost priceless doors, stand in front of these great office build-

DOORWAY OF THE UNIVERSITY CLUB, AT FIFTH AVENUE AND FIFTY FOURTH STREET, NEW YORK,
A FINE SPECIMEN OF CLUB HOUSE ARCHITECTURE.

annually erected scores of homes in each of which ten thousand dollars is far from unwisely spent upon a single doorway; and from our shops, too, have come the far costlier ones in the Boston Public Library and the Congressional Library at Washington. Overlooking the Hudson, far to the northward, copied from the famous old royal château at Blois, an antique lantern lights at

ings, and your eyes will find delight if they do not rise from the perfect entrances to the hideousness that is above. For if, in truth, we toil and live in caves dug in these lofty precipices frowning on either side of the city's ravines, our caves are at least most admirably entered. He that found here "nothing but squalor and confusion" was occupied in a study of our slums. Beauty

ENTRANCE OF THE TIFFANY HOUSE, AT MADISON AVENUE AND SEVENTY SECOND STREET, NEW YORK—
HIGHLY ORIGINAL IN DESIGN, AND VERY APPROPRIATE TO THE CASTLE-LIKE STRUCTURE
OF WHICH IT IS THE GATEWAY.

exists. Like misery, it must be sought. Our doors have not entirely cast off an old and repellent disguise.

THE DOOR—AND WHAT LIES WITHIN.

Do not demand that the door shall tell of the luxury within. You have the right to demand that it shall say a kindly word to those who pass, give welcome to those who enter, and God speed to those who leave. You have the right to expect the old time hinge, strong because it is not hidden, welcome because it is beautiful; locks, bolts, and nails that are not ashamed to be seen; doors that shall not be a source of pleasure to the present generation alone. Be prepared to appreciate harmony of design even in iron; to note how stone and glass and bronze have beautified a necessity.

And, after all, what do we care for entablatures or pilasters, architraves or corbels, merely as such? It is not the technical architecture of our doorways that interest us, but the idea of hospitality they typify, the associations that surround them. Upon the story of a romance, a tragedy, a broken heart and a ruined home, more than one Fifth Avenue door is closed, only to be opened when, a century hence, the gossipy letters of some Walpole of today are unearthed. But the idea of the outhanging latch string, the conviction that Dante's " All hope abandon, ye who enter here," above the entrance to his Inferno, is the last that could be written over the doorway of a New York home —these are the thoughts that are uppermost as one wanders through New York's streets; remembering, too, that in Dante's day they placed above the doorway mottos carved in wood or stone, and that the threshold was of such import that the priest came to give it blessing. We retain the quaint custom of placing a horseshoe where was once the motto over the door; and I would give little for the man who does not tenderly kiss his bride and ask for a blessing on their future at the moment she first crosses the threshold of their home.

30
The
Evolution
of Manhattan

THE DUTCH TRADER OF NEW AMSTERDAM AND THE INDIAN WHO SOLD HIS BIRTHRIGHT FOR A MESS OF POTTAGE.

The Evolution of Manhattan.

BY FRANK S. ARNETT.

THE SEVEN AGES OF NEW YORK—HOW THE INDIANS SOLD THEIR BIRTHRIGHT TO THE DUTCH; THE COMING OF THE BRITISH, AND THE BIRTH OF INDEPENDENCE; THE NEW YORK THAT DICKENS SAW, THE NEW YORK OF THE CIVIL WAR, AND THE NEW YORK OF TODAY—NEVER WERE THERE SHARPER CONTRASTS, NEVER A MORE MARVELOUS CIVIC DEVELOPMENT.

THERE is as little cause to envy the dwellers along the Rhine when we have the Hudson at our feet, as to envy the historic glories of European cities once we are familiar with our own. With swift mutations of form and color, the scenes have been changing throughout Manhattan's annals—even from that day, nearly four centuries ago, when a band of frightened red men, clad in skins, crouched in the bushes at what we call the Battery and watched the approach of the first white man's ship they had ever looked upon. Can you bemoan the absence of romance in the city's history when that scene was its commencement—sublime like the crea-tion of a continent, wonderful like human birth? Europe has nothing more picturesque than the earliest periods of Manhattan, nothing more overwhelming than its latest.

IN THE DAYS OF PETER MINUIT.

There are memory haunted nooks and corners which to every New Yorker, even to every American, should be sacred. There are pavements that still echo the footsteps of men who rank with the heroes of the world. There are still existing houses in which occurred the most dramatic events in the story of the republic. Can you pass the Bowling Green, tipping the southerly end of

397

Broadway, and not recall that here the giant city had its birth; that here one day, two hundred and seventy six years ago, Peter Minuit, earliest of our Dutch governors, stood with his aides, gay in

Here was the Government House. Here were the May Day dances. It knows no gatherings now save those of the lonely families of the skyscrapers' janitors; and the nearest dancing is that

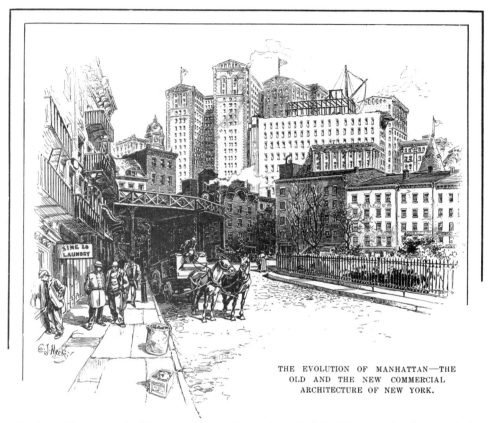

THE EVOLUTION OF MANHATTAN—THE OLD AND THE NEW COMMERCIAL ARCHITECTURE OF NEW YORK.

velvets and laces, and with a payment of tawdry trinkets, estimated—by the payer —to be worth twenty four dollars, purchased from the native chiefs the whole beautiful island of Manhattan?

The Bowling Green remains, and probably will remain until the city is no more; but today there is no trace of the old time architecture of New Amsterdam that surrounded it. Gone is even the row of quaint old houses which but yesterday looked up Broadway from the farther side of the green; yet if with loving care you seek in neighboring streets you will find some scattered evidence of the time when here were the residences of our early families of wealth and power.

From the first the Bowling Green was the center of the people's social life.

of frenzied brokers on the floors of the exchanges.

On the other hand, how strange that even in Minuit's time, when heavily wooded hills extended along the center of the island from the Battery clear to the northern extremity, when just above Wall Street were wigwams, cowpaths, and corn fields, and when at high tide the waters of the two rivers joined across the marsh where now is Canal Street—that even then, by a peculiar colonization which socially affects the New York of today, development went far above the limits of the island itself. For the great Dutch West India Company, whose imperial powers make twentieth century trust magnates seem like petty shopkeepers, granted the feudal title of "patroon," together with vast tracts along the Hudson, in return for planting there a colony of fifty people. And thus arose the Hudson's splendid estates and those old

Beyond, all is primeval forest. At nightfall the town herdsman drives the cattle within the wall, delivering each cow to its owner, whom he notifies by

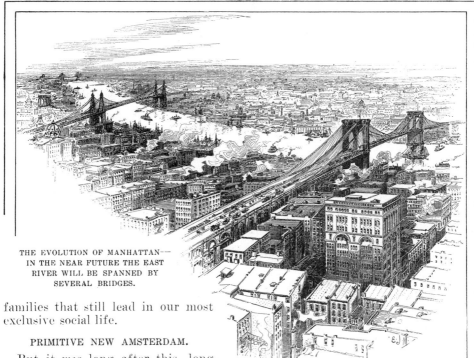

THE EVOLUTION OF MANHATTAN— IN THE NEAR FUTURE THE EAST RIVER WILL BE SPANNED BY SEVERAL BRIDGES.

families that still lead in our most exclusive social life.

PRIMITIVE NEW AMSTERDAM.

But it was long after this, long after Kiliaen Van Rensselaer, lord over seven hundred thousand acres, had married his niece to fat old Wouter Van Twiller, whom Washington Irving has so deliciously described, before the town itself crept northward even as far as the farm of Peter Stuyvesant. The town he knew—and does ever a Wall Street broker think of it?—ended at our financial thoroughfare, where then a palisade extended across the island. At its East River extremity one could pass through an arched gate to a country road, which, a short distance out, was joined by a footpath from Broadway, running beside a tiny, spring fed stream. Here rosy cheeked Dutch girls washed their home spun linen, making the path by oft going to the little brook. Hence it came to have the name of Maiden Lane —the street where now great jewelers annually import millions in precious stones to bedeck the fair descendants of those pretty barefoot girls.

the blast of a horn. The curfew tolls from the fort, the city gates clang to— and old Dutch New York goes to sleep. What think you of that, midnight revelers miles and miles north of the spot where that quaint gate clanged but two centuries ago? Wolves then prowled where now your glasses clink, and—but so do they today, for that matter.

THE PASSING OF DUTCH RULE.

Then, in a setting of the sun, without bloodshed, almost as if by magic, we became English. Dutch democracy passed away, and we had our first aristocracy— the patroons excepted, and they became lords of the manors. It was the heyday of Captain Kidd. Pirates and privateersmen swaggered through the streets, lavish with gold, bringing African slaves and marvelous products from the east. And the Sunday show on Broadway was far gayer than our Easter pa-

THE EVOLUTION OF MANHATTAN—MODERN IMPROVEMENTS HAVE THEIR PENALTIES, AS THE SLIPPERY ASPHALT SHOWS ON A SLEETY DAY IN WINTER; BUT THIS PROBLEM WILL BE SOLVED WHEN THE AUTOMOBILE SUPERSEDES THE HORSE FOR CITY TRACTION.

THE EVOLUTION OF MANHATTAN—THE HUGE UP TOWN APARTMENT HOUSES WHICH ARE MAKING NEW YORKERS A RACE OF CLIFF DWELLERS.

rade on Fifth Avenue, notably so as regards the men, strutting towards old Trinity in embroidered silks and satins, silver buckles and whitened wigs. Even more resplendent were they at the governor's residence on the Battery, wherein was much stately festivity, particularly on the occasion of a royal birthday.

And then, but not in a day, not without bloodshed, and sadly unlike magic, we became American. Even then all the country above the present Union Square was a wilderness, broken here and there by farms and tiny villages. We advance another half century to find an unceasing stream of stages running from the Battery to Greenwich, Yorktown, and elsewhere. The old families on State Street, or Canal, attended the fashionable Park Theater, near the City Hall, or spent the evening at Vauxhall Gardens, extending from Broadway to the Bowery.

THE TAVERNS OF OLD NEW YORK.

Now was the glory of the old time road houses, whose passing was sadly significant of the city's awakening to giant growth. Vanished are even many of the roads themselves, along which New Yorkers once sped behind fleet trotters, or the lumbering coaches to Boston and Albany scattered the dust. The old Bloomingdale Road is one such memory, with glistening vistas of the Hudson at every foot and the best of cheer at a dozen hotels and taverns. A Bloomingdale boniface—of a race now gone forever—once said of the dying out of driving on his road:

"There was no dying out. It just disappeared one afternoon all of a sudden, and that was the end of it. Central Park was opened, and one Sunday the whole crowd went through it and up Harlem Lane, and they never came back to old Bloomingdale!"

And that is typical of changes in New York. Things do not die out. They just disappear some afternoon all of a sudden, and that is the end of them. For a few weeks you remain away from the shopping, the theatrical, or the fashionable region. You again visit it, and it is not there. The bargain hunters, the thespians, the smart set, have gone elsewhere, never to return.

The passing of the road house was not a trivial matter. It was vital and prophetic. As to Colonial and Revolutionary New York, its whole history could be told in that of her taverns; of Cregier's, opposite the Bowling Green, the club house of the old Dutch merchants, each of whom had his long stemmed pipe in the rack of the public room; of Fraunce's, near the Royal Exchange, the scene of many a heart thrilling gathering in Washington's day.

NEW YORK'S NORTHWARD MARCH.

Where we have dined is here more pertinent than where we have fought. Seventy five years ago our forefathers frequented a little shop somewhere in the neighborhood of the Battery. It was kept by a Swiss with an Italian name, whose wines were of such excellence that his customers followed him to Beaver Street. Faithful even to his descendants, they followed again to Broadway and Morris Street, where Louis Napoleon, later Emperor of the French, supped with James Wallack and Jenny Lind. In the first year of the Civil War, New Yorkers were dining with the same Swiss family at Fifth Avenue and Fourteenth Street. In the Centennial year they had reached Twenty Sixth Street; and only the other day the old timer seated himself with a sigh of content, and for the first time as far up as Forty Fourth Street critically looked over the *carte du jour*. And that in a nutshell is the story of Manhattan's upward march—within the limits of one of its most characteristic phases.

But in the meanwhile, back there at the Battery, Castle Garden—where the Dutch had lowered their flag to the English, and where, long after, the Americans had given their hearts to the Swedish nightingale—had become an immigrant station, and the whole region fell upon evil days, vice and squalor holding high carnival in its low groggeries and lodging houses. And so at last the old families were forced from their homes to journey regretfully up town, taking only the memory of days when the Battery was the haunt of stately fashion and of happy poverty; the scene of Lafayette's landing and of Kossuth's,

of the triumphs of Jenny Lind, Mario, and Grisi. And as we walk in the reclaimed park, all of us may have the pleasant knowledge that it was the favorite walk also of Washington, Hamilton, Talleyrand, Jerome Bonaparte, Louis Philippe, and other actors in great dramas of the past.

A TIME OF SOCIAL TRANSITION.

Doubtless the period of this exodus was our worst—architecturally, morally, politically. We had just emerged from another—that in which Charles Dickens saw us—when, having forgotten the refinements of Washingtonian days, we were somewhat boorish and decidedly provincial. But more deplorable were the years immediately following the Civil War. Then we first had a hideously vulgarized society. Then we first saw the pauper in the twinkling of an eye become the millionaire. Then we first knew civic and corporate robbery on a colossal scale. And there were times when, noting how official corruption was taken quite as a matter of course, it seemed as if the republican form of government were a farce, and that it would have been a blessing if affairs in the long ago could have stopped short; if old Peter Stuyvesant could have continued indefinitely to stump along lower Broadway, or if the English royal governors for centuries of Sundays to come could have driven in their state coaches to the doors of old Trinity. But the evils were fleeting; and probably we should march to the Bowling Green to pull down King George's statue with our old time fury if we had it to do all over again.

Other results, less serious, appear permanent. In our up town march we have driven one of our most picturesque elements practically out of our midst. Magnificent houses are still erected—from habit, perhaps; but with the multimillionaire a town house is largely a storehouse. As a residence it is as obsolete as the unbounded hospitality of its old time New Year's Day receptions. Many families would never come to town but for the Horse Show or the opera, and even for these they put up at the hotels and their clubs. The city is gay. The hostelries, restaurants, and theaters are as splendid as any in the world. The life is brilliant, beautiful, alluring; but that of the old time New York home is gone except among the middle class —whose home, alas, is the flat! Fifth Avenue is no more what it was fifteen years ago than Wall Street resembles itself in the days when its gate led to the garden of the West India Company.

A CIVIC MONUMENT TO MODERNITY.

But weightier matters engross the New Yorker of today. From the Bowling Green of Peter Stuyvesant to the battlefields of Central Park and far beyond, the mighty city is a chaos. Men toil far beneath its streets, waving flags of red heralding the hourly dynamite explosion. On the surface entire blocks are razed, and palaces erected by merchant princes are cast aside as if mere cabins of the pioneers. Beneath one river men tunnel towards the Jersey flats. Far above the other, still other men, mere pigmies, creep along spider-like threads that swing from shore to shore. Where the red men sold the island for paltry baubles rises a stately custom house. From that spot to a point far beyond the lands they sold there is naught but the making and spending of millions. Millions are pouring into vast tunnels, are crushing down upon tiny triangles of earth, crystallizing in the beautiful lines of libraries and halls of government, rising in the grandeur of the cathedral on the city's Acropolis, and stretching out in the steel arms of huge bridges to welcome the outer boroughs to a more perfect union.

The universality of the pending metamorphosis, the way in which, of a sudden, the whole city seems bent upon self destruction as if with a grim faith in reincarnation—this is the first wondering impression. Even the staggering financial phase is all but forgotten, and the comparatively rapid evolution from cowpaths and wigwams is a secondary thought.

Never in the history of the world has a whole city so tortured itself in the eager desire for comfort, luxury, and beauty. For all is but in anticipation of a stupendous transformation that will make Manhattan unequaled as a civic monument to modernity.

31
The
Colossal
City

MUNSEY'S MAGAZINE.

MARCH, 1905.

THE COLOSSAL CITY.

BY EDGAR SALTUS.

HOW NEW YORK, ONCE A DUTCH TRADING-POST, THEN A BRITISH COLONIAL SETTLEMENT, AND LATER A SOMNOLENT AMERICAN PORT, HAS SWIFTLY EXPANDED INTO A WORLD METROPOLIS—ITS INTERESTING PAST, ITS AMAZING PRESENT, AND ITS INCALCULABLE FUTURE.

NEW YORK will be an extraordinary place when it is finished—when it is! But it has been in process of completion a pretty long time. At the start it was a little Dutch seaport. The island, at the lower end of which it squatted, had, a bit before, been purchased of the aborigines for a sum equivalent to twenty-four dollars. It is now worth at least two thousand million. That is rather a rise.

The first recorded sale of real estate was a lot thirty feet front by a hundred and ten deep, which fetched nine dollars and sixty cents. What the last sale will be, and what it will bring, no clairvoyant can foretell.

At the time of the first sale the town

NEW YORK IN 1790, FROM THE HARBOR—ON THE RIGHT, IN THE BACKGROUND, IS THE BATTERY PARK.
THE LARGE HOUSE NEAR THE CENTER OF THE PICTURE IS NO. 1 BROADWAY, SIR HENRY
CLINTON'S RESIDENCE DURING THE REVOLUTION—ON THE LEFT IS TRINITY CHURCH.

From a lithograph by Hayward.

extended from the Battery to Wall Street, with large and beautiful farms between. These farms produced everything imaginable, including fine manners and pretty girls. The manners are no more, neither are the farms, but pretty girls are a local specialty still. In some respects New York is eminently conservative.

At that time it was particularly so.

was a reason for that price. There was a reason quite as good for the prices of a hundred years ago. From a somnolent seaport, remote, obscure, and miasmatic, the town was beginning to experience the primal tremors that were to lift it among the metropoles of the world.

From the conclusion of the war of 1812 this impulsion may be said to date. With that date coincides the passing of old

| Pulitzer Building | Tract Society Building | Park Row Building | St. Paul Building | | Central Building | Washington Life Building | Bank of Commerce | Queen Building | American Surety Building |

THE SKY-LINE OF THE COLOSSAL CITY—A VIEW OF LOWER NEW YORK FROM THE HUDSON RIVER—

Beyond Wall Street was a wilderness. Within was the élite. The latter comprised ten families—the upper ten. Some of them were very rich. Their wealth ran into hundreds of dollars. In addition to the fine folk, there were others. At the beginning of the eighteenth century there were as many as five thousand in all. Fifty years later, the population had doubled. When the Revolution occurred, it had doubled again.

FROM VILLAGE TO METROPOLIS.

Meanwhile the town had expanded. On the west side it extended above Warren Street. On the east it extended farther yet, to what is called Broome Street to-day. Beyond these limits were swamps, salt meadows, infrequent country seats, partridge, woodcock, and a sense of being alone in the world.

That is only a trifle more than a hundred years ago. But already prices had jumped. Near Broome Street it was all one could do to get a decent lot for a penny less than five hundred dollars. On Fifth Avenue, recently, a strip fifty by a hundred brought over a million. There

New York and the parturition of the present city. The great act of flipping a sovereign across the sea was succeeded by the greater act of opening a continent. In the establishment of steam service, in the subsequent building of railroads, with, ultimately, the telegraph for overseer, a transformation ensued which was comparable only to wizardry. But the magic, however marvelous, was lack-luster beside that which the taming and domestication of electricity, together with the tossing up of skyscraping towers of Babel and Bedlam, was to produce.

In the advent of these surprises, New York has developed into the noisiest city in the world. In its sedater days it was subdued, neutral-tinted, down at the heel, careless, cheap, agreeable, and unhealthy. It is more sanitary to-day, far dearer, less neutral and livable. Its original brick and brown are going. As they go, in their place comes white. Occasionally an artist in architecture provides a touch of canary. But along Fifth Avenue, which formerly was almost somber in its brown-stone respectability, one new structure after another presents a façade of cream.

CYCLOPEAN CLIFFS, CROWDED CANYONS.

Beneath the sempiternal blue of the sky the effect is gracious. Were the avenue itself but wider, it might ultimately suggest the Paris Elysian Fields—might, we say, yet never will, if only because of the cyclopean scarps of the buildings.

is the uproar of trains, cars, tooting motors, clanging ambulances, and demon draymen, combined with the semioccasional tornado of fire engines, that it is quite insufficient to be acrobatic; it takes intrepidity, enthusiasm, and strategy to get about. Men who have gone through wars unscathed have lost their lives there, others perhaps their reason. It is a very unholy place, and though not

Gillender Trinity   Empire Manhattan   Hudson Standard Welles   Bowling Washington   Army
Building Church   Building Life   Building Oil Building   Green Building   Building
           Building   Building   Building

—SHOWING THE MOUNTAIN-RANGE OF HUGE BUILDINGS BETWEEN THE BATTERY AND THE CITY HALL PARK.

Without effort you may foresee the day when Fifth Avenue will be a dark lane, flanked on either side by sheer white heights, with, above, a slender stretch of tender blue. As with Fifth Avenue, so with the other arteries, thoroughfares, and even side streets of the town. They will line up giant hotels, gigantic office buildings, Gargantuan department stores, through which growing crowds will cascade.

The existing subway, together with the other subways and tunnels projected, will, it is said, lessen and deflect these crowds. But it is wrong to believe everything we hear. It is more probable that the crowds will increase. At each effort to facilitate transit, whether by new lines, larger cars, or longer trains, always are there greater swarms. Every convenience adds to the inconvenience. About New York last year there were conveyed a hundred million more passengers than were conveyed five years ago.

As it is, surface cars follow each other so continuously that it takes an acrobat to cross the street. In certain sections —in Herald Square, for instance—such

unique—there are other choice spots we wot of fully as emotional—it is rather typical of what all New York some day shall be.

A CITY OF THE HOMELESS.

Meanwhile, how are increasing hordes that collaborate in these horrors to be housed? Apart from tenement districts adjacent to the river fronts, all New York below Twenty-Third Street—a street, parenthetically, which in the memory of men who are not yet Methuselahs was once regarded as suburban— will, before long, be wholly composed of mountain ranges of office and dry-goods buildings, with wind-swept, sunless ravines between. The homeless will find no shelter there. Nor between Twenty-Third and Forty-Second Streets will there be much hope for them, either. For a while yet that region will not be wholly uninhabitable; but in a period relatively brief, there where now are surviving homes will be skyscrapers, department stores, apartment hotels. There are plenty of them already in this once suburban region. Shortly there will be more. Then there will be practically nothing else.

These things multiply with the insect rapidity of crowds. Already the annual increase in skyscrapers alone is counted in hundreds. Already the entire middle division of Manhattan is punctuated by them. At present their height varies from twelve to thirty stories; but there is one now planned that is to be thirty-five. It will be duplicated, of course, triplicated, imitated indefinitely, and then exceeded.

And why not? Builders assure us that short of eighty stories there is no engineering or economic limit to height, provided that the basic area be sufficient, and that the municipality, together with the as yet tolerably unknown quantity which we call vibration, omit to interfere. Assuming the possible and therefore probable construction of these little things, they may add a Babylonian beauty to the city, without, however, providing any of Babylon's charms.

THE ENDLESS PROCESS OF RECONSTRUCTION.

In any event, edifices more vertiginous than those existing are presumable. In the past five years new buildings have been going up at an average outlay of a hundred and twenty millions a year; and this not to entertain, or house, or even office a population steadily increasing at the rate of a hundred thousand per annum—or, at least, not primarily for such purposes—but because available area is so small that owners are constantly compelled to improve their holdings to the toppest notch.

Individually they are occupied not simply in building, but in demolishing and rebuilding. Individually that is what they are about; but conjointly they are reconstructing the entire town. In this process, during the past five years, there have been built more than one hundred and thirty apartment hotels, varying in height from nine to twenty stories, equipped with every imaginable luxury and discomfort, with rooms too small to change your mind in, with restaurants that do not restore, but with powdered flunkies, orchestral diversions, roof-gardens, and swimming-pools, together with the minimum of ease at the maximum price. Parallelly, there have gone up department stores, in a single one of which forty thousand people shop daily, with four thousand employees to help them at it; where at any moment between eight and six, two thousand shoppers can be fed.

Of these buildings, whether office, hotel, or drygoods, the majority display plenty of taste, and some of it pretty bad. But their general effect is suggestive. Half a dozen of them here and there may surprise; often they disconcert; yet when New York is covered with them, as ultimately New York will be, when they have ceased to be the exceptional and have become the inevitable, they will have acquired the serenity of a natural law, and with it a beauty titanesque in grandeur. Save in the uplands of dream and the hallucinations of poets, nowhere, at no time, will there have been any thing like unto it.

A PERPETUAL HOUSE FAMINE.

Meanwhile, and particularly then, how shall it fare with the homeless and increasing crowds? Every year, and for that matter every month, the supply of private dwellings diminishes. Those that remain will not endure forever. Those of recent construction are designed only for the rich, who each year are retreating more and more conspicuously to their country seats, and who occupy their town residences for but brief periods, generally for four months out of the twelve. We do not blame them for that. On the contrary.

But the point is elsewhere, or rather it is here. A trifle more than a century ago there were, relatively speaking, so many people in New York, and, speaking relatively also, so few homes, that a house famine occurred, as a result of which a lot of people were obliged to put their effects in the City Hall and go to jail for lodgings. That historic famine may seem sporadic. It is constant, with this difference: People nowadays, to whom private dwellings, apartment hotels, and country seats are equally impossible, put their effects in storage and jail themselves in flats. There is progress!

Yet somewhere there is always light, and for the "flatters," too, there are gleams. The gleams radiate from rapid transit. But the light is in the outlying districts, which improved communication will reflect. There, in lieu of infrequent and expensive dwellings, will rise multitudes of inexpensive homes—squares and crescents such as suburban London knows, mile after mile of houses, league upon league of villas, all of them unpretentious, distressingly similar, but convenient, accessible, secure from the noise and perplexities of the colossal city, and each of them to some human being the center of the universe, the one spot really cherished, the home in which loves and lives unfold.

WHERE IS THE HEART OF NEW YORK ?

Incidentally, in the mammoth metropolis another and a more notable change will have occurred. Pathology is familiar with a malady known as displacement of the heart. Of this complaint one of the symptoms, or, more exactly, one of the results, is loss of memory. The patient forgets. He becomes aphasiac. At first he cannot remember names; then words, then faces desert him. Finally the consciousness of his own identity escapes.

What happens to men is happening now to New York. Where is the heart of Manhattan?

Originally at Bowling Green, upward with the stream of life it has moved, halting only to be displaced anew, at Broome Street, at Bleecker and Bond, at Washington and Madison Squares, until now diagnosis locates its social angle at the Plaza. From one end of the town to the other it has moved, the result being that to-day New York is aphasiac. There are names and places and faces that she remembers no more. But when, the various subways and projected tunnels aiding, New York, merged in outlying districts, shall have lost her identity, the displacement will be complete.

From the Battery to Harlem, Manhattan then will be comparable only to what the City is in London, yet differing from the latter in this—that it will be the business center not of a metropolis but of a nation, a great mart, the greatest in the world, from end to end wholly commercial, thronged by day, vacant at night, a cyclopean inferno with a blue sky, into which, each morning, from West Chester and New Jersey and Long Island, hordes

NEW YORK IN THE PERIOD BEFORE THE CIVIL WAR—A VIEW OF BROADWAY AT THE CORNER OF GRAND STREET, IN 1840. THE BUILDINGS OF THIS PERIOD WERE MOSTLY TWO-STORY AND THREE-STORY WOODEN HOUSES. MANY PUBLIC STAGES PLIED ALONG BROADWAY.

From a lithograph by Hayward.

A CITY OF SKYSCRAPERS—THE HEART OF NEW YORK'S FINANCIAL DISTRICT, AT THE CORNER
OF WALL AND BROAD STREETS—IN THE FOREGROUND IS THE ROOF OF THE OFFICES OF
J. P. MORGAN & COMPANY, 23 WALL STREET; TO THE RIGHT, ACROSS WALL
STREET, IS THE ROOF OF THE UNITED STATES SUB-TREASURY.

From a photograph by Brown Brothers, New York.

of human beings will descend and scheme and fight and lie and die for gold.

Such will be the heart of New York. Meanwhile gold is very obvious, and, it may be added, highly requisite.

THE MOST EXPENSIVE CITY.

"To live in New York costs," said Mark Twain, "a trifle more than you've got." It pleased Mr. Clemens to be facetious. It pleased the late Mr. Lorillard to be precise. "In New York," he declared, "it is not possible to live like a gentleman on less than a thousand dollars a day."

Though Mr. Lorillard was precise, he was not perhaps what you would call profound. A gentlemanly mode of life can certainly be achieved on less. Yet given such a sum, and though you pay, as you may, if you care to, a hundred dollars a day for two rooms and a bath in a Fifth Avenue inn—and particularly if you economize in a fifteen thousand per annum flat—you will still, if you are careful, have a surplus.

But not much of a surplus if you propose to have a house on Fifth Avenue, an opera box, a stable, a chef, milliners' bills, jewelers' also, and, with them, the other necessary adjuncts of smart existence. In that case you will find that a thousand dollars a day will just about keep the wolf out of the drawing-room, without, it may be, even getting your name in the papers. In any event, on a thousand a day, which is nearly what ten million at three and a half per cent produces, you may be regarded as leading a gentlemanly life, but you will not be accounted wealthy.

No, indeed. Rent-rolls which anywhere else would spell opulence do not take one very far in New York. Save in fairyland and old Rome, never, at any time, in any form of society, however dis-tinguished or extinguished, has civilization beheld greater lavishness than that which our metropolitan plutocracy displays. More ornate than the swirl of London and more resplendent than that of Paris, it is only royalty that can vie with it, and not always with success. In Europe there is many a palace that would hide its diminished roof beside the sheer luxury of Fifth Avenue homes. In other European palaces, overlords and overladies are served with greater pomp, but not with greater perfection than that which these homes attain; and in them you will see women on whose necks are stones by comparison to which crown jewels are lack-luster. The bank accounts are as startling as the gems, and these accounts aiding there has resulted a general gorgeousness that is really stunning—a gorgeousness of which the uninitiated get in Central Park barely a glimpse and but a vision at the opera.

In its construction, New York is a colossal city. But in the wealth exhibited in the upper reaches of its auriferous stream it is not merely colossal, it is unique.

32
A New Era for the Metropolitan

A NEW ERA FOR THE METROPOLITAN

THE OLD SOUTH FRONT OF THE METROPOLITAN MUSEUM, WHICH WILL ULTIMATELY BE ENTIRELY SURROUNDED BY THE NEW BUILDINGS.

From a photograph by Charles Balliard.

BY ARTHUR HOEBER.

NEW YORK'S GREAT ART INSTITUTION PROMISES TO DEVELOP MORE RAPIDLY THAN EVER WITH J. PIERPONT MORGAN AS ITS PRESIDENT AND WITH THE ROGERS BEQUEST AS AN ENDOWMENT FUND—ITS NEW DIRECTOR AND ITS PLAN FOR A MAGNIFICENT GROUP OF BUILDINGS.

IN our strenuous American life, nothing may hope to escape the march of progress. It is in the air of this western hemisphere to advance, improve, readjust, reorganize. The recent development of our Metropolitan Museum of Art, and its promise of still greater development in the near future, may be cited as instances of the tendency.

In the world of art, things necessarily move more or less slowly. It takes many years to equip a great art institution. The preliminary work is enormous, and in a new country it must be accomplished under many disadvantages and in the face of discouraging apathy. It can be done only by the aid of public-spirited individuals who are able and willing to go down deep into their pockets. Moreover, the man who is profoundly interested in exploiting things esthetic is not apt to be intensely practical.

In view of the difficulties to be overcome, the growth of the Metropolitan Museum has been phenomenally rapid. It has been in existence for only thirty-five years. The movement for its creation was first suggested by the late John Jay, then United States minister to Austria. In the enthusiasm of a Fourth of July banquet in Paris, in the late sixties, he declared that New York should possess an art gallery comparable to those of the chief European cities. Later, some of the American residents in the French capital came together, talked the matter over, and addressed a letter to the Union League Club, of New York, advocating Mr. Jay's idea. In the mean time, that gentleman had returned home, and had been elected president of the club. When the letter from Paris came, he turned it over to the art committee of the Union League, and the result was a public meeting for consultation, which was held November 23, 1869.

THE BIRTH OF THE METROPOLITAN MUSEUM.

A committee of one hundred and sixteen gentlemen proceeded with the organization, and on April 30, 1870, the State Legislature incorporated the association under the name of the Metropolitan Museum of Art. A year later, the State appropriated half a million dollars for the construction of a suitable building in Central Park.

Meanwhile, as early as March, 1871, the trustees had acquired a collection of pictures of various schools, mostly of the sort referred to as "old masters"—and

hundred. In contrast to these scanty figures may be set the fact that last year nearly a million people visited the museum.

THE GREAT MUSEUM THAT IS TO BE.

By May, 1879, the central part of the present group of buildings in Central Park was finished. The new structure

THE NEW DIRECTOR OF THE METROPOLITAN MUSEUM, SIR CASPAR PURDON CLARKE,
AT PRESENT DIRECTOR OF THE ART DEPARTMENT OF THE VICTORIA
AND ALBERT MUSEUM, SOUTH KENSINGTON, LONDON.
Drawn by W. M. Berger from a photograph.

certainly they were old, if not always by the masters. To house these, along with other possessions, they leased the building at 681 Fifth Avenue. John Taylor Johnson, a well-known art patron, was made president, and thus was the museum formally started.

Two years later a move was made to the old Cruger mansion on West Fourteenth Street, near Sixth Avenue. At this time the public was admitted free on one day in the week. On that day the attendance averaged a little more than a thousand; on pay days, it was less than a

was inaugurated with imposing ceremonies, the President of the United States assisting at the function. Wings on either side were subsequently added, and finally what is known as the new East Wing, which cost nearly a million dollars, was opened two years ago. This really magnificent extension is the work of the late Richard M. Hunt, left uncompleted at the time of his death, and carried on by his sons. It gives an idea of the splendid proportions and imposing appearance to which the museum will attain when the plans for its architec-

ONE OF THE PICTURE GALLERIES (NO. 11) OF THE METROPOLITAN MUSEUM—AT THE END OF THE GALLERY, ON THE RIGHT, IS ONE OF THE MUSEUM'S MOST VALUABLE
PAINTINGS, "THE RETURN OF THE HOLY FAMILY FROM EGYPT," BY RUBENS.

Drawn by C. D. Williams from a photograph.

THE NEW EAST FRONT OF THE METROPOLITAN MUSEUM, FACING FIFTH AVENUE—THIS FINE
STRUCTURE IS SHORTLY TO BE EXTENDED TWO HUNDRED AND FIFTY FEET DOWN THE
AVENUE, AND WILL ULTIMATELY FORM A GREAT QUADRANGLE SURROUNDING
THE OLDER BUILDINGS.

From a photograph by Charles Balliard.

tural development are completed. Ultimately the original brick edifice is to be enclosed within a great quadrangle of handsome stone structures extending from Fifth Avenue, on the east, to the main driveway of the park, on the west. The cost of the completed museum is estimated at about twenty-two million dollars. Two and a quarter millions have already been appropriated for the next addition, which is to extend down Fifth Avenue for two hundred and fifty feet, and the architects are now perfecting the working plans.

Mr. Johnson continued at the head of the Metropolitan until 1888, and after that we find him carried on the annual reports as "honorary president for life." He was succeeded by Henry G. Marquand, to whose energy, good taste, and princely liberality the museum is greatly indebted. Mr. Marquand was a connoisseur in the true sense of the word and his judgment on a work of art was almost final. He presented many treasures to the galleries, among them paintings by Rembrandt, Van Dyck, Velasquez and Hals. Under his régime the museum was almost a personal possession. Trustees came and went, but his word was law. When he died, in February, 1902, he was

succeeded by F. W. Rhinelander, who survived him but two years, when J. Pierpont Morgan was elected to the chair.

MR. MORGAN'S PRESIDENCY.

Up to Mr. Morgan's incumbency, the museum had been managed along somewhat haphazard lines—the lines, perhaps, of the least resistance. This is not likely to continue. The value of specialized work has long since made itself evident, and nowhere is the specialist so necessary as in the management of a museum. Executive ability there must be, and the power to impress men of wealth to make liberal contributions; but nowadays much more than this is demanded from a managing director. He must be a man of erudition, of experience, of artistic intuition and training, and the training must be the result of years of· serious application and practical labor. Furthermore, he must be supported by men endowed with broad notions and liberal art education, and possessed of ample money and the courage to spend it promptly when proper opportunities present themselves.

In European countries, whose government is more paternal than ours, the matter is easier. Over there they have the advantage of the years behind them. The art idea, in a measure, is engrafted in the make-up of the public men who stand at the head of the state. There are no Congressmen from the "'way-back deestricts" to be placated when it comes to an appropriation. The glory of the French artistic tradition is part of the equipment of every Gallic statesman.

having passed successfully through the various ills of childhood, has emerged into vigorous manhood. It is no longer a struggling infant, but a virile personality with the claims and the needs of a full-grown individuality. Mr. Morgan, coming to the presidency at just the appropriate moment, has injected into the institution that intelligent business spirit

IN THE GREAT NEW HALL OF THE METROPOLITAN MUSEUM, IN WHICH ARE EXHIBITED MODERN SCULPTURES AND CASTS OF FAMOUS ANCIENT STATUES—THE STATUE IN THE FOREGROUND IS "THE BEAR-TRAINER," BY PAUL WAYLAND BARTLETT.

Drawn by C. D. Williams from a photograph.

We in America have still a formidable number of legislators who would object to paying out good money for a cracked canvas, dim with age and shadowy with color, because it bore the marks of some old master, or a statue with a broken nose and an arm missing, even were it pure Greek. Moreover, our tariff on works of art is so intelligently arranged that it keeps out good things and permits the entrance of much vile stuff, in the end offending and hampering the artist whom it is popularly supposed to assist.

However, the Metropolitan Museum,

which has made his name a synonym for successful organization.

THE MUSEUM'S NEW DIRECTOR.

An important epoch in the history of the museum was marked by the recent death of General Louis Palma di Cesnola, who had been managing director of the institution since its foundation. When Mr. Morgan chose Sir Caspar Purdon Clarke to fill this important vacancy, he probably made a very wise choice. The fact that he went out of his own land for the selection is a matter of no moment whatsoever. Unlike poets, directors are not born; they are made. Naturally and obviously, they must have a predilection for the work, but they must also, as has been said, go through a special course of study and experience. The facilities for such a curriculum do not exist in America. We have been occupied with the

It does not suffice to roll up an enormous bank account; there is something else in this life of ours. It is gratifying, after all, to have one's name associated with the cause of art.

MILLIONS FOR THE MUSEUM.

Curiously enough, this sentiment crops

ART STUDENTS COPYING PICTURES IN THE METROPOLITAN MUSEUM—THE GALLERIES ARE OPEN TO COPYISTS ON MONDAY AND FRIDAY OF EACH WEEK, ON PAYMENT OF A SMALL FEE.

problems of empire-building. In building the structure of the great republic, art has come last.

But to-day conditions are rapidly changing. We have emerged from the primitive state. We are heaping up unprecedented wealth. Having all the creature comforts, men begin to look about for the luxuries and the elegancies.

up where it might be least expected. One day about four years ago, the directors of the Metropolitan rubbed their eyes as they read in their morning paper that one Jacob S. Rogers, a manufacturer of locomotives in the rather prosaic city of Paterson, New Jersey, had died and left to their institution an amount estimated at from five to seven millions of dollars.

Such a colossal bequest perhaps is only possible here in America, and even here it staggers the average man. Yet there was no mistake about it. In time Mr. Rogers' will was admitted to probate, and it was found the income of the fund thus created was to be used for the purpose of purchasing rare books, fine pictures, and other works of art. Such a splendid endowment will, of course, greatly aid the museum's development.

Sir Purdon Clarke, the new director, will begin his new duties in the coming autumn. He is at present in charge of the art department of the South Kensington Museum in London, educationally the most important of the art institutions of the English metropolis. Of course he made no financial sacrifice in accepting the call to New York, but undoubtedly he was also attracted by the enormous possibilities he saw in the future of the American museum. His schooling has been thorough and diversified. He was graduated from the National Art Training School in 1865, and has steadily advanced from one position to another until he succeeded the late Sir Philip Owen in his present post. He has practised as an architect,

he has designed museums, he has organized exhibitions, and he has traveled over most of Europe and Asia as a purchasing agent in quest of works of art. He seems preëminently fitted to cope with the problems of organization, of extending the field of our museum, and generally of putting it on a more modern and scientific basis.

Sir Purdon's interest in American art, publicly expressed, gives the greatest encouragement to the native worker.

"Americans," he is reported to have said, "fail to recognize their own geniuses. The country is full of talent. Some of the best of the artists are American-born, but Americans demand that they shall be hall-marked in Europe before they will pay American prices for their work. I found foreign art everywhere I went in the United States; but I hope the day will come when American art will be most sought after by Americans."

A cheerful, hopeful note this for the American artist—one which will incline him to watch with the liveliest interest the policy of the director under whose guidance the Metropolitan Museum of Art enters upon a new and most promising chapter of its development.

33
The Basis
of New York
Society

MISS ALICE ATHERTON BLIGHT.

THE BASIS OF NEW YORK SOCIETY.

By Mrs. John King Van Rensselaer.

FASHIONABLE life in the good city of New York has at various periods presented such ever-changing, ever-varying features, that it requires elastic wits to keep pace with its rapid revolutions, which from time to time hold up for admiration and imitation features and novelties only to discard them before the mass of people, who are always ready or alert to follow social leaders, have had the opportunity to digest and adopt them.

This restless seeking for change, which is now the dominant characteristic of society, is due, firstly, to the women who, wishing to be leaders, are always on the lookout for novelties, in order to attract guests to their entertainments or to excite admiration for their own daring flights of fancy. This is generally obtained by laying out vast sums on a social function, which is not attractive from any point of view other than the amount of money that it has cost the hostess. The abandonment of the different forms of entertainment, one after the other, is owing to the disagreeable discovery that others, with equally well-filled purses, can do likewise, and therefore fashionable leaders of to-day tire rapidly of their own enterprises, and become completely disgusted with them when imitated on any large

Photograph by Taber.

MRS. W. K. VANDERBILT, JR.

427

MRS. H. BRAMHALL GILBERT.

scale by persons whom, according to their own standards, they would describe, in language that is all their own, as "not in the swim."

It is seldom that any one can remain what is termed "the leader of society" more than ten years. Either health or money gives out during the incessant pursuit of pleasure, and one of the two, and for preference both, are needed to lead successfully the butterflies of modern days through the giddy mazes of fashionable life.

During the leadership of each succeeding matron— and hitherto the reins have not been grasped by any unmarried woman—the marks of her own individuality have been strongly impressed on the form that the amusements of her time have taken. So much so, that to the onlooker, or historian, epochs can be easily classified, and distinguished by the name of the prominent personages of the day, with as much ease as the reigns of the monarchs of Europe. It must be said for the leaders of the past, that they were always noted for a strict regard for the proprieties of life. They were devoted mothers and exemplary wives, and the standard of morality in the community was a very high one. Charities and church-going were the first duties of even the most prominent of the social leaders who one after another have reigned with gentle sway over the amusements of New York city.

Looking backward over the last century in New York, traces of each social leader may be found by a close study of the most characteristic entertainments given during that time. But the records of those functions are not to be found by consulting the pages of the daily press, as would now be the case, for it was considered indecorous to have private affairs published, and it was only the most extraordinary entertainments that ever crept into the daily papers, and then all names were carefully eliminated, so that none but the initiated could understand them at the time; and few can comprehend them in

MISS ALICE MORTON.

the present day, unless they possess the key to the enigma.

It is to private journals or family traditions, therefore, that one must turn in order to describe the area of fashion during the past century. After the war with England that resulted in the independence of the American colonies, the seat of the newly formed government was for a short period stationed in this city, a condition of affairs that gathered here all the most brilliant men of the day, anxious to take part in the public offices, who, with their wives and families, gave an intellectual bias to society that it has never since that time rejoiced in. But that glorious epoch in the social life of

MRS HARRY WHITNEY TREAT.

MRS. VAN RENSSELAER CRUGER.

New York was previous to the dawn of the nineteenth century, and when the seat of government was transferred to a sister city, the sparkle of social life went with it, and the inhabitants of the old Dutch town settled down quietly, and seemed to care but little to entertain, or for being entertained, and therefore the life they led was intensely dull, and hardly worth recording. This state of affairs did not last long, however, as the wife of an opulent gentleman found she had not only the will, but the means, of entertaining her friends, and she soon made herself famous by giving handsome parties, that became the talk of the town. Having traveled considerably in foreign countries, the couple had a fine collection of works of art, and their house was filled with pictures and statues, which were objects of the keenest interest to the members of the social world, who at that time were but little wont to travel far from the banks of the Hudson, and had, therefore, seen few paintings and those generally of staid citizens and their wives in the fashionable attire of their day. To many of these worthy people, the nude statues and undressed nymphs that adorned the home of this social leader were most startling

MISS MARY CAROLINE WASHINGTON BOND.

surprises, and they considered these works of art little better than a disgrace to the community; therefore, to please their tastes, the complaisant mistress of the house was accustomed to drape her statues with pocket-handkerchiefs before throwing open her home to her friends.

About this time it became the fashion in Europe to give fancy-balls, and in imitation of this a magnificent one was held in the city of New York by the mother of one of the most fashionable leaders in the society of to-day. To this ball all that was brightest and most beautiful in the city was bidden, all vying with one another in friendly rivalry as to which character should be most thoroughly sustained by the presenter.

The fashion set in this way, of giving balls in which fancy-dress should be worn, incited among the fashionable

Photograph by Aimé Dupont.
MRS. H. K. BLOODGOOD.

Irving, N. P. Willis, Drake, Halleck, Cooper, Miss Sedgwick and many others were emulating them in New York. Thomas Moore and Mrs. Jameson came to visit this country and added spurs to the intellectual life that had had no time for cultivation during the exciting years preceding, during and directly after the Revolution. Mrs. Jameson came, it is true, not to cultivate taste in America, but was in involuntary exile, forced to share it with an uncongenial husband, but she, nevertheless, like the genius she was, contrived to utilize her time in study and in the exercise of a new accomplishment, and has left as an undying record of her achievements some most beautiful etchings, which are probably the first ever designed by a woman in America. Thomas Moore's professional business did not long detain him in this

world a study of poetical works and those of fiction. At that time Sir Walter Scott, Lord Byron and many others were filling the minds and imaginations of the English reading public with their beautiful fancies, and while their vogue extended not only over their native land, but to all others where their works could be understood and appreciated, Charles Bristed, Washington country, but both of them gave an impetus to the study of literature and its kindred arts, this being excited by the transitory visits of such talented people, and afterward, fortunately, kept alive by visits from Lord Morpeth and other shining lights from Europe, Fanny Kemble, Jennie Lind, Forrest, Macready and other celebrated lights of the stage, who each

MRS. OLIVER ISELIN.

gave in turn a flip to social ethics, so that all these brilliant personages, who passed a few weeks at a time in the city, left deep impressions on the society of the day, which at the time was small enough to receive and assimilate most thoroughly any such pleasant addition to its circle.

All these causes served to help mark the most brilliant literary epoch of the social life of the city of New York during the first half of the century. Up to that period dancing had been confined to the stately minuet, or to the more energetic contra-dance, but, strange to say, the simple introduction of a Polish national dance was destined to revolutionize society, and this was done, not by a leader in New York, but by a young man attached to the Russian legation at Washington, who introduced the waltz, which he taught

MRS. RICHARD TOWNSEND.

MRS. EDWARD LYMAN SHORT.

to some New York young ladies, who imported the foreign dance into the staid old place, and upon this a revolution in the social amusements took place.

It had been customary for the intellectual part of the community to meet frequently and with but little formality, in order to exchange verses, essays and other light literary articles, the best of which were read or recited at the houses of the different members of the set. Some of the brightest of the group started a magazine for private circulation only, and an immense amount of amusement was caused by one of the numbers, to which twenty of the most popular of the young people of the day contributed their private views

MRS. LORILLARD SPENCER.

on the language in which a proposal of marriage should be couched. One of the wits of society wrote a series of letters which described the foibles and follies of the set, in a sarcastic, but by no means an ill-natured, vein.

For many years the principal functions had been the public balls, called the assemblies. These were subscription entertainments, and were held in the City Hotel, or some other equally large and convenient hall. The subscribers inherited their positions, and extended the right to attend the balls to prominent persons, distinguished strangers, et cetera, and as the entrance into this society was almost distinctly hereditary, and had been handed down in certain families in unbroken lines since the first introduction by the Dutch founders of the city, it followed that those balls were very select, and at them were the best representatives of the old families of the place.

Although at these balls dancing was the principal amusement up to the year 1830, the waltz was not permitted within the sacred precincts, and its introduction at other parties created an immense sensation, calling forth stern denunciation from the pulpit and, what was more peculiar, from the press of the day, one editor of a daily paper being most abusive in his description of waltzing, which he feared would lead to the complete demoralization of society, and he was gross in his description of the terrible consequences that might ensue if this dance were practised by the young people in social life. In the light of later days, we may hope that none of the evils pictured by the worthy gentleman ever came to pass.

The assemblies were attended by persons of all ages. The ladies of the family were expected to grace the ball with their presence, and open it themselves by treading "one measure" in the first contradance with the most distinguished persons present. While the ball was being opened in a decorous and seemly manner, all the young persons present stood modestly in the background, contented to admire their elders, and to wait patiently until they were exhausted by such unwonted exertion, and desirous of retiring to the card-rooms, that were always provided for those who wished to enjoy a sober game of whist, and it was not until the last of the older ladies had left the dancing-floor that the juniors ventured on taking a prominent part in the festivities on their own account.

Private parties were conducted on more simple principles than at the present day, and were often little more than informal dances to the music of an itinerant fiddler. It was seldom that large entertainments were given during the season, and the assemblies were the great social functions of the year.

In families where there were a number of young people, impromptu parties were of

Photograph by James L. Breese.

MRS. WALTER PEASE.

frequent occurrence, but most of the citizens of New York contented themselves by keeping open house, and having frequent dinners, the hour for which was never later than five o'clock, and for the more formal of which there was generally an excuse, such as a present of some fine game, a stranger in town, who must be hospitably entertained and properly introduced, or the regular meeting of a society of bons vivants, noted for their wit and good fellowship, whose doings have been recorded in that valuable journal by their founder, the gentleman for whom the club was named — Philip Hone.

The most popular form of entertainment in the early part of the century were waffle parties, and these were given with persistent frequency by all hostesses in New York, and were a noteworthy feature of the place, marking as they did the survival of early Dutch entertainments, that were cherished by their descendants. The hostesses of the day were none of them particularly anxious for social leadership, but all were noted for warm-hearted hospitality that made them delight to gather around their square mahogany tables all their most intimate neighbors, friends and relations. Waffle parties were held at eight o'clock in the evening, and when

this sweet cake, baked in especially prepared irons, had been disposed of, the company would gather in the parlors and play simple intellectual games, such as "capping verses," or else indulge in more romping amusements, like blindman's buff, pillows and keys, et cetera, which are now relegated to the nursery.

Life in those days was simple, unaffected and easy. There was no question of handsome decorations or expensive entertainments. Things were done for comfort and not for show. It would have been considered the height of absurdity to adorn the table with flowers, as the gourmands of the day, who had a keen relish for tastes and flavors, considered that the perfume of highly scented vegetables, however beautiful they might be, interfered with their enjoyment of rich sauces, or the more delicate essence of clarets, Madeira and other wines, which to them constituted the charm of a dinner, and they deemed that their sense of taste was to be esteemed and placed before its kindred sense of sight, which was according to their opinion to be devoted to the enjoyment of scenery, works of art, or the products of the garden when in their own sphere, and they did not consider that flowers

Photograph by Aimé Dupont.

THE HON. MRS. CABELL.

MRS. CLARENCE MACKAY.

were in their proper place when on the dinner-table.

After the set of literary people had become scattered, by those mysterious acts of disintegration that separate social sets, after a life that seldom extends over a decade, waltzing, that at first had been frowned upon and discouraged, was gradu-

MISS HAY.

their young people to attend these functions, only providing suitable matrons for the girls, who were not always grateful for this protection.

The old-fashioned waffle parties, followed by simple games or by music, were voted by the youngsters very dull; therefore, by the middle of the century the principal entertainments in the good city of New York were dancing-parties, attended exclusively by juveniles, while elder members of families seldom troubled themselves to appear at any public function. This state of affairs was much to be deplored. Large entertainments that are wholly devoted to twirling masses of draperies are without balance or stability, unless graced by the presence of well-dressed matrons, who, at least, if they are relegated to the back-

MRS. JOHN VINTON DAHLGREN.

ally introduced, even within the assemblies, and finally this new dance reigned triumphant and revolutionized society, and shook to its very foundations the old-fashioned notions of the proper forms of social entertainments.

Several ladies who were willing to contribute their share to the amusement of society, and perhaps with aspirations of social leadership, encouraged the new dance, and invited to their houses only young and frivolous people, who were delighted to have opportunities of amusing themselves in this way, far from carping objections on the part of maiden aunts, whose faces and figures prevented them from being successful performers as dancers, and who, therefore, while occupying seats of observation, were disposed and ready to make ill-natured remarks. Others of the older members of families, finding but little amusement in attending balls at which no arrangement was made for their entertainment, preferred their ingleside, and left

ground, give value and effect to the picture.

In fact, the social element in New York during the forties and fifties was scarcely what could be called an intellectual one, but a society leader arose who was descended from some of the oldest families in the colony, and who had married a rich man with a feeling of responsibility as to the disposal of the great wealth he had inherited, and this estimable pair were the first to recognize that it was in their power to create a better element in the social life of the city, and they drew around them a charming circle of the brightest literary lights, scientists, artists, actors and actresses, so by deftly mingling them with the more intelligent of the fashionable community, they marked a decade in the social world

Photograph by Pach Brothers.

MRS. ARTHUR KEMP.

ancestors, and that it required only encouragement to develop wit and originality. She accordingly founded a literary club of ladies, who met biweekly in the parlors of the members, at which each one was expected to contribute an article from her own pen, to be read before her confrères and discussed by the society. The wisdom of this social leader has been well proved by the success of the modest little society which she founded, and from which have sprung many others of more or less distinction, the original society being an exclusive association to which few are admitted, and to attain entrance to which confers a certain social distinction. This society is so quietly conducted that but few people know of its existence, beyond the circle of old-fashioned New Yorkers,

that had a more durable effect than they lived to be aware of. It was this gracious hostess who declared that there was much latent talent among the butterflies of the gay world, as she well remembered the brilliant efforts of their of whom it is chiefly composed. About the time that the reins of fashion were falling loosely from the hand which cared but little to hold them, a new era dawned in the city, from which dates all the luxury of display that now reigns dominant in the society of the metropolis. Up to the middle of the century, the subject of wealth was one that was little considered or discussed. Every one lived in about the same simple style; every one was supposed to have the same number of servants, that was increased only when one family was larger than another and required more service. It was considered the height of vulgarity to spend money lavishly on unnecessary luxuries, simply for the sake of making a display and thereby exciting the envy of others. Quiet, unostentatious hospitality marked the character of each household in which the wit and education of the hosts were the standard of excellence and not the size of their bank account. Families were well known in all their branches and ramifications, and there were but few persons in society who had not been born and bred in the city.

The civil war attracted many persons

Photograph by Aimé Dupont.

MRS. JULES J. VATABLE.

from all parts of the country to New York. Immense fortunes were made with astonishing facility, and these new-comers set up a standard of their own and a society of their own making, that fell like an avalanche on the original inhabitants of the place, and completely overwhelmed the sober-minded citizens, who up to that time had been contented with their quiet lives, had firmly believed that honesty was the best policy, and had encouraged no interlopers in their society who were not thoroughly correct in morals and manners. This mass of new-comers in the city speedily created a new order of things, and carried all things before it in the commercial, as well as the social, world.

Photograph by Aimé Dupont.

MRS. CLARENCE ANDREWS.

There was little place for intellectual people in a set composed entirely of self-made people, and the old-fashioned New Yorker at first stood on one side in great amazement at the new régime, and then

MRS. CHARLES A. ALEXANDRE.

with amusement realized that the army of new-rich people who were gathered in the city, from every state in the country and from every class of society, had taken possession of social life in New York, setting a fashion of lavish display, unwonted luxuries and unbridled excesses that completely upset all previously conceived ideas of right and wrong.

Even the sex of the social leader was changed under the new order of things, and for a time a self-elected dictator from a Southern state ruled social functions in the city. Under his direction the scale of social membership was regulated entirely by the extent of a bank account. Knowledge, education, good breeding, et cetera, being unappreciated, were relegated to the background. The hostess who could spend the most money on an entertainment was the one to be the most highly commended and flattered. All this was a most delightful standard for the new-comers. As they could well live up to it, and had no other claims to distinction, the god of Mammon was speedily erected in the city as its most popular deity, before whom all must cringe and through whose portals only the qualified might enter, regardless of manners

MRS. JOHN JACOB ASTOR.

and morals, to find within a debatable arena on which each might fight for social distinction, armed with sinews of war made of gold and silver, and where the most heavily provided might slaughter all others by the sheer weight of their arms.

That this state of things could long con-

tinue is hardly to be credited. The city, elevated into a metropolis by the vast accumulation of wealth, has attracted others besides rich people within its borders. Clever artists, scientists, actors, eminent literary men and women, have come to the great hive, and found to their astonishment that there was no social life for them in the halls of Midas. With minds devoted to the accumulation of wealth, what could such persons have in common with intellectual beings who care little for Midas, and would not seek him, except to find a market for their wares?

The Midas of to-day is not inclined to encourage the arts and sciences, unless it adds in some particular way to his own glory. He finds no pleasure in the perso-

MRS. HENRY SHRADY.

Photograph by Aimé Dupont.
MRS. GOULD BROKAW.

nality of the people, who by him are to be considered only in the light of so much machinery that produces articles for him to purchase, and while Midas pays for the wares offered to him, he does not condescend to associate with the creators. So artist and musician, scientist and author, go their own ways, finding congenial society elsewhere, and content to see little of Midas, who already begins to find himself bored in the society of those who are as rich as he is, and who, therefore, will not give him the meed which each thinks due to himself only. Each one is jealous of the possessions of the others, and for lack of other employment breaks the Tenth Commandment, which he seems to consider was made for the poor and not for the rich.

The sober-minded, old-fashioned New Yorker is not as yet totally extinct, however, but stands aside amazed at this condition of affairs.   A new class in the rising generation, descendants of those who have invaded the city, is now growing up and soon will have to be most seriously con-

sidered.   Children of rich parents who have been educated by a different standard from the one used by the Cavaliers, the Dutch and the Puritans, are an element that will require new directions and new laws. It is true that their chief occupation is not that of their fathers, to accumulate wealth carefully, but is that of distributing it carelessly, and while so doing, to kill the chief enemy of their class— old Father Time. These youngsters often receive a foreign education, or are brought up by the worst class of French or English nurses, their fashionable mothers having had no time to superintend their education, as old-fashioned mothers were wont to do. For this reason they imbibe in infancy a contempt for their fatherland and a longing to identify themselves with one of Europe, where they may, by purchasing a title or large estates, deceive themselves into believing that they in truth belong to the gentle classes of the place, and try to believe, and to make others do so, also, that they are "to the manner born."   It is

Photograph by Davis & Sanford.
MRS. EDWIN GOULD.

true that some of the most fashionable men of the day did redeem their class by bravely offering their services to their country and endured unnecessary hardships with the courage of martyrs. But the men who went from New York in this patriotic way, were the children of the best and most loyal of its citizens, who had inherited from their forefathers true instincts of duty and manliness, and they rushed to the standard of their country, when it was raised, with devotion and loyalty; but where was the son of Midas in the fray?

Society as it exists to-day is full of many different entertainments, the mere recital of which would make matrons and maidens of the past giddy. Pleasure is indeed at the prow, but there are also a large number of the community who are eagerly desirous of doing good to their fellow-creatures, and these self-sacrificing people find time to devote to the great charities of the city,

Photograph by L. Alman & Co.
MISS LEONOR MILMO.

in the midst of all their amusements, and are willing to spend large sums of money on those who have not as much of the world's goods as they have themselves. To these ladies who are keeping up the traditions of charity in the city too much praise cannot be given, and they redeem the butterflies of fashion, who think only of themselves and of their own pleasure.

There is a marked difference in the marriage festivities observed in the social world at the beginning of the century and at its close. In former days the public announcement of the wedding was drawn up in a family conclave and sent by the groom for insertion in the daily papers; it was brief, and the custom was inherited from early days and followed the rulings of an old Dutch law regarding marriage. This notice, short, businesslike and to the point, was the only public announcement of the marriage, and was quite different from the blatant descriptions that fill the papers of to-day when a wedding takes place in a family of

MISS MADELINE GODDARD.

MISS CATHERINE GILL.

more or less social distinction, gathered by persistent reporters who dog the footsteps of bride and groom, publish lists of the gifts received, the clothes worn by each member of the family, and pictures more or less flattering of many of them, with so many minute details that the account of a fashionable wedding takes as much space as that of a battle, a murder or a railway accident.

This wide-spread publicity is abhorrent to people of refined tastes, and it would have been frowned down a few years since, but to-day it is the fashion, and its usage sanctioned by the most chic leaders of the social world, although it would have shocked some of these same ladies some years ago had they seen these private details published in the daily papers.

Still, the old folks had some peculiar notions of their own, and the published notices varied. Sometimes the bare announcement of the marriage was accompanied by a notice of the business of the groom, or it was casually mentioned that "the beautiful Miss Patty" had married "the son of Mr. Chase, the great merchant." One thrifty bridegroom published an announcement of his marriage in the New York "Evening Post" that ran as follows: "On Thursday, the 27th of May, by the Rev. Mr. Beach, Mr. George C., late counsellor-at-law in the Island of Bermuda, and author of a work entitled 'Lex Mercatoria,' to Mrs. Cornelia V., wife of the late" so and so. The bridegroom had evidently a keen sense of the commercial value of an advertisement under circumstances of so tender a nature, and took advantage of the occasion to insert a notice of his literary work. But this record is unique, and probably excited much comment at the time, for the public announcements of weddings in the early part of the century were marked by their simplicity and brevity.

Whenever it was possible, weddings were conducted at the home of the bride's parents. The custom of being married in church was not introduced until the middle of the century. The ceremony took place in the evening, and was attended with much festivity, and the occasion was the signal for a gathering of the family, who flocked to the wedding from far and near. The gifts were generally presented only by the closest relations,

and although rich and valuable, did not include the variety of useless toys that swell the list of the bride of to-day. The groom usually presented his future wife with a handsome watch and chain. A few pieces of silver were presented by his family, and a chest of table-silver was given by that of the bride.

The trousseau was made of linen and cambric of the finest quality, but it was made with the greatest simplicity. Brocades, silks, laces and camel-hair shawls were always part of it, and if the bride was descended from one of the Dutch settlers of the colony the wedding outfit included all the necessary plenishing of the linen cupboard, which was considered an integral part of the outfit and was contained in a large oak coffer or chest, this being sometimes as large as a wardrobe, and always carved elaborately and ornamented with hinges, locks, escutcheon, et cetera, of brass or silver.

Few persons in society married unless they were able to go to a home of their own, which was often built especially for the bride by her future husband and was his gift to her on their marriage, and few of the young couples of the beginning of the century ventured into matrimony unless well provided with what was then considered substantial means—which, however, their descendants would now scorn as genteel poverty.

Photograph by Aimé Dupont.

MISS HARRIETTE COLGATE.

34
The New
New York

THE PUBLIC LIBRARY (CARRÈRE & HASTINGS, ARCHITECTS), FIFTH AVENUE, BETWEEN
FORTIETH AND FORTY-SECOND STREETS.

THE CENTURY MAGAZINE

AUGUST, 1902.

THE NEW NEW YORK.

BY RANDALL BLACKSHAW.

WITH PICTURES BY JULES GUÉRIN.

WHAT has been done to make a great city, of which Manhattan Island shall be the heart, what is now doing toward that end, and what has been planned for the near future, it may be worth while to note thus early in the twentieth century.

New York may never weave for the human spirit the spell that was woven ages since by Rome and Athens. Though it should attain to the hoariest antiquity, its very name must prevent its becoming, like those of the Greek and Roman capitals, a synonym for age. Its history began less than three centuries ago, when traders from Holland bought the island from the aborigines; and while the founding of Rome by the foster-children of a wolf may be an incident less well authenticated than this "deal" in real estate, it appeals to the imagination with far more potency. The identification of the town with the name and fame of the Father of his Country is a fact of cardinal interest, and one that the local historian justly emphasizes; yet the story of any one of a hundred Old World cities surpasses that of the New World metropolis in its attractiveness to lovers of the romantic and picturesque. Color and warmth are sadly lacking in the mental picture that rises at mention of the city's name. The chronicler may dazzle by the magnitude of figures expressing municipal growth and commercial achievement; but statistics, no matter how amazing, can never take the place of legend or ancient history.

But to-day a new New York is coming to birth which bids fair to vie, if not in historic interest, at least in magnificence and beauty, with even so splendid a capital as that of France. The fair new city lies in the embrace of the old one like the new moon in the old moon's arms, throwing into high relief the harsh parental outlines. One might almost fancy that the town had been bombarded by a hostile fleet, such rents and gashes appear everywhere in the solid masonry, ranging from the width of a single building to that of a whole block front, nay, even to a succession of blocks, as where the new East River bridge has made foot-room for itself on the Manhattan shore. The very spine of the island has been split by dynamite in preparing the way for rapid transit; and where excavations are being made in preparation for certain new buildings, it looks as if lyddite shells had exploded, ripping up tons upon tons of bed-rock and gravel.

THE HALL OF FAME (McKIM, MEAD & WHITE, ARCHITECTS), UNIVERSITY OF THE CITY OF NEW YORK.

THE APPELLATE COURT-HOUSE (JAMES BROWN LORD, ARCHITECT) AND THE TOWER
OF MADISON SQUARE GARDEN.

Reckless as all this seems, wasteful as some of it undoubtedly is, by far the greater part of the destruction wrought has been commercially inevitable, and in accordance with a law of growth that involves the reconstruction of the city's central and more crowded quarters simultaneously with the pushing forward of its frontiers. A hundred thousand dollars must be sacrificed, if necessary, to provide for the advantageous investment of a million. The sweeping away of blocks of tenement-houses is a mere incident in the making of an indispensable bridge or creating new parks for the poor; the old inadequate reservoir at Fifth Avenue and Forty-second street is yielded cheerfully when a site is needed for the great central building of the Public Library; and no protest is heard when the Egyptian temple in Center street, yclept the Tombs, makes way for a larger prison, constructed on strictly modern lines, or when St. Luke's Hospital at Fifth Avenue and Fifty-fourth street gives place to a club-house and private dwellings that adorn and enrich the neighborhood. The old Columbia College buildings at Madison Avenue and Forty-ninth street, recently replaced by handsome houses, had outlived their usefulness; and the extension of such a mansion as that of the late Cornelius Vanderbilt at Fifth Avenue and Fifty-seventh street fully justified the tearing down of the adjacent "brownstone fronts." But the pecuniary, or even the esthetic, gain is less obvious when a fine new house in the same avenue, overlooking Central Park, is destroyed to make room for a somewhat larger one; or a dwelling of the palatial character of the Stewart house at Fifth Avenue and Thirty-fourth street is demolished in the interest of purely commercial structures; or so new and costly a building as the Progress club-house at Fifth Avenue and Sixty-third street is destroyed to furnish a site for a pretentious private residence.

The longest and most important step toward beautifying the city was taken when Central Park was created from the island's rocky ribs. That was over forty years ago; and one might say that rather more than had been given with one hand, by the making of the park, was taken away with the other, some fifteen or twenty years later, when the elevated railways were allowed to be built. Had such a tunnel as is now being constructed been a financial or engineering possibility a quarter of a century ago, four of the city's main avenues

might have escaped disfigurement by the railroads on stilts that deface them to-day. The esthetic blight inflicted by these unsightly structures was by no means offset by the subsequent laying of subways for the telegraph and telephone wires formerly festooned overhead along many of the principal streets and avenues.

The need of Central Park is more obvious to-day than it was when the transformation of a midurban desert into an oasis was begun; and the laying out of Riverside Park and Drive—the pictorial effect and accessibility of which have just been doubled by the construction of two viaducts, one at Ninety-sixth street, and the other, on a vaster scale, over the valley through which One Hundred and Twenty-fifth street goes down to the Hudson River—and the creation of Van Cortlandt, Bronx, Pelham Bay, and other parks beyond the Harlem River, were measures of equally far-sighted civic wisdom. So, too, was the making of the Harlem River driveway, or the "Speedway," as it is popularly called; for the provision of a long and wide and level road on which thoroughbreds should be allowed to show their paces every day removed an ever-present menace to the integrity of Central Park, since the owners of fast trotters, many of them members of the ruling Tammany ring, were unable to contemplate unmoved the adaptability of certain portions of the park to racing purposes. Only less important in degree were the northward extension of the East River Park at Hell Gate, the metamorphosis into a shaded lawn of the sandy East Side waste known as Tompkins Square, and the wholesale destruction of human rookeries, most notably at the Five Points and Mulberry Bend, to make room for small parks in the heart of the tenement-house district.

Hand in hand with the provision of small parks for the people has gone the creation of school-houses on greatly improved lines, thoroughly fire-proof, handsome and dignified in appearance, provided with roof playgrounds, and inclosing courtyards spacious enough to insure a permanent abundance of light and air. The City College is to abandon the inadequate building, which has long been a local landmark, at Lexington Avenue and Twenty-third street, in favor of a spacious home at Amsterdam Avenue and One Hundred and Thirty-eighth street. As the distance between the two locations is over six miles, this step is one of the most significant indications of the city's growth. And a sign of its growth in commercial conse-

COLUMBIA UNIVERSITY LIBRARY (M^CKIM, MEAD & WHITE, ARCHITECTS).

THE WASHINGTON ARCH IN WASHINGTON SQUARE (STANFORD WHITE, ARCHITECT).

quence is to be seen in the establishment of a free high school of commerce, to be housed in a large and costly building in Amsterdam Avenue, the corner-stone of which was laid last December.

Recreation piers have been erected at several points along the North and East rivers, and the building of others has been arranged for. They are brightly lighted at night, and on certain evenings in the summer music is provided for the delectation of the crowds that fill them; and as there is no charge for admission by day or night, they admirably supplement the service of the small parks as breathing-places for the poor. Incidentally, they are an ornament to the water front. The same impulse that prompted the building of these piers has led to the establishment of public baths and public comfort-stations, and the adaptation of the old Castle Garden to use as an aquarium.

Piers for commercial purposes, more nearly adequate to the needs of a great port than the old ones in use these many years, are being constructed on both sides of the city. Along the North River, from West Washington Market, at the foot of Gansevoort street, to the foot of West Twenty-second street, a new sea-wall, 3000 feet long, is to be built, with ten great two-storied piers, 800 feet long by 125 feet wide, at the foot of the intervening streets. As the river cannot be narrowed without the permission of the Secretary of War, the building of piers of this size, skirted by a street 250 feet wide, will necessitate the condemnation and removal of several blocks of property, the price of which, added to that of the piers themselves, each of which is expected to cost about $300,000, and of the sea-wall, will make the total expense of this improvement something like $8,000,000. And an effort will be made to gain the approval of the new administration for a plan to improve the docking facilities for half a mile or more farther northward. Along the East River, between Whitehall and Montgomery streets, a sea-wall and eight piers have been constructed at a cost of $5,000,000 or so; and new piers have recently been built at Seventeenth and Eighteenth streets.

When the underground railway (the so-called "Rapid Transit" system) finds itself in running order, at the close of next year, one of the most vexatious problems that confront great municipalities will have been solved for New York, and one that has been exceptionally difficult of solution here, owing to the island's length and narrowness. When the tremendous feat has been carried to a successful issue, and the greater part of the city's appropriation of $35,000,000 has been converted into steel and concrete and fire-proofing, there will be little to show for it to wayfarers in the street. They will note, perhaps, the entrances to the subway stations, except those that are hidden in certain newly built hotels along the route; and between One Hundred and Twenty-fifth and One Hundred and Thirty-fifth streets, spanning Manhattan Valley, and at One Hundred and Forty-fifth street, crossing the Harlem River, they will find a steel viaduct carrying the railway-tracks. But the road, as a whole, will be as inconspicuous as a penknife in a pocket, and what is now the most useless and obtrusive feature on the city's face will have shrunk into a beneficent invisibility.

From City Hall Park, near the lower end of Manhattan Island, the Rapid Transit tunnel will carry four tracks to One Hundred and Third street and the Boulevard (Broadway), a distance of nearly seven miles. The left-hand fork of the Y will follow a northerly course, for another seven miles, to Bailey Avenue, on the farther side of Spuyten Duyvil Creek, carrying three tracks as far as the station at One Hundred and Forty-fifth street, and two from that point to its terminus. The other branch, with its two tracks, will trend to the northeast, passing beneath the Harlem River and terminating at Bronx Park. This terminus, also, will be nearly fourteen miles from the original starting-point. At about One Hundred and Ninety-fifth street, on the west side, and a mile north of the Harlem on the east, what has been up to those points an underground will become an overhead road, running on elevated tracks. In other words, about five and a half miles of the Rapid Transit line will be in the open air. At Manhattan Valley, elevators will carry passengers *up* to the stations; at certain other points they will carry them *down*—in one or two instances to platforms nearly a hundred feet below the level of the street. This depth is reached in the Washington Heights region, where for a distance of nearly two miles the building of the tunnel has involved mining operations very different from the open-cut excavations that have sufficed for the greater part of the work. Similar boring has been done under the northwest corner of Central Park, the total length of the "drift" in that neighborhood

THE ELECTRIC POWER-HOUSE, SEVENTY-FOURTH STREET AND EAST RIVER
(GEORGE H. PEGRAM, CHIEF ENGINEER).

being about a third of a mile, and its greatest depth about sixty-five feet.

It will not be long before spurs of the underground road will be carried down Broadway and beneath the East River to Brooklyn, at an expense of $8,000,000; and perhaps to Bay Ridge, and thence, by a plunge under the Narrows, to Staten Island. By the time this is achieved, the Pennsylvania Railroad will be carrying out, at an estimated expense of $50,000,000, its stupendous project of a four-track railway, in two eighteen-foot tubes, extending beneath the mile-wide North River from the Hackensack Meadows in New Jersey to New York city, where it will open out into a station 1500 by 520 feet in size, between Tenth and Seventh avenues and Thirty-first and Thirty-third streets. Above this enormous underground station a bridge 100 feet wide will stretch between Thirty-first and Thirty-third streets. The end of the bridge will be approached by evenly graded carriageways; and stairways will connect the bridge with the platforms below, which will be skirted by twenty-five tracks. Eastward of Seventh Avenue, the Long Island Railroad, now a branch of the Pennsylvania, will lay three single-track tubes—one each under Thirty-first, Thirty-second, and Thirty-third streets—to and beyond the East River, where they will come to the surface in Brooklyn at a point seven or eight miles from the New Jersey entrance to the tunnel.

This great undertaking involves tunneling the island on a lower level than that of the Rapid Transit subway. Its significance is far-reaching, and so will be its effects. By adding immeasurably to the city's accessibility from the mainland, it will vastly increase its commercial importance; incidentally it will increase real-estate values, and lead to a radical improvement in the architectural quality of the buildings in the neighborhood of the proposed station, which is to be modeled, in a general way, on the Gare d'Orléans in Paris.

It is worth noting that the disclosure of

the Pennsylvania's plans has led to the incorporation of a company which talks of spending $40,000,000 to parallel that corporation's tunnel and to accommodate certain other railroads that are seeking entrance to New York. It is also announced that a new company, capitalized at $8,500,000, has been formed to complete the unfinished tunnel beneath the Hudson River from Jersey City to Morton street, New York, for use in connection with the Metropolitan Street Railway of New York and the Jersey City and tributary electric railroads. Of the 5580 feet under water, 4000 had been excavated when work was discontinued, several years ago. The New York terminal station of this tunnel will be in the West-Side block bounded by Christopher, Tenth, Greenwich, and Hudson streets.

President Cassatt's declaration that electric traction will be adopted in the Pennsylvania tunnels, as being " in every way the most practical, economical, and the best for the interests of the railroad company and the city," coming just before the recent fatal collision in the smoke-and-steam filled tunnel in Park Avenue between Fifty-sixth and Ninety-sixth streets, was promptly followed by the announcement by the New York Central Railroad Company of its intention to use electricity in handling its suburban traffic within the city limits—that is to say, between Mott Haven, beyond the Harlem River, and the Grand Central Station at Forty-second street. This will involve the construction of a tunnel beginning to descend from the present track-level at the lower extremity of the tunnel now in use for all trains, and thereafter to be used for through trains only, and extending beneath the train-yard to the station, with an underground landing-place connecting with the Rapid Transit tunnel station at Forty-second street, as well as with the railroad-station overhead. The new tunnel, which will form a wide loop under the Grand Central Station, will be large enough to carry several tracks, and its construction will virtually double the present capacity of the terminus. To the many thousands of passengers on the several lines that use the Central's tracks, this too-long-delayed reform will be an incalculable boon. The carrying out of its various plans in this connection, necessitating the acquisition of whole blocks of valuable real estate, the purchase of which has been under way for some time past, will of course involve very heavy outlays, and the railroad company has arranged to raise

$43,750,000, or more, by the issue of new stock.

The use of electricity on the Pennsylvania, New York Central, and Rapid Transit lines will follow hard upon its adoption on the elevated roads, on which the experimental trips of a train made up of motorcars and "trailers" were made in January last. An enormous power-house for the generation of 100,000 horse-power (twice as much as is produced by the immense dynamos at Niagara Falls) has been built beside the East River above Seventy-fourth street, with seven substations scattered about the city; and as the new motive-power will enable trains to start and stop on a curve, a station costing $100,000 will be built at Manhattan Avenue and One Hundred and Tenth street, and equipped with eight large electric elevators to carry passengers to the dizzy height of the tracks at that point.

Second in importance only to the actual and projected tunnels are the bridges that will bind the city to Long Island, if not to the mainland also. The gigantic union railway-bridge that has been dreamed of as a link between Manhattan and New Jersey may have had its death-blow in the adoption of the plans devised by a clever English engineer for the Pennsylvania road alone; but the Brooklyn Bridge in use for the last nineteen years is to be supplemented by three others, one of which is expected to be in commission before the close of 1903. From its anchorage near the foot of Delancey street, New York, it stretches 2800 feet to its anchorage in Brooklyn, E. D., with a clear span of 1600 feet between its open-ironwork towers, and at its lowest point an elevation of 135 feet above the water. The estimated cost of this picturesque structure, which, when completed, will have been a little over seven years in building, is approximately $15,000,000. This was about the cost of the first Brooklyn Bridge, which took over thirteen years to build.

The new bridge is officially known as No. 2, owing, not to its location, but to the date of its construction. Between this and the old bridge (No. 1), another (No. 3) has been arranged for. It is to be of the suspension-bridge type, a few feet wider than the one at Delancey street, and, including its approaches, a quarter of a mile longer, yet its cost will be about the same ($14,750,000). And yet another band is to link together the opposite shores of the East River. Bridge No. 4, as it is called, will be a cantaliver affair, having a central pier on Black-

HALF-TONE PLATE ENGRAVED BY R. C. COLLINS.

CHAMBER OF COMMERCE (JAMES B. BAKER, ARCHITECT).

well's Island, and costing about $11,000,000. And besides the recently constructed bridge spanning the Harlem at One Hundred and Forty-fifth street,—the latest of the many by which that stream is crossed,—one of unusual height is some day to overleap the great gap between Inwood, at the northern extremity of Manhattan Island, and the Spuyten Duyvil heights beyond, joining Riverside Drive with the new transpontine parkway from which it is now cut off by Spuyten Duyvil Creek, the outlet of the Harlem ship-canal into the Hudson River.

Fortunately for the architectural future of the city, the temptation to overtop the highest building previously erected is resisted now and then, in circumstances where it would be easy to yield to it. Notable among the monumental edifices that might have vied, had they so wished, with the heaven-aspiring Park Row Building, are the home of the Produce Exchange, facing Battery Park, the Herald Building in upper Broadway, the Appellate Court-house overlooking Madison Square,—a block below the immense and ornate Madison Square Garden, with its soaring tower tipped by St. Gaudens's " Diana,"—the Bank for Savings in Fourth Avenue, and the New York County Bank in Eighth Avenue (these two, like the court-house, of snowy marble), the Greenwich Savings Bank in Sixth Avenue, and the Bowery Bank at Grand street and the Bowery.

It is natural that the skyward tendency should manifest itself least strongly in the case of public buildings, where pecuniary returns on the investment in steel and stone are not looked for. Thus, the vast new Custom House (for which Congress has appropriated $3,000,000, and is asked to appropriate $1,750,000 more), now in course of construction immediately south of Bowling Green and east of Battery Park, at the lower end of Broadway, is to be limited in height to half a dozen stories. The present ponderous and imposing structure in Wall street (from the steps of which Garfield addressed the crowd when Lincoln was assassinated) was sold, with its site, for $3,265,- 000; yet the First National Bank, which bought it, is undecided whether to occupy it, on taking possession two or three years hence, or to replace it with a modern office building!

Among the nation's real-estate holdings in this city, the Post Office, to be erected when Congress appropriates the necessary $2,500,- 000, will rank next to the new Custom House. It is understood that the site of the new office will be farther up-town—that is, nearer the local center of population—than that of the present building, erected at enormous cost less than thirty years ago, yet long since antiquated and outgrown. When the old office was built, the local postal receipts were $3,000,000 a year; now they considerably exceed four times that sum.

The most important municipal buildings now in course of erection are the Tombs prison and the Hall of Records, both well down-town, in Center street. Each of these new structures, the cost of which will run into the millions, will take the place of a noted landmark; the original prison, demolished to make room for the new one, having been one of the most picturesque, and, though not old, yet one of the oldest-

looking buildings on the island; while the present Hall of Records, which is to be preserved, is the oldest, if not the most interesting, public building in the city, being a noted relic of old New York.

Of non-official buildings projected or already begun, none is more important in its indirect bearing on the commercial greatness of the city than the home of the Chamber of Commerce at Liberty street and Liberty Place, the corner-stone of which was laid last year, and which is to cost $1,500,- 000. It will be interesting to compare this magnificent building with Fraunce's Tavern at Broad and Pearl streets, which was the birthplace of the Chamber in 1768, and has ever since existed as a public house. The new building will be, in a sense, a companion to that of the Clearing House Association in the next street (Cedar); and only two blocks farther down-town, linking Wall street with Broad and New, is rising the highly ornamental home of the Stock Exchange, where last year's sales of 265,000,- 000 shares of stock are likely to be eclipsed before long, and where the cost of a membership certificate has reached the " record " price of $80,000. About two millions of dollars will be expended on this building, and every modern invention will be utilized in it by which time can be saved to men engaged in a business wherein, preëminently, time is money.

None of these buildings is of the sky-scraping class; and what that means to their neighbors was strikingly illustrated in Pine street, the other day, when a private banker's decision to erect a three-story building for his own use added $75,000 to the value of the two lots in the rear. In this connection it is worthy of note that the Park Bank is to make large lateral additions to its present home in lower Broadway, in the form of L's extending to Ann and Fulton streets, without imitating its more ambitious rivals by providing office-room for outsiders. When a bank houses itself in a sky-scraper, it is usually with a view to the making of a safe investment of its funds. When an insurance company does the same thing, it is largely with a view to attracting the public eye. Imposing architectural effects are often the result, as in the case of the Equitable, the Mutual, the New York, the Home Life, and the Manhattan, down-town, and of the Metropolitan in Madison Square, which is extending its broad-based marble headquarters over the site of the recently demolished Academy of Design at Twenty-third street

THE STOCK EXCHANGE (GEORGE B. POST, ARCHITECT).

and Fourth Avenue, and of the Lyceum Theater adjoining.

The almost simultaneous removal of Columbia College from Madison Avenue and Forty-ninth street to Morningside Heights, overlooking the Hudson River, and of New York University from Washington Square to University Heights, beyond and over-looking the Harlem, led not only to the replacing of the old college buildings with valuable buildings of modern type, but, especially in the case of Columbia, greatly accelerated the development of the new neighborhoods. Already there is ample promise that Morningside Heights will become, from an architectural point of view, what its natural features predestined it to be —the most beautiful section of the city. Only a little way from the impressive Low Library and lesser Columbia buildings, the story of which is as yet by no means told, the great Episcopal Cathedral of St. John the Divine (which will compare not unfavorably in size and beauty with the famous Old World shrines) is gradually taking shape, after ten years of halting progress; and between the cathedral and the college stands the vast bulk of St. Luke's Hospital, built only a few years since from the proceeds of the sale of the hospital building and grounds at Fifth Avenue and Fifty-fourth street. Even nearer to the university are the stately buildings of Barnard College, for women (now an almost integral part of Columbia), and the Horace Mann School, erected at a cost of half a million, which was first occupied in December last.

The most conspicuous and most famous of the many striking edifices in this neighborhood is the tomb of General Grant in Riverside Park, opposite One Hundred and Twenty-third street, where it rises 160 feet from its base-line and nearly 300 above the level of the Hudson. This has waited five years, and may have to wait many more, for the equestrian statue and portrait panels that are ultimately to embellish it. In the meantime, the Soldiers' and Sailors' Monument at Riverside Drive and Eighty-ninth street, on which the city has spent $250,000, has become an actuality; but the attempt to perpetuate, by popular subscription, the Naval Arch of 1899 has been abandoned. As yet, therefore, the beautiful Washington Arch in Washington Square, designed in 1889 by Mr. Stanford White, is the only monument of its kind in the city. A notable improvement in the neighborhood of the tomb was the recent substitution of a formal colonial garden for the unsightly sheds in the rear of the hotel on Claremont Heights, as the upper end of Riverside Park is called.

As an architectural monument, the next place to the Cathedral of St. John will be held by the Public Library, the foundations of which have just been laid on the site of the old reservoir in Fifth Avenue, from Fortieth to Forty-second street. This vast white marble building, 366 feet long by 246 feet wide, standing a little back from Fifth Avenue, will be not only a thing of beauty, but the latest expression, in equipment and organization, of modern thought on library problems. And it will not be long be-

fore its power for good in the community will be reinforced by the sixty-five branch libraries that Mr. Carnegie is to build at an outlay exceeding $5,000,000, the estimated cost, by the way, of the central building alone. Of the branch buildings—to be designed by some of the most artistic architectural firms in the city—thirty-seven will be allotted to the borough of Manhattan. The contract for the building of the first of these, in East Seventy-ninth street, was let in February last.

Before the end of the present year, the new wing of the Metropolitan Museum, extending to Fifth Avenue at Eighty-second street, will be thrown open to the public. The recent completion of this addition, at an expense of $1,000,000, has drawn public attention to the fact that the sketch plans for the museum as a whole, drawn by the late Richard M. Hunt, call for a series of similar extensions, wherewith the large original building is to be completely surrounded. As the city bears the expense of building, a large part of the income from the recent princely inheritance of over $5,000,000 from the Rogers estate will be available for the purchase of additions to the museum's art collections. On the opposite side of the park, in Manhattan Square, the Museum of Natural History is constantly undergoing enlargement to accommodate its increasing stores of animal, vegetable, and mineral wealth.

It may be some time before the local art societies, nobly discontent with the comparatively new Fine Arts Building in Fifty-seventh street, can carry out their ambitious project of a union building for exhibition purposes, for which they are looking heavenward, just now, for a windfall of $1,500,000; yet it is reasonably certain that before many years the National Academy of Design will have further improved the site it already occupies in part, in Amsterdam Avenue between One Hundred and Ninth and One Hundred and Tenth streets, where the realization in stone and steel of the designs for a highly ornamental edifice awaits only an adequate addition to its building-funds. And it will not be very long before the New York Historical Society, now at Second Avenue and Eleventh street, begins to establish itself on the block front in Central Park West extending from Seventy-sixth to Seventy-seventh street, which is to be the scene of its activities during the second century of its existence. A wing will be

GENERAL GRANT'S TOMB (JOHN H. DUNCAN, ARCHITECT) AND RIVERSIDE PARK.

constructed first, pending the completion of the fund of $800,000 necessary to carry out the building plans.

A striking improvement has already been noted in the architecture of the public schools recently erected in New York; and some idea of the activity of the movement for providing seats for the many thousands of pupils hitherto crowded out may be had from the latest reports of the Board of Education, which has recently removed from its former simple quarters in Grand street to a huge new building at Park Avenue and Fifty-ninth street, more than three miles farther up-town. During the year ending July 31, 1901, eight new school-houses were completed in the boroughs of Manhattan and the Bronx, at an expense of over $2,000,-000; during the same period contracts were let, to the same amount, for the construction of seven more, including the Commercial High School; and two others, previously contracted for, were in course of building. One of the two delayed school-houses—No. 171, extending from One Hundred and Third to One Hundred and Fourth street between Fifth and Madison avenues—is a fine example of the new type of such buildings in this city; and the East Side is soon to be ornamented with a high school for boys, extending from Fifteenth to Sixteenth street between Stuyvesant Square and First Avenue, which will appropriately illustrate the old Dutch ideals in architecture. This will be a huge affair, costing over half a million and accommodating 3400 pupils.

Progress is making on the Episcopal cathedral on Morningside Heights; an addition is being made to the Catholic cathedral in Fifth Avenue; the four colossal statues recently placed in niches on the exterior of the tower of Trinity Church in Broadway may be said to complete that old-looking, though far from ancient, edifice; St. Ignatius's Episcopal Church is rising gradually beside the Methodist St. Paul's in West End Avenue; the Church of Our Lady of Lourdes is nearing completion in Amsterdam Avenue, where the stone facing of the late Academy of Design in Fourth Avenue is to take a new lease of life, saving some $50,000 to the thrifty parish; the unfinished Russian (Greek) Church in Ninety-seventh street between Fifth and Madison avenues adds a new and striking note to the architectural tone-color of Manhattan; and the Broadway Tabernacle, which has yielded to the overwhelming commercial pressure at Sixth Avenue and Thirty-fourth street, will soon make a new stand at Broadway and Fifty-sixth street—its third site in sixty years' existence. This list of churches building, or to be built at once, makes no claim to exhaustiveness, but is sufficient to give some impression of the extent to which New York city is being made over.

By the 1st of April, 1903, the Young Men's Christian Association, which has sold its old home at Fourth Avenue and Twenty-third street, expects to be housed in a new one, eight or nine stories in height, extending from Twenty-third to Twenty-fourth street between Seventh and Eighth avenues. Its appropriation for building purposes is $450,000. The Lying-in Hospital at East Seventeenth street and Second Avenue, overlooking Stuyvesant Square,—the gift of Mr. J. Pierpont Morgan,—has just been finished at an expense of about $1,250,000, and the New York Infant Asylum has taken possession of its new home at Sixty-first street and Amsterdam Avenue; the Manhattan Maternity Hospital is to build in East Sixtieth street between First and Second avenues; the Mount Sinai Hospital will leave Lexington Avenue this year for new and more spacious quarters in Madison Avenue, extending from One Hundredth to One Hundred and First street; the purchase by the New York Central Railroad of the two Park Avenue and Lexington Avenue blocks between Forty-eighth and Fiftieth streets will make it necessary for the Woman's Hospital and the Episcopal Orphan Asylum to seek new homes; the Hebrew Sheltering Guardian Society is raising $250,000 to add a wing for

HALF-TONE PLATE ENGRAVED BY S. M. NORTHCOTE.

SOLDIERS' AND SAILORS' MONUMENT (C. W. & A. A. STOUGHTON, AND
P. E. DUBOY, ARCHITECTS), RIVERSIDE DRIVE.

THE METROPOLITAN MUSEUM (THE LATE RICHARD M. HUNT, AND RICHARD H. HUNT, ARCHITECTS).

educational and library purposes to its buildings at Broadway and One Hundred and Fiftieth street; and the Jewish Theological Seminary is to remove from Lexington Avenue to new quarters in One Hundred and Twenty-third street near Broadway; while within the last few years the Charity Organization Society (with its affiliated associations), the Episcopal Church Missions, and the Society for the Prevention of Cruelty to Children have found permanent and almost luxurious homes in Fourth Avenue, the

THE NEW NEW YORK.

465

Society for the Prevention of Cruelty to Animals at Twenty-sixth street and Madison Avenue, and the Presbyterian missionary societies at Fifth Avenue and Twentieth street.

Nothing of late years has more strikingly emphasized the growing importance of New York as a social center than the increase of the number, membership, and wealth of its clubs. The first of these to yield to the demand for a building of the monumental type was the Union League, whose home at Thirty-ninth street has been one of the landmarks of Fifth Avenue since 1881. The Century Association followed it up-town, from its modest but cozy quarters in East Fifteenth street, ten years later, and now occupies a handsome house in West Forty-third street. The Metropolitan had not long been organized when it moved into its Italian Renaissance palace at Fifth Avenue and Sixtieth street. Then came the University Club's removal in 1899 to a many-storied granite mansion, Italian of another type, at Fifth Avenue and Fifty-fourth street; and two years later the New York Yacht Club moved into a building in West Forty-fourth street worthy of the prestige of this greatest of boating associations, and a fitting repository for the America's cup. The Union Club, after long resisting the northward tendency that had proved irresistible to its rivals, has yielded at last, and having sold its old home at Fifth Avenue and Twenty-first street, is erecting a splendid new one at Fifth Avenue and Fifty-first street, on the corner next above St. Patrick's Cathedral. The City Club, devoted to the cause of good municipal government, has arranged for the erection of a home of its own in West Forty-fourth street; the Republican Club has accepted designs for a handsome ten-story building in Fortieth street, overlooking Bryant Square, on the site lately occupied by St. Ignatius's Church—"a typical New York club-house of the latest type," with kitchen on the top floor behind a summer roof-garden; the Sons of the Revolution have planned a dignified edifice, only two stories high, which will probably be built in West Fifty-fifth street; the Progress Club, having disposed of its spacious home at Fifth Avenue and Sixty-third street, will build a still more commodious one at Central Park West and Eighty-eighth street; and the City Teachers' Association is raising a fund for building purposes. The Harlem Club, at Lenox Avenue and One Hundred and Twenty-third street, occupies one of the most notable buildings in the upper part of Manhattan; the Catholic Club's quarters in Central Park South may fairly be regarded as permanent; the local clubs of Yale and Harvard graduates are sumptuously housed on opposite sides of West Forty-fourth street; the Arion Society of music-loving Germans can adequately entertain a royal prince in its home at Park Avenue and Fifty-ninth street; and some of the large athletic clubs, such as the New York, the Knickerbocker, and the Racquet and Tennis, have local habitations in keeping with their size and wealth.

Among the private houses now in course of erection are such notable examples of domestic architecture as those which Mr. Carnegie and a United States senator from another State are building in Fifth Avenue, overlooking Central Park. The former is noteworthy for its comparative simplicity, the amplitude of open space about it, and the effect of seclusion secured by surrounding it with well-grown forest trees. The progress of the latter has been marked by the incidental purchase of the quarries from which the stone is cut and of the foundry where the bronze-work is making. That such a house should cost $2,500,000 is less surprising than the fact that the recent alteration and redecoration of a neighboring Fifth Avenue "mansion" should have involved the expenditure of $600,000 or more. A private dwelling, princely in size and appointments, is to replace the Progress club-house at Fifth Avenue and Sixty-third street.

Many millions are involved in the plans for new hotels of the largest and most modern type soon to supplement such new and typically metropolitan hostelries as the Waldorf-Astoria, the Holland House, the Imperial, the Manhattan, the Savoy, and the New Netherland. Among these are the nineteen-storied Hotel Terminus, to be built by the Subway Realty Company, opposite the Grand Central Station, at Park Avenue and Forty-second street; the great caravansary that the Astor estate is demolishing the St. Cloud at Broadway and Forty-second street to make room for (both of these will have direct underground connection with the Rapid Transit tunnel); the new Astor building in Broadway between Forty-fourth and Forty-fifth streets; a twelve-storied structure at Seventh Avenue and Forty-ninth street; and the hotel that is to form a part of the projected Pennsylvania Railroad station in West Thirty-third street. Then there is the slowly growing Hotel Martha Washington, for women, in

MUSEUM OF NATURAL HISTORY (CADY, BERG & SEE, ARCHITECTS).

Twenty-ninth street near Madison Avenue —an ornate twelve-story affair, to cost, with the land it stands on, $750,000.

But no less typical of the New York of to-day than these hotels proper are the so-called apartment-hotels, where suites of rooms are engaged by the year by families that either use the dining-room of the building or go out for their meals. Many of these peculiarly modern compromises between the hotel and the apartment-house are going up in all the residential parts of the city, including even Harlem, hitherto the stronghold of the class of tenants that prefers the apartment-house proper, with its individual dining-rooms and kitchens. These hotels range in height from eight to twelve stories or more, and sometimes occupy the entire front of an avenue block. Most notable among the newer buildings of this type is the one completed this year, under the direction of the Astor estate, at Fifth Avenue and Fifty-fifth street.

Of theaters, large and small, there are at least threescore in the borough of Manhattan; yet such is the demand for additional accommodations that at least eight new ones have recently been planned. One of these will be built next door to the Republic and the Victoria theaters in Forty-second street at Seventh Avenue; another on the opposite side of the street; a third in West Forty-fourth street; yet another in the same neighborhood, the Longacre Square district; a fifth on a site not yet announced; a sixth in One Hundred and Twenty-fifth street near

St. Nicholas Avenue; a seventh (the new Lyceum) in Forty-fifth street east of Broadway; and an eighth in the Bowery.

It would be an endless task to enumerate the buildings for business purposes that are rising with mushroom-like celerity and frequency in all parts of the city, though mention may be made, in passing, of such as are to replace familiar landmarks. First among those which by virtue of their size and situ-

ation are likely to become landmarks themselves must be counted the Cumberland Building in the triangle at Broadway, Fifth Avenue, and Twenty-third street, nicknamed "the Flat-iron." Then there is the Knickerbocker Trust Company Building, soon to occupy the site of the Stewart house at Fifth Avenue and Thirty-fourth street; the trust company building that is to confront the Metropolitan club-house across the Fifth

THE UNION CLUB (CASS GILBERT, JOHN DU FAIS, JOINT ARCHITECTS)
AND ST. PATRICK'S CATHEDRAL.

HALF-TONE PLATE ENGRAVED BY H. C. MERRILL.

"THE FLAT-IRON," TWENTY-THIRD STREET AND BROADWAY (D. H. BURNHAM, ARCHITECT).

Avenue end of Sixtieth street; the Bank of the Metropolis in Union Square; the store which has replaced the Star Theater (formerly Wallack's) at Broadway and Thirteenth street; and the business buildings being erected on the site of the residence of the late Marshall O. Roberts at Fifth Avenue and Eighteenth street, Chickering Hall on the diagonally opposite corner, the Union Club three blocks farther north, and Colonnade Row (formerly La Grange Terrace) in Lafayette Place. A notable structure is the Windsor Arcade, that marks the site of the burned Windsor Hotel at Fifth Avenue and Forty-seventh street, and emphasizes the fact that height is not indispensable to striking architectural effects.

The various railway plans that have been in the air for some time past have concentrated attention on the neighborhood of Herald and Greeley squares, where Broadway, Sixth Avenue, and Thirty-fourth street intersect one another. Here two whole block fronts have been swept away, and while one is to be occupied by a "specialty" store, the other, with an annex across the street, is to be the site of a vast department store. On the opposite side of the avenue, the Broadway Tabernacle and adjacent buildings are to be razed and the site dedicated to the god of trade. Nothing could better illustrate the tendency of the large retail shops to follow the northward movement of population than the fact that a shop in Grand street, that ten or twelve years ago did an annual business of $6,000,000, was closed last year for want of patronage, while in Sixth Avenue, from Fourteenth to Thirty-fifth street, whole block fronts are constantly being removed to make room for department stores that cut deeper and deeper into what may be called the *hinterland*.

The original purchase-price of Manhattan Island—sixty guilders—was equivalent to $24. Building-sites in the Wall street district have been bought of late years at more than $240 per square foot, and the assessed valuation of the real estate in Greater New York is to-day $3,237,777,260. Building-plans filed during the year 1901 called for the expenditure of about $150,000,000; and there are no signs that this hitherto unparalleled expansion—which is shared in a measure by the other chief cities of America—has reached its bounds.

To recapitulate: First in significance among the changes now making or soon to be wrought in Manhattan must be put the actual and projected railway tunnels, the East River bridges holding a good second place. Next to these comes the erection of such magnificent buildings as the Episcopal cathedral, the Public Library and its many branches, the proposed Post Office and the Custom House, the Chamber of Commerce and the Stock Exchange. The municipality's contribution to the growing greatness of the city is not restricted to the building of bridges, but includes the Zoölogical Park and Botanical Garden sites and buildings, bridgeways and viaducts, parks and parkways, improved school- and fire-houses, recreation piers and piers for commercial purposes, free baths, public comfort-stations, and smooth street pavements. Private initiative provides new university and college buildings, churches, club-houses and theaters, hotels, apartment-houses, and private dwellings, and office buildings that rival the tower of Babel not only in height but in linguistic diversity of their occupants. This lavish expenditure of wealth and energy, both collective and individual, must result within a very few years in the creation of a virtually new New York. And if we succeed in retaining an enlightened local government, and the admonitions of the Municipal Art Society and the Municipal Art Commission are duly heeded, the proposed tricentennial celebration of the discovery of the Hudson River will find us in 1909 prouder than we have ever had reason to be of the magnificent city that in three centuries has been reared on Manhattan Island.